THE COMEDY OF ROMANTIC IRONY

D0992875

Morton Gurewitch

University Press of America,® Inc.
Lanham · New York · Oxford

Copyright © 2002 by
University Press of America,® Inc.
4720 Boston Way
Lanham, Maryland 20706
UPA Acquisitions Department (301) 459-3366

12 Hid's Copse Rd.
Cumnor Hill, Oxford OX2 9JJ

Library of Congress Cataloging-in-Publication Data

Gurewitch, Morton, 1922-
The comedy of romantic irony / Morton Gurewitch.
p.   cm
Includes bibliographical references and index.
l. Romanticism. 2. Irony in literature. I. Title.

PN603 .G87 2002
809'.145—dc21   2002021483 CIP

ISBN 0-7618-2299-2 (paperback : alk. ppr.)

⊖™ The paper used in this publication meets the minimum
requirements of American National Standard for Information
Sciences—Permanence of Paper for Printed Library Materials,
ANSI Z39.48—1984

For Daniel, Alexander, Nicholas,
Noëlle, and Eric

Contents

Preface

To describe romantic irony as an enigma would be something of an exaggeration. Few literary concepts, nevertheless, are capable of evoking the kind of perplexity which is engendered by a more than passing acquaintanceship with romantic irony. Assessments of romantic irony, it is true, often appear to be expressed with a good deal of confidence. Consider the following specimens: Romantic irony is a pathologically egotistical denial of actuality.[1] Romantic irony is "a fantastic symphony of contradictions," a "bacchanal of chaos."[2] Romantic irony reveals a disjunction "between inner and outer," for example, between outer caprice and inner sadness.[3] Romantic irony is a species of "esthetic nihilism."[4] Romantic irony conveys "a despairing disillusionment generated by the juxtaposition of an ideal possibility and prosaic reality."[5] Romantic irony is a "cultural faith," heroically serviceable in salvaging "a saving remnant of civilizing illusion."[6] Romantic irony is self-reflexive, self-conscious illusionism.[7] Romantic irony is a gloomy combination of "sentiment and cynicism," a "despondent idealism," a "metaphysical despair," and also a "narcissistic, onanistic, and potentially solipsistic discourse."[8] Occasionally one hears a cautious note, as in the statement that romantic irony perhaps reveals "ancient dichotomies" of the soul.[9]

Despite some astonishing discrepancies in these judgments, two claims recur a fair number of times. The first is that romantic irony is the product of a dualistic psyche. The second is that romantic irony is proof of a rather unhappy disposition. But is this the case? Is a dualistic mentality indispensable to romantic irony? (Yes) And are sadness, gloom, and despair inevitable traits of the romantic-ironic temper? (No)

It is almost universally taken for granted that the chief source of enlightenment in regard to romantic irony is accessible in the writings of Friedrich Schlegel, who has been described as a revolutionary figure in the history of literary and philosophical irony.   Yet definitional problems persist. The trouble is that Schlegel's provocative assertions about irony (the phrase "romantic irony" became enshrined only after Schlegel's death) are extraordinarily, and at times mystifyingly, capacious. It is by no means whimsical to advance the idea that German (that is, Schlegelian) romantic irony has so comprehensive an embrace that it cannot possibly be boiled down to a lucid, simplified interpretation. Nor is it likely that such an interpretation would be other than anathema to proponents of German romantic irony, who are convinced that Schlegelian irony would be drastically impoverished, if not cretinized, by any narrowing of its fecund, multiple suggestiveness. A brief unitary formulation of romantic irony would be quickly tagged as no more than a single aspect of Schlegelian ironic totality.

The almost perverse many-sidedness of Schlegelian irony has been blessed by a seemingly invincible prestige. Yet it is perfectly plausible to argue that if Schlegel's ideas were (unfortunately) deleted from literary history, it would still be possible to arrive at a valid definition of romantic irony – a definition based on practice, not theory. I am alluding here to a number of European romantics who engage in an unprecedented comedy of ambivalence, and on whom the influence of Schlegelian theory is null. These romantics include Byron, Carlyle, Musset, Gautier, Stendhal, Heine, Pushkin, Lermontov, Baudelaire, Flaubert, and Dostoevsky, all of whom may be identified, at least in some of their works, as comedians of romantic irony.

But why should romantic irony be construed primarily as a mode of comedy? (Schlegel himself pays homage to comedy in the form of "humor" and "wit"; these play a more than marginal, but less than dominant, role in his theorizing.) The answer to this question lies, to begin with, in the Pyrrhonic perspective of the ironic temper. Through the ages the radically sceptical ironic temper has been especially marked by its subtle derogation of the ideal, of grand illusions. When it is exercized in the world of comedy, the ironic temper not only undermines the idealisms and illusions of mankind, but brands them as incurably absurd and hence ineluctably subject to risible collapse. (This is the theme of a previous work, *The Ironic Temper and the Comic Imagination* [1994].)

What is striking, indeed original, about the European romantic ironist – it is the central argument of this book – is that he cannot help prizing the idealism he amusingly trashes; he cannot help sanctifying exalted aspiration while laughingly dismissing the process of enchantment. The romantic ironist is thus a creature of ambivalence. He is a romantic antiromantic.

Yet romantic irony, whose lightness can turn dark and even morbid, cannot be isolated from other modes of comedy. The atmosphere of Byron's *Don Juan* and Carlyle's *Sartor Resartus*, to take but two examples, is often governed by romantic irony. But both works are also frequently energized by satire and farce. (Nor is that all.) Still, it is romantic irony, with its fervent idealizing and comic disenchantment (and re-enchantment) that constitutes a unique contribution to the history of literary comedy.

After an introductory section, most of this book deals with English, German, French, and Russian writers in whom romantic irony is either an abiding proclivity or a temporary, though potent, inclination. The purpose of the Appendix is rather different. In it I trace the fortunes of romantic irony in Anglo-American criticism of the last half-century. I do so by focusing, more or less chronologically, on shifting critical reactions to a single, key work of romantic irony, Byron's *Don Juan*. I have tried to do justice to a large number of critical books and essays in this analytical survey; but on more than one occasion justice has not been deprived of polemical enhancement.

Chapter 1

In Search of Romantic Irony

1.

Though no one has recently claimed that romanticism's production of comedy verges on the prolific, the notion that romanticism is inherently hostile to comedy appears to be safely dead. Carl Dawson points out that romanticism's reputation for niggardliness in comedy is inaccurate, and that a significant number of writers in the romantic period establish a strong sense of comedy. "We are not inclined," he declares, "to think of the generations of Wordsworth and Coleridge, Shelley and Keats, as times of comedy; and in an age of muddled theater, comedy had a hard time finding a voice. In fact Byron, Austen, Peacock – not to mention humorists like Charles Lamb, Isaac Disraeli, Leigh Hunt – are accomplished writers of comedy and very much characteristic of their age."[1] Of course every period has its (more or less characteristic) comic writers; and no one is likely to prophesy the end of comedy in human culture.

Still, Dawson is right. The romantic sense of comedy, we can assume, is in little danger of suffering further neglect, especially if it is understood that satire is one of the essential elements of comedy. When Marilyn Butler underscores the presence of satire (and self-satire) in romantic works ranging from Shelley's "Alastor" to Hazlitt's *Liber Amoris,* she wryly introduces her subject by observing that "the Romantics didn't know that they were not supposed to be satiric."[2] It is amply recognized by other critics that Blake was a master of funnily corrosive irony, that

Wordsworth composed more than just scraps of owlish levity, and that Keats could produce jokes, enjoy wit, ponder the incursions of laughter in despondency, and celebrate Elizabethan "bards of passion and of mirth."[3]

It is true that the romantic sublime is hardly associated with laughter. Wordsworth, for example, often seems gravely smitten by a sense of divine solemnity, even when recalling moments of youthful, Chaucerian gaiety. In a passage later removed from the 1850 version of "The Prelude," Wordsworth advocates a "religious dignity of mind" which, conceived as the "very faculty of truth" (1805: Bk. 4, 1. 297), is able to humanize an otherwise predatory mankind. [4] Such dignity appears to leave little room for spontaneous lightness. Yet Wordsworth is capable of exploiting a jocular tonality. So is Shelley. Peacock observed that Shelley "often talked of the 'withering and perverting spirit of comedy,' " though he delighted in Mozart's *Marriage of Figaro*[5] and admired Byron's *Don Juan*. Shelley himself, furthermore, had a fine talent for satire, though his satiric poems have not had a particularly rewarding afterlife. A poem like "Peter Bell the Third," a witty, if occasionally labored, mockery of Wordsworth's poetry and morality, handsomely escapes the stupendous dullness that not only paralyzes Peter's satanically reactionary versifying but also deadens the very springs of life and earth. Shelley's light touch – for all his prankishness, he once declared that "perhaps no one will believe in anything in the shape of a joke from me" [6] – may not be one of his paramount powers, whether exercised as criticism or as blitheness for its own sake; but it cannot be ignored.

Shelley's ambivalent attitude toward comedy may remind us of Rousseau's. In his *Letter to d'Alembert* Rousseau condemns comedy in the theater for habitually subordinating moral integrity to worldly maxims. He even scolds Molière for favoring those who are cunning over those who are deserving. Yet despite his ethical strictures, Rousseau enjoys Molière's plays; the fact that they are morally questionable does not become an aesthetic deterrent. Nor are Rousseau's *Confessions* devoid of self-mockery. Consider an incident that he recounts in Book 7 of *The Confessions* – an incident which, according to Rousseau, furnishes a key to his character.[7] As secretary to the French ambassador in Venice, Rousseau is introduced to Zulietta, a bewitching Venetian courtesan. There is much to adore in this divinely sweet, vivacious, witty Zulietta; and Rousseau quickly becomes a worshipper. But Rousseau is also a contemplative; and thought now spreads a canker over the goddess. He reflects that Zulietta, after all, is morally tarnished; she is on sale to everybody. (Zulietta herself seems to attach little value to money, and has embraced Rousseau because he reminds her, or so she claims, of a former lover.) How can Zulietta, accustomed to the commonplace, rude souls of her other clients, recognize and appreciate Rousseau's poetic temper, his refined open-heartedness, his delicate moral being? Further brooding succeeds in completely chilling Rousseau's passion, which then yields to tears, enriched by a strong dose of narcissistic vanity.

Unable any longer to idealize Zulietta's qualities or trust that she will discern his own exceptional merits, Rousseau concludes that his heart (aided by the promptings of the flesh) has been intolerably duped by a slut. Or perhaps (nay, probably) this seemingly perfect, piquant, paradisal beauty is being gnawed by some secret, repulsive defect. (Not by a sexual disease, though, for Zulietta is so lovely and her health so radiant that Rousseau wonders whether he himself is sexually sound enough for her.) This agitation brings on more tears. Zulietta is of course perplexed by his behavior. Her mirror, however, reassures her: she is a masterpiece of graceful sensuality. And so she is willing to practice her erotic charms on this baffling species of lover. She is so successful that Rousseau, his intrusive idealism quashed and his meddling intellect forsaken, swoons with pleasure and prepares to sink down on what appears to be a virginally unblemished bosom. Thereupon he makes a disturbing discovery: Zulietta has only one nipple.

This mammalian deficiency so astonishes Rousseau that the detached observer in him becomes fully awakened once more. Uneasily, naggingly, and quite stupidly, he is driven to associate this physical abnormality with a deeper, spiritual imperfection. He is even prepared to regard Zulietta as a monster of unnaturalness. But it is Rousseau's imagination that has turned monstrous. Zulietta, who has hitherto exhibited little taste for Rousseau's elliptical conversation, now feels exasperated by his probing for dark significance. Without further ado, she disdainfully advises him to give up the ladies and dedicate himself to mathematics. Nature, Rousseau mournfully realizes, has not equipped him to enjoy simple, sensual, unanalyzed pleasures.[8] His pathos is partly checked, however, by his awareness that he has been manipulated in this episode by some sort of comic idiocy.

Rousseau is thus capable of subjecting his poetic imaginings (modified by an inappropriately inquisitive mind) to self-satire. One of the reasons *The New Héloïse,* concerned though it is with the vicissitudes of desperately romantic love, is not entirely encased in sobriety is that Rousseau on several occasions resorts to a worldly, playfully ironic, antiromantic guardedness. Consider the following editorial note, which is designed to distance him from the impassioned sentiments of Julie and St. Preux: "I think I hardly need to mention that in this second part and the one that follows it, the two separated lovers do nothing but speak irrationally and deliriously; the poor creatures no longer have any presence of mind."[9] In *The Confessions* Rousseau more than once recounts anecdotes, in a self-ironizing mode, that are meant to explain his romantic propensities, that is, his various attractions to naïveté and folly. Yet Rousseau does not permit his sense of humor to contaminate his emphasis on himself as a unique human being. [10]

2.

Had his mockery of the romantic sensibility been other than incidental, Rousseau would perhaps now be associated with Byron or Musset or Heine, writers who may be described as romantic ironists. The European romantic ironist, a comedian of ambivalence, laughingly subverts the romantic temper while explicitly or implicitly retaining his allegiance to it.

It is not difficult to distinguish such romantic irony from the more customary mode of Pyrrhonic irony. The Pyrrhonic ironist comically, and irrevocably, dissolves the cant of the ideal and the mendacity of illusion. (In the perspective of Pyrrhonic irony, idealism and illusion stem from the irremediable follies of unruined innocence.) The romantic ironist, however, holds fast to romantic idealization and romantic passion even as he sceptically or cynically makes fun of what he consecrates. Together, Pyrrhonic irony and romantic irony constitute one of the primary components of the comic imagination.

Comedy does not, however, dominate center stage in contemporary accounts of romantic irony. These generally take as their point of departure a number of Friedrich Schlegel's theoretical Fragments (as well as certain of his dialogues and essays), especially those published in the *Lyceum* and the *Athenaeum* at the close of the eighteenth century. These Fragments, which can be both provocatively mysterious and stimulatingly lucid, are often indicative of critical genius; but they can also be numbingly abstruse (and occasionally pedestrian). Several of these Fragments combine to establish irony, not as a comedy of ambivalence, but rather as an all-embracing, infinitely creative-destructive paradoxicality.

Yet Schlegel is far from being insusceptible to the power of comedy. Nor is intellectual levity merely one of his peripheral concerns. It is notable that among the contradictory elements Schlegel's program for romantic poetry (which includes the novel) calls for, analysis is wedded to spontaneity, spiritual profundity merges with humorous tendencies, and idealism is fused with wit. The significance of self-aware playfulness in Schlegel's Fragments, then, cannot be understated – at least at the level of theory. *Lucinde* (1799), Schlegel's creative effort to incorporate (and virtually sanctify) the uses of lightness in romantic literature, exemplifies a boldly liberating disposition; and the novel provides many palpable delights. But *Lucinde* hardly represents a landmark in the history of comedy. Nor is Schlegel's concept of irony a potent notable catalytic agent in European romanticism.

Schlegel's speculations on irony, which appear to encompass the paradoxical coupling of all possible contradictions (therein lies both its fascination and its weakness) are admired by many critics; but such speculations are not a beacon that illuminates the ironic literature of the romantic period. If we set aside the rather misty question of cultural osmosis, it is evident that neither Byron nor Heine, neither Stendhal nor Pushkin, nor any other important practitioner of European romantic irony, derives his animus or his strategy from Schlegel's theorizing.

The "true poet," Robert Penn Warren asserts, earns his vision by submitting it to "the fires of irony."[11] This tempering of vision by the fire (or ice) of irony operates in both romantic irony and New Critical irony. But the peculiar equilibrium of New Critical paradox is not marked by the internecine warfare of romantic irony. More importantly, neither New Critical paradox nor Schlegelian theory is predicated on the sovereignty of comedy. The affirmatives of romantic irony are familiar – for example, lyrical love, the spontaneous self, impassioned idealism, natural harmony, the spell of innocence, intuitions of perfection, the imagination of wonder, heroic dreams of liberation, spiritual transcendence, the vision of the infinite. The comedy-inducing negatives of romantic irony are few and murderous: sceptical candor, realistic deflation, cynical dismissal. The domination of comedy persists even when romantic irony's negatives are ousted by its affirmatives. In either case, romantic and antiromantic elements remain entrenched in opposition. The romantic ironist who balances nineteenth-century expansive imagination and feeling, on the one hand, and eighteenth-century rational restraint and mocking worldliness, on the other, is faithful to both enchantment and astringent reality. He salvages the one in his rhapsodies and promotes the other in his ironic comedy.

3.

It is not unusual for a romantic ironist to purge himself, quite unsuccessfully, of the stigma of romanticism. He may be tempted to describe romanticism as a linguistic orgy, a vacuous sublimity, a gratuitous maiming of classical calm, a preposterous counterfeiting of idealism, an elephantiasis of the emotions, a maddening surrender to obscurantism, a narcissistic pathology of the soul, even a spiritual vampirism afflicting an entire nation. Complications and concessions inevitably set in, however.

Stendhal offers a relatively mild version of such attempted exorcism. He wishes to purge his prose of a fault he views as all too patent in French romanticism: a lyrically messy sensibility. Yet for all his cult of coolness, Stendhal is captivated by Italian romanticism (it is not passionately sincere). Moreover, in *The Life of Henry Brulard,* Stendhal traces an early infatuation with a "Spanish" romanticism whose principal tenets are conscientious honor and heroic nobility of soul. [12] With a mixture of regret and pride, Stendhal underscores the follies into which this elevated "Spanish" sentiment has led him. At the end of *Brulard* he admits that he has carried the "weakness" of romantic exaltation "to the verge of madness... The romantic element in me extended to love, to courage, to everything" (373). Stendhal also believes that the Spanish spirit prevented him "from having the comic genius" (168). That this is a wildly inaccurate opinion (Stendhal, it is true, was thinking of stage comedy) is made especially clear in *The Red and the Black,* where a genius for comedy jostles the near-lunacy of romantic emotion.

The logic of Stendhal's early interpretation of romanticism as a historical phenomenon, explainable by evolutionary trends, attenuates to some extent the defects (including his own) that he ascribes to the (French) romantic ethos. His *Racine and Shakespeare* (published in 1824, long before the reminiscential *Life of Henry Brulard*) metamorphoses all epochs of modernism, whether in ancient Greece or seventeenth-century France or nineteenth-century Italy, into eras of romanticism, which, he writes, "is the art of presenting to different peoples those literary works which, in the existing state of their habits and beliefs, are capable of giving them the greatest possible pleasure." [13] (Classicism, he goes on, supplied such pleasures for their great-grandfathers.) Though the impurities of French romantic sensibility (or his own surrender to

"Spanish" sentiment) continued to be questioned by Stendhal, in principle he could hardly fail to acknowledge that what struck him as egregious in current literature, for example, "the false sensitivity, the pretentious elegance, and the compulsory pathos of that swarm of young poets who exploit the *dreamy vein* and the *mysteries of the soul,*"[14] was presumably a significant source of contemporary pleasure.

Heine, a far more consistent romantic ironist than Stendhal, finds in the legacy of German romanticism certain dubious ingredients that enormously outweigh the undesirable elements in French romanticism. In *The Romantic School* (1834), Heine declares that French romanticism is no more than charmingly muddled and innocuously eccentric. German romanticism, in contrast, is vitiated at its very core. Whereas French romanticists treated medievalism (a dead thing) as only a Gothic fad, German romanticism's wholesale obsession with medievalism (conceived as still alive) became, Heine maintains, its special type of madness, one which can to some extent be grasped by visiting the insane asylum at Charenton.[15] Similarly, French folk legends are beautiful and tame, while German folk legends are bloodily monstrous. The French, Heine explains, no longer threaten Europe with Napoleonic nightmares. Their patriotism, which has become wise and generous, unalarmingly embraces the entire civilized world. German patriotism, on the other hand, is as perverted as German romanticism: it is parochial, contemptuous, and bellicose.

Even in his *History of Religion and Philosophy in Germany* (1835), Heine, while enthusiastically noting the astonishing ascendancy won by the grand elements of the German spirit, is prone to express misgivings about reactionary tendencies in German culture. Like Byron in his treatment of the Lake poets in *Don Juan*, Heine is scarcely held back by a divine sense of fairness. After lauding Kant, Fichte, Schelling, and Hegel – Germany, Heine observes, achieved its greatest revolution in philosophy, not, as in France, in politics – he stresses Schelling's apostasy: "He has forsaken the altar consecrated by his own hands; he has slunk back to the religious kennels of the past." Schelling "goes cringing about in the antechambers of practical and theoretical absolutism, in the dens of Jesuitism he lends a hand in forging intellectual manacles."[16] Yet despite certain instances of romantic philosophy's reversion to intolerant religion, and for all his belaboring of the hazards of German romanticism (his repudiation of its medieval bias is mitigated by ambivalence or even sympathy for several of its representatives, especially Uhland), Heine, a strong partisan of the Enlightenment, judges himself to be the last of the German romantics and hence complicit in its graveyard nostalgia.

4.

Like Byron, Stendhal, and Heine, Leopardi did not find it difficult to demonstrate antipathy toward certain allegedly virulent features of the romanticism that had entered upon the cultural scene. In an early, injudicious, posthumously published essay on the new romantic poetry, Leopardi stabbed melodramatically at the extremism of aberrant Italian romantics: "Until now," he declared, "poets have been swans and not vultures that sweep down on carrion."[17] Neither swan nor vulture, Leopardi owes allegiance to the romantic world (though not to the official, bizarre romanticism he prematurely despised) through the passion, pain, and gloom of his poetry, deeply influenced though that poetry was by the patrician mystique of classical purity.

Leopardi is a romantic marked by profound ironic propensities (for one thing, he cannot help thinking of Italy's past glory and present humiliation); but, unlike Byron, Heine, and Stendhal, he cannot be viewed as a romantic ironist. Leopardi's irony can be grim; and it does not always alleviate his sense of disillusion, which is far more morose than that of Byron. Stendhal, or Heine. Nor does his preoccupation with "noia" (ennui) make for buoyancy. "Noia," that great intensifier of disenchantment, is described in Leopardi's *Zibaldone* (Sept. 30, 1821) as "the most sterile of all human passions. It is the child of nullity and thus the mother of nothingness."[18] Yet "noia" presupposes the potency of illusion (just as Baudelaire's "spleen" presupposes the potency of the "ideal"). In an earlier comment in the *Zibaldone* (Aug. 18-20,1820), illusion is described as undefeatable by balked aspirations. "Illusions, however weakened and unmasked by reason," Leopardi comments, "always stay with us and form the major part of our lives ... Nor, once lost, are they lost in such a way that their vital roots are also destroyed: if we go on living they are bound to flower again despite all our experience and certitude"(5). In the *Pensieri*, Leopardi even remarks that "'noia' is in some ways the most sublime of human feelings" (113), since it proves that the human mind has an urge to be nobly inventive, even if that urge is doomed to frustration.

Yet over and over again, with an insistence that is more prophylactic than pathological, Leopardi accentuates not only the doom of splendid urges but the omnipresence of human vanity, wretchedness, and baseness. In the poem "To Count Carlo Pepoli," for example, "noia," so far from being "the most sublime of human feelings," is ranked as life's supreme perversity. It transforms dreams into ordure, and the voyage of the ideal into circumambient grief. Worst of all, it drives us to assuage our misery by inflicting suffering on others.

Negations of this sort explain why it is that when illusion and disillusion collide in Leopardi's poetry, the results is not apt to be a romantic-ironic tug-of-war between untempered promise and destructive reality. Rather, Leopardi's mordancy is transmitted through traditional modes of irony, either circumstantial or cosmic. Consider "Sopra il ritratto di una bella donna" ("On the Portrait of a Beautiful Woman"), where ironic pessimism conveys a hideous comedy of disintegrated beauty. The poet ponders the luminous architecture of a lovely face (carved on a sepulchral monument) that cannot escape crumbling. Does not Fate, the poet dolorously yet maliciously asks, dissolve even an angel's brightness into dirt and a foul pack of bones? If humanity is destined to become only dust, what is the point of feeling exaltation? Neither Fate nor man is spared Leopardi's sardonic mockery; nor is there any trace of ambivalence here.

Similarly, romantic illusions about Nature are not unscathed. These illusions (together with man's reliance on Providence) are shredded in Leopardi's supremely ironic poem, "La quiete dopo la tempesta" ("Tranquility after the Storm"). The titular storm has just swept by, apparently enacting a spasm of cruel forgetfulness on the part of Nature. But now Nature reassuringly resuscitates her basic sweetness. Life is again gracious and gay: the sun smiles, birds delight, hearts rejoice. But is this renewed radiance, the poet wonders, more authentic than Nature's fits of darkness and terror? Is this semblance of a boon merely a lure? The nature of Nature, the poet concludes, is duplicity: her moments of peace and beauty serve only to screen the absurdity of life. Human joys themselves are merely delusive, functioning as irregularly permitted respites from torment. Leopardi's tone in puncturing Nature's pretense of fostering mankind is not brutally repudiative. His final lines proceed to ruin the myth of Nature's benevolence, along with Eternity's regard for the human condition, with delicately cutting ironic politeness:

O bounteous Nature, these
Are then your gifts, and this
The happiness you offer
Us mortal Men! The issue out of pain
Is happiness enough;
And pains you scatter with a generous hand,
While sorrow springs even of its own accord;

And pleasure, which by some odd miracle
Is born from trouble, is great gain. O human kind,
Dear to the eternal powers, happy indeed
If granted pause for breath
After each grief; most blest
If even these are cured at last by death.[19]

The sardonic animus of these lines is beautifully, bitterly restrained. But Leopardi has not written a romantic-ironic poem; he has not communicated the idea that Nature is both supernal and infernal, and that it should be both celebrated and denounced. The double vision in his poem stems uniquely from man's victimization. Nature only seems to be a paradise; in actuality it is a scourge. The poet's unillusioned ironic lucidity suggests an even more odious misuse of power: the main drive of Nature (and the cosmos), whether convulsively or with ingenious nuances of voracity, is the sadistic maiming of man's spirit.

Indeed, with the exception of a heroically disdainful elite, the human race, Leopardi believes, is destined to squirm rather than revolt, to endure pathetically rather than laugh defiantly. Laughter itself is not for Leopardi a sure indicator of courageous resistance. In his essay "In Praise of Birds," laughter is more readily perceived as a symptom of physical and psychological laceration than as an innate reflex of high spirits. The essay presents the meditations of the solitary philosopher Aemilius, who extols the joy of birds, seemingly an analogue of human laughter. But the joy of birds, Aemilius reflects, is energetically innocent; human laughter is not. In their seizures of laughter, men brood and ache, crack and bleed. It may be "a wonderful thing that man, the most tormented and wretched of all creatures, should possess the faculty of laughter," Aemilius sums up; yet laughter remains "a sort of temporary madness or else raving or delirium – since men, who are never fully satisfied or delighted by anything whatever, can have no reasonable or just cause for laughter." [20]

Not surprisingly, mankind, according to the philosopher, forms the chief staple of mockery for the ignoble theatrical gods. Nevertheless, Aemilius's meditations do not end on a totally sour note. A few valorous human beings have indeed achieved an ironic, adversarial smile that lessens the power of divine jeering. The philosopher also believes that a paradox has developed within laughter itself. This usually reliable symptom of crucifixion has somehow generated a meliorative force, a movement toward social reform. Yet it is difficult for the reader to feel that this conviction is more than half-hearted. (Baudelaire's vaguely similar essay "The Essence of Laughter" is much more promising and certainly more persuasive. Baudelaire's essay may begin with the notion that laughter is evidence of madness and damnation; but it ends with the idea that comedy – not the satiric, socially improving sort, but rather the kind that Baudelaire calls the "absolute comic," rich in varieties of irrationality and the grotesque – can become a source of redemptive energy.)

Leopardi is not the only ironic romantic who cannot usefully be described as a romantic ironist. Blake is another. No one can deny Blake his often sulphurous sense of comedy, whether in his epic-apocalyptic poems or in the relatively tidier framework of "The Marriage of Heaven and Hell." Yet in "The Marriage of Heaven and Hell," Blake's astonishing unorthodoxy – his exposure of sham, hypocrisy, and abysmal pseudo-religiosity – is crucially dependent on the orthodox methodology of ironic inversion. Thus angels are not inspiringly spiritual; they are tamely pious, repellently respectable. Devils do not mar one's soul; if they are piercingly destructive, that is because they are blazingly creative. The "Proverbs of Hell" section is not a collection of satanic dicta but rather a unique manual of romantic drives and intuitions.

The contrapuntalism of Blake's *Songs of Innocence and Experience* would seem to lend itself more obviously to the dualities of romantic irony; for Blake's innocence and experience, like Carlyle's transcendentalism and descendentalism, often resembles or parallels romantic idealism and antiromantic disaffection. Yet the clash between innocence and experience in Blake is usually too melancholy or too bitterly ironic to sustain the comedy that is indispensable to romantic irony. (Thus the irony that counterpoints the vision of apparently radiant, flower-like "thousands of little boys and girls raising their innocent hands" in St. Paul's in the first "Holy Thursday" and the dark portrait of children in the second "Holy Thursday" who are victims of unholy, eternally wintry misery produces a shattering pathos.) Nor does the permanent ambivalence of romantic irony lend itself to Blakean "progression" via contraries.

Lightness may be the final test, and ambivalence the initial premise, of European romantic irony. However, perceptions of comedy and assessments of ambivalence are hardly unproblematic. Is it plausible, for example, to describe the conflict between romantic urge and antiromantic control in Jane Austen's *Sense and Sensibility* as proof of romantic irony? To put the issue more precisely, if one is convinced that Austen, consciously or not, has assigned more or less equal value to Marianne's rebelliously expansive sensibility and Elinor's prudentially contractive good sense – sense and sensibility, however, mingle in surprising ways in both young women, for good or ill – and that the author has also maintained a comic (if at times poignant) atmosphere in the novel, may one not fittingly regard *Sense and Sensibility* as a work of romantic irony?

Elsewhere in Jane Austen, cool, disciplined judgment is not, for the most part, exactly balanced by frank, engagingly irrational exuberance. *Sense and Sensibility* is something of an exception. A. Walton Litz probably speaks for most readers when he says that though "ostensibly the author's sympathy is with Elinor ... running counter to this is Jane Austen's obvious admiration (reflected in lively description and dialogue) for Marianne's vitality and candor. It is as if Jane Austen's own sensibility were all on the side of Marianne, but her judgment had to decide for Elinor."[21] So far as romantic irony is concerned, however, the chief consideration must be that Jane Austen seldom relinquishes the tone of an assured, if brilliantly subtle, satiric mentality. Expressing itself in perpetually keen analyses and witty discriminations, this mentality does not naturally give way to romantic irony's unstable, risky interplay of romantic enthrallment and comic disengagement.

Still, a faint nexus can be discerned between Austen's *Sense and Sensibility* and Goethe's *Faust: Part I*, where Faust's exalted reveries and Mephistopheles' trenchant, malicious belittlements more compellingly exemplify romantic irony's intersections of romantic exaltation and comic derogation. It is true that Faust's idealism is to some extent spoiled by his moral lapses. Nevertheless, it remains potent enough and provocative enough to serve as a perfect foil for Mephistopheles' cynical laughter (especially in regard to the spiritualization of love, which for Mephistopheles has a solid animal basis.) On the other hand, Faust's emotional sublimity effectively disparages (though not always) Mephistopheles' vulgar comic realism. Each of them, in scenes inflected with startling tonal dissonance, is thoroughly capable of exploding the other's pretensions. (*Faust* has also been viewed as a Schlegelian synthesis of "tragedy and comedy; intellectual brilliance and emotion, irony and lyricism.")[22]

Faust's romantic irony, in turn, does not measure up to *Don Quixote's*. Cervantes' novel plays the game of enchantment and disenchantment not only far more consistently than *Faust* but also with vastly greater comic resourcefulness. Don Quixote's idealism, which is rarely collapsible, and his visionary optics, which are seldom altered, are notoriously contested by the external world's hilariously punitive corrections, and by Sancho Panza's own bluff dismissals of fantasy (that is, when Sancho Panza is not himself caught up, as he increasingly is, in his master's chivalric ardor.)

So singular and so masterfully deployed is the romantic-ironic dualism in *Don Quixote* that it may seem strikingly inappropriate to associate Byron's comedy in *Don Juan* with that of Cervantes. (Byron, incidentally, carelessly overestimated the dissolvent effect of Cervantes' novel. It is now widely believed that no work more resoundingly keeps chivalric romance alive than *Don Quixote.*) Yet Don Quixote's romantic soaring into the ideal (which is not quite divorceable from his search for fame) and his subsequent antic tumbling into reality is to an appreciable degree matched in the early cantos of *Don Juan* by a Byronic dichotomy of romantic and antiromantic impulses.

5.

This kind of dichotomy has not, of course, always been applauded as a sign of psychic resilience or a symptom of creative flexibility. Irving Babbitt, for example, in *Rousseau and Romanticism* (1919) considered romantic irony, like romanticism itself, to be a profound threat. His bias against romanticism (he welcomes romantic literature only for its recreational pleasures) is strikingly recognizable not only in his chapter on romantic irony, but in others that concentrate on romantic melancholy, romantic love, romantic genius, romantic imagination, and romantic morality. All of these chapters are intended to seal off the perverse distillate of romantic intoxication.

In an earlier study, *The Masters of Modern French Criticism* (1912), Babbitt had twice, each time briefly, broached the question of romantic irony. In the first of his two comments, Babbitt locates the source of "true romantic irony" in the mid-nineteenth century breakdown of revolutionary fervor, when romantic idealists (pseudo-idealists, in Babbitt's terminology), emerging from their shattered evangelism, were crushed by the sight of "the deepest materialism the world had seen since the Roman decadence."[23] Despite a certain fondness for hyperbole, Babbitt plausibly puts his finger on the historical nerve of romantic irony: the destruction of social and political idealism by resurgent illiberal governments, accompanied by a massive defection to middle-class acquisitiveness. Yet chronological elasticity is lacking in this observation. When the failure of idealistic aspiration is seen, not as encapsulated in a single historical event (the aborted revolution of 1848, which is what Babbitt had in mind), but as a recurrent phenomenon in the period 1789-1848, we acquire a broader context for the play of historical forces that helped generate the ambivalence of romantic irony.

As it happens, the validity of Babbitt's insight into the historical sources of "true romantic irony" becomes diluted in the very passage from *Masters of Modern French Criticism* that has just been cited; for Babbitt also remarks that Napoleon was the "ironical reply of the Nature of things to the utopias of the French Revolution"(129). By conjuring up the irony of things – the inescapable, mocking circumstances that throughout history undermine not only visionary hopes but justifiable expectations of all sorts – Babbitt allows his critical focus to slip into a platitudinous universality that denies romantic irony a measurable historic correlate.

The second of Babbitt's two reflections on romantic irony in *Masters of Modern French Criticism* is imbedded in his analysis of the ironic temper of Anatole France and Ernest Renan: "The sense of universal illusions," Babbitt writes, "does not result, in the case of M. France, so much in metaphysical anguish as in an extreme form of romantic irony that abounds in the later work of Renan – the irony of the man who hovers over all points of view and refuses to be bound by any because every point of view is necessarily relative and transitory" (318-19). The phrase "romantic irony" in this passage is quite misleading. The ironic temper of Anatole France and the older Renan, with its smilingly sceptical rejection of treacherous absolutes and abiding illusions, is Pyrrhonic in nature. (The older Renan believed that since god is the perpetrator of a huge joke-world, a mortal ironist would be well advised to arm himself with a countervailing gaiety of detachment.) It is Pyrrhonic irony that comically subverts the apparently immortal errors of idealism without seeking to re-animate the illusions it shatters. It is romantic irony, on the other hand, that comically presents an irresolvable civil war of the mind and the imagination. The ambivalence of romantic irony belongs to the earlier part of the nineteenth century. Pyrrhonic irony gains renewed strength in the later nineteenth century, when the depletion of romantic idealism becomes more and more pronounced.

Babbitt probably has Schlegelian theory in mind when he speaks of ironic hovering in Anatole France and Renan. Certainly Schlegel is the villain in Babbitt's chapter on romantic irony in *Rousseau and Romanticism,* a work whose constant charge is that European romanticism is fundamentally de-civilizing, that it represents a divorce from moral reality. According to Babbitt, romanticism's "despotism of mood" [24] exploits the emotional deviations of the personal, purely exploratory self, and inevitably regresses to an emphasis on adolescent wonder. This failure of maturity, of self-command, is relentlessly imaged by Babbitt as an unruly, often pathological drifting, an anarchic truancy from an ethical norm. Romanticism's "infinite indeterminate desire," he complains, stems from "an endless and aimless vagabondage of the emotions with the imagination as their free accomplice" (74). As a representative of humanism, Babbitt calls for an Aristotelian wisdom of centrality, restraint, and proportion, virtues which are nourished by what Babbitt calls an imagination of vital control.

In Babbitt's chapter on romantic irony, the supreme romantic vagabond is Friedrich Schlegel, whose conception of romantic chaos (inexhaustibly pregnant) and romantic originality (outrageously intolerant of interference) Babbitt flintily derides. Two *Lyceum* Fragments, nos. 42 and 108, and one *Athenaeum* Fragment, no. 116, afford Babbitt all the evidence of damnation he needs. *Lyceum* Fragment no. 42 hymns the "divine breath of irony" in certain works, both ancient and modern, whose mood of "transcendental buffoonery" enables the poet to rise "infinitely above everything limited, even the poet's own art, virtue, and genius." [25] *Lyceum* Fragment no. 108 pays homage to Socratic irony as a union of jest and seriousness, openness and dissimulation. It embodies "the insoluble conflict of the absolute and the relative, of the impossibility and necessity of total communication"; and since it is "the freest of all liberties," empowering us "to rise above our own self," Socratic irony tends toward "constant self-parody" (131). *Athenaeum* Fragment no. 116 defines, among a host of dizzying promulgations, the first principle of romantic poetry, which "recognizes that the arbitrariness of the poet endures no law above him" (141). Such are the elements, in Babbitt's view, that account for the unholy career of the egomaniacal romantic imagination.

For many contemporary critics, as has been noted, Schlegel's Fragments are intellectually stimulating challenges (if at times enigmatic or too sweeping) rather than so many signposts to the spirit's perdition. Butt Babbitt is convinced that he is alerting the reader to the danger of an infatuation with fantastic paradox – the intolerable Schlegelian paradox, for example, that the romantic ironist can carry out a quest for transcendental illumination while making light of his own artistic limitations. This kind of self-division, Babbitt somewhat stodgily avers, is an invitation to crazily irrational, self-destructive play. The result can only be an erratic and interminable "pilgrimage in the void" (203). Earlier in the chapter, Babbitt had disparaged Nietzsche's (allegedly reckless) idea in *Beyond Good and Evil* that "objection, evasion, joyous distrust, and love of irony are signs of health; everything absolute belongs to pathology" (quoted, 190). Schlegel's irony is deprecated as a comparable intellectual scandal.

What particularly irritates Babbitt is Schlegel's attempt to fortify his case for "vagrancy of spirit" (205) by relying on the example of Socrates. Such linkage is untenable, Babbitt argues, inasmuch as Socratic irony respects the mind's need for unity and hence aims at a centrality of ethical meaning. Schlegelian irony, on the other hand, exhibits a purely dispersive, centrifugal tendency. The situation is somewhat different with Ariosto and Cervantes, whom Schlegel also recruits for the purpose of corroborating his theory. Babbitt admits that these two masters belong on the margins of romantic irony because of their dualistic proclivities; they love yet also burlesque medieval tales of chivalry. Nevertheless, Babbitt maintains that Ariosto and Cervantes dwell too close to the foundations of human nature to exemplify Schlegel's anomalous interpretation of the lawless creative mind.

In rejecting what he deems to be Schlegel's intemperateness, Babbitt seeks support in various literary studies, the most significant of which is George Brandes's *The Romantic School in Germany.* Though Brandes's critique is much milder than Babbitt's, his comments on Schlegel's "notorious romantic irony"[26] clearly resemble Babbitt's later attacks on psychic self-splitting. Brandes too is put off by a theory that glorifies the ego's illicit potentialities and encourages the growth of a capricious unreality. Like Babbitt, Brandes frowns on the belief that true art is self-shattering to the point of self-parody. As a Dane, moreover, Brandes is prepared to quote Kierkegaard's objections to Schlegel. (Kierkegaard, not without considerable assistance from Hegel's views on Schlegelian theory, even though Kierkegaard suggests that Hegel got the theory wrong, regards Schlegel, in *The Concept of Irony,* as the subjectivistic, ahistorical, irresponsible proponent of a psychological and cultural pathology camouflaged as irony.) Yet Brandes finds a "fundamental resemblance" between Schlegel's ironic, arbitrary subjectivity and Kierkegaard's aristocratic, paradoxical refusal to be merely understood. [27] Unlike Brandes, Babbitt does not cite Kierkegaard; but he does allude to Hegel's distaste for Schlegel's ruinous idea of irony.

Brandes and Babbitt see eye to eye on Schlegel, but not on Byron. In *Naturalism in Nineteenth-Century English Literature* (a non-Zolaesque title), a work published after his study of German romanticism, Brandes applauds Byron as the quintessential symbol of romantic revolt. In doing so, he does not fail to emphasize Byron's propensity to exploit extraordinary tonalities; these are construed by Brandes as evidence, among other things, of Byron's restless, heroic unorthodoxy. The poet "bounds," he writes, "from one feeling to another, by preference its exact opposite, in order to make each as strong as possible, and then hacks and hews at them – the harder, the extremer the tension he has produced." [28] This recognition of creative-destructive rhythms does not, however, incline Brandes to associate Byron with Schlegel, perhaps because *Don Juan* "contains the whole wide ocean of life, with its storms and sunshine,"[29] whereas Schlegel's *Lucinde*, though never moribund since it contains many intellectually charming passages, is a comparatively bloodless fiction. Babbitt, on the other hand, though with curious ambiguity, identifies *Don Juan* as a "masterpiece of romantic irony" (207).

Most of the humanistic starch in Babbitt's rejection of romantic irony's "gypsy laughter from the bushes"[30] – the kind of laughter that supposedly betrays ethical and spiritual insolvency – sagged long ago. Nevertheless, several of Babbitt's unfashionable perceptions are hard to dismiss, especially his insight that the romantic ironist embodies, in a unique way, the Rousseauistic warfare between heart and head. Babbitt claims that the romantic ironist dreams, then dismantles his dream; he idealizes, then self-mockingly distances himself from his ideals. In this process, Babbitt wryly concedes, there is at least one value, albeit a desperate one: by clinging to his dream and yet practicing aloofness from it – by refusing that is, to remain the dupe of his illusions – the romantic ironist can escape the madness which excessive disillusion might otherwise cause (206). Babbitt, no lover of paradox, is oddly suggesting that romantic irony, the product of a "grave psychological weakness" (205), has the strength to fend off lunacy.

Babbitt inadvertently spoils this interesting analysis when he intimates that the romantic ironist evolves from a stage of intoxication to a state of irreversible sobriety. "Everyone knows," Babbitt remarks, "with what coldness [Heine's] head came to survey the enthusiasm of his heart, whether in love or in politics" (206). But romantic irony is not a one-way temporal process that leads from naïveté to harsh realistic awareness. Heine's sceptically mature head did not forsake once and for all his youthfully romantic heart. Nor was his romantic temper a neurotic affliction of youth therapeutically eliminated by advancing years.

The motif of a heart no longer susceptible to a rebirth of illusion is sounded once again when Babbitt alludes to Renan's early idealism and late irony, and also to the ironic mind of Anatole France. (This allusion echoes his comments on these two writers in *Masters of Modern French Criticism.*) Babbitt once more fails to distinguish between the Pyrrhonic irony of Renan and Anatole France and the romantic irony of Byron and Heine. (The irony deployed by these two poets is of course not confined to the romantic version.) In Pyrrhonic irony, the visionary qualities of youth do indeed surrender to the disabusements of age, or at least to the disillusions of experience. In European romantic irony, however, amused disbelief does not extinguish strong leanings toward re-enchantment. If the romantic ironist clings to his dream while disavowing it, as Babbitt believes, that is because the dream remains an active force. European romantic irony is an expression of profound (though hardly unfathomable) ambivalence. It is as little a capitulation to the heart's enfeeblement as it is to moral fatigue or psychic exhaustion.

It is somewhat surprising that Babbitt, having pronounced Byron and Heine to be the pre-eminent romantic ironists of England and Germany, respectively, does not assign the author of *Madame Bovary* the title of French master of romantic irony. In an earlier chapter on the romantic imagination, Babbitt had pointed out that Flaubert is dominated by an "acrid disillusion," the result of a continuing conflict between his intellect and his emotions. Flaubert, Babbitt states, "oscillates rapidly between the pole of realism and the pole of romance," and is thereby left philosophically "suspended in the void" (95) – the familiar habitat, we recall, of the romantic ironist. The fact that in *Madame Bovary* Flaubert mocks "the ideal that he craves emotionally and imaginatively" (95) would seem to position him fairly close to Byron and Heine.

Had Babbitt argued that Flaubert is France's principal romantic ironist, he might not have been convincing. But Babbitt is surely right in designating Heine as the "true German master" of romantic irony (206). Yet his discussion of Heine's romantic irony is disappointing. Babbitt claims that there are two ways in which Heine manifests his romantic irony. The first is through tonal disruption ("Stimmungsbrechung"), that is, the "swift passage from one mood to another" (207). To reinforce this claim, Babbitt cites Jean Paul Richter's judgment that his own novels contain "hot baths of sentiment … followed by cold douches of irony" (quoted, 206). But tonal disruption is of various sorts. Thus a sudden swing from tenderness or pathos to levity is hardly the equivalent of a startling reduction of romantic idealism to laughable rubbish. As for the quotation from Jean Paul, it interestingly evokes the rapid, often grotesque transmutations that occur in his fiction. Equally interesting is that the observation about hot baths and cold douches is an indictment generously composed by Jean Paul himself on behalf of readers protesting against his failure to write straightforward narrative.[31] In any event, Babbitt's quotation, far from sufficing to explain the workings of European romantic irony, shows only that for this critic, an emphatic tonal disruption is the primary stylistic quirk of the kind of writer who is "subject to no centre" (207) and who goes about perpetuating disorientation by promoting extremes.[32]

The second presumptive technique of a romantic ironist like Heine is "the sudden breaking of the spell of poetry by an intrusion of the poet's ego" (207). Here again, however, we must make distinctions. Sudden authorial irruptions into a text may signify a good many things, for example, eccentric teasing, or diabolic leg-pulling, or premeditated (or perhaps unpremeditated) double attitudes. The point is that an unexpected authorial expulsion of "the spell of poetry" does not automatically herald a jolting split between a romantic aspiration and its mocking repudiation. Moreover, a self-conscious, self-referentially interruptive playfulness is not unique to romanticism. It can be found in the eighteenth-century novel; and it has become a frequent tactic, if not an entire strategy, in contemporary metafiction.

Though he supplies no illustrations of "Stimmungsbrechung," Babbitt informs us that "some of the best examples" of tone disruption "are located in *Don Juan*," a work which Babbitt, we remember, has categorized as a "masterpiece of romantic irony." (Babbitt adds that the poem also contains plenty of Swiftian satire and irony.) Inasmuch as Babbitt equates romantic irony with the moral imagination in a state of disgrace, and also depicts it as a kind of metaphysical hoboism, a "masterpiece of romantic irony" seems a rather strange compliment, as though Babbitt were accrediting a marvelous specimen of literary gangrene.

A typical example of romantic irony's (suspect) procedure in *Don Juan* is located, we learn in an endnote, in stanzas 107-111 of Canto III. If we glance at these stanzas, we see that Byron has indeed contrived a considerable tone disjunction. But what kind of disjunction? Is he thrusting upon us, perhaps to obviate narrative staleness or simply to cater to a destructive whim, a seriocomic passage in which a charge of emotion is suddenly devalued, or a solemn atmosphere is brusquely unsettled? Or is he embracing a romantic ideal or an intense romantic passion which is then comically nullified? (Or is he nullifying an ideal with is then resurrected? In European romantic irony a comic purging of the ideal may be followed by its whole-hearted rehabilitation.)

The substance of the five stanzas (misleadingly) recommended by Babbitt for their romantic-ironic typicality may be briefly schematized. The first (107) is an evening pastoral that celebrates the domestic satisfactions of tranquility, good cheer, and parental love. The next stanza (108), similarly tender, trails some anxieties from Dante's Purgatory as it evokes journeys both secular and religious, touches on the inevitability of separation and change, and finally curves toward decay, death, and grief. The stanza offers a comforting note, however, by adducing the universality of mourning. A specific elegiac instance occurs in stanza 109, which is how Nero suddenly slips into Byron's lines; for even Nero the destroyer, though richly deserving his doom, was lamented by some grateful wretch (fact, not fantasy) who strewed flowers on his tomb. [33]

The mention of this notoriously decadent Roman emperor in the midst of stanzas devoted to the pleasures of gentle repose and the melancholy of unassisted extinction is of course a jarring intrusion. In stanza 110, the narrator (Byron's twin, by and large) wakes up, with disingenuous tardiness, to the incongruity of this historical allusion and at once annihilates the tone of the preceding stanzas: "…what on earth has Nero, / Or any such like sovereign buffoons, / To do with the transactions of my hero,…?"[34] Evidently his powers of invention, the narrator apologizes, have sunk down to zero. In the last stanza (111) he belittles his talent once more, accusing it of having lapsed into tediousness. This self-accusation then licenses a nonchalant disparagement of the stature of epic poetry, for Byron hints that continued tedium on his part will prove "too epic." He will therefore abbreviate the threatening bulk of Canto III and, in doing so, garner laurels from the critics.

By the end of the fifth stanza (111), Byron has not only irreparably jangled the sad music of mortality but has blatantly indulged in self-irony. He has also wittily desanctified the dignity of the epic, the grand literary form he has explicitly (mock-) adopted. (Epic solemnity is more than once cavalierly deflated in *Don Juan*. Canto III itself, ending in the stanzas just discussed, begins with a truncated, saucily disrespectable apostrophe: "Hail, Muse! et cetera –.") Yet Byron's literary misbehavior (his radical tone disruption and mischievous authorial intrusiveness) is not inherently a demonstration of romantic irony.

6.

Byron's unseemly capsizing of delicate or rapturous feelings into an abyss of harsh comic dissonances produced imperfect admiration or downright hostility long before Babbitt composed *Rousseau and Romanticism.* The poet's deviations from tonal stability and decorum, especially in the early cantos, were often judged, at best, as perilously piquant and, at worst, as ignominiously deficient in moral discrimination. In 1831, Macaulay shrewdly explained that Byron's literary tendency toward doubleness was the product of his allegiance to both the old and the new poetic sects. But Macaulay's calm perspective on Byron's "strange union of opposite extremes"[35] had not been widely shared. Leigh Hunt, for example, though writing for the nonce as a liberal ally of Byron in the *Examiner* (1819), was unhappily obliged to note the poet's recurrent use of a "sudden transition from liveliness or grandeur to ridicule or the mock-heroic" (174), a tactic Hunt believed was used with mortifying recklessness. Yet in accounting for the disunity not only in *Don Juan* but in its author's temperament, Hunt perceptively underlined the conflict in Byron between the blight of disillusion and the power of authentic feeling. When the latter threatens to become unbearably pronounced, Byron "dashes away and relieves himself by getting into another train of ideas" (176).

Though praising Byron in the *Edinburgh Review* (1822), Francis Jeffrey finally proffers a damning diagnosis of *Don Juan*, precisely because the poem interlinks sublimity and cynicism, exalted emotion and sardonic heartlessness. The poem, he remarks, transmits a "fatal power of corruption" (201). The nobility that might palliate or even supply an antidote to Byron's pernicious scepticism "is mingled with the poison, and the draught is the more deadly for the mixture!" (202) Shifting from this alarming medical metaphor to an equally dismaying religious simile, Jeffrey likens Byron to a priest who pleads for purity while zestfully joining in debauchery. The shock suffered by goodness is irremediable. Jeffrey recognizes, however, that in certain persuasively idealizing passages it is impossible not to credit Byron with a devotion to "sweet and lofty illusion" (203), that is, until the poet abruptly, jokily abolishes his own fineness of feeling.

Jeffrey offers four illustrations of what he finds objectionable in *Don Juan:* 1) the combination, in Canto I, of Julia's shameless antics in her bedroom and the holy warmth of her epistle to Juan; 2) the immediate switching in the shipwreck episode, in Canto II, from a father's pitiful agonizing over his dying son to the cannibalistic facetiousness of slicing up Juan's tutor; 3) the instant juxtaposition, in Canto III, of the glorious invocation of Greece with dull, ignoble ribaldry; and 4) the close sequence, in Cantos IV-V, of the anguishing death of Haidée and the seraglio masquerade. These examples of Byron's tendency to yoke incompatibles together confirm for Jeffrey the poet's excessive inclination to endorse the abolition of dream and the death of virtue. True, Jeffrey admits that Byron is witty enough and knowledgeable enough to make his cynicism "irresistibly pleasant and plausible" (204); but Byron remains guilty of outrageous ethical lapses.

Byron's predilection for moral nihilism is also emphasized, and in much the same terms as Jeffrey's, in Hazlitt's *The Spirit of the Age* (1825). Hazlitt contends that Byron prostitutes his talents in a unique self-travesty effected by a droll, "utter discontinuity of ideas and feelings." (This lightness of temper, Hazlitt believes, is characteristically aristocratic in its arrogance and irresponsibility.) The result of this anarchic poetizing is to make "virtue serve as a foil to vice." Hazlitt's righteous formulation of Byron's allegedly demonic craft is memorably melodramatic (this adverse judgment was later recalled, however):

> He hallows in order to desecrate; takes a pleasure in defacing the images of beauty his hands have wrought; and raises our hopes and our belief in goodness to Heaven only to dash them to earth again, and break them in pieces the more effectually from the very height they have fallen....When he is most serious and most moral, he is only preparing to mortify the unsuspecting reader by putting a pitiful hoax on him. This is a most unaccountable anomaly. It is as if the eagle were to build his eyry in a common sewer ... (275)

Hazlitt adds in a footnote that "the censure applies to the first cantos of *Don Juan* much more than to the last" (275n1). Yet these first cantos, for those who were not overbearingly moralistic, were particularly fascinating. Thus Lockhart in "John Bull's Letter to Lord Byron" finds Canto I and Canto II wonderfully animating, while Macaulay's verdict is that the first cantos are the best part of *Don Juan*. The audacity and variety of Byron's tone disruptions evidently struck some readers not as a satanic hoax but as a delightful liberation from inert decorum and the cant of consistency. (When Hazlitt, incidentally, drops the charge that Byron is dissolving morality and concentrates instead on purely literary matters, he becomes an early discoverer of self-reflexive literature. "*Don Juan,*" he writes, "has been called a *Tristram Shandy* in rhyme; it is rather a poem about itself" [275n1]).

Whatever their personal relationship to Byron, and whatever the power of their critical acumen, Hunt, Jeffrey, and Hazlitt variously suggest that there is something unforgivably rotten about Byron's levity.

Thomas Moore is more flexible. In the *Letters and Journals of Lord Byron: with Notices of his Life* (1830), he indicates how extraordinarily multiplex Byron's personality is. Yet he locates within the poet a basic duality (essentially supported by Macaulay's review in 1831) that derives, not from a deranged eagle's lust for the sewer, but from a creative temper that combines the "wit of a Voltaire" with "the sensibility of a Rousseau." Byron conjoins "a susceptibility to all that is grandest and most affecting in human virtue, with a deep, withering experience of all that is most fatal to it, – the two extremes, in short, of man's mixed and inconsistent nature, now rankly smelling of earth, now breathing of heaven" (283). Moore's insistence that antithetical elements prevail within the human imagination, and that man is nothing if not a creature of contrast, reflects a psychological commonplace of the time. Yet Moore himself shies away from a disorderly duality. What he finally accentuates is the need for a controlling, purifying power of judgment. Byron's bias toward "incongruous juxtapositions...between the burlesque and the sublime," he declares, may be faulted because it runs the danger of vitiating "the mind's relish" for nobility; it risks encouraging only a "sceptical indifference" (284) in the matter of moral choice. Nor can Moore unregretfully accept the incursions of mockery in Byron's portrayal of human suffering and baseness.

Though Moore echoes, somewhat more mildly, the complaints of his critical predecessors, his description of Byron's duality as a blend of Voltairean wit and Rousseauesque sensibility retains a good deal of cogency. A number of Byron's twentieth-century critics find this old-fashioned bipolar perspective on Byron not only useful but quite convincing, though they usually substitute "heart" or "idealism" for Rousseau and "head" or "satire" or for Voltaire.

Of course psychic dualities were hardly a discovery of the romantic period. The Renaissance, above all, had provided masterly illuminations of psychic incompatibles. Montaigne, a frequent expositor of human inconsistency, discovered in himself innumerable contradictions. In his essay "Of Glory," he writes that "we are, I know not how, doubled within ourselves, with the result that we do not believe what we believe, and we cannot rid ourselves of what we condemn."[36] Montaigne's speculation, echoing Plutarch's idea of the "discontinuous self" in the *Moralia,* probably helped to intensify Shakespeare's perception of the ego's extraordinary incongruities.[37] And not only Shakespeare's. Hiram Hayden claims that the divided self in the Elizabethan age became an "epidemic dichotomy." "In no other period in any literature with which I am familiar," he goes on to say, "is there such a schizophrenic tendency. Nowhere else will one find such a strange mingling – in the same men, even in single passages – of affirmation and rebellion, idealism and cynicism, aspiration and pessimism, delicacy and grossness, exuberance and despair."[38]

Though it would be going a bit far to describe romantic dichotomies (whether psychic or aesthetic) as epidemic, it is clear that extraordinary polarities of mood abound in the romantic period. Yet romantics who cultivate dissonance are not axiomatically romantic ironists. When Victor Hugo wrote his preface to *Cromwell* (1827), he was proclaiming the need, long overdue, for interfusing vital antitheses on the French stage. Hugo's scheme of literary evolution is not especially reliable – after a primitive epoch of lyrical naïveté, followed by a period of epic simplicity in antiquity, the modern age of drama arrives – but his justifiable theme is the truthfulness, the authentic reality at the core of (ever modern) Shakespearean drama, a reality frustrated by the rigidities of old-guard French theater. Romantic drama, Hugo insists, must be faithful to what is characteristic of the modern, unstable, paradoxical temper: it requires a "harmony of opposites," a blend (or at least an intersection) of "the grotesque and the sublime, the terrible and the farcical, tragedy and comedy. . . ." This kind of drama would "make the audience switch constantly ... from buffoonish antics to harrowing emotions. . . ."[39]

Such tonal disruption is not equivalent to the kind of ambivalence that is generated by a convergence of visionary and sceptical impulses. Nor is a visionary-sceptical duality, for that matter, necessarily a mode of comedy. The distinction between tone disruption in general and romantic irony in particular may be stated as follows: tone disjunction transforms specifically into romantic irony when it both supports and laughs at a romantic ideal, when it both ardently advocates and comically discountenances a lyrical imperative.[40]

Chapter 2

Byron, Carlyle, and the Comedy of Ambivalence

1.

It is essential to differentiate between romantic irony and the ironic mockery of romanticism. The latter mode of comedy accentuates the sublime-to-the-ridiculous, where the sublime functions, not as the component of a genuine ambivalence, but merely as a set-up for its own unexpected, funny demolition. Thus Peacock's comic critique of romantic oddities in *Nightmare Abbey* (1818) is virtually unhedged, whereas the creation and disintegration of romantic imperatives in the early cantos of *Don Juan* (1819-23) are recurrently sustained.[1]

Peacock also launched an essayistic critique of romanticism in "The Four Ages of Poetry," which is customarily regarded as an indissoluble mixture of the serious and the facetious. This essay, which induced Shelley to write his "Defense of Poetry," attacks romanticism primarily for its weird anachronism. Peacock scores the irrelevance of a regressive romantic literature in an age of science and utility. His comments are not substantially different from those of later Victorian critics who protested that romanticism, trafficking in foggy unreality, was the socially irresponsible product of a warped sensibility.[2]

Nightmare Abbey, however, deals not with a ridiculously obsolescent romantic enclave in the domain of positivism, but rather with certain modish representatives of romanticism who embody either revolutionary fervor (Scythrop) or romantic shadowiness and doom (Flosky and Cypress). The comedy in *Nightmare Abbey* does not particularly ply the reader with ambiguity. In the epigraph to the novel, Peacock makes it clear that the figures in his book (a number of them, like Mr. Listless and Mr. Toobad, are preposterous non-romantic types) are likely to resemble Jonsonian humor characters.

The young hero of Peacock's novel is Scythrop Glowry, a kind of Coleridgean Shelley,[3] a caricaturally ardent spirit disordered by "metaphysical romance and romantic metaphysics."[4] Author of a short treatise entitled "Philosophical Gas: or a Project for a General Illumination of the Human Mind," Scythrop is absorbed by chimerical schemes for mankind's emancipation. However, his passion for reforming the world becomes tangled, and then decisively unravels, in an ordeal of amorous temptations. Combining romantic agony and (eventually) histrionic skill, Scythrop oscillates ingloriously between two beauties, the coquettishly light-hearted, musical Celestina O'Carroll, who plays havoc with his emotions, and the somberly intellectual, impassioned yet sphinxlike Stella (Celina Toobad) who reinforces his most ambitiously idealistic reveries. For some time Scythrop finds himself incapable of choosing between them, that is, until the two ladies learn of each other's existence and speedily abandon him. Scythrop then prepares a Wertherian suicide (*The Sorrows of Young Werther* is one of his favorite books) in case neither lady is willing to re-embrace him. In fact, neither is prepared to do so. Marionetta intends to marry Mr. Flosky, while Stella aims to become Mrs. Listless. There is no suicide, of course. Scythrop's mock-desperate resolve (this is not his first experience in amorous woe) is easily liquidated by a soothing glass of Madeira and a pleasant lapse into emotional shallowness. Romantic revolutionary idealism proves to be more Gothically gaseous than heroically inflammatory; in addition, the romantic philosophy of soulful love is hilariously discredited. Romanticism apparently involves, not an authentic quest for a paradisal infinite, but rather a grappling among different kinds of adolescent posturing.

Yet for all its devastating drollery, Peacock's farcical satire is essentially genial. Indeed, the atmosphere of the book has been described by J. B. Priestley as "golden, smiling, Epicurean" (ix). This is conspicuously the case when Mr. Hilary, a champion of the "cheerful and solid wisdom of antiquity" (68), as well as an enthusiast of the filled bumper, "the only symbol of perfect life" (65), good-naturedly incriminates modern despair and misanthropy. According to Mr. Hilary – predecessors like Lucian dispensed much the same advice – one must, in an unstable world, moderate one's expectations, but without ceasing to cultivate buoyancy and balance. It is evident that Mr. Hilary, a purveyor of temperamental sunshine, is Peacock's overt (though not especially memorable) source of rebuttals to the fashionably morbid ravings of contemporary romanticism. Far more powerful, however, are Peacock's indirect assaults against a literature that is fatally undermined, in his view, by unreliable visions of ethereal love and perfected humanity.

The antipodes to Hilary's festive disposition are represented by two flagrant exponents of the romantic ethos, Mr. Cypress (Byron, though not the creator of *Don Juan*), who has a small but pungently misanthropic part to play, and Mr. Flosky (a character saddled with the ideas of Coleridge), who has a more important and much funnier role. Byron-Cypress is a restless, disenchanted, "lacerated spirit" (64) for whom life, once luminous but now insufferable, has become an unabating procession of failures and betrayals (inevitably inaugurated by the French Revolution). Life is "an all-blasting upas" (67) beneath whose sway ideals, and especially love, can only wither. Cypress's funereal ejaculations are usually, and almost uncontrollably, distilled from the dark dissonances of *C hilde Harold.* (Peacock generously footnotes references to the poem's prevailing gloom; and in one early, extensive note he piles up, with mordant urbanity, multiple specimens of the mythological mishmash in *Manfred.*)

In his own cultivation of despair Coleridge-Flosky is far more laughable than Cypress. Catapulted all the way back to the shadows of feudalism by the French Revolution's aborted promise of political liberty, Flosky has been writing, and endlessly orating, about things tearful and fearful, miserable and blighted. A connoisseur of the minutiae of human wretchedness and ghastliness, he admiringly describes contemporary literature as the "morbid Anatomy of Black Bile"(35). Much of the visionary fog Flosky is wrapped up in is due to his having lain "several years in transcendental darkness, till the common daylight of common sense became intolerable in his eyes"(7). That is why he shuns the procedures of analytical logic; and that is why this thinker, convinced that the health of the mind requires an interminable anti-factual pursuit of abstractions, is averse to seeing connections between ideas. (He is also aware that intellectual coherence would hurt his reputation.) Yet Flosky, like Scythrop, is allowed several just observations on matters political or psychological – but not to the point where his ideas become more celebrated than mocked.

Peacock's burlesque of romanticism's delinquencies (sickly misanthropic introspection and dismal irrationality) does not encourage an obliquely resistant polemic in favor of the romantic temper. There are few hints in *Nightmare Abbey* that romantic idealism, though tending toward derangement, may still in some degree be viable. Byron's *Don Juan,* on the other hand, visibly juggles the pros and cons of the romantic mentality.[5] Byron's romantic irony does not, however, require an immediate contiguity of polar positions. A perfect, transitionless, back-to-back counterpoise of contradictory tendencies in the vein of romantic irony occurs (in an inversion of the usual pattern) only once in *Don Juan,* in stanzas 113-14 of Canto I.[6] In stanza 112, the narrator, who has been seriocomically approaching the initial, blushful-anxious embrace between Juan and Julia, directs the reader's attention, less compassionately than slyly, to the despairing timidity of all young lovers. At the beginning of stanza 113, the moon, that matchless luminary of romantic love, rises up – only to be ousted at once from its glamorous role. It is described as a peeping pander, the falsely coy superintendent of a cozy ambiance of sin:

> The sun set, and up rose the yellow moon:
> The Devil's in the moon for mischief; they
> Who call her CHASTE, methinks, began too soon
> Their nomenclature; there is not a day,
> The longest, not the twenty-first of June,
> Sees half the business in a wicked way,
> On which three single hours of moonshine smile –
> And then she looks so modest all the while.   (I. 113)

The cynically amusing derogation of a prime symbol of romantic feeling is countered, however, in the very next stanza, whose tone at once capsizes that of the preceding lines. The vital illusion of the mysterious moon's serene yet gently disquieting aura of beauty, love, and even sanctity is fully restored:

> There is a dangerous stillness in that hour,
> A stillness, which leaves room for the full soul
> To open all itself, without the power
> Of calling wholly back its self-control;
> The silver light which, hallowing tree and tower,
> Sheds beauty and deep softness o'er the whole,

Breathes also to the heart, and o'er it throws
A loving languor, which is not repose.   (I. 114)

This unusually tight juxtaposition of clashing perpsectives is not so much an illustration of Coleridgean balance or reconciliation as it is a miniature version (and neat objectification) of the stand-off in Byron's temper between high romantic and comically low antiromantic attitudes.

Yet Byron's vision is not consistently bifocal. Nor does romantic irony proliferate so tenaciously in *Don Juan* that it overwhelms Byron's other comic drives. The poet's satirical and farcical forays into the precincts of propriety, marriage, education, war, custom, politics, religion, and other areas of prevailing cultural cant (or dementia) dominate all other modes of comedy in the poem. Even Pyrrhonic irony, which deems illusion and idealism to be amusingly and incurably absurd, is more prominent in *Don Juan* than romantic irony. But though satire, enhanced by farce, is ubiquitous and prepotent in Byron's comedy, and though even Pyrrhonic irony is a more visible entity (and a far more traditional mode of disenchantment) than romantic irony, it is the flashes and jolts of Byron's romantic-ironic contraries in the first few cantos that exert a special appeal to the dissonance-prone modern imagination.

Byron's romantic irony flourishes in the early cantos in large part because the pleasures and problems of the adolescent Juan elicit an entire idiom of seductive feelings and provocative ideas which kindle, or rekindle, Byron's unexpired romanticism. Yet they also stir up a recalcitrant, comically oriented counter-romanticism. Fledgling experiences of love, beauty, Nature, exoticism, religious awe, acute danger, and near-death supply the narrator with a host of opportunities to initiate conflicts between lyricism and factuality, dream and desecration.

After the first half-dozen cantos or so, however, Juan's adventures seldom supply the kind of material that nourishes Byron's most compelling romantic-ironic proclivities. By then Juan is well on his way to becoming, and remaining, an urbanely attentive, gallantly tactful, highly resourceful character whose rapidly achieved immunity to youthful, amorous idealism (or even fervor, its dubious psychic surrogate) is sustained by Byron's making unavailable to him, or simply withdrawing him from, potential romantic passion. This does not mean that Byron is tempted (or at least not very often) to reduce Don Juan to his traditional status as a fickle, emotionally sterile amorist, a blasé burglar of boudoirs destined for infernal punishment.

Byron viewed the process of sophistication in Juan as inevitable.[7] By the time Juan reaches England, he is already possessed of a heart that "had got a tougher rind" (XII. 81). Tenderness has become largely irrelevant, however, since in the late English cantos Juan serves primarily as a satiric lens for the disclosure of Byron's long-ruminated animadversions on English society. The final cantos demolish English social predilections, prejudices, and superstitions with superb wit and verve. Nevertheless, as many readers have sensed, the narrator's zest for comic disorientation remains unexcelled in the early cantos. Perhaps that is why the epigraph from *Twelfth Ninth* that prefixes Cantos VI-VIII – the lines glorify cakes-and-ale frivolity – seems a bit belated.

The comic instability of the opening cantos of *Don Juan* is engendered by a narrator who is in no sense bedeviled by customary author-reader accommodations. In the guise of a chameleonic impresario, he juggles miscellaneous roles, ranging all the way from gay impenitent to stiff-necked puritan.[8] However, his favorite role, when he is not moved by a romantic afflatus, becomes transparent soon enough: the narrator has pre-empted the character of the legendary, jestingly irreverent, quasi-demonic Don Juan. This appropriation of the traits of a lawless voluptuary and cynic by the narrator makes for a fine paradox: for the most part, the privileges of Don Juanism are denied Byron's titular hero. The youngster remains for some time a scarcely spotted lamb, though some readers find in him rather large libertine spots from the very beginning of the comic epic.[9]

The Don Juanesque penchant of the narrator, on the other hand, is evident early on when he drops the mask of a diffidently respectable family counselor and assumes the features of a perspicacious man of the world. This change in attitude is nicely illustrated in Canto I (78-79), where the narrator, pondering the difficult issue of Julia's emotional vicissitudes (she is deeply attracted to the young Juan but is married to a complacent clod twice her age), plays tartly and deviously with sacrosanct morality. He primly recommends that young ladies caught up in the lovely Julia's quandary ought to prove their virtue by taming temptation. Moreover, there exists in this world, he helpfully adds, an angelic, immaculate, Platonic love, which happens, luckily enough, to be precisely the type of pure emotion Julia feels for Juan – or so she has convinced herself. The narrator now plunks down a disconcerting parenthesis:

And so I'd have her think, were I the man
On whom her reveries celestial ran.   (I. 79)

Although the narrator quickly switches back to the pose of responsible ethical guardian, the comic damage has been done: Platonic love is a fantasy that can be conveniently danced with all the way to the bedroom. (Reinforcement of this view arrives in I. 116, where Plato is non-comically condemned as a pander, preposterously blind to the imperious requirements of both heart and flesh.)

Byron's relaxed view of the human propensity to err (especially erotically) is conveyed from the very outset of *Don Juan*. Consider Canto I. 18, where the narrator wonders (un-Miltonicly) how Adam and Eve, two beings burdened with tedious spiritual perfection, ever managed to get through Edenic nights without sex. Illusion-dissolving Pyrrhonic irony – paradise, its creator, and the unnaturalness of spirituality are all ironized – is the chief comic impulse at work here. Later, in an equally unspiritual mood, Byron reduces the sexual mores of our naughty world to a by-product of latitude and longitude. The indecent sun, heating up the human thirst for sex, makes nests of immorality out of tropical climates, whereas the cold temperature of England is a warranty of proper conduct:

> Happy the nations of the moral North!
> Where all is virtue, and the winter season
> Sends sin, without a rag on, shivering forth. (I. 64)

Though this subordination of morality to locality was one of the platitudes, however lightly held, of the era's cultural geography (Montesquieu, among others, connected climate and culture), Byron's Pyrrhonic hypothesis about the frailty of human virtue whimsically transcends a merely mechanical joke.

It is owing to his Pyrrhonic, and often prankish, recognition of the heart's incorrigible fluctuations and the body's unsuppressible yen for pagan pleasures that Byron is so often capable of exposing the ideal as a comic masquerade. Take, for instance, stanzas 209-12 in Canto II, where the narrator is preoccupied with the question of the authenticity of Juan and Haidée's love. The stanzas are part of a cluster of passages dealing with fidelity and fickleness, a theme launched by the (apparently shocked) narrator's speculation that perhaps Juan has somewhat hastily forgotten Julia, who has been left behind in Spain. The stanzas suddenly shift ground as the narrator's insouciantly presented amorous credo (faithfulness is best) is put to the test. A farcical tussle develops between philosophy, who urges adherence to the principle of sacred ties, and the narrator, who, after fervidly insisting on his detestation of inconstancy, nevertheless rambles on about his recent attraction to an extremely pretty creature, "fresh from Milan / Which gave me some sensations like a villain" (II. 209). Philosophy's peremptory command that he persist only in single, sublime devotion brusquely wins out. But her conquest is fragile. This can be grasped as soon as the narrator begins theorizing, in the manner of Molière's Dom Juan, that the romantic ideal of constancy is surely best fulfilled by paying homage to Nature's cornucopian supply of beautiful women:

> This sort of adoration of the real
> Is but a heightening of the *beau ideal.*   (II. 211)

That the exponent of this beautiful idealism is not exactly quivering with sincerity is made clear by the sleight-of-hand maneuvre in the next stanza, where the narrator continues to define "the adoration of the real," but not without several dollops of teasingly sophisticated ingenuity:

> 'Tis the perception of the Beautiful,
> A fine extension of the faculties,
> Platonic, universal, wonderful,
> Drawn from the stars, and filtered through the skies,
> Without which Life would be extremely dull;
> In short, it is the use of our own eyes,
> With one or two small senses added, just
> To hint that flesh is formed of fiery dust.   (II. 212)

If the opening lines of the stanza skillfully camouflage carnality, the emphasis in the fifth line on the threat of boredom smoothes the way for the rationale of libertinism smuggled into the last three lines. Yet carnality is curiously redeemed – it becomes virtually synonymous with the human spirit – through the nobility of the last phrase, "fiery dust," which squashes the imputation that mere concupiscence rules manly blood.

The next three stanzas (213-15) continue to undermine the ideal of romantic fidelity that is supposedly being propped up. The narrator introduces the notion that romantic fidelity has coincidental material benefits for which any idealist would be grateful: if "one sole lady" could forever charm us, not only would our hearts and livers be gratified, but the state of our finances would be tolerably improved. At the end of this section on inconstancy, which concludes Canto II, Byron chooses to focus on the havoc usually wrought in stormy hearts and envenomed livers by human passion. In doing so, he sacrifices comedy temporarily to melodrama. Yet the sequence of stanzas is lighthearted enough, on the whole, to minimize this final spasm of gravity.

There is a more hectic comedy of inconstancy early in Canto II, where Byron appears (for a while) to avail himself of the dualism of romantic irony. Having begun his reformatory travels – after the scandal of her adultery with Juan, Julia is secluded in a convent, while Juan is sent pedagogically out of Spain – Juan rereads, on the deck of his ship, Julia's letter of farewell and swears splendidly that he will never forget her, never resign her fair image: "Sooner shall this blue Ocean melt to air, / Sooner shall Earth resolve itself to sea" (II. 19). But as his ship starts lurching, he is forced to curtail his paen to everlasting loyalty. Indeed his dismissal of all other woes as meaningless in comparison with the loss of Julia is conspicuously belied by his physical discomfort: "'Beloved Julia, hear me still beseeching!' / Here he grew inarticulate with retching" (II. 21). The narrator apparently clinches this debunking of the romantic temper by informing us that though love may contest, and even thrive on, noble maladies, it must succumb to such vulgar ailments as a cough, a sneeze, or a turmoil in the bowels (II. 22-23).

It would seem, then, that the bowels must triumph. In fact, Juan's intestinal fortitude and integrity of heart prove to be potent enough to nonplus even the narrator, so that the last word on this entire incident returns Juan to romantic grace. His passion, successfully resisting his nauseated stomach, demonstrates the essence of perfect love (II. 23). But this is a tongue-in-cheek conclusion. The gastric distress that has been plaguing Juan is so burlesque in nature that it reduces romantic protestations of fidelity (for all their ultimate triumph over emesis) to clownish nonsense.

Byron's duplicitous antics can subvert a burgeoning romantic temper much more simply, in the form of sudden cynical disclaimers or subtle sexual innuendoes. Thus in Canto I. 95-6, the narrator seems to be utterly in tune with his young hero's mystic yearning to lay his head upon the bosom of his beloved Julia. However, in the final couplet of stanza 96 – the last two lines of the *ottava rima* in *Don Juan* are notorious booby traps – the narrator blithely sophisticates Juan's restlessly immaculate mood by insinuating that physical appetites, even more than the spiritual kind, would be catered to if Juan's longings were fulfilled. In an earlier stanza (I. 93), the narrator belatedly explodes Juan's ethereal speculations by suggesting that puberty, not philosophy, is the main feeder of adolescent sublimity. And in a still earlier stanza (I. 87), the narrator proclaims his sympathy for the pensive, romantically tormented Juan, who is wandering, befuddled, in Wordsworthian woods, by declaring that he too has a predilection for solitude – the kind of solitude a sultan enjoys in his harem. In each of these three instances, the narrator's persumptive affinity with Juan's romantic moods serves only as a springboard for the perpetration of worldly, if companionable, amusement. Such arch though kindly trifling with the idealistic reveries of love-smitten youth is a warm-up for the sabotage of rapt emotion and idealistic innocence that Byron later effected in his authentic romantic irony.

Yet "authentic" examples of romantic irony may not be beyond suspicion. What looks to one reader like the genuine article may seem to another a case of pseudo-romantic or perhaps only quasi-romantic irony. Consider, for example, the tactics employed in Canto II. 136, where, after delicately describing Haidèe's incipient love for the shipwrecked Juan, the narrator abruptly anesthetizes our response to Haidèe's feelings by introducing servant realism in the person of Zoe, for whom nature on their Greek island is less a setting for romantic love than a seminary of sense, fact, and sex. For Zoe, food takes urgent priority over mooning about at the sight of a stranger's handsome, if woefully weakened, form. Haidèe's heavenly mood may be resonant enough in the reader's mind to survive Zoe's practical preoccupation with fried eggs. If not, the juxtaposition of irreconcilables (quiet ecstasy and smelly cooking) will give evidence only of a quasi-romantic irony not significantly divorceable from the comic technique of the sublime-to-the-ridiculous.

The distinction between genuine romantic irony and the sublime-to-the-ridiculous may be troublesome but not, by and large, unduly so. In an eighteenth-century novel like *Tom Jones,* where lyricism has its limits, disparities of mood are not hard to judge. One doesn't have to puzzle over whether Fielding at a given moment is laughing at romantic awe or faithfully recording its impressive power. When Tom Jones's rhapsodic apostrophe to the nonpareil beauty of his beloved Sophia yields almost immediately to the pleasures of fornication in the bushes with the pretty but vulgar and malodorous Molly Seagrim, Fielding's revelation of Tom's inconsistency (hot-bloodedness has supplanted dreaminess) expresses, not ambivalence toward romantic flights, but rather a cheerful, if sloppy, lapse into healthful hedonism. But Haidèe is neither a Sophia Western nor a Molly Seagrim; the Juan of Byron's early cantos is not a Spanish copy of Tom Jones; and Byron cannot be counted on to view the absurdities of violent contradiction with the easy candor of a Fielding.

There is a further complication, one that has already been mentioned: in romantic irony there may be a noticeable gap between contrarieties. In

Canto II. 183, for example, the venerated sun unambiguously lends its dying radiance to a lovely, tranquil, mysterious atmosphere. But this celestial scene has been salvaged for romantic purposes by a narrator who had earlier, in stanzas 139-40, joshingly assaulted romantic addictions (as well as other kinds) to sun-worship.

Canto II. 183 also provides a glimpse into a much smaller romantic-ironic gap. The sizable preamble to the sun romanticism of this stanza, a preamble which bridges several other stanzas and dispenses much anarchic mischief, suffices by itself to establish a comic collision between antiromantic deflation and romantic rapture. Most of the preamble's mischief originates back in stanza 178, where the narrator professes a pagan credo untouched by spiritual refinement or by the inconvenience of a conscience: "Let us have Wine and Women, Mirth and Laughter, / Sermons and soda-water the day after." This credo is expanded in stanza 179, where the narrator recommends, and celebrates, many valuable kinds of (generally non-liquid) intoxication, such as glory, gold, and love. These constitute the best of life. Still, they each produce hangovers, headachy ordeals whose disvalue the narrator, not at his logical best here, manages (almost tipsily) to shrug off.

At the beginning of stanza 181, the demonstrably inconsistent narrator suffers a momentary attack of oblivion. What was it he was describing just before his digression on the reasonableness of drunkenness? Oh, yes, the island coast. And now, getting his bearings once more, but shifting radically from pagan irresponsibility to a sense of the ineffable, he manifests a relish for natural wonder. As Juan and Haidèe wander forth, hand in hand, the ineffable is incarnated in the redeemed romantic sun:

> It was the cooling hour, just when the rounded
> Red sun sinks down behind the azure hill,
> Which then seems as if the whole earth it bounded,
> Circling all Nature, hushed, and dim, and still,
> With the far mountain-crescent half surrounded
> On one side, and the deep sea calm and chill
> Upon the other, and the rosy sky
> With one star sparkling through it like an eye. (II. 183)

As in the moon stanzas in Canto I (though the latter are virtually cemented together), an ironic-romantic, rather than a romantic-ironic, polarity prevails. In this less familiar form, romantic irony is likely to be more than usually disconcerting, perhaps for the same reason that resurrection is more arresting than interment.

The most notorious of the ironic-romantic disjunctions in *Don Juan* involves the bedroom farce and Julia's farewell letter in Canto I. (There is a large interval between these two sections of the canto.) In accordance with the imperfect law that newly adulterous women in literary comedy quickly become endowed with wondrous powers of deceit, Julia elaborately attempts, in stanzas 140-57, to ward off her husband's suspicion that she may have bedded another man. The role of insulted, ferociously outraged, marvelously eloquent virago suits her so vibrantly that her romantic image seems utterly marred. Sallies to the tune of

> Has madness seized you? Would that I had died
> Ere such a monster's victim I had been!
> What may this midnight violence betide,
> A sudden fit of drunkenness or spleen?
> Dare you suspect me, whom the thought would kill?
> Search then the room!' Alfonso said, 'I will. (I. 142)

or

> Ungrateful, perjured, barbarous Don Alfonso,
> How dare you think your lady would go on so?   (I. 146)

are too cunning and too shrill, however needfully histrionic, not to constitute a blazing negation of romantic sensibility.

Yet after a number of intervening stanzas, in several of which the imbroglio of adultery is protracted by a ludicrous wrestling bout between the near-naked Juan and Julia's husband Alfonso, Byron introduces Julia's farewell letter to Juan (I. 192-97). The brazenly guileful scold in the bedroom farce melts away before the image of a self-consciously fallen, poignantly subdued but still passionate woman, for whom, even though she is sequestered in a convent, the transfiguring power of romantic love (not merely carnal inebriation) will forever erase all cautionary tales about the correct conduct between men and women. True, there is a tinge of mockery (or else a very odd exactitude) in the narrator's description of Julia's elegant writing materials. And there is also an element of rhetorical and even melodramatic commonplace (which should be distinguished from calculated artifice and premeditated pathos) in the letter itself. (Cf. "'Man's love is of his life a thing apart, / 'Tis a woman's whole existence.'" [I. 194].)[10] But passionate sincerity, as Flaubert, that obsessive recorder of triteness, observed in *Madame Bovary,* cannot do without some resort to clichés, whether plain or enhanced. In any event, the fact that Julia's letter is one of Byron's accretions to his text suggests not that Byron's romantic irony is adventitious, but rather that it is irrepressible.[11]

Romantic irony is energetically deployed in Canto II, not long after Haidée, who is essentially devoid of artificial feeling (though she is not unpracticed in minor theatrical arts), first performs her ministrations for the convalescing Juan. From then on, Canto II makes consistently patent an ambivalence which powerfully supports but also comically repudiates the romantic spirit, especially as it is embodied in spontaneous passion. Byron unmistakably gives his blessings to Juan and Haidée,[12] and just as unmistakably retracts that blessing in amusingly blatant or nuanced disparagements. (Both the blessing and the retraction are coordinated with hints of forthcoming disaster, which is of course true love's fatality.)

At times Byron's romantic irony in Canto II consists, in effect, of a mere footnote that slyly qualifies a carefully fostered romantic atmosphere. Thus every bit of food and drink that is meant, under Haidée's vigilant care, to stimulate Juan's recovery of his health becomes a divinely nutritional offering of love – until the narrator undercuts the fascination felt (or about to be felt) by the convalescent hero and the ministering angel. Initially the narrator concurs in the universal opinion that food is a mighty restorer, not only because it regenerates the body but because, like wine, it is indispensable to love's survival. Indeed health, much like idleness – here the tender romantic voice casually takes on the accents of a seasoned sensualist – is "true love's essence" (II. 169):

> While Venus fills the heart (without heart really
> Love, though good always, is not quite so good)
> Ceres presents a plate of vermicelli, –
> For love must be sustained like flesh and blood –
> While Bacchus pours out wine, or hands a jelly: ...   (II. 170)

The ironic significance of these comically gastronomic, mythologically enriched lines (the ingredients of which are not original with Byron) lies in the narrator's parenthetical homage to the heart. The parenthesis violates the core of romantic feeling by making of the heart an organ whose powers exist primarily to improve the function of the genitalia. This kind of homage is better suited to eighteenth-century amatory perceptions than to nineteenth-century romantic intuitions. (In Crébillon fils's sophisticatedly licentious *The Night and the Moment*, for example, Cidalise and Clitandre, two past masters of amorous suavity, end their dialogue on various refinements of fleshly delight by extolling the power of lyrical feeling. Why? Because they recognize that such lyricism, which is actually a curious mixture of momentary sincerity and abiding theatricality, is conducive to greater voluptuousness in bed.)

The most radiant (or poignant) passages in Canto II are similarly at risk of being intersected by lines that playfully or mordantly adulterate the intense yet sweet dignity of romantic love. One might think, when the love of Juan and Haidée moves to the verge of fulfillment, that Byron will at last dispense with gleeful, debonair, or cynical disavowals of romantic passion. At first this seems almost certainly to be the case. The consummation of love is presented as though it were impermeable to contamination by levity, though not by a slight shadow cast by the last lines of the following stanza:

> And now 't was done – on the lone shore were plighted
> Their hearts; the stars, their nuptial torches, shed
> Beauty upon the beautiful they lighted:
> Ocean their witness, and cave their bed,
> By their own feelings hallow'd and united,
> Their priest was solitude, and they were wed:
> And they were happy – for to their young eyes
> Each was an angel, and earth Paradise.   (II. 204)

This sanctification of the romantic heart is not, however, allowed to linger in the reader's consciousness. It is immediately blasted by an army of facts, both literary and historical, which the narrator adduces, in a mixed tonality of gravity and lightness, to remind us, in the event that we are spilling over with emotion, that love is the very deity of evil and that throughout history it has been busy spawning madness, slavery, and suicide – not to mention permissive philosophy and the ridiculous perils of adultery. A further de-idealizing note is struck when Juan's forgetfulness of Julia, like every other man's wickedly delightful inconstancy, is ascribed to the influence of lunar caprice.

Nevertheless, the romantic ethos in Byron's view finds its unique justification, and its special grace, in the season of youth. The spontaneous emotions of Juan and Haidée are bewitching precisely because they are alien to bookish and borrowed passions. However much the narrator's antiromantic maturity, shaped by his all-too-ripe, disenchanted, self-mocking consciousness, may impel him to cauterize romance as fantasy and romanticism as illusion, advancing age cannot dissipate his nostalgia for innocence – an innocence immune to the sham of literary imitation and to the stale projects of the over-civilized mind.

That such guileless love is subjected to the gratuitous cruelties of mischance is conceded by the poet. Romantic passion, as Byron cannily yet delicately indicates in convincing detail in Canto IV, is famously hostile to longevity.

The romantic-ironic ambivalence that consecrates yet also funnily rescinds the ideal, whether of the heart or the mind, is scarcely restricted in *Don Juan* to the experience of love. In Canto III, the poem entitled "The Isles of Greece" (another of Byron's accretions) is a notable, if not vey neat, specimen of romantic irony applied to a large, trans-personal context. For the most part, the poem elegizes the long historical collapse of the Hellenic-romantic ideal of heroic freedom and cultural glory. However, unlike the lines on Greece's decayed honor and bankrupt grandeur plangently voiced in *Childe Harold,* "The Isles of Greece" is sandwiched between digressive, derisory passages that almost destroy the poem's ultimate call for deliverance. The narrator is not responsible (though Byron is) for the elegy. According to him, the poet who composed "The Isles of Greece" is an astonishingly supple political turncoat who has been hired as a festive entertainer to heighten the pleasure of Juan, Haidée, and their attendants. This ingratiating, ingeniously protean trimmer is willing, at least for the present occasion, to "agree to a short armistice with truth" (III. 83) by evoking his youthful enthusiasm for Greek independence. But as if the morally questionable character of the trimmer poet were not scandalous enough, the narrator compounds the suspect quality of the proceedings by forgetting (this is not his first slip) what his current topic is, and even the number of the canto he is composing.

This jokey double devaluation serves as a prelude to "The Isles of Greece," which begins as follows:

> The isles of Greece, the isles of Greece!
> Where burning Sappho loved and sung,
> Where grew the arts of war and peace, –
> Where Delos rose, and Pheobus sprung!
> Eternal summer gilds them yet,
> But all, except their sun, is set.

However, the shame of Hellenic degeneration momentarily vanishes as the singer nobly affirms, and valorously reiterates, his rejection of enslavement. His affirmations are necessarily weakened, however, as Malcolm Kelsall points out, by the substitution of wine for action. What damages the ideal of freedom for Greece even more tellingly, Kelsell suggests, is the poem's anacreontic sentimentalism.[13]

Yet the singer's appeal for a resurgence of heroism is much more rudely punctured by external shock than by internal irony. The modern epigone of Orpheus, having been mildly praised by the narrator for his infectious emotion, is branded as a perverter of truth – not because he is opportunistically catering to the celebratory pleasures of Juan and Haidée but because he is a poet; and all poets are creatures of mendacity:

> His strain display'd some feeling – right or wrong;
> And feeling, in a poet, is the source
> Of others' feeling; but they are such liars,
> And take all colors – like the hands of dyers.   (III. 87)

This failure of bardic integrity, which implies more sins than political shiftiness, at once surrenders to its antithesis. The narrator, whose temper, however mutable, cannot be compared to the weathervane mentality of the Greek versifier (scepticism, cynicism, and ambivalence are not easily classifiable as exploitative guile), abruptly eulogizes, instead of impugning, the mighty liberations achieved by poets. Yet his paean to the inseminating power of literature ends on a somewhat melancholy, somewhat frivolous note:

> But words are things, and a small drop of ink,
> Falling like dew, upon a thought, produces
> That which makes thousands, perhaps millions, think;
> 'Tis strange, the shortest letter which man uses
> Instead of speech, may form a lasting link
> Of ages; to what straits old Time reduces
> Frail man, when paper – even a rag like this,
> Survives himself, his tomb, and all that's his!   (III. 88)

As the idea of inspirational literary power stretches into the next stanzas, it becomes more dubious, and then even mortifyingly insufficient, so that before long the narrator has wiped out even the dimmest of messianic conceits relating to the influence of words. This flagrant diminution of value is linked to the Ecclesiastian all-is-vanity theme, which, adorned by allusions to the unheroic aspects of various scribes (and conquerors), leads to a venomous attack on the literary and political demerits of the Lake poets.

The post-"Isles of Greece" stanzas represent for Jerome McGann a "typical Byronic gesture of resolute irresolution." This is not deemed a weakness. McGann suggests that "paradoxically Byron's cynicism is a liberating rather than a defeatist move because Byron is aware that the past ... cannot be appropriated to the present through the simple gestures of mobility or chameleonic acts. Byron turns a mordant eye on the inheritance of greatness (especially of poetic greatness) because he knows its ideal apparitions conceal human, equivocal truths. Indeed, when those equivocal forms do not appear, the ideals enter the world as monsters."[14] McGann's cogent insight into Byron's "resolute irresolution" and emancipatory cynicism is adaptable to European romantic irony; that is, one may claim that romantic idealism unqualified by antiromantic mockery may wind up as a perversely partial, even monstrously bogus, vision. However, one has to remember that the romantic ideal is never definitively quashed in romantic irony and may itself repudiate the errancies of subversive laughter.

The pre- and post-"Isles of Greece" stanzas can hardly be surpassed as an illustration of complicated ambivalence. But a more compact group of internecine romantic-ironic stanzas may be found not much further along in Canto III. Their theme is not heroic emancipation but rather the beauty of Nature, especially as it elicits the soul's yearning for spiritual loftiness. In stanza 101, the narrator reports that Juan and Haidée, left alone after much feasting and revelry, are admiring "the rosy flood of twilight's sky." The moment appears propitious either for aesthetic or religiously tinged appreciation, or both. Yet it is improbable, after their happily pagan festivities (whose oriental luxury has for the moment damaged the lovers' primal innocence), that Juan and Haidée's admiration (translatable as awe) is touched by a sense of the holy. Even if they are moved by a religious sensibility, they are not likely to meditate silently on matters of doctrine, or earnestly subscribe in their thoughts to current or classical gods. The narrator, however, takes it upon himself to intone an "Ave Maria" that sensitively Christianizes the heavens Juan and Haidée are raptly gazing at. The sixteen lines (extending from stanza 101 to stanza 103) that distill the fervor of the "Ave Maria" section allow not the slightest suspicion of a smile to appear. Yet the "Ave Maria" atmosphere of delicate natural beauty, mysterious spirituality, and heavenly love is immediately, intrusively, and vulgarly revoked by the first five lines of stanza 104:

Some kinder casuists are pleased to say,

> In nameless print – that I have no devotion;
> But set those persons down with me to pray,
> And you shall see who has the properest notion
> Of getting into Heaven the shortest way;   (III. 104)

The supposed end-product of such preposterously undignified competitive prayer – a certain economy (even velocity) in getting into heaven – relegates religious faith to little more than a trickster's virtuosity. However, the last three lines of the stanza bury this foolery in a swift return to spiritual exaltation as the narrator declares his allegiance to the religion of natural wonder:

> My altars are the mountain and the ocean,
> Earth, air, stars, – all that springs from the great Whole,
> Who hath produced, and will receive the Soul.   (III. 104)

This romantic-mystical reverence, which echoes similarly grave lines in Canto III of *Childe Harold*, is not at once giddily reversed. Yet shortly thereafter, Canto III ends with the seriocomic stanzas (including the lines on Nero) that Babbitt mistakenly took to be representative of Byron's romantic irony.

It is in Canto IV that the romantic irony of innocence and experience is climactically embodied. Once again the ideal of romantic love is flawlessly crystallized and beautifully buttressed. And once again, at almost every step of the way, it is jocularly recanted. Still, Byron's oscillations are so packed with surprises that they seldom risk becoming exasperatingly obsessive. Byron begins Canto IV by recording two closely related, disturbing metamorphoses, both of which register the inescapable truths of maturity. The first of these radical changes has converted "what was once romantic to burlesque" (IV. 3). The second has reconfigured pathos and pain, for Byron has been self-protectively obliged to transmute tears into laughter (IV. 4). These two transformations are far from irrevocable, however. Canto IV will prove that the romantic ideal can wrestle with, be obliterated by, and yet energetically survive (though not forever), the incursions of burlesque. And Byron's laughter will range far beyond the clichés of psychic therapy, as is soon made clear by his self-defined status as an amateur of literary comedy who is prepared to promote merriment in modern affairs the way Pulci, the "sire of the half-serious rhyme" (IV. 6), made merry with medieval chivalry. (But in Byron's own translation of Pulci, the latter comes across as rather wooden.)

That the prolonged apothesis of romantic love which follows these introductory musings is shadowed by melancholy and by forebodings of catastrophe is not, as has been mentioned, much cause for surprise. Byron construes modern love, even in the form of Juan's and Haidée's sinless sinning, as having its roots in the ineluctable bargain with damnation made by Adam and Eve. More to the point, Byron splendidly reformulates the familiar romantic perception that though irreparable loss and death are haunting reminders of love's brevity, they are also perfect insurers of love's authenticity. Juan and Haidée, the narrator affirms once more, are not meant to exemplify mere literary love; nor are the innately romantic "fairy pair" (IV. 17) destined to be encumbered by age or dragged down by the routine accommodations of the social world:

> Their faces were not made for wrinkles, their
> Pure blood to stagnate, their great hearts to fail;
> The blank grey was not made to blast their hair,
> But like the climes that know nor snow nor hail,
> They were all summer: lightning might assail
> And shiver them to ashes, but to trail
> A long and snake-like life of dull decay
> Was not for them – they had too little clay.   (IV. 9)

The celebration of undiluted romantic love continues from stanza 8 to stanza 23, and only infrequently does it succumb to realistic or sportive asides. However, Byron's disruptive energies have never been in danger of shriveling up. In stanza 24 he dissolves the tranquil rapture of the two lovers at a moment when fear of the future has unsettled them. When Haidée attempts to comfort Juan by defying augury with a kiss, the narrator suddenly becomes interested in the comparative power of kisses and wine to dismiss omens:

> Some people prefer wine – 'tis not amiss;
> I have tried both; so those who would a part take
> May choose between the headache and the heartache.   (IV. 24)

The narrator's relapse into the role of blasé hedonist, nonchalantly (but also a bit plaintively) ready to level off differences between heartache and headache, remains unaltered in the next stanza, where the nuisance of a woman's love vies for low-class honors (perhaps in the category of mental numbness) with the dismal after-effects of wine:

> One of the two, according to your choice,
> Woman or wine, you'll have to undergo;
> Both maladies are taxes on our joys:
> But which to choose, I really hardly know;
> And if I had to give a casting voice,
> For both sides I could many reasons show,
> And then decide, without great wrong to either,
> It were much better to have both than neither.   (IV. 25)

This hemorrhaging of romantic transcendence ceases even more startlingly than it began; for in the next two stanzas Byron resuscitates the potency, and especially the urgent transiency, of delicately incandescent love:

> Mixed in each other's arms, and heart in heart,
> Why did they not then die? – they had lived too long
> Should an hour come to bid them breathe apart;
> Years could but bring them cruel things or wrong;
> The world was not for them, nor the world's art
> For beings as passionate as Sappho's song;
> Love was born *with* them, *in* them, so intense,
> It was their very spirit – not a sense.   (IV. 27)

Such dissociative sequences signalize romantic irony's double postulation; on the one hand, dedication to exalted feelings, aspirations, and ideals; on the other, skeptically or cynically comic distrust of the seductions of enchantment. The order of this double postulation cannot, as we have seen, be taken for granted. If Byron often hallows the ideal and then comically diminishes or defiles it, he also (irregularly) resanctifies it.

Byron's seriocomic practice of profound concern and brisk disengagement need not, of course, take the form of romantic irony. Consider the section in Canto IV that recounts Juan's capture by Lambro (Haidée's unexpectedly returning piratical papa) and his subsequent consignment to the slave market in Constantinople. This harrowing episode provokes the drama of Haidée's resistance, collapse, madness, and death. But after detailing the brutally expeditious manner in which Juan is wounded, bound, and dragged away to be shipped abroad, the narrator snuffs out any hint of tragedy in the making by becoming ruthlessly aloof:

The world is full of strange vicissitudes,
And here was one exceedingly unpleasant:
A gentleman so rich in the world's goods,
Handsome and young, enjoying all the present,
Just at the very time when he least broods
On such a thing, is suddenly to sea sent,
Wounded and chained, so that he cannot move,
And all because a lady fell in love.   (IV. 51)

This stanza, transmogrifying Haidée's love into a damnably inappropriate female whim, flippantly drains off any emotion that might have arisen from the hero's plight and the heroine's dismay. Nor do the following lines modify this extinction of empathy. The narrator claims, to be sure, that he has been so much moved by the pathos of Juan's servitude (the claim is negated by his suddenly icy imperviousness to tender sentiment) that he is compelled to take leave of his hero – presumably to recover his equilibrium. We at once discover, however, that the "pathos" felt by the narrator has in fact been caused by his excessive consumption of green tea, "the Chinese nymph of tears" (IV. 52). This depersonalizing of tears into tea not only solidifies, so to speak, the narrator's detachment from the Juan-Haidée crisis but leads to an even more distancing editorial digression (IV. 52-3) on the physical and psychological effects produced by various kinds of potations, from coffee to cognac. The result is a strong reinforcement of the narrator's anomalous, cavalier, indeed callous levity.

It is true that the narrator's disprizing of sentiment is a good deal mitigated when he attends, at length, to Haidée's grief, derangement, and death. In the tribute he pays to her romantic destiny there is not an iota of tonal duplicity. Yet after describing the desolate, dirge-haunted island where Haidée and her father are buried – here, we suppose, Byronic comedy must surely abdicate – Byron dispatches poignancy with a much more radical evasion than that provided by allusions to Chinese tea. He obliterates romantic-elegiac emotion by raising an ungallant mock-alarm at appearing to be affected by Haidée's unhinged mind. This unbeguiling tactic is supported by a familiar, frivolous yen for aesthetic irregularity of design (somewhat qualified by the need to get back to the hero of his epic):

I don't much like describing people mad,
For fear of seeming rather touch'd myself –
Besides, I've no more on this head to add;

And as my Muse is a capricious elf,
We'll put about, and try another tack,
With Juan, left half-killed some stanzas back.   (IV. 74)

Juan will recover. Romantic irony will not. Indeed the destruction of romantic-ironic ambivalence occurs in the very next canto, which is driven mainly by (first-rate) sexual farce. The fun begins when the old Negro Baba, whose mission is to smuggle Juan into the Sultana Gulbeyaz's quarters, suggests to Juan and the Englishman Johnson that " 'T would greatly tend to better their condition, / If they would condescend to circumcision' " (V. 69). Johnson, Juan's diplomatic, stoically shrewd fellow captive, pretends to entertain the idea, but Juan steadfastly (and somewhat grandiosely) rejects the barbarous suggestion that circumcision would come in handy in their present condition: " 'Strike me dead, / But they as soon shall circumcise my head!' "(V. 71)

The next indignity confronting Juan is a travesty of transvestism that he almost fails to surmount. Though Juan finds a female disguise, which is indispensable to Baba's scheme, outrageously demeaning, he is soon tripping over his petticoat, sporting a crown of false tresses, and submitting to various cosmetic embellishments. By the time Juan and Johnson bid each other farewell, they have entirely surrendered to a carnivalesque spirit of masquerade. Johnson's facetious recommendation: " 'Keep your good name; though Eve herself once fell' " is capped by Juan's jocosity: " 'Nay,' quoth the maid, 'the Sultan's self shan't carry me / Unless his Highness promises to marry me' " (V. 84). This bit of self-conscious buffoonery on Juan's part is rather unusual. It is the narrator who has hitherto monopolized excursions into zaniness.

Zaniness quickly evaporates, however, when Juan feels compelled to spurn the required ritual homage to oriental sovereignty. The Sultana Gulbeyaz's offensive question/command: " 'Christian, canst thou love?' " (V. 116) elicits from Juan memories of Haidée, and these are attended by a flood of tears. The ravishing, tigerishly sensual, balked Sultana is at first confounded by this strange exhibition of the heart's sincerity, for she has been accustomed only to sycophantic praise and prayer. Unschooled in even the most trivial of miseries, she now feels her eyes glistening with a most undespotic sympathy. Gulbayez is thus trapped between the imperatives of royal power and a wholly novel impulse of good Samaritanism (which the narrator, with habitual tongue-in-cheek, ascribes to all females). Yet the Sultana's inchoate kindness is not strong enough to erase the embarrassment of having wasted precious time with an inhibited infidel; nor is her patience durable enough to nullify the risk of martyrdom if she is caught entertaining the young Spaniard.

While Gulbeyaz hesitates, the narrator forestalls any assumption on the reader's part that her incipient urge to betray tenderness may lead to Juan's third genuine affair of the heart. Ludicrous circumstances alone suffice to rule out the possibility that Gulbeyaz might occupy a niche in a romantic triptych: Julia – Haidée – Sultana. The narrator hardly encourages such a development as he coolly and concisely engages in comparative cultural counseling. He cautions occidental gentlemen accustomed to leisurely erotic pursuits that they would do well to declare their intentions rapidly in torrid zones, for there sexuality is likely to be tindery. There is no question now of romance, especially when the narrator more than half invites us to look askance at Juan as a victim of amorous gaucherie who remains troubled by a residue of sentimental moonshine:

> But he had got Haidée into his head:
> However strange, he couldn't yet forget her,
> Which made him seem exceedingly ill-bred. (V. 124)

The narrator now arranges what will shortly turn out to be the definitive demise of romantic love and, coincidentally, of romantic irony, in *Don Juan*. To begin with, however, Juan's lofty self-defense – " 'The prisoned eagle will not pair, nor / I serve a Sultana's sensual phantasy' " (V. 126) – buckles before Gulbeyaz's beauty, which the narrator glibly, if teasingly, assures us is possessed of the divine right to command obedience. Such obedience will be (more or less) forthcoming from the backward Juan, but only after Gulbeyaz has, as the narrator suggests, comically competed with Potiphar's wife, Lady Booby, and Phaedra:

> Her first thought was to cut off Juan's head;
> Her second, to cut only his – acquaintance;
> Her third, to ask him where he had been bred;
> Her fourth, to rally him into repentance;
> Her fifth, to call her maids and go to bed;
> Her sixth, to stab herself; her seventh, to sentence
> The lash to Baba: – but her grand resource
> Was to sit down again, and cry of course.   (V. 139)

Gulbeyaz's tears melt Juan's scorn so effectively that he (almost) peremptorily dismisses thoughts of Haidée. He is even prepared to believe, with insufficient warrant, to say the least, that he has been confusing romantic fidelity with prudish virtue, which he now bluntly dismisses, consigning it to outmoded history. It is at this moment that Juan's new career of chivalrous, sweet-tempered sensual sophistication with the ladies is about to be inaugurated. But there is an impediment. Old Baba hurriedly enters the scene to warn Gulbayez – " 'he hopes not too soon' " (V. 144) – that the Sultan is coming. No further encounter between Gulbeyaz and Juan will take place, for the Sultana, after a most uncommon spell of agonizing sleeplessness, will become murderously incensed by reports of Juan's nocturnal hanky-panky with the amiably carnal harem girl Dudù. Between the single tear Juan sheds at the beginning of Canto V as he thinks of Haidée and his lost paradise, and the flood of tears wept by Juan toward the end of the canto as the image of Haidée reaches his consciousness a second time, only to recede somewhat rapidly, Juan's romantic heart fitfully re-emerges, briefly and none too nobly questions its own validity, and conclusively subsides. Juan's erotic impulses, fugitively and funnily stirred by Gulbeyaz and Dudù, will in succeeding cantos be further de-romanticized, indeed smoothed down from a natural yet idealizing urge to a mode of suavity. The poet's romantic-ironic ambivalence will concomitantly (with some resurgence here and there) fade away.

The final stanzas of Canto V toy with the benightedness and cruelty of oriental despotism, though they end with a satiric assault on occidental cultural conceit. Byron pounces on two allied themes which have generously circulated within the first five cantos: morality and marriage. Stanza 157 reiterates the nexus between climate and conduct established in Canto I (and reinforced earlier in Canto V). This allows Byron once more to strip morality of its bogus absolutes, and in particular to mock the artificial virtues of the very cold and therefore puritanical (English) north. In the penultimate stanza (158), which tips the commentary toward the grotesque condition of marriage, the narrator seemingly deplores the polygamy of the East in favor of the monogamy of the West. But it is the latter that should be shunned, for it comes close to being a form of institutionalized beastliness:

> Thus in the East they are extremely strict,
> And *Wedlock* and a *Padlock* mean the same; ...
> But then their own polygamy's to blame;
> Why don't they knead two virtuous souls for life
> Into that moral centaur, man and wife?   (V. 158)

In the final cantos of *Don Juan*, where the moral centaur takes the shape of Lady Adeline Amundeville (who has several redeeming qualities) and her husband Lord Henry (who has fewer), Byron's satire elatedly skewers the petty ordeals and abundant shenanigans of English society. It is here that Byron also dangles before us the portrait of Aurora Raby. The narrator suggests that Aurora-as-gem may be regarded as a cultivated version of Haidée-as-flower, and that Aurora's virginal, bemused gravity is capable of renewing certain "perhaps ideal," even "divine" feelings in Juan (XVI. 107). But these are decidedly muffled feelings, which Lady Fitz-Fulke's mischievously erotic manipulation of the fable of the Black Friar will (presumably) quickly eradicate.[15] Further erotic developments in *Don Juan* remain unarticulated simply because Byron's comic epic was left unfinished. But though the petering out of Byron's poem can ratify no firm assumptions, we may surmise, given Byron's plans for Don Juan's further exploits (to be terminated by the guillotine), that his hero's career was not going to move toward a second immersion in Edenic purity, and also that Byron's narrator would probably have little cause (though such speculation is shaky) to resume exercising the ambivalence of romantic irony.

2.

Byron's comic impieties in *Don Juan* would seem to belong to a totally different literary universe from those occupied by Carlyle's *Sartor Resartus*. Yet *Sartor,* which at times is almost as suffused with comic energy as *Don Juan,* is the only other (equally extraordinary) work in English romanticism that comes within the orbit of romantic irony. Byron's romantic soaring and antiromantic sinking have their analogue in Carlyle's transcendentalism and descendentalism. *Sartor,* to be sure, carries a great deal of redemptive freight that would be repugnant to the artistic consciousness at work in *Don Juan*, a consciousness that only fitfully, and at a much less wondrous level, accepts romantic visions as transcendental revelations. Yet the fact that the romantic temper in *Don Juan* does not connote the striving toward spiritual unity conveyed in *Sartor Resartus,* or that the antiromantic current in *Sartor Resartus* points to a moral abyss never permitted significant exploration in *Don Juan,* does not mean that romantic-ironic parallels between the two works are difficult to sustain.

After its early prominence in *Don Juan,* romantic irony is more or less eclipsed by unabating Pyrrhonic and satiric worldliness. In *Sartor Resartus,* however, romantic irony is only dimmed (not abandoned) by the requirements of salvation. In *Don Juan,* it is the narrator who conveys authorial self-division. In *Sartor,* self-division derives, first, from the gulf between Professor Teufelsdröckh and the Editor, and second, from the transcendental-descendental duality of Teufelsdröckh himself. The latter source of romantic irony is (apparently) impermanent, while the first seems inexhaustible. That is because the contrast between the visionary, exhortative, yet curiously jokey German professor and the seemingly common-sensical and conservative but equally saturnine English editor remains a constant. (It has been argued, however, that Carlyle's play with polarities is only superficial, that the Editor is the Professor's sturdy ally, despite fits of resistance, from beginning to end.)[16]

Carlyle's Editor is convinced that Germany, despite its recurrent infatuation with metaphysical meanderings that have been responsible for much fruitless, misdirected energy, offers a harbor for constructive thought. England, on the other hand, though commercially great, is morally stunted and spiritually torpid, owing to a bias toward practicality that "cramps the free flight of Thought."[17] That is why the Editor has assumed the (almost impossible) task of domesticating and propagating (with much astonishment and dismay) the marvels and murkiness of an often rebarbative soteriological clothes-philosophy. And that is why, for all that he ridicules hazy German idealizing, the Editor is at times so effervescently enthusiastic about the Professor's creed.

That transcendental creed, which fulfills Carlyle's "need for belief," though it is balanced by his "need for skepticism,"[18] pierces through flesh and matter and exalts man's spiritual cohesion with divine love and power. Its opponent is descendentalism, which veers toward mechanism and skepticism, in the process lowering mankind "below most animals." Transcendental wonder is constantly being threatened by a squalid world. Indeed, the imperative of faith may slacken and virtually dissolve beneath the impress of a descendental obeisance to the materialistic, trivializing, godless cash-nexus element in modern life.

A transcendental-descendental dualism (not to be banally classified as a dialectic between commitment and detachment)[19] might conceivably have activated in Carlyle far more melancholy that mirth. As it is, there are many dark, soul-wrenching passages in *Sartor,* as well as black thunderings against the abominable condition of England. Yet Carlyle's ambivalence has produced a unique religious-metaphysical-social comedy. The Professor's mysteriously elevated yet whimsical pronouncements and the Editor's stern but sound reservations about the dense language and mangled structure of thought he is obliged to deal with supply, to begin with (and end with), a quenchless source of comic friction.

In contending with an unfamiliar, puzzling conceptual world, the Editor is pleased to view himself as something of a martyr. To bring order out of the Professor's chaos, he must first decipher baffling German phraseology, then build bridges in English across the Professor's teeming medley of ideas. This tiresome job, the Editor grumbles, is slowly undermining his health. Yet the hermeneutic work he has undertaken is not unrewarding. There are pearls in the Professor's phantasmagoric, wearisomely capricious prose – "invaluable ore" is buried in "much rubbish" (28). At its best, moreover, the Professor's prose exhibits "indomitable defiance" and "boundless reverence," though at its (frequent) worst, his prose can be fiendish, "almost like diluted madness" (205).

The Professor's tumultuous, nebulous, prolix, "multiform perversities" (29) also demonstrate, the Editor is convinced, that he is a "wild seer" (30), so deficient in the social graces that it would not be amiss to describe him as an inhabitant of the moon. Too much of the Professor's dawdling, enigmatic, unsocial dreaming, the Editor insists, issues from his lamentable transcendental habit of "looking at all matter…as Spirit" (29) – and at man himself as essentially a naked Spirit. (Yet this vision conveys precisely the essence of the Professor's clothes philosophy.)

The Editor is obviously the butt, at least intermittently, of Carlyle's satire, especially when he claims, somewhat stiffly, to be the representative of a "sounder British world" (62). In this self-congratulatory role, the Editor rebukes the German professor for espousing Sansculottism, a drastically un-English, malignly irreverent, crazy proneness to destroy the sacred fabric of society. Though he has the grace to realize that his mocking criticism may be at times ill-advised, the Editor nonetheless regards the Professor as a darkly, at times pestilentially "speculative Radical" who is ready to reduce to flimsy rags "the solemnities and paraphernalia of civilized life" (63). (He concedes, however, that the Professor's political radicalism is combined with an inner, princely courtesy.) The practical men of England, in the Editor's opinion, are too clear-sighted to view as other than delusory what the Professor thinks he has witnessed in society: a gross, disastrous discrepancy between the perishing poor and the decadent rich, two groups who exist cheek-by-jowl in a collapsing world ruled by mechanically-minded unbelievers.

Though the Professor's "deep, silent, slow-burning, inextinguishable Radicalism" (250) remains a disturbing problem for the Editor, the latter more than once indicates that the Professor is nevertheless far from being a firebrand, that indeed he is basically an indifferent, even placid, iconoclast. What makes the Professor's Sansculottism even more unusual is his transcendental-descendental polarity. According to the Editor, the Professor's being transmits both the "Song of Spirits" and "the shrill mockery of fiends" (31).

This fantastic "diabolico-angelical" duality is almost deafeningly announced in the Professor's name: Diogenes Teufelsdröckh, god-begotten and devil-bedunged. A high, heavenly, transcendental Diogenes is destined to consort with a low, sublunary, descendental Teufelsdröckh, at least until the moment arrives when this hybridized being is capable of unifying his contradictory leanings into a single source of conviction. In the meantime, the carping Editor will keep reminding us that Teufelsdröckh is temperamentally unreliable, and that if he seems to be a bearer of angelic love and compassion, he also appears to be an "incarnate Mephistopheles," "imperturbably saturnine." The Professor's sense of the comic is equally suspect: it may strike one as tender and loving; but it also betrays a "malign coolness" indicative of a bitter, sardonic spirit (32). The Editor's further description of the Professor as "prophetico-satiric" and "mystical-whimsical" (185) allows us to speculate that Teufelsdröckh's psyche, not to mention Carlyle's, is well attuned to the dualities of romantic irony.

The genesis of such dualities is especially evident in two biographical-autobiographical chapters in Book II, "Romance" (ch. 5) and "Sorrows of Teufelsdröckh" (ch. 6). "Romance" reflects the more persistent mode of romantic irony in *Sartor*: the interplay of Teufelsdröckh's mystical-romantic idealism and the Editor's deflationary antiromanticism. "Sorrows of Teufelsdröckh," on the other hand, illustrates Teufelsdröckh's own grasp of romantic irony. This understanding is reached in one of two ways: either Teufelsdröckh is seized by a radiant vision which disintegrates upon further meditation and is then sardonically dismissed; or some unholy agency of the external world subjects a supernal ideal to an infernal let-down.

In "Romance," Teufelsdröckh rhapsodizes retrospectively on the marvels of falling in love, which he regards as the most immediate revelation of heaven on earth. It is "a discerning of the infinite in the finite," which discerning, he sensibly reflects (but only in passing) "again may be either true or false ... either inspiration or insanity" (141). His former beloved, Blumine, had once uplifted his soul and provided him with "unutterable joys" (142). Her love had surrounded the young, hitherto thwarted and penniless Teufelsdröckh with unearthly music, so that "pale doubt fled away into the distance; Life bloomed-up with happiness and hope." A new "Apocalypse of Nature unrolled to him" (143).

Of course the censorious Editor, no exponent of the religion of sensibility, is not satisfied by all this poetizing. He views it as a Circean anomaly, a product of deranged Petrarchism and Wertherism – in a word, as a flirtation with pure madness. While Teufelsdröckh in his innocence (and indigence) is at a loss to account for Blumine's subsequent estrangement (economic and social pressures are largely to blame), the worldly Editor supplies a down-to-earth explanation: "What figure, at that period, was a Mrs. Teufelsdröckh likely to make in polished society? ... Will any yet known 'religion of young hearts' keep the kitchen warm?" (144) In his reproof of Teufelsdröckh's elegy on his lost love ("Their lips were joined, their two souls...rushed into one, – for the first time, and for the last!"), the Editor adds a bit of allusive, not overly imaginative, fun: "Thus was Teufelsdröckh made immortal by a kiss" (145).

In the following chapter, "Sorrows of Teufelsdröckh," romantic irony is engendered, not by a firestorm of seraphic love chilled by an amused Editor's sense of domestic realism, but by the dispensations of shocking circumstance. The lonely, miserable young Teufelsdröckh, wandering far and wide, finds himself at one point spellbound by the solemn beauty of nearby mountain peaks. Gradually he succumbs to the feeling that he is holding communion with the living spirit of Nature, "his mother and divine" (151), and that the blight of his protracted isolation has been finally eliminated. (There is not the slightest authorially guided hint of caricature here.) In the midst of this magical transport, however, he is alerted to the sound of carriage wheels, and soon afterward is stabbed by the sight of his beloved Blumine (who had wept fluently at being wrenched from Teufelsdröckh) and Towgood, his best, most loyal friend, rushing by, apparently on their honeymoon. This distasteful surprise produces a far more desolating ejection from God's bosom than Teufelsdröckh's earlier separation from Blumine, since he has just been celebrating the revelation of the divine in the entire visible world. The Editor cannot resist contributing his own amusement to this unusual juncture of events by willfully equating (he realizes he is being somewhat cruel) genuine nature worship with its sham derivative. This he does by quoting Teufelsdröckh's own disparaging comments, taken from the philosophic volume on clothes, on the current epidemic of sentimental sighing and swooning amidst natural scenery.

Yet the divine in the visible world is authentically revealed when Teufelsdröckh awakens, after a "healing sleep" in "The Centre of Indifference" (Book II, ch. 8), to a "new Heaven and a new Earth" (186). Teufelsdröckh now definitively triumphs – or so it seems – over disenchantment, dread, and disbelief. This miracle, affirmed in "The Everlasting Yea" (Book II, ch. 9), does not, however, induce the Editor to drop once and for all his diagnosis of the Professor's dichotomous personality. Teufelsdröckh's psychic imbalance, the Editor hints, will perhaps survive his extraordinary spiritual metamorphosis. In Teufelsdröckh's account of his wholesome repose and subsequent regeneration, is there not, the Editor asks, still "more of riancy, even of levity, than we could have expected! However, in Teufelsdröckh, there is always the strangest Dualism: light dancing, with guitar-music, will be going on in the forecourt, while by fits from within comes the faint whimpering of woe and wail" (186-87).

Teufelsdröckh's fusion of riancy and woe cannot be divorced from his apprehension of life's tragicomedy. The Professor frequently observes, though never with academic blandness, that existence is a compound of joy and sorrow, of praying and cursing, and that the knotty conditions of life have been enormously magnified by social injustice. (Carlyle's own later, militantly aggressive ideals would do little to alleviate such injustice.) In "Reminiscences" (Book I, ch. 3), for example, Teufelsdröckh notes that while the rich disport themselves in "gay mansions," the "heaped and huddled poor" are hardly better off than those in "condemned cells" (23).

In "Pedagogy" (Book II, ch. 3) the grotesque motley of life's "strange scaffolding, where all at once harlequins dance, and men are beheaded and quartered" (116), is described as the fearful truth of things, though youth is still resilient enough to cope with it. To an older Teufelsdröckh, such motley is plainly the consequence of lunatic social and economic disparities. In "Old Clothes" (Book III, ch. 6), Teufelsdröckh's portrait of the grim yet antic chaos of life, with its "wail and jubilee, mad loves and mad hatreds, church-bells and gallows-ropes, farce-tragedy, beast-godhood – the Bedlam of Creation!", does not derive from psychic instability or metaphysical malady, but rather from the unassailable recognition of the "terrible indictment which Poverty and Vice bring against lazy Wealth" (242). In the Editor's view, of course, this critique is "overcharged."

But there is something more baneful in Carlyle's universe than social and economic inequities, and that is spiritual drought. Dereliction of spirit permits chaos to fester; and chaos, especially in the earlier part of *Sartor*, is often seen, not as a Schlegelian world-energy pregnant with creative possibilities and ceaseless renewal, but rather as a dark world-lunacy, a ghostly-ghastly mingling of imposture, sterility, unbelief, and terror. Nevertheless, chaos also functions as the seedbed for the ultimate fruition of Teufelsdröckh's transcendental philosophy, when the "mighty Spinx-riddle" of the universe will be sufficiently unlocked to reveal the overwhelming wonders of Natural Supernaturalism – wonders that remain masked to those deluded by malignant materialism.

The wonders of transcendental spirituality seldom deflect Byron's mockery in *Don Juan*; but the poet is in any case quite capable of recovering from numinous sensations. He can continue to enjoy the friction of clashing perspectives (including those generated by romantic irony) and to recurrently inculpate man, society, and even the cosmos Teufelsdröckh's passage from the Everlasting No through the Centre of Indifference to the Everlasting Yea (and Natural Supernaturalism) cannot, however, be regarded as a repeatable performance. Teufelsdröckh is not meant to revert to moral incertitude – or to the kind of comic sensibility that is so often a product of inner dualism.

Teufelsdröckh is familiar with, and deeply disapproves of, the poetry of the aggrieved non-comic Byron. When he urges the reader to overcome Byronic pathology and become receptive instead to Goethean renunciation and practical self-realization, he is not entertaining thoughts of a cyclic process whereby Byronic morbidity may be susceptible to continuing doses of therapy. What is needed, he argues, is a definitive spiritual transformation. Yet despite Teufelsdröckh's attainment of spiritual oneness, Carlyle, in the role of Editor, is still free to practice the Byronic dichotomies of romantic-ironic comedy. Moreover, the transfiguring power of the Everlasting Yea does not succeed in solemnizing or even starching the Professor's own comic temper. Both before and after the Everlasting Yea, Teufelsdröckh is characterized by a love of satire, though it is frequently softened into a lumbering playfulness or a roguish whimsicality. (*Sartor Resartus* itself seems often enough governed by a titanic puckishness.)

Once upon a time, to be sure, the Professor's attraction to the ludicrous was not much modified by an indulgent humor. He was for a while an ironist in a pure (that is, poisonous) sense. The mature Teufelsdröckh may appear at times to be smugly cocooned in his mockery while forecasting the inexorable devastation of a sick society – a society which, the Editor asserts, has nourished him and therefore, despite its shortcomings, deserves his gratitude. But the young Teufelsdröckh once viewed society as the great enemy, and therefore deployed against it, without any admixture of gentility, a pulverizing irony. This species of irony, which Teufelsdröckh translates as "sarcasm," served as a shelter from his exasperating wounds. No longer, though. In his spiritual maturation, he claims, he has forever renounced this "language of the Devil," though not without somewhat fondly recalling the "torpedo powers" (129) of ironic, socially dangerous youth.

The period in Teufelsdröckh's life during which his sarcastico-ironic alienation from society was supplanted by a healthier sense of humor is recounted in "The Centre of Indifference" (Book II, ch. 8). After repudiating the diabolic principle of "The Everlasting No" (that is, contemptuous cynicism, universal disbelief), Teufelsdröckh was enabled to shed his diseased introspective romanticism and to adopt instead a curative-comic attitude. His subsequent, wholesomely buoyant trivialization of life is captured in the observation, which Teufelsdröckh admiringly assigns to Hugo von Trimberg, that "God must needs laugh outright, could such a thing be, to see his wondrous manikins here below" (181). The journey that finally causes Teufelsdröckh to disgorge his destructive mockery and attain the divine perspective of the curative-comic does not, as we know, cancel out romantic irony in *Sartor Resartus*. (Nor does Teufelsdröckh's redemption from the divisiveness of transcendentalism and descendentalism ultimately rob him of his sense of humor.)

Romantic irony is not, however, the principal component of comedy in *Sartor Resartus*.[20] G. B. Tennyson, among others, declares that the core of comedy in *Sartor* is to be found in the Richterian theory of humor expounded by Carlyle himself in his first essay on Jean Paul.[21] "The essence of humor," Carlyle states in "Jean Paul Richter" (he is leaning here on Jean Paul's *Vorschule der Aesthetik,* or *Preschool for Aesthetics*), is "warm, tender fellow-feeling with all forms of existence." "True humor," unlike shallow, soulless irony, "springs not more from the head than from the heart; it is not contempt, its essence is love; it issues not in laughter but in still smiles, which lie far deeper. It is a sort of inverse sublimity exalting, as it were, into our affections what is below us, while sublimity draws down into our affection what is above us."[22]

According to Carlyle, the greatest English humorist is Sterne, though "the purest of all humorists" is Cervantes (17). As for Jean Paul (who was himself much influenced by Sterne), "he is a humorist from his inmost soul" (14), whether he is being tumultuously sportive, tenderly quaint, or sunnily benevolent. In a later essay, "Jean Paul Friedrich Richter Again," Carlyle emphasizes a much greater range in the humorist's moods; "humor" now covers virtually the entire gamut of comedy – "from the light kindly-comic vein of Sterne – to the rugged grim farce-tragedy often manifested in Hogarth's pictures."[23] In his essay on Schiller, whom he finds excessively grave, Carlyle again points to the primary virtues of humor (affection, condonation) when he remarks that humor "has justly been regarded as the finest perfection of poetic genius."[24]

Recently, Elizabeth M. Vida, assessing the influence of F. Schlegel and Jean Paul on Carlyle's sensibility, concluded that while Schlegel's ideas on irony had no particular impact on *Sartor Resartus,* Jean Paul's theory of humor is decidedly relevant to Carlyle's masterwork.[25] Of course, one may judge that Carlyle's theorizing about humor, for all its dependence on Jean Paul, is more benign than his practice of it. Albert J. La Valley writes that "Carlyle tried to lift himself by Richter's bootstraps, and it is probably fair to say that he only occasionally reached the ideal of humor that he sketched for himself in the essay on Richter. In fact, the very irony he denounced and polarized against Richter's humor came far more easily to him."[26]

3.

That Carlyle was "well-versed in romantic multiplicity" is Karl Miller's useful perception in *Doubles: Studies in Literary History* (1985),[27] a work which, though it is explicitly rooted in the dualistic literature of the romantic period, fails to discuss *Sartor Resartus.* Miller explores the romantic comedy of duality – specifically the "irony and humour" that "flow from the affairs of the fissile and mutable self"(91) – in a chapter entitled "Comic Turns," though the chapter is in fact largely given over to an analysis of eighteenth-century "pioneering instances" of the literary presentation of inconsistency, notably Diderot's *Rameau's Nephew* and Wieland's *The Private History of Peregrinus Proteus the Philospher.* A major thesis in "Comic Turns" is that "satires on romance can themselves be romantic, and that humor, so far from being fatal or inimical to it, could accompany, in Schlegelian synthesis, the romantic surge of the 1790's. Schlegel explained that romance could criticise itself"; indeed, Miller concludes, "humour and irony, and the modern mingling of genres, made this possible" (93).

A "romantic surge" that is prepared to mock itself approximates the mode of European romantic irony. But, as will be shown in the following chapters, European romantic irony cannot be reduced to a concretization of Schlegelian theory. In any event, the romance that "could criticise itself" is represented in Miller's chapter on romantic duality mainly by Jane Austen's *Northanger Abbey* and E. S. Barrett's *The Heroine,* novels in which satiric criticism of Gothic romance substantially outweighs any interfusion of genuine romantic idealism and comically oriented antiromanticism.[28]

Byron's *Don Juan* is mentioned by Miller only in passing; nor are Byron's truths of inconsistency anywhere dubbed "romantic irony." Yet romantic irony (so specified) does play a small role in *Doubles,* in connection not with Byron but with Keats. Miller, like many other critics, selects as the key to the romantic sense of contrast and multivalence Keats's "negative capability," which "can be regarded as an aspect of duality, and it can also be regarded as an aspect of the divided self." Miller goes on to say that the "poetic character of the romantics is no split personality, but it is not too much to say that the ethos which was to produce a Jekyll and Hyde had already produced – in its perception of the capacity to take an equal delight in the creation of both – an Iago and an Imogen" (79).

Miller does not attempt to establish a casual sequence in European romantic "dualistic and dialectical outlooks"; yet he might almost be proposing cause and effect when he speaks of "the German notion of romantic irony ... and the ensuing English notion of negative capability" (80). If no direct (highly dubious) transmission of ideas, notions, or outlooks is being signaled here, Miller is perhaps alluding to the operation of European cultural osmosis. In either case, Miller assigns Friedrich Schlegel a leading part. His significance is ascribed to his "theoretical justification" of protean fiction, his belief in "the duality of man" (88), his insight into Socratic irony as a union of jest and seriousness, ingenuousness and dissembling, and his understanding of irony as the apprehension of "a paradoxical reality" (89). Miller also cites Schlegel's late comment, made in 1829, on "our intrinsic dualisms and duplicity" (quoted, 89). Such are the perceptions from which evolved, Miller declares, "the currency of the term 'romantic irony' "(89). Obviously it is time to take a closer look at the Schlegel phenomenon.

Chapter 3

The Beatification of Friedrich Schlegel

1.

Anglo-American students of literature who are captivated by modern irony but feel somewhat insecure about its alleged origins in German romanticism have been able to avail themselves, in the last few decades, of several admirably accessible introductions to Schlegelian theory. D. C. Muecke, for example, has an interesting chapter on romantic irony in *The Compass of Irony* (1969). Muecke points out, to begin with, that Schlegel's critical terms fluctuate, so that at times "Ironie," "Witz," and "Arabeske" substitute for one another. He also notes that Schlegel's concept of irony is "only rarely and only in his notebooks" called "romantische Ironie."[1] In outlining the major postulates of this concept, Muecke focuses on the figure of an ironist-artist-god who is both immanent and transcendent, who is free to create or destroy (the destruction will be restorative rather than nihilistic), and who is dynamically aware of the universality of irreconcilable contradictions and paradoxes, whether in Nature or man or art. In art, the chaos of these contradictions promises endless creative fertility. Though the ironic work of art acknowledges its limitations (which it may nevertheless transcend), it is capacious enough and liberated enough to deploy both subjectivity and objectivity, instinct and deliberation, spirituality and sensuality, fun and earnest, love and the demolition of what is loved. In short, "the Romantic Ironist will be consciously subjective, enthusiastically rational, and critically emotional" (200).

Muecke nominates as the only substantial heirs of Friedrich Schlegel's irony three romantics: Ludwig Tieck, E. T. A. Hoffmann, and Heine. The nomination procedure is not without flaws, however, inasmuch as Muecke manages to draft Tieck twice. On the basis of his three motley plays (the most famous of which is *Der Gestiefelte Kater,* or *Puss-in-Boots*), composed between 1797 and 1799, Tieck is judged to be a full-fledged romantic ironist. But this judgment does not fit logically into Muecke's earlier assignment of Tieck's three fantastic plays, along with Sterne's *Tristram Shandy* (1760-67) and Diderot's *Jacques le fataliste* (1783) to the special category of "proto-Romantic irony" (172). What these three ingeniously jesting writers have in common is that they advertise the artifices of their fictive worlds and thus play havoc with the tradition of aesthetic unity and "illusion." In a word, they make light of the validity of the literary forms they work with. Their "so-called destruction of artistic illusions" (164-65) – as Muecke realizes, no thoroughgoing disruption, no actual confusion of distanced life and immediate art, ever takes place – is what Muecke specifies as "proto-Romantic irony." But Muecke, who has made Tieck both a romantic ironist and a proto-romantic ironist, violates logic a second time: he calls the destruction of artistic illusion both "one aspect of Romantic Irony" (164) and "only a step in the direction of Romantic Irony" (165).

The "proto" in Muecke's phrase is designed to highlight the historical prelude to a fully achieved romantic irony. Yet Muecke refers to so many authors, ranging from Aristophanes, Chaucer, Shakespeare, and Cervantes to Pirandello, Gide, Musil, and Beckett, who have played, in varying degrees, with the "double level of art" (165) – that is, their works "shift amusingly or disconcertingly from one imaginative level to another, seemingly more realistic one" (170) – that "proto-romantic irony" is no more useful a term than "post-romantic irony" would be if the latter phrase were applied to twentieth-century literary experimenters who revel in the zany athleticism of self-conscious, self-challenging, self-disruptive art.

A more persuasive text is Hans Eichner's *Friedrich Schlegel* (1970), whose third chapter lucidly examines Schlegel's thinking about irony and romantic poetry.[2] Eichner reminds us that romantic poetry in Schlegel refers basically to "works written in the period from Dante to Cervantes and Shakespeare."[3] But it also refers to modern, non-realistic novels by writers like Sterne, Diderot, Goethe, Jean Paul, and Tieck; for in Schlegel's vision, the spirit of romantic poetry will be carried into the future by works that are more imaginative and more poetic than novels deformed by realism. That future, as it turns out, emerges in the twentieth century, not in the historical period of European romanticism. Schlegel, Eichner suggests, "would have hailed such novels as Joyce's *Ulysses* or Thomas Mann's *Magic Mountain* as the beginnings – merely the beginnings – of a return to the great tradition" (67) subverted by nineteenth-century unilinear realism.

The great tradition of the idiosyncratic comic novel, from Cervantes to Sterne, is of cardinal interest to Schlegel, Eichner remarks, because it rejects authorial constraints. Schlegel is convinced that romantic literature, especially the romantic novel, is too episodic, too digressive to submit to classical prescriptions. Tristram Shandy's declaration that he will confine his writing to no man's rules that ever lived anticipates, indeed is reincarnated in, Schlegel's statement in *Athenaeum* Fragment 116 that the romantic author's "caprice" (Willkür) is subject to no rule (61). This does not mean, however, that what is being proposed is aesthetic anarchy in a void. Romantic caprice is only apparently anarchic; in reality it is artistically arranged, wedded to method. The result is variously described as wit, arabesque, confusion, or chaos (62). The capricious, fantastic work of art is also "sentimental"; that is, it is informed by the spirit of love. Indeed the romantic work of art mirrors the chaos of the universe, which is an organic whole and an expression of divine love (68).

The "synthesis of apparent chaos and underlying order" that Schlegel, as Eichner indicates, "envisaged as the ideal form approximated by the great poets of the romantic tradition" (64) is intimately tied to a sense of irony, which stems from universal paradox – from the duplicity of things. This sense of irony, this paradoxical frame of mind, enables the artist to be "both detached and involved, deeply serious about his art and yet full of critical, conscious awareness" (70). In other words, irony is a process of "alternating self-creation and self-destruction," a phrase which some Anglo-American critics hold in awe, as though it betokened a double biblical apocalypse. Eichner points out that Schlegel plays more than once, and somewhat ambiguously, with this phrase; but it basically means that the work of artistic inspiration is inevitably modified by self-consciousness, by self-criticism. The artist who realizes that he cannot attain perfection acknowledges his inadequacy through ironic depreciation of his work, and thus negates his failure (72).

Eichner collects a number of interrelated, more or less synonymous phrases Schlegel employs to denote the meaning of irony: alternating self-creation and self-destruction, constant self-parody, permanent digression, consciousness of infinitely full chaos, fusion of involvement and detachment (or seriousness and playfulness), awareness of infinite paradox (73-74), and so on. Another such phrase, "transcendental buffoonery," is likely to be troublesome, since it seems to exude an aura (generally attenuated in critical discussion) that is both metaphysical and farcical.[4] But romantic digressive (especially Shandean) caprice, Eichner suggests, suffices to explain the nature of such buffoonery. "Transcendental," we are told, is Schlegel's word for "constant reflections of the work of art in the work of art itself" (73) – a notably Shandean practice. Indeed, Sterne is a master of "transcendental buffoonery." Moreover, "it is striking," Eichner comments, "how many of Schlegel's countless definitions of irony apply quite literally to Sterne's narrative manner." (Eichner adds, it is true, that "a similar case could be made for the novels of Jean Paul, and for any novel in which the technique of the interposed narrator is used for humorous purposes"[73].)

If *Tristram Shandy* so well incarnates (in advance) the features of Schlegelian irony, would it not be appropriate, however anachronistically, to enthrone the detachedly involved and playfully serious Sterne as the pre-eminent German romantic ironist? That is precisely what Peter Conrad does in *Shandyism: The Character of Romantic Irony* (1978), and what Lillian R. Furst has far more cogently accomplished in *Fictions of Romantic Irony* (1984). Yet Furst considers "romantic irony" a misnomer from which Sterne should be liberated, owing to his eighteenth-centuryness. The applicability of the term "romantic irony" to Sterne does not faze Peter Conrad, however, who claims that *Tristram Shandy*, by ingeniously fusing genres, dismantling what it worships, laughing gloriously, and enduring subjection to no law, "would seem to be Schlegel's ideal romantic form."[5]

In his chapter on the romantic novel in *The Romantic Period in Germany*, ed. Siegbert Prawer (1970), Hans Eichner, no longer engaged in aligning Sterne with Schlegel, has no trouble locating Schlegelian "fantastic form" in Bonaventura's *Die Nachtwachen (Nightwatches*, 1804), Brentano's *Godwi* (1801), E. T. A. Hoffmann's *Lebens-Ansichten des Katers Murr (Murr the Tomcat's Views on Life,* 1822), and of course Schlegel's own novel *Lucinde* (1799). However, in his illuminating introduction to *The Romantic Period in Germany*, Prawer rightly refuses to address German romantic irony as though it were a high-powered mystique: "From the first," he writes, "Romantic writers were highly conscious artists, writing with a critic (another self!) always at their elbow, prone to that *irony* which is one of the pillars of literary theory and practice in this period. Aesthetic distance, free play of the mind, relativizing, self-criticism within the actual work of art, the teasing and mystifying of potential readers, conscious experimenting with form and modes of expression, shifting tone, multiple reflections through tale within tale – these are but some of the shapes in which we encounter irony in Romantic writing."[6]

For all its varieties of style, multitudinous genres, and intermittent invitations to lightness, Schlegel's *Lucinde* can hardly compete with *Tristram Shandy*. Peter Firchow, who in 1971 published a translation of *Lucinde,* together with Schlegel's complete Fragments and the "Essay on Incomprehensibility," writes in his introduction that Schlegel's novel, oddly shaped but not devoid of subtle symmetry, is meant to be both an unpruned, natural growth, a sort of literary plant (in "An Idyll of Idleness" the protagonist celebrates the many virtues of the higher vegetative life), and at the same time a self-reflective work whose narrator exercises the interruptive technique cultivated by writers like Cervantes and Sterne.[7] However that may be, Firchow does not contend that Schlegel's interest in levity has resulted in a first-rate comic novel.

In praising the seriocomic temper of Goethe's *Wilhelm Meister's Apprenticeship* – few modern readers of the novel will be able to detect reliable signs of that temper; even Carlyle, Goethe's own translator, found the work deficient in its power to amuse – Schlegel asserts that Goethe "seems to take the characters and incidents so lightly and whimsically, scarcely ever mentioning his hero without irony and smiling down upon his masterpiece itself from the height of his spirit. But one should not let oneself be deceived by this into supposing that he is not religiously in earnest."[8] In *Lucinde,* Schlegel strives to attain more palpable comic effects than Goethe's, without sacrificing a sense of serene gravity.

Initially Julius writes to his beloved Lucinde about a beautiful dream full of "romantic confusion." (The charm of "beautiful chaos," lovingly but incontestably destructive of conventional order, is obviously a supreme Schlegelian motif.) In Julius's opinion, this dream, marked by "wit and rapture," as well as a spiritualized sensuality, characterizes their united life and their religion of love. In "A Dithyrambic Fantasy on the Loveliest Situation in the World" (temporarily transposed sexual identities), Julius indicates how pleased he is with the "sublime frivolity" of their "marriage."[9] Indeed the fire which consumes them is so intense that it requires cooling by "playful good humor" (49).

The trouble with Schlegel's attempted synthesis of the earnest and the lighthearted, however, is that it is more often preached than enacted.

There are, to be sure, plenty of pointers to levity in the novel, including Julius's conviction that, as "Wit's beloved son" (62), he is writing a daring, fantastic, "mad little book" (60). Nor does Julius scant Nature's "incredible humor" (120), expressed in the exuberant caprices of the cosmos. Yet only occasionally is lightness brilliantly illustrated, as in the pages of "Fidelity and Playfulness," where Julius and Lucinde carry on a witty conversation on jealousy that seems to emerge from a positively Wildean mental complexion. Julius remarks, for example, that "man is inherently a serious beast. But one should fight this shameful and abominable inclination with all one's might and in every way" (75).

It was not a wanton comic spirit but rather the scandal of (alleged) soft pornography that provoked many early readers of the novel. *Lucinde* is no longer alarming to the genteel, but the novel, as Julius might put it, is nevertheless challenging in its moral positions. *Lucinde* is certainly not, as Kierkegaard construed it, palpably obscene. (Hegel also found the novel ignoble.) In *The Concept of Irony*, Kierkegaard admits that *Lucinde* reveals instances of enchanting talent. But he damns the book's "free play of ironic arbitrariness,"[10] which encourages the abolition of ethics, a sensual dead-end, an aesthetic anesthetization of the soul, and a self-centered, cowardly wallowing in an imaginary world. Before launching this attack, Kierkegaard examines the enormous vacancy of the almighty Fichtean ego, then passes to the perversity of a Schlegelian irony of eccentric, subjunctive, pathological subjectivity flourishing in a supposedly divine (but in fact irresponsibly reckless and ultimately boring) freedom that unforgivably dissolves historical actuality.

If *Lucinde* has moments of Wildean wit, Schlegel's Fragments (in Firchow's translation) may strike one as autocratically willful, surprisingly banal, wittily luminous, strangely profound, thrillingly audacious, and impenetrably obscure. At times, as in *Athenaeum* Fragment 196, Schlegel can be both incisively aphoristic and amusingly perceptive: "Pure autobiographies are written either by neurotics who are enthralled by their own egos – a class that includes Rousseau; or out of robust artistic or adventurous self-love, like that of Benvenuto Cellini; or by born historians who consider themselves nothing more than the raw materials of historical art; or by women who are playing the coquette with posterity as well as with their contemporaries; or by worrisome people who want to clean up the least little speck of dust before they die and can't bear letting themselves depart from this world without explanations" (188).

The essay "On Incomprehensibility," the last Schlegelian item Firchow translates, offers a multitude of both ironic and non-ironic reflections on diverse modes of irony, some so entangling as to require rescue by the gods. Incomprehensibility of course does not always have irony as its source. But when it is allied to paradox, chaos, and self-parody, incomprehensibility becomes a grace, a virtue, a seminal stimulus to the spirit. It becomes, Schlegel writes, the imagination's rebuke of the mind's pitiable need for complete understanding. Indeed mere rationality may destroy the essential mysteries of life. There is of course a mixture of teasing and sobriety in all of this; but since Schlegel commends paradox as a renovator of the greatest truths, it is not all that surprising that he is capable of praising incomprehensibility as a potentially salvational power.

Schlegelian irony, evoking sociable wit, paradox, transcendental buffoonery, and the vibrations of humor, could easily, one might assume, assimilate the dualistic comedy of European romantic irony.[11] The trouble is that Schlegelian theory is hospitable to a great number of dualities. Nor do such dualities focus on a unique mode of comedy. Most important, however, is that the ambivalence of European romantic irony – its pattern of enchantment and disenchantment (and re-enchantment) – is verifiable rather than merely speculative, and is far more significant in the making (and interpreting) of literary romanticism, from Byron and Heine to Pushkin and Baudelaire, than Schlegel's frequently awesome abstractions. Muecke himself concedes that the concept of Schlegelian irony had little aesthetic impact, that it "did not make much headway" during the romantic period (183). The results, he admits, is an embarrassing gap between Schlegelian theory and the paucity of works in German romanticism that fully exemplify that theory: "Romantic Irony in Germany," he sums up, "was ... a programme for literature, rather than literature itself" (184).

That particular program for literature seems, as Eichner observed, to have been designed for the twentieth century, not the romantic period. In Muecke's opinion, the German writer who best illustrates Schlegel's formulations is Thomas Mann, especially in *Doctor Faustus* (185-86). Erich Heller in *The Ironic German* had earlier emphasized the belated, astonishing consummation of Schlegel's theorizing on irony and romantic poetry in Mann's *The Magic Mountain*.[12] In Heller's view, Schlegel is basically a literary prophet. He may have enrolled certain authors of the past, especially Shakespeare and Cervantes, under the aegis of irony, thereby making the glory of literary irony largely a matter of retrospection; but he is primarily a "great diviner of the historical probabilities of literature,"[13] probabilities that would materialize not in German romanticism but in the modern European novel.

In "The Rhetoric of Temporality," Paul de Man remarks that in Germany "The advent of a full-fledged ironic consciousness ... certainly does not coincide with a parallel blossoming of the novel. Friedrich Schlegel, writing on the novel, has to take his recent examples from Sterne and Diderot and has to strain to find a comparable level of ironic insight in *Wilhelm Meisters Lehrjahre* and in Jean Paul Richter. The opposite is true in France and England, where the spectacular development of the novel is not necessarily accompanied by a parallel interest in the theory of irony; one has to wait until Baudelaire to find a French equivalent of Schlegel's penetration."[14] De Man goes on to interpret Baudelaire's "The Essence of Laugher" as essentially an essay on irony, particularly in its stress on what Baudelaire calls the "absolute comic." But in fact Baudelaire associates the absolute comic not with irony but with grotesque, unself-conscious buffoonery, or with conscious literary fantasticality of a high comic order. The absolute comic has much more to do with riotous disinhibitions and magical metamorphoses than with the temper of irony.[15]

De Man claims that the absolute comic arouses an especially deep sense of differentiating self-awareness, of one's "plurality of worlds" (195). The movement of ironic consciousness, moreover, is so perilously unsettling, in de Man's view, that it ends up unraveling the self with extraordinary acceleration. But where Baudelaire conjures up the breath of the marvelous, invokes a dizzying fairy tale imaginativeness, and underscores the regenerative power of the absolute comic, de Man, persistently and willfully confusing the absolute comic with irony, concludes that "irony is unrelieved *vertige,* dizziness to the point of madness" (198). De Man then quotes Baudelaire's comments on the extravagant superiority complex of the insane and on the tendency of madness to expose itself in laughter.

It is true that at first Baudelaire interprets laughter as a sign of original sin – of hateful pride, satanic superiority, and even insanity. This perspective is sustained in the early part of his essay. However, a quite different orientation is stressed in the latter part of the essay, which concentrates on the embodiment of the absolute comic in an English pantomime and in certain of Hoffmann's tales. The absolute comic is represented as a restorative force that purifies the fallen nature of man and wipes out the diabolic stigma of laughter. In de Man's analysis, however,

its own textuality. Thus Victor Terras in *A Karamazov Companion* (1981) defines romantic irony as a device by which "the narrator alternately steps in and out of his narrative, once identifying with it and then again treating it ironically as mere fiction."[18] Though Anthony Winner is ready to entertain more than one view of romantic irony in *Culture and Irony: Studies in Joseph Conrad's Major Novels* (1988), he sounds much like Terras, if more gravely so, when he remarks that romantic irony involves "a fiction's apprehensions about the epistemological and ethical status of its own fictionality."[19] The *Bedford Glossary of Critical and Literary Terms* (1997) supplies the same kind of understanding: "as defined by the nineteenth-century philosopher Friedrich Schlegel," romantic irony "is present in poems and prose works whose authors or speakers at some point reveal their narration to be the capricious fabrication of an idiosyncratic and highly self-conscious creator." Romantic ironists like Chaucer, Cervantes, Byron, Pirandello, and Nabokov, the *Glossary* informs us, "*want* their readers or audiences to 'see through' them, i.e., to appreciate the manipulative nature of their art and the slightly comic quality of even their most serious artistic endeavors."[20]

Proponents of Schlegelian theory, however, maintain that the idea of self-conscious literature by no means exhausts the meaning of romantic irony. In "Coda: Ironies Domestic and Cosmopolitan," the final chapter in *Romantic Irony* (1988), Frederick Garber, editor of the volume, concurs in the view that (Schlegelian) "romantic irony is one of the primary modes of self-reflexive literature." Nevertheless, he adds, "romantic irony is not simply self-reflexive"[21]; it is more than a self-pondering temper hovering over the making and unmaking of fictionality. Romantic irony is also, Garber asserts, an open-ended encounter of the free, supple, sovereign (but also vulnerable) consciousness with irreconcilable incompatibles and omnipresent instabilities (which the self-destabilizing of the romantic-ironic text symptomizes). Thus Blake's romantic-ironic polarities in *The Marriage of Heaven and Hell* point, like Schlegel's theoretical Fragments, to a necessary and fruitful, if also threatening, "war of contraries" ("the essence of existence") against fixity and finality (377).

If, as Garber appears to be suggesting, self-reflexiveness (textual self-subversion) and the war of contraries (resistance to delusory organicist unity) are at the core of romantic irony, an exemplary romantic ironist would very likely be a combination of Sterne and Shakespeare. The Sterne component of this hybrid writer would activate constant self-creation and self-destruction, while the Shakespeare component, though similarly gifted in playing games with the artifices of art, would voice the permanent dialectic of antagonistic values, unstable forces, and incompatible assessments. Who, then, is Garber's candidate for this ideal figure of romantic-ironic suppleness? Or, rather, who, in his view, has most tellingly conveyed the gist of romantic irony? In Garber's anti-climactic opinion, "the single most influential figure in the practice of Romantic irony remains Ludwig Tieck" (360). Thus Tieck's (at times rather facile) theatrical illusion-breaking is obliged to prop up the provocative, mind-teasing theories of Friedrich Schlegel. (Three decades earlier, René Wellek, relying on the work of Raymond Immerwahr, had noted that "at the time that Schlegel formulated his ideas on irony he did not know Tieck's comedies and he never considered them realizations of his ideals. Goethe, Shakespeare, and Cervantes were his ironists, not his fellow romanticists."[22] If, as Garber further indicates, the Schlegelian romantic ironist, for all his stress on incompatibles that are "endemic to experience" (375), reaches for the transcendence of all contingencies, it is hard to imagine how this mysteriously grand, liberating urge can ever be allied with the tactics of Tieck's topsy-turvy plays.

The preceding remarks are not intended to question the appeal of Tieckian disruptive fantasticality. *Puss-in-Boots,* which is more than a little strange, is a delightful play. Its necessarily improbable cast of characters includes Hinze, the clever tomcat who will gain a kingdom for the young peasant Gottlieb; a "sensible" bourgeois on-stage audience that voices pleasure in certain scenes and speeches but more frequently expresses dissatisfaction with what seems to be a cockeyed theatrical piece; a king, a princess, a court scholar, a court fool, etc.; finally, several stage assistants and the author himself; who from time to time eloquently solicits the on-stage audience's indulgence toward the peculiarities of his play and the mishaps of its production.

Tieckian maneuvers may suggest to some critics a relativistic reaching for the absolute, but there is a clear kinship, long recognized, between Tieck and the eighteenth-century creator of theatrical fantasies, Carlo Gozzi. It has even been claimed that "the German romantics came to view Gozzi as their spiritual and artistic predecessor, A. W. Schlegel finding in the Venetian his own concept of irony, [Jean] Paul his view of humor, Tieck his own technique of mixing levels of reality, and Hoffmann a model for his fantasy."[23] The on-stage audience in *Puss,* at any rate, may remind one of Gozzi's *La Fiaba dell'amore delle tre melarancie (The Love of Three Oranges)*, a play that mixes fairy tale and commedia dell'arte and manages to sport with both.[24] Gozzi's on-stage audience (most of it, at least) quarrel about the values of comedy, tragedy, romance, and farce. However, a minority among the audience (they are the Eccentrics) intervene effectively to control the plot, which is solidly inaugurated when the hypochondriac Prince of Clubs finally laughs but also suffers the curse of falling hopelessly in love – well, not quite hopelessly – with three oranges.

The members of the on-stage audience in *Puss* wrangle even more vociferously. Yet they can also be swayed by mellifluously modest appeals to their charitableness, even if only momentarily, so busy are they emitting exasperated, "sensible" objurgations at the presentation of the fairy tale. Not all the members of the on-stage audience, however, ventilate hostility. A learned character named Bötticher, for example, is pedantically (and ludicrously) obsessed with the finesse of the actor playing the cat. Another character, Schlosser, has passed beyond ordinary grumbling: after concluding that he is either dreaming or drunk, Schlosser is willing to believe he has a punctured brain and is on the verge of being pushed into insanity; this, he presumes, is doubtless the play's aesthetic intention. In the epilogue, however, the author assures the audience that his intention has been only to transport them back to their childhood years. This comment elicits rotten fruit, not sympathy. Yet the author is right. The madcap moments of the inner, fairy tale play are potent enough to release a real theater audience from the grip of excessive maturity. Even the on-stage audience's contrapuntal vocal complaints (mixed with occasional expressions of enjoyment and a few vacuously neutral statements) are funny enough, by themselves, to shatter the restraints of adulthood.

Of course we are not likely to forget that the delights of nonsense in *Puss* coexist with a host of satiric aims. Tieck pokes fun at silly, volatile monarchs, casts his ridicule at the splintered condition of Germany, directs his hits at late eighteenth-century cultural attitudes and topical literary and musical oddities, and, most important of all, shafts the on-stage audience's middle-class mentality, which is so limited that it requires orderly, reasonable literary procedures, that is, good taste and rational theatrical illusion, not adventurous dramaturgy (which is not to deny that this same middle class can get sodden with sentimentality).

Nevertheless, Tieck's satiric mockery in *Puss* remains irrevocably interlocked with the play's fundamental buffoonery. Today it is the zaniness of *Puss,* its farcical confusion of perspectives, that wins our attention, not its alleged embodiment of the physics and metaphysics of German romantic irony. Some of the clowning is less than brilliant, to be sure. In Act I, the King and the foreign Prince Nathanael, who is courting the King's daughter in vain, fracture "illusion" by raising the question of how it is that the audience accepts the Prince's perfect fluency in a language he doesn't even know. In Act II, Hinze the cat tells Gottlieb he has to be patient while awaiting good fortune, for "in the real world things don't go so fast" (71). (This realistic remark by an unreal creature induces a brief apoplexy in the on-stage audience). When the curtain is accidentally raised just before Act II – we discover the author and a technician almost at each other's throats on the stage – Hanswurst, the court fool, kills some time by addressing the audience and agreeing with it that the author has written a miserable play. Gottlieb tells Hinze in Act III that his promised happiness had better arrive before 8:00 p.m., for the comedy will be over by then. In the same act, the court scholar and Hanswurst argue about the merits of a play called *Puss-in-Boots,* which Hanswurst declares is a wretched work, though he claims not to be acquainted with it. The argument is capped by Hinze's support for Hanswurst, after which Hinze is "quite dismayed. – I myself helped the fool to a victory over a play in which I'm performing the chief part" (111). This kind of self-reflexive foolery hardly warrants touting Tieck's theatrical oeuvre as a force that produced a significant alteration in Western consciousness.

3.

Tieckian dishevelment may be dizzying, at least temporarily; but it does not involve unplumbable mysteries. However, mysteries of non-finality are apparently destined to adhere permanently to the Schlegelian theory of irony. Garber, uneasy about limiting Schlegelian romantic irony to only two or three dominant characteristics, hints more than once that such irony is too subtle and too complex to be definitively pinned down. Not surprisingly, Schlegelian irony has become remarkably malleable. It is capable of assimilating much more than the techniques of metafiction and the everlasting war of contraries.

A striking example of such assimilationism is Lloyd Bishop's *Romantic Irony in French Literature from Diderot to Beckett* (1989). Bishop believes that "the range of romantic irony is vast; it extends from the most obvious overt devices – the Pirandellian parabasis and the destruction-of-illusion effect – to the self-conscious texts of Mann and Nabokov and to the subtlest forms of unsignaled irony."[25] Moreover, romantic irony "is the predecessor of all forms of black humor in this century, of the modern tragic farce and the antihero (e.g., the passive hero and the hero as clown), of the unreliable and imperceptive narrator of contemporary fiction, of the post-modern novel's urge to dispel representational illusion and to question its own strategies and presuppositions, of the sad clown in modern painting, even the Satie-like autoparody in contemporary music. It has been termed a prelude to the philosophical notion of the Absurd."[26] Bishop makes some interesting comments on authentic French romantic ironists (Musset, Gautier, Stendhal, Baudelaire); but little save critical indigestion is likely to be the outcome of his tentacular claims for romantic irony.

Clyde de L. Ryals also sees romantic irony proliferating mightily. In *A World of Possibilities: Romantic Irony in Victorian Literature* (1990), Ryals examines Carlyle, Thackeray, Browning, Arnold, Dickens, Tennyson, and Pater – all in the light of Schlegel's concept of irony. According to Ryals, if a Victorian text mixes genres and styles (to whatever degree), engages in self-reflexiveness (mildly or blatantly), avoids fixed meaning by apparently deconstructing (in some measure) the world it has represented, and presents characters (if there are any) and makers (or narrators) who are conscious of theatrical make-believe (whatever the depth or range of that consciousness), it is to be labeled a work of romantic irony. Presumably tying all, or most, of these traits together is an ancient philosophical sagacity about indeterminacy that Ryals converts into a nineteenth-century epiphany: the need to suspend judgment in the midst of contradictory views. In other words, a familiar classical, Pyrrhonic scepticism – a refusal of subjection to mental fixity (judgmental certitude) in a world of conflicting evaluations – is interpreted by Ryals as the fundamental romantic-ironic stance. Thus, he declares, "the kind of irony that Thirlwall describes – suspended judgment required by the indeterminacy of the case [Connop Thirlwall, writing in 1833, had in mind Sophocles' presentation of equal but opposing truths or rights in *Antigone*] – is that now known as romantic irony."[27]

Ryals gets closer to Schlegelian ideas when he elevates process – the dialectical stage of becoming – as the prime reality of romantic irony. Yet as he shifts from Schlegel to the Victorian *Zeitgeist*, problematically rife with ideas of change – it has been frequently observed that "diagnosticians of Victorian society ... experienced their time as exceptionally unsettled,"[28] marked by pervasive anxieties born of intractable social problems – Ryals's thinking again becomes formulaic. "Once the doctrine of becoming, eternal change without telos, was embraced," he writes, "it followed as the night the day that an ironic, a romantic ironic world view was the result" (14). The certainty Ryals extracts from his clichéd analogy is perhaps a measure of his statement's intellectual frailty.

Because Ryals wishes, despite his emphasis on eternal non-teleological change, to signalize Victorian promise, based on a healthily sceptical cultural mentality, he regards "acceptance of contradictions and paradoxes" (131) among the great Victorians as an index of cultural confidence, of Whitmanesque potentialities in an age of transition. Instances of cultural malaise, of shaken faith in the idea of progress, of grinding doubt, fear, dismay, and pessimism are not exactly scanted; but Ryals's main point is that romantic irony, "revealing itself in different styles, forms, modes, and perspectives," and underscoring provisional, developmental (reconstructionist as well as deconstructionist) meaning, embraces the process of becoming as a great enabling power, releasing a "world of possibilities" (15).

In such a world, the very process of change, validated by instability and contradiction, suffices to identify romantic irony. Thus Arnold's poetry, which is described as uncommonly self-reflexive (but only in the sense that the poet splits himself into different selves), qualifies as romantic irony mainly because "all is in course of change" (61). Ryals may insist that Arnold "presents not certainties but possibilities," yet some of those possibilities are famously dark, and not to be expunged by a jesting self. When Ryals states that Arnold's "favorite situations are those that are intrinsically ironic" (63), such intrinsicality, one might surmise, does not augur well for a world of refreshing possibilities. Yet what Ryals chooses to emphasize is "an ironic posture that permits toleration of indeterminacy" (65) and the co-existence of right and wrong. When Ryals tells us that the later Arnold often uses the elegiac mode "because it allowed for the irony of reversal," (70) we are meant to think that elegiac irony is not essentially mournful; it signifies beneficial flux. (Lycidas is dead, yet he beautifully survives.)

Melancholy attitudes, embattled positions, and pessimistic proclivities in Arnold are thus allowed little currency by Ryals, who suggests that Arnold's gloom is thoroughly penetrated by his playful, even laughing, acceptance of life's universal ironies: Arnold "exhibits his conflicts ironically – so as to transcend them. Far from being a poet of 'sincerity,' Arnold is self-conscious, seriously playful, problematic, and equivocal. His, in sum, is the art of the romantic ironist that presents a self always in process and always relishing and extolling its own self-activity" (75). The romantic ironist may be a problematic and equivocal self; but he delights in luminous becoming and aesthetic bliss.

Indeed Ryals is prepared, in Schlegelian fashion, to associate romantic irony with the relish of the creative process itself. The "imaginative donnée" of "The Scholar-Gypsy," Ryals declares, is "not the scholar-gypsy and his quest, or modern life with its ills, or meaning of any kind; rather, it is ... romantic irony, which permits the poet to rise above his finite subject matter to a realm of aesthetic consciousness" (71). But it is possible that this realm (which seems somewhat vacuous in its aeriality, as though aesthetic consciousness did not also initiate and sustain a work of art) meant less to Arnold than his poignant recognition of lapsed heroism and lost coherence in modern life.

The Idylls of the King is another work that is held to be romantic-ironic: Tennyson, like God (and Thackeray and Dickens) "is both immanent and transcendent"; "he is also like God in that he is inscrutable, presenting us with ambiguities, contradictions, and paradoxes" (112), all of which are essential elements in the doctrine of becoming. Collapsed ideals and a perishing kingdom reeling back into the beast may seem to characterize the ending of the *Idylls,* but indeterminacy still reigns. Assertions and intimations are undermined by other intimations and assertions. Pessimism is balanced by optimism. Furthermore, Tennyson "calls attention to his poem as a literary artifice and thereby to himself as the artist" (112). Hence Tennyson, despite his sadness, is a romantic ironist.

Walter Pater's *Marius the Epicurean,* another self-mirroring, "self-conscious linguistic construct" (128), is construed by Ryals as a work of romantic irony mainly owing to its "idealist doctrine of becoming" (114). Marius himself turns into a romantic ironist when he begins to feel receptive to Christianity's very special principle of becoming, that is, its doctrine of a (non-provisional) mutation from death to immortality. The very embodiment of romantic irony in the novel's Christianity is "the true Heraclitean doctrine of becoming" (123) – hitherto obscured by Marius's epicureanism – wherein death is treated as birth. Nevertheless, the "truth" released by this insight remains hypothetical, indeterminate, and profoundly enigmatic. In Ryals's pages, "becoming" (romantic irony) signifies both ineradicable scepticism and "unlimited possibilities" (123).

God, celebrated more than once by Ryals in *A World of Possibilities* as an ironic artist, is clearly the ultimate, the supreme romantic ironist, and the spiritual father of Friedrich Schlegel. As it happens, theologizing German romantic irony had already been officially carried out in

Romantic Irony (1988), edited by Frederick Garber. But this effort (sponsored by the International Comparative Literature Association) to beatify Schlegelian theory (bonded to Tieckian practice) was scarcely an unqualified success. *Romantic Irony* contains, it is true, a number of major essays, especially those by Behler, Garber, Gillespie, and Furst. On the other hand, the uneven conclusions reached by many of the contributors make the volume virtually self-defeating.

In the preface to *Romantic Irony,* Garber avers that "though the major Romantic impetus [of romantic irony] came from German sources Romantic irony had a rich, if scattered, life in European and Anglo-American literature, a life which took that Germanic impetus and made it into matter for local consumption."[29] This generalization, to say the least, is misleading. In the chapter entitled "Imagination and Irony in English Romantic Poetry," Anthony Thorlby certainly does not substantiate the notion of a "Germanic impetus" that was "made into matter for local consumption" in English romanticism. Thorlby does find irony in all the principal English romantic poets, but his basic position is that a "discrepancy of word and thing" is primarily responsible for such irony: "The irony consists in the fact that [the poets] could feel, and thus imaginatively visualize, the inadequacy of utterance to actuality, of creative consciousness to lifeless fact without meaning or identity, and yet could seek to escape from it and in their poetry to overcome it" (142). In a word, the English romantic ironists, though seeking "the lost state of paradisal oneness of being" (143), remain conscious of the "ironical status" of their imaginative but inevitably duplicitous words.

This may sound vaguely Schlegelian, but a drastic secession from Garber's thesis begins to take place when Thorlby points out that "the literary works of Friedrich Schlegel and Tieck which supposedly exemplify [romantic irony] are considerably inferior in quality, even in the quality of their ironic vision," to the works of English romantic ironists. A dissimilar psychology and "dissimilar socio/political circumstances and traditions" (149) account for such differences. The English romantics have an "ethically more realistic and responsible conception of the self. Precisely their grasp of actuality rendered their imagination of it so poignant: an alternating or contrastive vision … is the source of … their Romantic irony, with all its attendant modes of longing and loss, attentiveness to common detail and sublime moments of exaltation" (150). There is little in Thorlby's essay (whether one agrees with it or not) that can reconcile German and English romantic irony, let alone corroborate the idea that German romantic irony somehow invigorated English romantic irony.

A number of other chapters in *Romantic Irony* bear similarly lukewarm or deflationary messages about the influence of German romantic irony. Nor is this a question of minor vs. major national literatures. (Some major national literatures – Spanish and Italian – do not even make an appearance in the book.) In their chapter on "Thorbecke and the Resistance to Irony in the Netherlands," Wim Van den Berg and Joost Kloeck conclude that "neither knowledge of the theoretical conception of Romantic irony, nor literary phenomena corresponding to it, can be perceived even in germ" in the romantic period in the Netherlands (176). In "Pushkin, Lermontov, Gogol: Ironic Modes in Russian Romanticism," Roman S. Struc ultimately finds that "the Russian literature of the Romantic age does not seem to include irony [that is, German romantic irony] as one of the firm constituents of its poetics" (249).

Other contributors, to be sure, find potent influences at work. For example, in "The Development of Romantic Irony in the United States," G. R. Thompson is certain that the fiction of Irving, Poe, Hawthorne, and Melville, writers creatively stirred by literary ideas (especially, even if only indirectly, German literary ideas), may be securely approached through a romantic-ironic conspectus. These writers abundantly exhibited "ambiguities or disruptions in the text"; they "playfully or ironically manipulated narrative frames"; and they exercised "philosophical scepticism of humankind's attempts to penetrate the inscrutability of existence" (271). (Thompson is far from suggesting that romantic irony has to do with a world of encouraging possibilities.) Frederick Garber believes, in addition, that contemporary American literature is, in part, also indebted to Schlegelian irony; at least he is ready to snare Thomas Pynchon and John Barth within the international complex of romantic irony (8).

One of the few Anglo-American critics prepared to offer a cool, unawed, realistic assessment of Schlegel's probable impact on literature is Stuart Curran, whose comments on the putatively influential dissemination of Schlegelian ideas were voiced shortly before the publication of *Romantic Irony*. "It is perhaps natural for later historians," he writes, "to see in the *Atheneumsfragmente* the foundation of a Romantic aesthetics. But a meticulous historicism must paint a more complicated picture ... the ideas of the Jena circle were virtually ignored by Italian culture, generally disavowed by British empiricism and skepticism, and rather splendidly distorted the minute they crossed the borders into the France of the Bourbon Restoration. We might even infer that Schlegel's circle had a comparatively minor influence on the actual achievements of German Romanticism, since for all its energetic spirit of creative innovation, its pronouncements came a quarter of a century after Goethe's own frame was established, and he and Schiller dominated the European view of German Romanticism. Against those titanic presences the effusion of brilliant but gnomic ideas whether in short-lived periodicals, through an extensive but unpublished correspondence, or in untranslated philosophical lectures could not compete on a European stage – nor, for that matter, among the general reading public of the German-speaking states."[30]

4.

Scholars of German literature, on the other hand, tend to pay ritualistic homage to Schlegelian ideas and to regard German romantic irony as enormously influential. Recently the validity of such devotion to German romantic irony has been sharply questioned by Joseph A. Dane – not because German romantic irony is hokum, but because in his view it is ill defined and historically shaky. Lacking unity and a consistent theme, it presents a bundle of critical concepts (often dichotomies) that can be indulgently shaped and conveniently re-shaped. In *The Critical Mythology of Irony* (1991), Dane examines the manipulations by which critics, especially in the last two centuries, have managed to plant, rather than discover, irony in literary works. As for German romantic irony – no other kind is "more crucial ... in the history of irony" – Dane concludes that it "cannot be reduced legitimately to a definition, nor can the claims for it be taken at face value."[31]

The assertion that German romantic irony is a mythic entity that has evolved scripture and dogma (118) is hardly the product of a superficial assessment. Dane has studied the work of nineteenth- and twentieth-century German scholars, from Hettner and Haym to Strohschneider-Kohrs, Behler, and Japp. He has scrutinized twentieth-century evaluations of German romantic irony in English, from Lussky and Immerwahr to Furst and Handwerk. (Only Babbitt's *Rousseau and Romanticism* and *Romantic Irony,* edited by Frederick Garber, are missing.) He has also carefully inspected the relevant writings of Schlegel, Karl Solger, Hegel, and Adam Müller.

Schlegelian scripture, Dane observes, is bound to be untidy if only because critics have inventively ransacked Schlegel's notebooks (unpublished until fairly recently) in order to corroborate perceptions about irony extracted from a handful of Fragments that appeared chiefly in the *Lyceum* and the *Athenaeum*. Schlegel's (conceivably rejected, but certainly provisional) notebook formulations on the subject of irony are in Dane's judgment radically experimental, often contradictory, "enigmatic, and difficult to relate to his contemporary published fragments" (74). Moreover, the coherence attributed to the published Fragments themselves is dubious; it is a coherence "about which Schlegel himself seems to be skeptical" (102). Nevertheless, the "myth of coherence" (75), much of which depends on "critical sleight of hand" (102) – especially the unrigorous acceptance of apparently interchangeable terms (wit, paradox, arabesque, parody, irony) – has continued to prevail, though by 1800, Dane is convinced, the "Letter About the Novel" ("Brief über den Roman") suggests that Schlegel "no longer considers irony central to a theory of romantic poetry, or to a theory of the novel" (104).

Though "most scholars agree" that Schlegelian irony "involves at least the self-conscious relation of the artist to his work and the destroying of artistic illusion" – Garber, we recall, would also focus on the war of contraries, but would declare that any kind of strict definition is bound to miss certain (perhaps undefinable) nuances in German romantic irony – Dane finds that "little of Schlegel's original thought develops in conjunction with the word *Ironie*" (106). Nor does he believe that advocates of Schlegelian irony wish Schlegel's writings to be judged on the criteria of disinterest, logic, and consistency (92).

One might argue that Dane, perhaps over-committed to lucidity, logic, and consistency, has allowed insufficient room for subtle, imaginative, expansionist implications in some of Schlegel's famous pronouncements. Dane observes, for example, that *Lyceum* Fragment 42 (on "the divine breath of irony" and "transcendental buffoonery") and *Lyceum* Fragment 108 (on the "unresolved conflict of the indefinite and the definite, of the impossibility and necessity of a complete communication") derive explicitly from Socrates. Such pronouncements should not, therefore, be permitted to take on, in the minds of romanticists, an unwarranted richness of mystery. But if Dane, scrupulously dry, perhaps underestimates the possibilities that can be teased out of Schlegel's texts, his readings are by no means oppressively restrictive. On the contrary, Dane's strong point is analytical rigor, which serves as an indispensable corrective to a good deal of loose speculation. Indeed it is difficult not to agree with Dane's argument that German romantic irony exists only in the realm of literary myth.

The myth, nevertheless, seems more firmly entrenched than ever. Consider recent works by Kathleen Wheeler and Ernst Behler. In *Romanticism, Pragmatism, and Deconstruction* (1993), Kathleen Wheeler puts to rout any suggestion that German romantic irony is a fuzzy, misleading, or over-valued concept. Her basic assumption is that German romantic irony, which is represented, she declares, by Novalis, Friedrich Schlegel, Ludwig Tieck, Jean Paul Richter, and Karl Solger, is a supremely potent force in the making of modern literature and criticism – a force inspired, above all, by Socratic and Shakespearean insights and expressive modes, and in turn inspiring, or significantly helping to shape, pragmatic and deconstructive ideas.

A key motif in Wheeler's diachronic web of inspirations is the triumph of dynamic becoming over the arid search for fixed meanings, final results, ultimate truths, and transcendent realities. But the writers Wheeler puts in the limelight are so bereft of individualizing traits that they seem virtually interchangeable in their critical postulates and literary practice. According to Wheeler, Novalis's *Heinrich von Ofterdingen,* Tieck's *Der gestiefelte Kater* and Schlegel's *Lucinde* all belong in the same category of romantic irony because all three demonstrate "what today we might call disruption, Verfremdung, or defamiliarization," as in Brecht or Beckett.[32] That is all we get to know about any of these extraordinarily diverse works. Yet the apparent digressions in *Heinrich von Ofterdingen* (essayistic dialogues, tales, poems, fables), which either chart or shape Heinrich's poetic-spiritual education, are not the equivalents of Tieckian disruption, though they do involve some subtle metafictional play. The final, excessively lengthy cosmic fairy tale spun out by Klingsohr may be gratuitously convoluted; but the symbol-laden triumph of goodness, love, peace, poetry, wisdom, and order over chaos and evil is meant to strengthen, like the luminous words of the sage miner and the hermit sage, Heinrich's deepening awareness of the mysterious spirit of life and the universe. That mysterious spirit does not easily harmonize, moreover, with baffling, daringly unorthodox comedy, though Heinrich, a preternaturally gifted apprentice in the realm of art and thought – he is endowed with almost as many transcendental insights as the novel's official dispensers of wisdom – is obviously capable of sublime joy and exaltation (and also of compassionate tears). If *Heinrich von Ofterdingen* has moments of serene joviality, those moments do not stem from a cornucopia of scandalous paradoxes, in the manner of *Lucinde;* nor is the novel ever propelled by the sort of anarchic mischief that flourishes in *Der gestiefelte Kater.*

With Schlegel at her side, Wheeler avows that German romantic irony is forever fluid, forever agile, forever provisional, forever paradoxical, and forever (it seems admissible to add) uncapturable. Wheeler believes, moreover, that there is no great discrepancy of conviction between German romantic ironists and English romantics like Shelley, Coleridge, and Blake. One major instance of deep affinity, she suggests, is Coleridge's reconciliation of opposites, which is like the tension of opposites (the rational and the irrational, the finite and the infinite) in German romantic irony. Like Blake, she adds, the German romantic ironists have in mind a permanent, integrative interpenetration of contraries.

In another, earlier publication, Wheeler had quoted from a letter Tieck wrote to Coleridge, in which Tieck commented that the English poet never degenerated into "shallow sentimentality." Wheeler concluded that Tieck "viewed Coleridge's style as truly 'ironic' in the high German romantic sense. Sentimentality was a sign that the artist was not in control of his material and was unable to gain the necessary objective distance of a detached, reflective, and self-conscious spectator of the process of his own composition."[33] But irony in the "high German romantic sense" of the word turns out, we learn from Tieck, to be characteristic of the drama of Sophocles and Shakespeare.[34] There is no interchange between the two correspondents regarding Schlegel's concept of irony in the Fragments.

Wheeler's zealousness in according sovereign significance to German romantic irony is especially detectable in the various functions she ascribes to the Fragment. In German romantic irony, she declares, Fragments reveal that art (like life) offers a limited perspective.[35] But Fragments also underscore "the irresolvable mystery of being" (31). Moreover, like Nietzsche's in *The Will to Power*, Fragments are inspiriting "fields of energy" (16). They are seeds that fertilize the imagination (27). Fragments are parodic, paradoxical, symbolic refutations of the sterile quest for transcendence. Fragments are oracular models of incomprehension designed to stimulate the reader to engage in an endless activity of inconsistent and contradictory decipherment whose Socratic goal is self-knowledge, self-criticism, and self-cultivation – that is to say, "a clear consciousness of 'eternal agility' and of an indefinite 'teeming chaos' " (32).

Socrates might have found this kind of self-cultivation rather awesome. Nevertheless, Socrates is often obliged by Wheeler (as well as by Schlegel) to reinforce (or perhaps originate) much of German romantic irony. The Socratic inspiration of German romantic irony, Wheeler remarks, involves "an entire way of life" (27), which is expressed literarily as paradox and absurdity (29) and also as "the fantastic, marvellous and grotesque" (30). Socratic scepticism, furthermore, is the ancestor of Nietzschean perspectivism: both Socrates and Nietzsche reject transcendental unities and falsely authoritative absolutes. So do the German romantic ironists, who are convinced that both mind and universe evolve organically and unpredictably (5).

German romantic irony, Wheeler argues, is very far from being a parochial literary idiom; indeed, it makes us aware that all art is intrinsically, productively ironic (28). Wheeler establishes an immense congruence between romantic irony, European literature, and modern thought – a thesis which she supports by networking liberally in intellectual and literary history. (Too liberally at times. Thus she states that the nexus between romanticism and Socrates' irony is affirmed by Kierkegaard [28]; yet she never hints that Kierkegaard's attitude toward German romantic irony is hostile.)

In sentences heavily loaded with cultural freight, Wheeler asserts that the modern counterpart of German romantic irony's dynamic relativism is the pragmatic view of art, language, and reality (27). In the "Socratic-German romantic tradition," irony includes the Deweyan idea of "art as experience," which is tantamount to a "Coleridgean-Barthean notion of aesthetic experience as primary and imaginative" (28). Wheeler also points to a "Deweyan-Derridean" deconstructive puncturing of attempts at fixity and the finalization of meaning (29), a process inaugurated by German romantic irony – that is to say, by Socrates. However, she rejects "nihilism and destruction" as "descriptions of the ironist's practice" (29).[36] In short, Wheeler sees German romantic irony as a literary-critical-philosophic agency that not only possessively yet fruitfully reinterprets the past but also, as a prodigiously influential force, encompasses the future in the shape of pragmatism and deconstruction.

While Wheeler clutters her discussion of German romantic irony with several decades' worth of distinguished names, Ernst Behler, whose scholarly mind has been mapping and re-mapping German romantic irony in German and English over the years, succeeds in condensing Schlegelian concepts of irony into only a handful of pages in his *German Romantic Literary Theory* (1993), a study that concentrates on the early, progressive period of German romanticism. For Behler, as for Wheeler, German romantic irony is a historical turning point for modern and postmodern literary criticism and philosophy. In Behler's judgment, moreover, Schlegel's position in the history of irony is of revolutionary, unparalleled significance.[37] This does not mean that the essence of German romantic irony can be summed up in a few accommodatingly rational axioms. German romantic theory as a whole, Behler admits, "eludes any final formulation and does not result in an ultimate doctrine." Nonetheless, it has served as a source of "actualizations" for many late critical developments, ranging from New Criticism to deconstruction.[38] (Behler omits pragmatism; but then, Wheeler leaves out New Criticism.)

Unlike critics for whom Schlegelian irony's incorporation of multiple dualities remains at the very least troublesome, Behler believes that Schlegel's Fragments on irony, both published and unpublished, "certainly show a coherence," despite shifts in "emphasis and approach" (142). If Behler is right, one need not be a Jamesian demon of subtlety to illuminate the master duality in German romantic irony. At the beginning of his book, Behler singles out the interesting process of irony's constant alternation of self-creation and self-destruction as the essential definition of Schlegelian irony (2). However, Behler is quite prepared to substitute simpler, more familiar wording, like "affirmation and negation" (149) for such continual fluctuation. This master polarity, Behler then affirms (not quite perspicuously), relates to most of Schlegel's other polarities, for example, "Classical and Romantic, poetry and philosophy, the Ego and the world" (149). It is also encapsulated, Behler continues, in Schlegel's description of Cervantesque-Shakespearean "artfully ordered confusion," "charming symmetry of contradictions," and "wonderfully perennial alternation of enthusiasm and irony."

This last "alternation" has always been rather peculiar. That is because the master polarity of German romantic irony involves both "enthusiasm and scepticism" and also "enthusiasm and irony." This means that irony is viewed as negative and sceptical, on the one hand, and as dual (affirmative-negative, enthusiastic-sceptical), on the other. But perhaps this paradox deserves to be ranked with the Schlegelian idea that the ironic artist can rise above his own art, genius, and virtue.

Behler does more than reshuffle familiar Schlegelian phrases. He also offers unhackneyed interpretations of a few celebrated Fragments. Thus he demotes an isolated, wholly untypical Fragment in the collection entitled *Ideen (Ideas)*, a Fragment which almost every admirer of Schlegel (Kathleen Wheeler, for one), seizes upon as an indispensable key to the wondrously supple nature of German romantic irony: "Irony is the clear consciousness of an eternal agility, of an infinitely abundant chaos" (quoted, 151). While acknowledging that this definition may be seen by some as an expression of confidence, Behler views it as a manifestation of melancholic irony, wherein "one's own insignificance, transitoriness, and fragmentation" are emphasized (151). Fragment-writing itself is approached by Behler without fuss or Wheeleresque euphoria. Intimately related to romantic irony, it reveals a "fragmentary, incomplete, perspectivistic, or asystematic outlook" (152). That is to say, "completion and totality in any realizable fashion are questioned by a type of writing that, from the outset, rejects any type of closure and postpones it to an unrealizable future" (153).

In the "Conclusion" of *German Romantic Literary Theory,* Behler writes that an early [German] Romantic is … someone who looks at literary texts with a good dose of irony, who in his relationships with other people displays an infinite amount of wit, and who in philosophy exercises constantly higher exponential series of thoughts" (300). Since even Nietzsche would probably fail such a summons to an ever-ripening, ever self-transcending intellect, perhaps we may assume that Behler is uttering a playful, neo-Schlegelian hyperbole.[39]

In defining German romantic irony, contemporary handbooks of literature, which strive for appropriate simplifications, usually rely on a formula that Wheeler and Behler would find restrictive, and that the reader is already familiar with. In *The Oxford Companion to the English Language* (1992), romantic irony is described as a mode in which "writers conspire with readers to share the double vision of what is happening in the plot of a novel, film, etc. … Henry Fielding interrupted the action in his novels to address his readers directly and comment on events. When engaging in this game, writers combine creative egotism with a suave and knowing self-mockery."[40] In *The Cambridge Guide to Literature in English* (1993), romantic irony is held to lie "in discrepancies of tone and statement that result from an authorial detachment from the created characters and action, which allows unexpected moods or comments to be expressed."[41] Is romantic irony, then, essentially a convoluted sabotage of linear narrative convention? Or is it basically a comedy of contradictory voices? Let us turn to two German romantics, E. T. A. Hoffmann and Heinrich Heine, each of whom has been seen as a perfect exemplar of German romantic irony.

Chapter 4

Proposed Exemplars: Hoffmann and Heine

1.

E. T. A. Hoffmann figures more prominently than any other German romantic, with the exception of F. Schlegel, in Ingrid Strohschneider-Kohrs's voluminous, presumably authoritative *Die romantische Ironie* (2nd ed., 1977). Exploring her subject as an intricately resourceful self-reflexive mode of art, Strohschneider-Kohrs, after a long introduction devoted to F. Schlegel, devotes almost 60 pages to a single Hoffmann novella, "Princess Brambilla," which, together with Tieck's *Puss-in-Boots*, becomes the chief representative of German romantic irony. In this scheme of things, Heine, whom Irving Babbitt long ago described as the master of romantic irony in Germany, is an irrelevance, a blank, except when he is occasionally cited as an example of inferior irony-making. To be specific, Heine is granted only four brief references that add up to no more than half-a-dozen lines. An example: Tieck (not the early Tieck), who admires Karl Solger as the great sage of ironic theory, mentions Heine as a practitioner of lower (that is, merely Swiftian) irony, not as a creator of higher artistic irony.[1] Elsewhere, Strohschneider-Kohrs suggests that Heine's irony is facile and limited (449) and indeed is tantamount to a cynical enjoyment of destructiveness (342). A somewhat random footnote also quotes Heine's displeasure with Hoffmann's narrative allegorizing (360n75).

Hoffmann's narratives, it has to be said at the outset, reveal a remarkably diverse tonality, ranging from tragic or demonic terror to farcical high jinks and Shandean whimsy. That is why he has been perceived as both an unsurpassed exemplar of the fantastic-grotesque in comedy – Baudelaire regarded him as the master of the "absolute comic"[2] – and as a "shattered self" whose vision is basically tormented.[3]

The work of fiction usually advanced to illustrate Hoffmann's identity as a romantic ironist is *The Life and Opinions of Kater Murr (Die Lebens-Ansichten Des Kater Murrs)* (1821), a feline autobiography which includes vandalized portions of the biography of Kapellmeister Johannes Kreisler. Hoffmann, for whom doubleness or self-division is a creative constant, has arranged the text so that the two completely different narratives (Murr's and Kreisler's) recurrently intersect each other. Thus the novel incessantly and disconcertingly tears itself apart – or, to put it more conventionally, destabilizes itself.

Kater Murr flashes a fiction-as-frolic signal almost as quickly as *Tristram Shandy*. Mock-anxiously playing the role of a not very competent editor, "Hoffmann" hopes the reader will forgive what may seem to be an incredible delinquency: he has overlooked the repeated interpolation of alien material in Murr's autobiography. Tomcat Murr had ripped this alien material (to serve as blotting paper, for example) from a printed though apparently unpublished book in his master's library, a book dealing with the extremely strange life of the musician-composer Johannes Kreisler. The hodgepodge formed by these incompatible lives has emerged as a finished product from the typesetter. Since the periodic markers, "s.p." for "scrap paper" and "M.C." for "Murr continues," must, initially at least, prove far more irksome than helpful, the book would appear to be an incredibly sloppy venture in publishing – that is, if its self-destructive format were taken as a genuine idiotic error rather than as a deliberate, fascinatingly crazy scheme to cut capers with textual integrity. The editor's anxiety is transparent camouflage for a complicated literary joke.

Now it is obvious that Hoffmann's artful skipping between feline Murr's adventures and the bizarre occurrences in Kreisler's life may be interpreted as a manifestation of the Schlegelian artist's freedom to "dissolve and reconstitute [his] own construction at will at any time."[4] But in fact, the potentialities for structural deviance in this split novel are pre-ordained, inasmuch as Hoffmann's text is based on a constant, unvarying alternation of its two components. Moreover, the pages of Murr's autobiography (written, according to the "Author's Introduction," for an élite of pure, sensitive souls) are generally lucid and follow each other with little chronological disruption. The Kreisler sections of the novel are rather different. Despite early "editorial" attempts at tracing Kreisler's artistic development coherently, missing or chronologically irregular chunks of narration are not infrequent. These may produce unbridgeable gaps, though they are not fatally injurious to the reader's comprehension. Still, the Kreisler text does become increasingly crowded with tantalizingly murky, mysterious events. Fortunately, however, they are offset by profoundly poetic meditations and mesmerizing bursts of zaniness, both light and dark.

The comedy, whether zany or not, which marks Murr's share of the book is consistently light in temper. In the "Author's Introduction," Murr presents himself as a modest, tremblingly idealistic student of literature who is striving to attain the heights of culture. (On the other hand, in the suppressed yet somehow plainly printed and proudly aggressive "Author's Preface," he advertises himself as a famous, pedagogically valuable man of letters and one of the great geniuses of the age; he also acknowledges Puss-in-Boots as his distinguished ancestor.) Murr may think of himself as an exalted seeker of the romantic ideal; but he generally comes across as a smug, inane, egomaniacal pseudo-romantic who apes literary masters of the past and present in unwittingly parodic form. Yet this is an incomplete picture. The celebrity-smitten young Murr is delightfully vain and endearingly shallow, not only in his hackneyed, soulful romantic attitudes and his success-oriented aspirations but especially in his adolescent cravings, pretensions, fulfillments, and disappointments. The great charm of Hoffmann's story derives from an amusing, uncanny merger of characteristic feline instinct and "refined" human behavior.

Murr's unusual appetite for education in the home of his owner Meister Abraham (Kreisler's friend and mentor) is stimulated by an "intellectual lust"[5] that sets him far apart from most other cats. Murr learns to comprehend human speech, to read, to cultivate poetic and scholarly pursuits, and, more rapidly than one might think advisable, to write "immortal works" (II.33). One of these is his autobiography, wherein Murr's self-infatuation and rhetorically disguised opportunism are often burlesquely chastised as he experiences the pains of emotional and intellectual growth. Consider, for example, Murr's speculations on eroticism. Murr theorizes that love in the human race – a race notably prejudiced, perfidious, and barbarous, as well as downright clumsy – is a psychic malady, a "partial insanity" (II.108) that blinds its victims to the true nature of things. But with the arrival of springtime, and despite his study of worldly Ovid, Murr begins seething with "an ineffable, erotic bliss" (II.154), a bliss whose naïveté, rudely shattered, will eventually get him "tossed into the gutter" (II.174). Erotic longing in Murr's career often results in misplaced, fruitless passion, especially when he falls in love with a beautiful canine (like Rousseau, Murr claims he will hold nothing back). What he reaps from this preposterous one-sided affair is sheer disaster. Yet at the same time Murr is aware that good poets seek out misery as a stimulus to creativity; and he is convinced that he is capable, "even in mortal anguish" (II.126), of engendering Shakespearean iambics.

Murr is apparently not resourceful enough, however, to survive all of his calamities. In a postscript, the editor, who from time to time has gently scolded Murr for his (parodic) plagiarisms, informs us that this precocious, lovable genius has been prematurely snatched away by death. That being the case, the interpolated Kreisler text is also destined to be brusquely cut off. The connection between Murr and Kreisler is fairly tenuous to begin with, nor does it ever become more substantial. We do learn, early in the novel, that Meister Abraham intends to leave his amusingly learned cat for a while with his friend Kreisler; and subsequently the editor does parenthetically remonstrate with Murr for having palmed off certain of Kapellmeister Kreisler's ideas as his own. But there is not much else available to link the lives of cat and composer. This may or may not be regrettable. In any event, it is not especially illuminating to note that Hoffmann has been offering us, in his two disjointed texts, antithetical portraits of the artist.

If Murr's sliced-up autobiography supplies enjoyable vexation, the arbitrary, though equally regularized, fragmentation of Kreisler's story leaves us captivated but at times maddeningly disoriented. The narrator himself complains that the Kreisler text is a thing of confusion that has to be patched together (II.177), though he assures us (not too convincingly) that the problem of coherence is readily resolvable. But in fact it is not. In any event, Kreisler's psyche is more provocatively enigmatic, at least for the student of comedy, than the physical dislocations of Hoffmann's text.

Kreisler may believe that the creative soul – he himself composes divinely – is properly moved by a spiritual love capable of giving birth to masterpieces of art, music, and literature. But neither his otherworldly artistic spirit nor his silent adoration of Julia (not to mention his attraction to the magnetic Hedwiga) is sufficiently insulated from his erratically mundane comic temper. Kreisler the comedian often lacks decorum and even psychic balance in social settings. His comic spirit is not inherently beguiling; indeed it is often ambiguous and baffling, and at times it strikes others as darkly mocking or malignly jocular. Madame Benzon, for example (her judgment does not issue from a neutral perspective) thinks Kreisler's sense of comedy is characterized essentially by "fantastic eccentricity" and "lacerating irony" (II.58), while his antics seem to Hedwiga, at first, to be those of a madman. Julia, however, thinks of Kreisler as a modern melancholy Jaques, upon whom cheerfulness often breaks.

Kreisler admits that he used to be excessively madcap, but only by way of reacting against his psychic ailments. Certain fantasies still obsess him; and he even fears that one day he will become the prey of insanity. In the meantime, his comic idiosyncrasies remain unpredictable. At one moment he is amiably humorous; at another, satanically mocking; and at still another, clownishly anarchic. Kreisler himself interprets his comic disposition as an ironic, though not especially mordant, mode of escape from life's "dark, unfathomable power" (II.59). This self-analysis is more or less corroborated by Meister Abraham, magician and master conjuror, whose awareness of certain destructive forces that lie hidden beneath Kreisler's whimsical wit – forces he is unable to exorcize – is not shared by other observers.

Meister Abraham is not, however, omniscient. Nor is the genealogy of Kreisler's comic impulses overly helpful. As an adolescent, Kreisler was guilty of several "brilliant idiocies" (II.80), which were apparently due in large part to the famous "mad whims" and "fantastic pranks" of Meister Abraham, then known as a marvelous organ-maker named Liscov. Though Meister Abraham's skill in highlighting whatever was ludicrously incongruous clearly influenced Kreisler's youth, the youngster was finally too tender not to shy away from Liscov's malice. The narrator nevertheless insists that "the eccentric organ-builder was really suited to protect and cherish the seed of the deeper humor that lay buried in the boy and which grew and prospered well enough." And what is this "deeper humor" that Liscov himself apparently lacked? It is a "rare, wonderful mood which is generated from a deep perception of life, in all its aspects, and from the conflict of hostile principles" (II.100). (Labeling this "rare, wonderful mood" would not be hazardous, since it involves either Schlegelian irony or Sternean/Jean-Paulian "humor.")[6] In an amplified version of his own original self-analysis, however, Kreisler himself suggests, much less reassuringly, that his comic temper derives from a tormenting, irrepressible yearning for a paradisal vision – a yearning born of an enduring sense of misery and barrenness. Only the purifying spirit of music can conquer that sense of wretchedness and obliterate his nihilistic impulses.

In the absence of that paradisal vision, or of its symbol (divine music), comedy, though defensive and escapist in its origins, becomes a formidable power, providing Kreisler with both civil and, more often, rebellious satisfactions. (Of course, for lesser mortals who are denied potential access to a higher world but who have enough to endure without worrying about unattainable ideals, a defensive, escapist sense of comedy is no less vital.) In drawing rooms, Kreisler's comic temper is bound to unleash anomalies. Yet that is how he gains an interesting convert. Princess Hedwiga, who has been feeling unusually ambivalent toward Kreisler, is suddenly, intuitively convinced that Kreisler's comic fantasticality is actually a sign of the profound perceptiveness which the narrator has already defined as "deeper humor." Kreisler is at first rebuked by the Princess, who is feeling somewhat edgy, for having introduced inappropriate, soul-tormenting music into a social gathering. Kreisler responds buffoonishly, begging pardon for hellishly blaspheming against social propriety. Fired with antic verve, he then urges Julia to sing a comic duet with him. This duet, in which Kreisler plays an Italian buffo, brings the house down with untranscendental roars of laughter. The Princess then joyously, even giddily, finds an affinity between her magnetism and Kreisler's: "Oh, I understand your leaping humor. It is exquisite, truly exquisite! Only in the conflict of the most contradictory emotions and of warring feelings does the higher life blossom!" (II.120) Though the Princess does not realize how quickly the absurdity which symptomatizes the "higher life" can be extinguished in Kreisler, and though, like the narrator's, her words are too benignly theoretical and might almost be viewed as parodic – Hoffmann more than once deflates pretentious commentary on irony and humor – she is well positioned to be an elucidator of dualities; indeed she is riven by discordant impulses and visions that make of her, it has been claimed, a Hamletesque competitor of Kreisler.[7] Julia's interpretation of Kreisler's sense of humor, we recall, is also favorable, though far more simply, even naïvely, posited. She is certain that Kreisler's "seemingly mischievous humor, which often wounds people, comes from the truest, the most wonderful soul" (II.165).

Though several amusing scenes mitigate the effect of sinister occurrences and labyrinthine complications, comic mischief, whatever its ultimate source, generally evaporates as the Kreisler text gets more and more involved in Gothic ramifications of secrecy, mystery, and terror. Yet Kreisler's sense of comedy continues to be subjected to analysis. Thus

Meister Abraham, discussing his friend's iconoclasm with Madame Benzon, defends Kreisler's comic spirit as a unitary force having a single beneficent aim. According to Meister Abraham, Kreisler's comic defiance of convention is evidence of meritorious mockery, totally divorced from cynical, angry, or mystifying bitterness.

Above all else, he maintains, Kreisler "loves the jest which arises from a deeper observation of human existence and which can be called nature's loveliest gift and which nature creates from the purest source of its being" (198). But Meister Abraham's judgment, not unlike the narrator's, is obviously deficient (in this case, to be sure, it is meant to be diplomatic). For Meister Abraham knows full well, as we have seen, that Kreisler's wounded heart is susceptible of being clawed by dark powers. That is why it is so difficult for him to anchor his wildly restless existence and release the godlike music within him. Kreisler's laughter is certainly not confined to the purposes of laudable satire. Yet it would be a mistake to define that laughter as basically a species of jesting purity arising from the sweet wellsprings of nature.

To the student of comedy, the complex, disconcerting nature of Kreisler's (and Hoffmann's) comic proclivities is far more challenging than the apparent structural lunacy of *Kater Murr,* that ingeniously contrived repeating mechanism whose self-disarticulation is so carefully articulated. *Kater Murr* may be viewed as an illustration of playfully self-conscious German romantic irony. But if Kater Murr's life and opinions had been served up linearly and uninterruptedly, instead of in bits and pieces, the evolution of this unfailingly anthropomorphized feline would have remained unchanged. And if a significant part of Kreisler's peculiar life had also been presented linearly, uninterruptedly, and integrally, his conflicted psyche's reactions to the curse and potential enchantment of life would have been no less fantastic, either in its eruptions of farce or in its release of ironic percipience.

The structural intricacies of "Princess Brambilla: A Capriccio in the Style of Jacques Callot" are much more bewildering than the scrupulously organized zigzagging between two artists' discrete lives in *Kater Murr.* "Princess Brambilla," indeed, reputedly furnishes German romantic irony's most authoritative credentials. Certainly the capriccio capers along freely, whimsically, arbitrarily, astonishingly – apparently as a pure expression of self-dissolving, self-reconstituting artistic sovereignty.

One of the major themes of "Princess Brambilla" has a reconstitutive power of its own; for the novella, among other things, is an eccentric paean to regenerative comedy. In his foreword, the editor of this fairy tale asks the reader to "forgo seriousness for a few hours and surrender to the pert and capricious sport of a hobgoblin who is perhaps overimpudent"[8] in his use of the resources of a musical cappricio and of Callot's commedia dell'arte drawings. It would seem, from these introductory words, that a large measure of fantastic, outrageous farce will be the tale's chief means of waylaying noxious gravity. Of course Schlegel's statements about artistic caprice and "transcendental buffoonery" may come to mind here. But it is also possible that a hobgoblin's sport may make German romantic irony a critical superfetation. That particular sport, moreover, is by no means mindless. The editor refers to Gozzi's comment – and Gozzi is a prime inspiration for Hoffmann, as well as for Tieck – that a fairy tale needs a profound idea to make it come alive, something that "a whole arsenal of absurdities and ghost paradings" will not accomplish (114). We are thus assured that forgoing seriousness will not mean scrapping psychological and philosophical ideas. As it happens, four profound, closely intertwined ideas circulate in "Princess Brambilla": the double nature of personality (prosaic and supernal), the search for authentic love, the transformative power of comedy, and the thaumaturgic gift of irrationality.

This last item, the thaumaturgic gift of irrationality, is much on the narrator's mind. At the beginning of the second chapter, and in a voice very much like the editor's, he asks the reader to surrender to the power of the marvelous, to give credence to vivid, fabulous images that will set him free from a narrow, humdrum mentality. Nor does the narrator's seductive message seem spurious. Has not the reader, he pertinently asks, already had strange dreams, beautiful and intense, that have cracked open his daily drabness and unlocked the gates of a magic realm, so that his inner being experienced a mystic marriage with the ineffable? And has not this kind of dream rapture remained more trenchantly real than the reader's muddled activities and dreary milieu?

In daily life, to be sure, certain penalties occur when one is absorbed by wonders; one stubs one's toes, bumps one's head, and so on. The penalties of absorption in fantasy that are suffered by the actor Giglio Fava, the main character in Hoffmann's story, are due to his transfixion by a dream vision of the intoxicatingly lovely and incredibly wealthy Princess Brambilla. Though she can be seen only through magic spectacles ground by an Indian mage named Ruffiamonte, Giglio Fava has been unexpectedly supplied with precisely such spectacles by a famed Roman charlatan named Celionati. The Princess, we learn, has come to Rome from Ethiopia in search of the Assyrian Prince Cornelio Chiapperi.

The Prince, the (possibly dazed) reader is free to speculate, is perhaps a distinguished dilettante or a famous patron of the arts seeking out the glories of Roman genius. But the Prince, before vanishing somewhere in the city, seems to have come to Rome only for the sake of having one of his molars extracted. (It is Celionati who managed the extraction and who is now hawking not only magic spectacles but simulacra of the princely tooth.)

In the Hoffmannesque fairy tale genre of the hilarious-fantastic (the genre that so appealed to Baudelaire), it is not unusual for dizzily proliferating marvels to be partnered by comic hyperbanalities, though ludicrous trivialities may conceal significant motives and meanings. The extracted tooth, for example, has been interpreted as a symbol of "false theatricalism"[9] – and play-acting, we have been informed, is Giglio Fava's specialty. In any event, Giglio's dream vision of Princess Brambilla so haunts his odd thoughts and involuntary actions that he is frequently convinced he is the victim of a devilish hoax rather than the recipient of a heavenly illumination.

If any kind of hoax is being perpetrated, it is owing to the seemingly benign magic (which may temporarily create discomfort and silliness) of that supreme puppet-master, buffoonish mountebank, and miracle-maker, Prince Batianello di Pistoja, known to us familiarly as Celionati. This magician, who takes an inordinate interest in Giglio Fava, is possessed of such mysterious inventive powers – his treasury of secret love is so dazzling – that mere rationality, which in "Princess Brambilla" is a species of aridity, is utterly impotent to follow the strange, swift metamorphoses promoted by this amazing capriccio character. Celionati's magic charlatanism flourishes with especial vigor because he is presiding over a Roman carnival atmosphere charged with the wildest of fancies and the most intemperate of gaieties. The pattern in this madness (if "pattern" is not too demeaningly realistic a term) ultimately has to do with the necessary reunion of Prince Cornelio and Princess Brambilla, who are frequently confused with, or merge with, Giglio Fava and the beautiful, if saucy, theatrical milliner Giacinta Soardi.

Not until the end of the novella does this coupling, or doubling, or self-dividing (in the cause of a transcendent unity) become more or less clarified. In the meantime Giglio Fava, whose career is that of a vain, foppish, pretentious, bombastic tragedian, is not only in haphazard pursuit of Princess Brambilla (Prince Cornelio is similarly attracted to Giacinta) but must also wrestle with a higher Self (Prince Cornelio) in all sorts of risible ways. He is caught up, to take a climactic example, in a duel with

Capt. Pantalone (actually Prince Cornelio), a duel in which signs of blatant enmity alternate with expressions of holy friendship. Giglio "dies" in this infantile commedia dell'arte duel, amid the carnival crowd's laughter; but the corpse turns out to be a cardboard dummy stuffed with atrocious tragic roles scripted by the Abate Chiari, whose talent may be gauged by the title of his latest tragedy, "The White Moor." As a result of this struggle with a more noteworthy Self (however cloaked in incarnational absurdities), Giglio finally emerges as a purified artist whose forte is comedy, not tragedy. He joins Giacinta in what appears to be a delightful, perfect marriage, for she too has been transformed and is now a richly talented comic actress.

What is at stake in this creation, or rather re-installation, of the better, comic Self of Giglio is of unique importance. It signifies the resurrection of a mythic spring of laughter in Urdar Land that ensures the salvation of humanity from destructive gloom.[10] The Urdar Spring, which for a while loses its magic freshness and is transmogrified into a fetid swamp, plays a role in several outlandish tales tacked on to the main fantastic story. But these subordinate, vertigo-inducing tales all wind up reinforcing the main event: the blessed, laughter-releasing, comedy-emancipating reunion of lovers in a redeemed land. Love, comedy, liberation, paradise – these are now (once again) all fundamentally inseparable.

Roguish, baffling Celionati is the chief theoretician of comedy in "Princess Brambilla." However, he is not without (inferior) rivals, quite ready to debate him. In Hoffmann's third chapter, the brilliant, cryptically droll Celionati becomes the spokesman for Rome's carnival jests, which a group of sober German artists in the Caffè Greco have criticized as the grotesqueries of a deranged mind. In the opinion of the most thoughtful member of the group, Franz Reinhold, the stage masks of the commedia dell'arte point only to the superficiality of carnival and hence do not get to the core of human nature. He tells Celionati that while he does appreciate the Italians' idiosyncratic virtuosity in farce, what is missing in their jubilant frenzy is a "jot of kindly sentiment" (158) – the sort that characterizes German "humor," which is so much more profound than Italian farce. (This is the kind of "humor," presumably more affirmative than irony, which is cited, not without some mystification, in *Kater Murr.)*[11]

Yet Hoffmann himself injects into his tale's lunatic mirth more than a jot of kindly sentiment. Of course, given its investment in Callot, the commedia dell'arte, and the heteroclite nature of capriccios, "Princess Brambilla" indulges far more obviously in anarchic exuberance (and tart satire) than in tender, profound, "humorous" feeling. It is true, however, that the novella's magic, zany elements are ultimately wrapped in sheer gentleness of heart. This synthesis Celionati himself will bring about. In the meantime, his response to Reinhold's criticism suggests that if German "humor" does not attend to the element of the fabulous, it will remain more than a little parochial. Indeed Celionati announces provocatively that his listeners will remain ignorant of the authentic meaning of comedy so long as they have not gazed at the waters of the Urdar Spring.

If the story of King Ophioch, Queen Liris, and the Urdar Spring, which Celionati then recounts to the German artists – they are familiar with the Italian's agreeable exotic, incredible tales – and which was communicated to Celionati himself by his "friend" Ruffiamonte a couple of centuries ago, seems to the reader irrelevant or even obfuscatory, the narrator is ready to justify his tactic. He cautions the reader to be aware that what appears to be leading him astray may in fact be heading straight for the central action. (This narrator clearly enjoys, like Hoffmann himself, exhibiting his skills in artful fictionality.)

The initial (main) section of Celionati's extravagantly convoluted tale may be reduced to its simplest, yet still awesome-preposterous, components. In the kingdom of Urdar Land, King Ophioch, who has been plunged into melancholy over man's intellectual dissension with Nature, and Queen Liris, who has been endlessly, pointlessly laughing her head off, are awakened from a deathlike sleep by the mage Hermod (actually Ruffiamonte), who creates the Urdar Spring of bright laughter, sparkling with a pure re-imaging of things. The King's melancholy is transformed into joy, while the Queen's mindless giggling is transmuted into ecstasy. Their subsequent loving laughter is more than emancipatory; it is salvational.

After listening to Celionati's sizable installment of this tale, Reinhold does not hesitate to equate the happiness-making Urdar Spring with German contemplative humor, which he now describes as harboring ironic self-reflection (a Schlegelian touch) as well as a delight in the follies of life. These follies are presumably more temperate than not, since Reinhold, whose judgment is bound to seem somewhat smug, now honors Celionati for transcending the limitations of Italian carnivalesque gaiety. Yet no single formula, even if it makes room for carnivalesque laughter and contemplative humor, is supple enough or comprehensive enough to fully capture the comic energies at work in Hoffmann's fiction.

One can, however, make the case that self-reflexive art is more resonant in "Princess Brambilla" than in *Kater Murr*. At the beginning of the fourth chapter, the narrator, in effect a super-Celionati, focuses on the therapeutic comedy his story-telling is designed to propagate. He draws the reader's attention (not for the first time) to the "bizarre hobgoblinery and dreamlike delusion" (173) that inhabit not only a capriccio-oriented fairy tale but also the human spirit, itself a nonpareil fairy tale. Artists are particularly blessed, he points out, because they are able to express the kind of inner radiance that is capable of effacing terrestrial grief. This (self-) eulogistic passage suddenly buckles, however, when the narrator admits that undisciplined authors too easily surrender to reflections precisely like those he has just uttered – reflections which may be pleasing flourishes but which are quite irrelevant to plot and characterization. This bit of self-deconstruction allows us to wonder (briefly) whether the fairy tale of the human spirit is largely rhetorical filler. Yet the narrator's whimsical aggression against his own authority is much too mild and fugitive to wreck our willing suspension of disbelief.

A far more drastic destabilizing of the text occurs when Celionati assures Giglio (addressed as Prince Cornelio) that "everything we are doing and everything that was done here is not real but rather a capriccio fabricated from beginning to end" (215). How can narrative normalcy be so radically disowned? How can a fabricated character like Celionati dance out of the author's confining text and feel free to serve as an interpretive intermediary while at the same time vouching for the unreality of his own being as well as everyone else's?

The dismantling of traditional narrative rituals is even more startling when Celionati declares that he perceives his function in the novella's thematic world so clearly that he refuses to bore the reader of "Princess Brambilla" by providing further details of the story of King Ophioch and Queen Liris. Celionati even claims that when the author created him as a deeply knowledgeable man who would be engaged in curing Prince Cornelio of his lingering illness – the illness is "chronic dualism" (232)[12] – he (the author) did not assign him (Celionati) the role of being a mere dispenser of comic fairy tales: "I tell you the author had something quite different in mind when he invented me, and if he should be looking on when you treat me so casually, he could very well think I had slipped out of character" (231). Celionati, that incomparable manipulator of the magic of unreality, is perfectly aware of his own fictionality. Yet he insists on the (Pirandellian) authenticity of his insight into the compositional origins of "Princess Brambilla."

Celionati avows, moreover, that the author "prescribed absolutely no time limit on our existence and actions" (233). So now we have a literary character who is both bound and totally free, a character who has virtually pre-empted the authorial will by certifying his ability accurately to assess his creator's inmost intentions. This presumptuous, if fabulous, puppet, assumes the guise of a superlative puppet-master and pulls his own strings. What would happen if he "really" risked his creator's displeasure by genially permitting a minor mutiny against authorial design? Whatever the answer – and the question is essentially crazy – Celionati enjoys considerable license in stepping outside the narrative frame and behaving like a co-author. According to Schlegelian theory, Hoffmann's shedding of narrative proprieties (construed as tyrannies) demonstrates the artist's caprice, freedom, and sovereignty, traits that betoken far more than the traditional artist's dominance over matter and form.

It is in the last few pages of "Princess Brambilla" – the improbable narrative line ends abruptly – that Celionati elucidates the story's confusing developments, though his clarification scarcely lessens the impact of the story's irreality. As the Prince di Pistoja, Celionati pays a visit to Giglio and Giacinta. These two are now happily married and are a prince and princess in their own right; that is, as celebrated stage comedians, they lord it over theatrical Rome. Giglio and Giacinta are able to recall the rapture of their mutual recognition as Prince Cornelio and Princess Brambilla in Urdar Land. But Giacinta is not quite clear about the business of simultaneously living a real, mundane life and a mythical, spiritual one. She is enlightened by the Prince di Pistoja, who rejects the idea that the purpose of his coming to see them is an all too convenient last-minute explanation of a disconnected narrative. Such a reparative visit, he suggests (launching still another flagrantly tricky operation outside the logical boundaries of conventional fiction), would surely be distrusted by the reader, who might even discredit or dismiss the characters in "Princess Brambilla" as the products of creative deficiency.

After thus (questionably) dispatching the issue of a lapse in narrative organization, the Prince goes to the root of the novella's complexity. It seems that a malicious demon once bewitched Queen Mystilis (Princess Brambilla), and that this spell required expunging by recourse to the little world of the theater, where a couple "animated by true fantasy and humor in their inner beings" (249) would project their curative animation into the larger world. The comic theater would thus become a soteriological force, akin to the miraculous Urdar Spring. "Princess Brambilla" itself cannot claim such preternatural homage; but in its own diminished way, it too signalizes the triumph of purgative, pain-dissolving mirth in a world of obsessive, denaturalizing sobriety.

In the introduction to their translations of *Kater Murr* and a number of the novellas, Leonard J. Kent and Elizabeth C. Knight inevitably suggest that Hoffmann's metafictional complications belong under the rubric of German romantic irony. Hoffmann, they write, "admired Sterne's apparently haphazard technique of narration and saw this purposeful breaking of illusion and 'detachment' (romantic irony) as a refined and subtle technique which found a parallel in the willful caprice of many of the German novels of the time, especially Jean Paul's" (I.15). Kent and Knight's standard definition of German romantic irony applies to Hoffmann in some fairly obvious ways. But security in addressing Hoffmann's comic temper is less easily attained. One may choose to locate the pulse of Hoffmann's comic art in Shandean self-conscious caprice, or in Tieckian illusion-breaking, or in Schlegelian irony's godlike refashioning of chaos – or in all three. But if so, one would have to admit certain reservations. Sterne does not supply the magical component of Hoffmannesque irrationality. Tieck in his topsy-turvy plays does not match the profundity and scope of Hoffmann's voyages into the fantastic. And Schlegel would perhaps blink at the proposition that "transcendental buffoonery" (that cryptically strong phrase for a tenuous notion) is wondrously represented by Hoffmannesque mutational farce.

2.

Heine's ironic practice of jarring romantic vision with renegade drollery (or the reverse) is associated only marginally, rather than commandingly, with Schlegelian theory. The critic who finds, as Jocelyn Kolb does, that there is an "uncanny correspondence between the theories of the early Schlegel and the poetic practice of Heine"[13] is clearly in a minority, as Kolb is well aware. More often, Heine's ironic temper has been dissociated from Schlegelian theory by critics who believe that German romantic irony, unlike Heine's, does not sufficiently connect with the terrestrial world. Max Brod, for example, states that German romantic irony is accustomed to "switch from the level of everyday reality to a dream level," while Heine's wit "rudely shatters the dream and switches back to everyday reality."[14] Similarly, Laura Hofrichter emphasizes that German romantic irony "was directed against reality," whereas Heine's tone-disruptions were "directed against escape from reality."[15] These verdicts are echoed by Hanna Spencer: "unlike the ironic flights of the romantics which allow them to escape from reality, Heine's irony has precisely the opposite effect: it bursts the idealistic bubble by confrontation with reality."[16]

In his two excellent books, *Heinrich Heine, the Elusive Poet* (1969) and *Heinrich Heine: A Modern Biography* (1979), Jeffrey L. Sammons permits himself only a single, oblique allusion to romantic irony. Yet one of the epigraphs in his biographical study – Gérard de Nerval's comment (uttered in 1848) that Heine is a Voltaire charged with feeling, an eighteenth-century skeptic caught in the silver glow of German moonlight – nicely evokes the divided allegiances that characterize European romantic irony. Sammons himself inevitably underlines the "very deep-seated" split in Heine between the romantic and the rationalist,[17] and just as inevitably introduces the psychological-historical concept of "Zerrissenheit," "the condition of being torn and disrupted" (35). And of course he cites long established affinities between Heine and Byron. Only once, however, in discussing the inextinguishable longing and mordant frustration expressed in Heine's love poetry, does Sammons define the poet's "Stimmungsbrechung," his "sardonic breach of mood," as romantic irony, and even then he calls it Heine's "anti-Romantic irony" (162). Sammons, at least (much to his credit), does not attempt to forge a link between Schlegel's theory of irony and Heine's dualistic poetry.

D. C. Muecke makes only a single reference to Heine in his chapter on (German) romantic irony, but his brief discussion inadvertently discloses a certain fuzziness in Schlegelian theory – or in critical adaptations of it. Bearing in mind *Lyceum* Fragment 37, Muecke states that the artist, "when possessed by creative fervour, is, as we have seen Schlegel saying, in an unfree condition. To recover his freedom he must impose upon his work the self-limitation of irony. Heine's 'Ocean Wraith' in *The North Sea* shows the poet abandoning himself to a romantic reverie and then withdrawing himself."[18] Muecke then quotes Heine's poem in full without further comment.

The conjunction of "creative fervour" (productive yet also imprisoning) with "romantic reverie" (inspiring yet likely to be delusionary) seems superficially apt. But creative energy in literature shapes images, actions, assumptions, and perceptions that are describable in any number of ways – as romantic, realistic, tragic, comic, baroque, naturalistic, lyrical, decadent, surrealistic, and so on. Is a sudden "ironic" withdrawal from the "creative fervour" of naturalistic rawness or baroque elegance or tragic passion also to be viewed as a variation on German romantic irony? What is required here is a narrower optics. European romantic irony, focusing on an authentic idealizing vision that gets comically derailed by disenchantment (though enchantment is renewable), provides a far more relevant, and far more manageable, key to Heine's poem than the creative intoxication and cool detoxification Muecke emphasizes in Schlegelian irony.

Let us take a closer look at "Ocean-Wraith" ("Seegespenst") or, in Hal Draper's translation, "Sea Apparition" (*The North Sea* I.10).[19] The poem presents the picture of a poet who becomes immersed, while leaning over the side of a boat, in the discovery of an antiquated yet busy city deep beneath the sea. No breath of levity ruffles this picture. Nor, in the lines that follow, is there any sense that the real world is being frivolously or dangerously erased, or that the dreamy poet would make a suitable subject for clinical insights. All is enchantment and pathos. Distant church bells and a great cathedral organ arouse within the poet both a "mystic awe" (142) and an infinite, sorrowful yearning for a lost love he has tormentedly sought throughout the world. The wounds in his scarcely healed heart open once more, as though under the impress of familiar kisses; and it seems that drops of his blood sink far down through the water to the very figure of his still faithful beloved, who now sits at a window, "like a poor forsaken child" (142). The poet is so enthralled by this vision that he prepares to abandon mere earthly life by plunging into the water to become united forever with his darling. In the last lines of the poem, however, a resurgence of reality arrests the poet's self-destructive impulse. The skipper of the boat, laughing maliciously and alluding to the devil's power over foolish mortals, grabs the poet's foot in the nick of time and hauls him back to safety. The poem thus shifts, in Byronic, ambivalent, tone-disruptive fashion, from the mesmerizing summons of romantic love, enhanced by myth and confirmed by suffering, to a burlesque recognition of the romantic imagination's deceptiveness. In Schlegel's terms (as transmitted by Muecke), a cooling of Heine's overheated creativity has been effected by a liberating, ironic self-consciousness. But this decontextualized, dethematized way of viewing the poem fails to register its specific dichotomy: the nostalgic bleeding and comic staunching of the romantic heart.

The romantic irony of "Sea Apparition" is perhaps best illuminated by contrast with "Night on the Beach" ("Die Nacht am Strande"), which is also from the first cycle of *The North Sea* (I.4), and which also tears apart illusion woven of enchantment. The poem begins with a prologue in which the North Wind babbles and bellows into the exultant sea a medley of songs and stories, some dark and magical, others wantonly droll. After these agitated, suggestively mixed atmospherics, a divine stranger appears along the seashore, his heart apparently wilder than the sea. Striding swiftly towards a fisherman's hut, where a lovely daughter sits by herself near the hearth, the confident god intends to resume yesteryear's marvelous alliances between immortals and mortal maidens – the kind of alliances that customarily engendered heroes and kings. But the god turns out to be as oddly susceptible to inclement weather as Ivan Karamazov's frail devil. He has been chilled by the night wind; and fearing a cough that will last throughout eternity, he requires of the fisherman's daughter, before commencing his supernatural love-making, some tea with rhum. The poem's dissonance is as debunkingly amusing as the discord in "Sea-Apparition." Heine has reduced a seemingly bold, gallant deity, trailing clouds of Olympian (and perhaps a wisp of biblical) glory, to a funnily prosaic, feckless, vulnerable quasi-hypochondriac.

The poet, one might think, following Schlegel/Muecke, has achieved a playful self-release from creative ardor. But in this case Heine's comic deflation of passion is not preceded by an intensity of aspiration that tests out as unarguably romantic. (Whether Heine felt himself partially embodied in a god saddled by familiar infirmities is both interesting and irrelevant.) What counts is that the antic evanescence of the pagan deity's nobility wrecks, not a fervent expression of the romantic temper, but rather an enfeebled, pretentious imitation of mythic grandeur. The tone disruption of "Night on the Beach" is therefore quite unlike that in "Sea Apparition," where the poet first embraces the mystery of romanticism, with its idealized yearning and its indissoluble pain, and then ruins it with the laughter of disbelief. What "Night on the Beach" displays is a comic collapse brought about by the sublime-to-the-ridiculous.

The example of Byron has already revealed how slippery the distinction between romantic irony and the sublime-to-the-ridiculous can be. But the distinction can also be clear-cut. Consider a poem entitled "Dialogue on Paderborn Heath" ("Gespräch auf der Paderborner Heide"), published in the early collection *Youthful Sorrows (Junge Leiden)*. Its initial version would have offered a simple interplay of ridiculous romanticism and laughable realism. The final version, however, is redeemed by its romantic-ironic dissonance. The first of the two speakers in the "Dialogue" exhibits what appears to be a mad romantic sensibility. This speaker maintains that he sees, or hears, only beautiful dancers, gallant hunters, heavenly songs, and a charming vision of his beloved. He is regularly interrupted, however, by a second speaker – perhaps the realistic, rationalistic side of the poet's split psyche – who attempts prosaically to dispel the first speaker's quixotic fantasy by pointing out that what he sees and hears are only squealing pigs, squalling geese, cowbells, and an old beldam with a crutch. Yet these repeated intrusions of the ordinary, gross world of sense experience do not cause the first, somewhat saddened, speaker to disparage his visionary perspective as a poetic delusion. In the end, he accepts the validity of the second speaker's corrective commentary. But at the same time he retains a Cervantesque double vision; comic fact and poetic ideal somehow merge, somehow fend off mutual cancellation.

This kind of merger is more complex in no. 13 of the early *Lyrical Intermezzo*. The speaker in the first half of the poem is evidently an ex-romantic who so values his new-found sensualism that he has completely discarded the need for idealization. He tells his mistress that he has faith in her kisses, not in her declarations of eternal love. Her lips, he informs her, are gratifying tangible, while amorous words and high-flown metaphors are merely air. The second half of the poem is a wryly comic reversal of this sensualist stance. Some sort of intervening revulsion from disenchantment has taken place; some kind of bruising, chastening experience, accompanied by anxiety-provoking introspection, has summoned the speaker back to the magnetisim of the ideal. Henceforth, he decides, as he sinks upon his mistress's breast, he will seize gratefully upon rhapsodies of language. Not that he will let tangible caresses go; but sheer carnality, having lost its self-sufficiency, must surrender to the heart's thirst for poetic certitudes. The speaker's willed recurrence of the illusionary world is both poignant and farcical. His initial nonchalant rejection and subsequent desperate retention of the ideal reveal a melancholy self-mockery that is characteristically Heinesque.

At times, to be sure, Heine's pathos in evoking the romantic spirit overwhelms even a rueful sense of comedy. In no. 44 of *The Homecoming,* the speaker recognizes that he needs to acquire some good sense, enough at least to abandon the romantic style of life he has worn too long as a mask. The glittering comedy of illusion, he admits, is over; he is now ready to put away his exquisite romantic passions and his splendid romantic props. Yet despite this wholesome, if belated, decision, the speaker is miserable. There is in his patched soul a melancholy realization that he is still contaminated by theatrical unreality, that having been so long in bondage to the basic folly and marginal bric-a-brac of romanticism, he cannot shake himself loose.

Elsewhere, however, pathos is purged through a more disinfectant sense of self-irony. In no. 55 of *The Homecoming*, the speaker recollects his grief at being maltreated by a potential mistress (the poem is addressed to her) who has laughed cruelly at his amorous, passionately romantic pleadings. Owing, however, to a history of similar disillusion and suffering, the speaker feels immunized against any impulse to self-destruct: "Don't think I'm so sad to recall this / That I'll shoot myself on that score! / You see, my sweetheart, all this / Has happened to me before" (98). Obviously Heine can handle the wreckage of lyrical illusion with flippant pathos, bitter frivolity, cavalier melancholy – or romantic irony.

In moments of retrospection Heine is capable of sardonically assessing his life as a history of romantic fulfillment (perhaps illusory) that inevitably undergoes antiromantic attrition. Perhaps his most outlandish retrospective view of the comically failed inspirations of romanticism occurs in the Prelude to "Vitzliputzli," in Book I of the late, magisterial *Romancero*. The poet reinvents America at the time of Cortez, painting it as pristine, fresh, undiseased, and hence utterly unlike nineteenth-century Europe, that graveyard of romanticism. Seemingly advertising *in propria persona* Goethe's dictum on the linkage of romanticism and malady, the poet is marked by a deathly pallor as he travels back to the colorful new world. Indeed he is obliged to explain to a frightened, pious Latin American monkey that if he looks weirdly decadent, that is because he has spent the best years of his life in the "Catacombs of Romanticism" (601).

There are no catacombs in "Forest Solitude" ("Waldeinsamkeit"), the first poem in the "Lamentations" section of Book II of *Romancero*. But though the poem provides an open-air, rather than a tomb-like, setting for the evolution of the romantic temper, the end result is comparably enervating. In sadly amused tranquility, but with a good deal of fanciful hyperbole, the poet recalls how, in his wooded solitude, his youth was inebriated with the magic of fairy tale romanticism. And now? Romantic mystery, verve, and reverie have all vanished. The poet feels drained in his disenchanted maturity, as though the romantic spirit had been essentially vampiric all along. Still, Heine's self-mockery keeps his pathos mostly in check as he faces up to a deromanticized world.

When the aberrations of romanticism are projected outside Heine's own psyche, the romantic temper is apt to turn wholly caricatural. "The White Elephant" ("Der weisse Elefant") in Book I of *Romancero* is a perfect example of self-irony safely externalized onto a preposterous object. The titular hero, the King of Siam's most precious, most delightful, most beloved treasure, is being gnawed by an apparently incurable illness: he is possessed of an all-consuming passion for the tall, godlike, incomparably white Countess Bianca of Paris (her image came to him in a dream). Thwarted elective affinities have robbed the white elephant of his mirth and his equanimity. Unfortunately, this four-footed Werther, the poet informs us, has neither the epistolary nor the suicidal talent of the original Werther. Barely nourished on a diet of noodles and Ossian, he just hangs on, longing inconsolably on moonlit nights for wings that will transport him to his Parisian Lotte.

What to do? The court astrologer advises the king to send the ailing white elephant on an immediate expedition to Paris, where the Countess Bianca's charms will no doubt heal the invalid. Besides, the elephant will have the chance to become truly civilized in the French capital (where a poet like Gautier knows something about the fascination of whiteness). The astrologer also advises that a fat letter of credit (a million ducats or so, drawn on the Rothschilds) should accompany a bursting passion. At the end of this saga of suffering, or, rather, of this burlesque of romantic agony, we learn that no news about the fate of the love-tormented elephant has been forthcoming from the orient. But then, Heine could hardly have supplied further details about the Paris-bound pachyderm without injuring the poem's already extravagant nonsense. Thematically, of course, the poem (lightly) bears a weighty symbolism: the career of the white elephant suggests that romanticism is a ludicrously overvalued legacy and that, notwithstanding the poem's Asian context, the romantic temper has thoroughly disordered the European imagination.

3.

In *The Romantic School,* Heine had already analyzed the self-debilitating German romantic temper. In doing so, however, he manifests as little regard for the Schlegels as Byron shows, in *Don Juan,* for Southey, Wordsworth, and Coleridge. Heine's animus is plain. He delineates the Schlegel brothers' contribution to German romanticism as a defossilization of medieval mysticism, a meddlesome digging up of ghostly lunacies: " 'Our literature,' said the Schlegels, 'is old, our Muse is an old woman with a spinning wheel ... our emotions have withered, our imagination has dried up, and we must renew our strength, we must seek again the choked-up springs of the simple, artless, medieval poetry, and the fountain of youth will gush forth.' "[20] The result, in Heine's view, was not a restored youth but a relapse into puling infantilism. Not always, of course. Heine writes admiringly of Tieck's translation of *Don Quixote;* and if he relates Cervantesque madness to the German romantic school's nostalgic, delusory cult of medieval chivalry (205), he does so with a delicate touch. Heine is even willing, temporarily at any rate, to suggest that "perhaps it was dissatisfaction with the present belief in money and disgust at the egotism they saw sneering out of everywhere that had first moved certain poets of the Romantic School in Germany with the best of intentions to flee from the present age to the past and to promote the restoration of medievalism" (247). Still, the German cult of the Middle Ages, Heine complains, was utterly divorced from the seminal ideas of the French revolution, which were replaced by reactionary politics and intolerant Catholicism. Whereas the French romantic school picked up Gothicism only as a passing fad, German romanticism turned sick fantasy into dogma: "German medievalism is not lying mouldered in its grave; on the contrary, it is often animated by an evil spirit and steps into our midst in bright, broad daylight and sucks the red life from our hearts" (271). It was owing to such pathological, repressive medievalism that Heine felt obliged to undertake almost single-handedly – or so he claims – a crusade against the pernicious elements in German romanticism.[21]

In *The Romantic School,* Heine remains taciturn in regard to his own romantic roots. In his *Confessions,* however, he presents himself as both a destroyer and a devotee of romanticism. He admits that though he has fought romanticism to the death, he has never been able to rid himself of its sorcery: "A witty Frenchman ... once dubbed me an unfrocked Romanticist. I have a weakness for all that is witty; and spiteful as was this appellation, it nevertheless delighted me highly. Notwithstanding the war of extermination that I had waged against Romanticism, I always remained a Romanticist at heart, and that in a higher degree than I myself realized."[22] This self-mocking "unfrocked Romanticist" – this romantic ironist who persists in being an ambivalent gladiator of the ideal – is frequently hobbled by unlucky transactions with reality. He tends to embrace exquisite dreams that are all too often eclipsed in a purgatory of banal and buffoonish frustrations. The union of romantic dream, agony, and clowning is Heine's celebrated harlequinade.[23]

The comedy of pain is not an outstanding feature of Schlegel's concept of irony. Though Schlegelian irony does provide theoretically for dark, self-destructive moods, such negation is apt to be an index not of decline but of vitality – of an essentially buoyant, dialectical self-consciousness. In Heine's irony, however, possibilities of blight are not merely speculative. Consider the difference between Schlegel's appreciation of Cervantes and Heine's. In Schlegel's view, *Don Quixote* is characterized by an "artfully ordered confusion," a "charming symmetry of contradictions," a "wonderfully perennial alternation of enthusiasm and irony" which "transplants us once again into the beautiful confusion of imagination, into the original chaos of nature.[24] (A return to the "original chaos of nature" seems like a remarkable achievement; but Schlegel has in mind the confluence of chaos and culture.) Heine, on the other hand, in one of his commentaries on Cervantes sees in the irony of *Don Quixote* a microcosm of the larger, agonizingly comic duality of heroism and clowning, of noble vision and ignominious defeat, with which God originally permeated the world and which has infiltrated more than one literary masterpiece.[25]

If the divine prerogative of wanton absurdity fails to charm Heine, it also fails to subdue him, even in his later years of devastating illness. In his *Confessions* the poet, with pained levity, analogizes the terrible irony which the "Aristophanes of Heaven" (a Self-plagiarist) has visited upon him in his confinement to a "mattress grave" with the cruelty He once inflicted on a fifteenth-century leprous priest whose beautiful, universally known songs enchanted the healthy listeners of this world but did not alleviate the priest's own desolate life.[26]

The nineteenth century, in Heine's judgment, is an especially torturous epoch for lyrical poets sensitive to God's ironic manipulation of the course of history. In *The Baths of Lucca,* Heine evokes, in his customary mode of facetious profundity, the specter of European dismemberment. He is in the company of Gumpelino, a prosperous compatriot who has been exhibiting his pinchpenny, pseudo-aesthetic personality by raving over the freely available beauties of the landscape. Nature, Gumpelino exclaims, is prettier than illustrated postcards. It is even more gorgeous than theatrical spectacles – and so much less expensive. His trumpery romantic outburst concluded, he discovers Heine standing coolly aloof. This is not the first time a philistine has insolently and childishly vulgarized Nature in the presence of the poet, who, like Diogenes Teufelsdröckh, is aware that Nature has become a picnic area, especially on weekends, for middle-class "artistic" redemption. Flushed in the religion and economics of natural wonder, and sensing the poet's mocking temper, Gumpelino retaliates (not very maliciously) by accusing Heine of being a "zerrissiner Mensch" – a distorted, dismembered being, a creature of Byronic morbidity. Seizing upon this hackneyed (yet regrettably just) criticism with despairing gusto, Heine relates his psychic disunity to a crucial European malaise: "Ah! Dear reader, if you would complain of dividedness and want of harmony, then as well complain that the world itself is divided. For as the heart of the poet is the central point of the world, it must, in times like these, be miserably divided and torn."[27] (For the European romantic ironist, the most significant disjunction in "times like these" is the gap between lingering revolutionary idealism and unremitting political reaction.) Heine is nevertheless conscious of the paradoxical blessing bestowed on him by his poetic martyrdom.

In chapter 11 of his autobiographically based *Ideas: Book le Grand,* Heine had once before correlated the dissonances of the poet with the discordances of modern history, though again he recognizes – it is a basic datum of the ironic perspective – that the theater of human events is always being roiled by the First Author's provision of tragicomic absurdities. It is in imitation of God's irony that a Shakespeare or an Aristophanes feels licensed to underscore a universal streak of lunacy and misery: "Aristophanes shows us the ghastliest picture of human madness only in the laughing mirror of wit . . . . Shakespeare puts the deadliest lament over the wretchedness of the world into the mouth of a fool, at the same time taking pains to shake the fool's cap and bells."[28]

God's creation of world tragedy in thousands of acts, interspersed with pungent reminders of world comedy, is particularly exemplified for modern man by the French Revolution and the post-Napoleonic era: "after the exit of the heroes, the clowns and harlequins enter with their fools' clubs and wooden swords. After the bloody scenes of the revolution and imperial battles, the fat Bourbons came waddling on again with their stale old jokes and nice Legitimate 'bon mots.' " In such tragicomic convulsions, ardent idealism collapses both woefully and funnily: "Comical touches slip into even the most exalted pathos of this world tragedy; the despairing Republican who thrust his knife into his heart perhaps smelled the blade first to see that no herring had been cut with it."[29] This hero-herring composite translates into the duality which stamps Heine's mature romantic irony: nobility wedded to farce, dream subjected to comic disfigurement, exaltation contaminated by the absurd.

The absurd, bloody staging of revolutionary and post-revolutionary tragicomedy is not, to be sure, a romantic-ironic discovery. In his *Reflections on the Revolution in France* (1790), Burke is also much disturbed by the theatrical recklessness and mad improvisations of the living moment: "It appears to me as if I were in a great crisis, not of the affairs of France alone, but of all Europe . . . . Everything seems out of nature in this strange chaos of levity and ferocity . . . . In viewing this monstrous tragi-comic scene, the most opposite passions necessarily succeed, and sometimes mix with each other in the mind."[30] To the ordered mind of Burke, and to the anitomian mind of Heine (self-proclaimed warrior for the liberation of humanity), the revolutionary epoch had become a vast theatrical heresy – a heresy whose turbulently novel arousal of contrary passions could scarcely be contained within the relatively mild Johnsonian doctrine of mixed literary genres that had enabled Johnson several decades earlier to approve of Shakespeare's fidelity to life's strange miscellaneousness.

Only a few years after Burke's pronouncements, F. Schlegel too was describing the French revolution as a grotesque, "fearful chaos," a "monstrous human tragicomedy."[31] (Schlegel seemed to be interested, however, in emphasizing that the revolution had crystallized the French addiction to paradox.) But this kind of tragicomic historical chaos (abhorred by Burke, theologized by Heine) has little to do with the chaos whose fullness and fruitfulness Schlegel celebrates in connection with irony. The Schlegelian ironist's (theoretical) achievement of successive illuminations issuing from the seedbed of chaos does not especially relate to historical actuality, as Kierkegaard less gently indicated.

4.

For the ironically-minded, revolutionary fervor had become by mid-century a pseudo-idealistic masquerade hiding an assortment of unclean motives and murderously opportunistic designs. Heine, as S. S. Prawer points out, "could see nothing" in the revolution of 1848 "but a crazy farce"; " 'I say nothing,' Heine wrote to his publisher, Campe, on July 4, 1848, 'about what is happening in these times; it is universal anarchy, the world turned upside down, divine madness made visible! If this goes on, the Old One will have to be locked up. The atheists are to blame for all of this, they have driven Him out of His wits.' "[32] God's bumbling dramaturgy in arranging human affairs had turned into pure delirium.

Several years before the revolution of 1848, Heine had lampooned a singular species of the historical grotesque that had grown wildly on native grounds. In *Germany: A Winter's Tale,* he had Aristophanically exposed the petty despotisms and intellectual backwardness shackling contemporary Germany, whose people hardly knew how thoroughly they had been roped in by benighted authority. In *Atta Troll: A Midsummer Night's Dream* (1841), a similarly large-scale work, political and social failures are also significant. Certainly they occupy the thoughts of Atta

Troll, a dancing bear deeply dismayed by the world's anti-republican, anti-egalitarian tendencies. However, the bear's liberal political ideas (some of which are far from being sound) and his soberly insistent virtues are mixed up with aesthetic liabilities and laughable prejudices.

Atta Troll is describable as both a satiric mock-epic and, in Heine's own words, the swan-song of German romantic lyricism. Yet this description is incomplete. The lyrical moods and fantasies of the swan-song are bonded on more than one occasion to a comedy of disavowed romanticism. The poem therefore also figures as a work of European romantic irony. When Heine suggests in the poem's epilogue, dedicated to Varnhagen von Ense, that he has composed perhaps "the wildwood's / Last free song of the Romantic!",[33] his tone is not precisely mournful. He knows full well that his old friend, while stirred by memories of romantic dreams, will not be able to resist laughing at some of the "crazy stuff" in the poem. Heine seems almost to be implying that the romantic imagination can be disinterred and reanimated only in the redemptive presence of folly.

Romantic irony in *Atta Troll* derives mainly from the comic wreckage of exalted moods intermittently produced by awe-inspiring Pyrenean scenes, or by fantastic visions of the supernatural. But from the beginning, a sense of pettiness unfavorable for romance and mythical glory is allowed to undermine a romantic yen for the sublime. The narrator exults in the ability of his winged poetic charger to ride into the "realm of fabled story" (426) and a long forgotten dream world. Yet he also wonders how any bard would dare to immortalize the kind of paltry, feeble deeds that he and his companion Lascaro (a Pyrenean witch's son, probably defunct but magically kept alive) perform while pursuing the escaped Atta Troll. They are only shipless Argonauts hunting a bearskin instead of a golden fleece. Jason, furthermore, never needed an umbrella in Colchis, whereas the narrator and Lascaro get drenched in the Pyrenees (463).

The narrator may paint ravishingly forested mountain scenes, but he also (more than whimsically) complains that despite all the dithyrambs poets devote to the divine temple of Nature, the stairs of the temple can be disgracefully inconvenient. After leaping over rocks and clambering uphill and downhill, he groans that his legs are exhausted – and so is his spirit (442-43). This denial of the very lyricism he is fostering is encapsulated, with a sense of pathos that (unusually) overrules purely comic disenchantment, in the lovely song of the mountain snow, which sighs to be released from its frozen white wasteland and become transmuted into a pearl. The narrator hints that the fate of the liberated snow may be only a metamorphosis into muck (450-51).

Lumbering, malodorous Atta Troll cannot be denied his own lyrical sentiments. These are expressed in his Petrarchan love-longing for his wife Mumma, whom he has helplessly left behind in his escape from servitude. (She will end up in the Paris zoo, the consort of a Siberian brute.) But the lyricism of this "ursine Ulysses" and "shaggy Roland" becomes principally material for drollery. Atta Troll's reformatory zeal is also (though not consistently and not unequivocally) a springboard for comedy. Atta Troll has the distinction of being a bear rationally inspired by the need for social and political justice; but his ideas are targeted for mockery primarily because the bear's magnanimity is often hollow, pretentious, or perverse.

In his 1846 preface to the poem, Heine scornfully refers to the miasmic atmosphere in Germany responsible for politicizing and moralizing literary composition, an atmosphere which *Atta Troll,* written in "the capricious dream-like manner of the romantic school" (421) was designed, in part, to make fun of. Heine, exemplifying the unfettered spirit of authentic literature, condemns a repressive school of insipid writers who betrayed their envy of a gifted literary élite by hitting upon the face-saving, fraudulent formula that poetic talent "entailed the suspicion of bad character" (420). In effect, socialized mediocrity was thus enabled to crucify the poetic imagination.

The tendentious Atta Troll, that piously moral, hirsute social democrat, is in fact full of character; but he is also devoid of talent. Nevertheless, he commands a certain sympathy. His righteous views on men and animals may be stale and pompous; but this lord of the forest, basely chained and victimized (before his escape) has good reason to believe that the doctrine of the Rights of Man means only cruelty to animals. Reacting against humanity's exploitative hypocrisy, Atta Troll envisions a new order, an earthly democracy of animals, all equal, regardless of odor, hide, or religion. (This does not prevent him from being anti-Semitic.) Yet Atta Troll's planned revolt against the tyranny of man (which was to be infamously successful a hundred years later in Orwell's *Animal Farm*) is robbed of much of its validity by the bear's farcically chauvinistic, narrow-minded reflections on superior animal braininess. Atta Troll's elevated character is further reduced when he reveals his revulsion from mankind's indecorous predisposition to laugh and smile. Still, the narrator, who tongue-in-cheek affirms his allegiance to the human race, gives a decent amount of space to the bear's indignation at mankind's degraded, pickpocket, atheistic ways.

The dancing bear receives, then, a somewhat ambiguous evaluation. Yet the poem's most significant ambivalence is largely independent of ursine affairs. Heine's romantic irony is best illustrated in the description of a nocturnal Wild Hunt, a "mad Cavalcade of spirits" (455). Three spectral presences especially fascinate the narrator: the once solemn Graeco-Roman goddess Diana (cast in a new, incongruous role), the laughing Celtic-Romantic fairy Abunda, and the seductive Judean queen Herodias, still possessed of the head of John the Baptist. The narrator's enchantment with these three illusory, divine, but unblessed "muses" is both genuine and prankish.[34] He is clearly drawn to, and awed by, this breathtaking triune vision. Yet he cannot avoid mischievously noting that the famously chaste Diana is now uncharacteristically consumed by lust and is apparently trying to make up for lost erotic time by consorting with a variety of gallants, all inferior to specimens of ancient Hellenic handsomeness. But if Diana "perhaps ... now makes up for / Quality with quantity," the lovely fairy Abunda, recognizable "By her smile's supernal sweetness / And the mad warmth of her laughter" (457), remains true to herself, needing no trans-generational catalyst of gaiety. Even the fevered oriental Herodias is not denied a sense of humor. At times, childishly laughing, she plays ball with John's adored head.

If Heine were less complexly romantic, less driven by contradictory impulses, perhaps the beautiful, joyous, eternally youthful Abunda would be the fairest of them all in the narrator's eyes. But it is Herodias, a more intense, tangled figure, that he cannot help worshiping, especially since she has been glancing at him coquettishly, langorously, enigmatically. With heart aflame, but with a mind still capable of dousing irreality in laughter, he urges her to love him. He is willing to admit that the dead Jewess may be damned; but this condition is not truly grave, he points out, since he himself is absolutely free of religious prejudice; nor is he expecting much in the way of personal salvation. His appeal is not heeded. Neither Herodias nor the other two phantomatic ladies are available for capture.

Atta Troll, however, is not an uncapturable fantasy. The bear is finally trapped and shot through the heart by Lascaro. We learn that the narrator's sweetheart Julia now owns the brown hero's hide, on which the narrator himself has often stood barefoot in her Paris bedroom, meditating in Schillerian fashion, though more playfully than melancholically, on how necessary extinction is as a prelude to poetic immortality.

Heine's assertion that he tried in the second half of *Atta Troll* to revive
the (persecuted) romantic temper "not in the soft key of the earlier school,
rather in the boldest manner of modern humor, which can and will take in
all the elements of the past" (907), would not be questioned by S. S.
Prawer, who amply indicates in *Heine: The Tragic Satirist* how often the
poet mocks his idealized self while precariously balancing cynicism and
genuine feeling.[35] Prawer observes that "with their nostalgia, their strange
blend of exoticism and elements from German folk-lore, their search for
ineffable sensations beyond the reach of ordinary existence, their
mingling of love and death, the 'Wild Hunt' chapters of *Atta Troll* present
most compellingly a *Romantic* view of life. They, more than anything else
in this work, justify Heine's contention that he had here written 'the last
free forest-song of Romanticism.' " Though he is also fully cognizant of
the comic elements in *Atta Troll*, Prawer is reluctant to assess the poem
as an example of romantic irony – that is, German romantic irony.
"Though the German Romantics had known," he remarks, "how to mingle
irony and satire with their ecstasies, Heine shows even in these 'Wild
Hunt' sections a detachment that goes beyond 'romantic irony' " (70).

Yet the poet – Jew and gentile, offspring of Germany and exile in
France, sensualist and quixotic adorer, believer and atheist, ardent idealist
and cynical comedian -- who almost succumbs to the lure of love and
death while at the same time laughing at his romantic impulses seems to
be more than suitably equipped to embody the ambivalence of European
romantic irony. A "detachment that goes beyond [German] 'romantic
irony' " signifies for Prawer a state in which the poet "is saved from
ultimate dangers and debarred from ultimate ecstasies by his ever-lively,
ever-mocking intellect" (71). But this is precisely the state of European
romantic irony, which is able to blunt the destructive edge of ultimate
romantic perils and to stall the invasion of ultimate romantic passions.[36]

Consider Heine's (more or less) balanced display of romantic
consecration and comic, antiromantic desecration in "The God Apollo,"
in Book I of *Romancero.* The shifting perspectives from which the
celebrated, eponymous Greek deity is envisaged both affirm and put at
risk certain priceless values: faith, love, art, and beauty. In this respect the
Greek god differs substantially from the godlike image of Sir Lancelot in
"The Lady of Shalott," although both figures inadvertently initiate an
erotic transfiguration on the part of an observer. In Tennyson's poem,
nothing is permitted to damage the vision of a sexually and heroically
magnificent knight – a vision which, appearing in the Lady of Shalott's
mirror, seizes hold of this fairy child's imagination, draws her to a

forbidden window, and causes her to die of a mortal curse. In "The God Apollo" it is a young nun, not a fairy child (though severe seclusion is their common lot) whose heart is bewitched. But the god who entrances her turns out to be curiously malleable.

In the first part of the poem, the nun sees and hears the splendid, golden-haired, melodically seductive deity, who happens to be sailing down below on the Rhine in the company, it seems, of the nine lovely Muses, dressed in garments distinctly Grecian. Apollo's song, which figures as the second part of the poem, dissolves the nun's inhibitions. The song is profoundly nostalgic: this exiled god of music, driven from his Greek mountains and his Castalian spring, evokes a golden age of harmonious airs and graces, an age of unspoiled laughter and luster. It is true, however, that his lyricism is somewhat marred by what has been described as "over-jaunty accents ... of the modern fairground, with geographical references that merge the Greek Parnassus with the Parisian Montparnasse."[37]

In the third and final section of the poem, the tremulously naive nun, her faith shattered, hurries from her convent in search of the Greek idol. Her distraught inquiries prove fruitless until she meets a slovenly old peddler who proceeds to paint a seedy picture of the "god." He indelicately informs her that "Apollo" is his relative, an ex-rabbi and former leading cantor named Faibisch (Phoebus) who lost his job owing to a predilection for gambling, free-thinking, and pork, and who is currently touring the country and its waterways in the role of Apollo – he has also played clowns and kings in market-places – accompanied by a troupe of low-grade casino entertainers from Amsterdam disguised as the Muses.

The poem succeeds as romantic irony insofar as the enthralling sight and sound of the beautiful Hellenic god (despite minor vulgarizations) are countered, but not repudiated, by the disreputable theatricality of Apollo's portrait in the final section. Had the (somewhat flawed) ideal image of Apollo in the second part of the poem been drawn not by the narrator but by an inflamed literary nun deflected from spirituality into amorous, sense-disordering rapture, the case for a subsequent cancellation of the ideal would be inarguable. But it is the poet's own vision that validates, admittedly with a touch of parody, the captivating song and sight of "Apollo," that is, until Heine permits classical (if not wholly pure) radiance to be funnily smudged by Jewish-bohemian lowlife. Though the romantic ideal of Hellenic beauty, art, and nobility is ostensibly replaced by grossly described comic charlatanism, the antithetical portraits of Apollo remain polarized; neither is capable of effacing the other.

The charms of Heine's irreverence undergo little strain in matters of faith, whether that faith is Hellenic, Christian, or Judaic. Consider the third chapter of *The Rabbi of Bacherach,* Heine's aborted prose fiction. Don Isaac Abarbanel, an urbane, renegade Spanish Jew, unexpectedly encounters the refugee rabbi of Bacherach and his wife in the Frankfurt ghetto. The faith of the rabbi, who evokes the legend of the Wandering Jew, forever outcast and forever persecuted, obviously enlists Heine's allegiance. But much is also granted to Don Isaac, the apostate possessor of a wandering Jewish nose. Don Isaac – like Heine, he is repelled by dour Hebraism – has shamelessly (yet somehow forgivably) adopted a gastronomic view of the enduring qualities of Judaism. He visits the Jewish quarter not to pray but to eat. Jewish cuisine has apparently outlasted Jewish beliefs, though in a sense Jewish cuisine itself constitutes a lingering version of such beliefs.

Heine's antic impertinence in the realm of faith may or may not be actualized in romantic irony; yet religious faith is almost as likely to elicit a dualistic response from Heine as his favorite target in the romantic-ironic comedy of ambivalence: romantic love. Both themes, faith and love, co-exist in surprising fashion in "Donna Clara" (*The Homecoming*), a poem which deals with the passion shared by a young knight and Donna Clara, a beautiful Alcalde's daughter. Donna Clara's declarations of love for the knight are infested with extraneous, recurrently expressed anti-Semitic prejudice, to which the knight seems to pay little attention. Eventually, however, the apparently devoted, ever so loving knight discloses to the lovely, passion-stricken despiser of Jews – he does this casually, smilingly, with calm dignity – that he is the son of the eminent Rabbi Israel of Saragossa. The revelation conveys an ironic shock, of course; but since the knight's love, seemingly so pure and sweet, turns out to be purely and sweetly vindictive, the irony in "Donna Clara" is no more than circumstantial. Heine's ironic comedy of course plays amply with bogus, as well as genuine, idealism.

Chapter 5

White Blackbirds: Gautier, Musset, Stendhal

1.

In pointing out that Alfred de Musset's temperament made him a perfect disciple of Byron – the Byron who exported both doom-laden romantic moodiness and witty de-romanticizing impulses – Phillippe Van Tieghem long ago used a binary formula which, despite its conventionality, still roughly applies to all practitioners of European romantic irony. Musset's psyche, Van Tieghem observed, contains in close relationship both irony and passion, both faith and skepticism, both ardor and doubt.[1] Earlier, Paul Bourget had linked Musset's temper to Heine's. He had depicted the two writers as "iconoclasts adoring the idols they break."[2] Théophile Gautier has been analyzed in similar terms: he manifests "the same curious dichotomy as Byron or Hoffmann, in whom skepticism and mockery were constant correctives of the lyrical."[3] Stendhal too has been seen as harboring a split psyche: he is both an "Enlightened Voltaire" and a "Romantic Byron."[4] (The same must of course be said of Byron himself.) Indeed certain Beylists "irreverently revere" in Stendhal "the tender cynic, the passionate ironist. . . . the lucid daydreamer."[5] Musset, Gautier, and Stendhal, in sum, are both subverters of romanticism and romanticism's proponents.

The element of ironic lucidity in ambivalence of this sort may of course yield to burlesque. This is the mode in which the young Gautier, for example, exposes the faddish singularities and follies created by a saturation in the romantic ethos. The spoofing of romantic obsessions in Gautier's *Les Jeunes-France: Romans Goguenards* (1833) – translatable as goofy tales of impassioned French youth – may remind one of *Nightmare Abbey*. Structurally, however, *Les Jeunes-France* differs from Peacock's novel inasmuch as it consists of unrelated stories and sketches. The lunacies of romanticism that Gautier probes include Hoffmannesque fantasticality ("Onuphrius"), Byronic egomania ("Daniel Jovard"), and the cult of medievalism ("Elias Wildmanstadius"). Though Gautier's exhibition of romanticism's charlatans and madmen (fictive characters all) corresponds to Peacock's travesties of Shelley, Byron, and Coleridge, Gautier's persona is also prepared (unlike Peacock) to incriminate himself as one of the perpetrators of romanticism's buffooneries.

In his introductory remarks, which suggest that prefaces may serve as charming uncorsetings of chapters to come,[6] Gautier's persona professes to have been an incurably Parisian loather of Nature, scorner of politics, and despiser of literature. His friends, however, have provoked him, in the interests of cultural decency (that is, fashion), to become a writer, and have helped to make him an accomplished member of the romantic generation. Physically, he fits the romantic image admirably. Women find his pale olive complexion a beautiful sign of disillusioned, tormented, satanic sensibility (xvii). (Actually, it is the result of gastritis.) Gautier's persona intends to exploit his sham erotic romanticism to the full. A volcanically impassioned seducer, he will become, in the guise of an irresistible fallen angel, the Napoleon of Don Juans. If only he were a bastard, he sighs, he would be perfect (xviii).

The caricatural theatricality of Gautier's versions of French romanticism – Gautier does not hint that English and German romanticism reach more persuasively toward the depths of the soul – is well illustrated in "Daniel Jovard, or the Conversion of a Classicist," a tale of the artist as a demented romantic, that is, a crazed consumer of the bogus qualities of romantic chic. In the beginning, however, Daniel Jovard is only a bourgeois mediocrity, a part-time neo-classical versifier utterly out of date in the new literary era of the late 1820s. After thundering against the romantic newcomers for having foisted on the public a barbarous corruption of taste, he falls under the spell of a dandified former schoolmate, Ferdinand de C---, who derides the idols Daniel has worshipped and instills in him not only heresy and revolt, but a tremendous hunger for glory. So fanatical is Daniel's conversion to romanticism that he indulges in a private holocaust of the classical age: he hurls his Boileau, Voltaire, and Racine into the fire and demands that all literary classicists be trundled to the guillotine.

The mocking narrator allows this former cultural fossil, now devastatingly infected with the virus of romanticism, very few prepossessing qualities. Nor does Daniel avoid sinking into an abyss of unreason and immorality as he dutifully learns from Ferdinand de C--- that the fashionable literary life requires the trickiness and mercenary aims of a prostitute, as well as brazen advertisements of one's unique self and a heavy reliance on plagiarized rhetoric (best accompanied by a handful of glamorous adjectives, such as pyramidal, phosphorescent, and transcendental).

Daniel's transmutation into the most furiously ambitious of bourgeois-reviling romantics is impeded, however, by a single, mountainous obstacle: he is stopped dead in his tracks by his cursedly antiromantic patronymic, Jovard. Months pass while he searches for an exalted pseudonym. Finally, he comes up with a massively polysyllabic foreign name loaded with romantic consonants. This laboriously forged romantic identity virtually deranges our non-hero. Trembling with wild, magnificent impressions, he is tempted to scribble his new name on walls (romantic graffiti are narcissistic rather than obscene). But he requires a more sensational means of attracting attention to his metamorphosed self. Should he commit suicide to gain the public's notice, or merely limit himself to assassination? He does neither. He decides to publish some poems in the current mode (pure folderol) and get in touch with the new artistic circles. Having made himself over into a complete Byronic personality, as well as a thoroughgoing publicity hound, Daniel zooms into the limelight. With his flowing beard, enormous brow (it is shaved), and rolling eyeball, he is henceforth able to command an adulatory audience. Such is Gautier's extravagant vision of the romantic as posturer and mountebank. (Some of the romantics in *Les Jeunes-France* are genuinely cracked, however.)

In Gautier's anecdotal *A History of Romanticism* (1874), hyperbole is less rank. Here he recalls nostalgically how the young idealistic romantics, dedicated to art, poetry, Nature, and liberty, fought to clear away the debris of palsied classicists while also contending with obstructive philistines. On February 25, 1830, at the first performance of Hugo's *Hernani,* "two systems, two parties, two armies, two civilizations"[7] famously prepared for cultural warfare. Ultimately, the youthful "flamboyants," invigorated by Shakespeare, Calderon, and Goethe (but also by Corneille and Molière) conquered the old "dullards." In those days there was no shortage of genuinely ecstatic romantics.

Among the young romantics so belligerently devoted to revolutionary art and poetry, authentic eccentricities inevitably flourished. Some of these echo the oddities on display in *Les Jeunes-France.* Gautier remembers, for example, that "it was the fashion for a man to be wan, livid, greenish, and somewhat cadaverous, for thus did one attain the fateful, Byronic, Giaour look of one devoured by passion and remorse."[8] This emaciated look, he reports, enticed women to give their love to the romantic rebels before the grave itself embraced them. Even if this account is only marginally accurate, Gautier's portrait of Daniel Jovard and other strait-jacketable romantic types cannot be ascribed uniquely to wildly inventive comedy.

Nor is ambivalence lacking in *Les Jeunes-France.* A double-edged attitude toward the romantic psyche is traceable in several of the tales. "Elias Wilderman," for example, portrays a sensitive young man singularly and totally ensconced in the culture of the Middle Ages. Romantic medievalism is detectable in his food, his clothing, his archaic speech – even in his handwriting. And since he is intimately in harmony with all aspects of the Gothic, he spends much of his anachronistic life meditating in cathedrals. But Gautier is not intent on exploiting a purely farcical send-up of still another romantic psychosis. His mockery is subdued by intimations of noble, if absurdly escapist, pathos. (The nineteenth century, after all, can be stiflingly pedestrian.) Similarly, in "Onuphrius, ou les vexations d'un admirateur d'Hoffmann," comedy is more than occasionally restrained. It is difficult to laugh at the young artist Onuphrius when he is driven mad by the demonic impulses of the romantic imagination. Indeed the weird Hoffmannesque details Gautier offers us are as surrealistically fearful as they are funny.

"Celle-ci et celle-là, ou la Jeune-France passionnée," the principal tale in the collection, comes closest to betraying sympathy with romantic tendencies. Yet such sympathy is dominated by ridicule of romanticism's delinquencies of temper and taste. Rodolphe, the chief character, is a young poet determined to live a tempestuously creative life by obeying the dictates of romantic idealism and romantic transcendence (that is, delirium). What he hankers after is a tremendously passionate love affair. Alas, it is not to be. Having envisioned love as poetically, hugely spontaneous, Rodolphe is reduced to using precise tactics – indeed, an idiotically mechanical, step-by-step program – in order to achieve a semblance of romantic intensity. The trouble is that the exquisitely exotic mistress he has chosen has not the slightest inkling of what a romantic sensibility requires. She not only fails to respond correctly to romantic cues but provides no stimulus at all for poetry-making of the right romantic sort. Furthermore, her aging husband proves to be a useless foil since he is too dense to recognize the high drama of infidelity. The result is that Rodolphe's adulterous affair evolves banally, not Byronically. Violent emotions and convulsion-engendering reversals of fortune are simply not to be had.

The witty narrator of "Celle-ci et celle-là" cogently remarks that dreamy youth – specifically, youth lacerated by a foolishly self-imposed induction into the celebrated but illusory emotional adventures of romanticism – must submit to gay good sense and to the refreshing poetry of real life. Still, Rodolphe's willfully concocted, calculatedly pursued, and platitudinously developed pseudo-passions are often charmingly depicted by the narrator, who in spite of his shrewd analysis of youthful folly is himself hardly immune to the intoxications of romantic literature. In short, there are pronounced traces of romantic irony in this and several other tales of *Les Jeunes-France* (as there are in other early works of Gautier).

But it is in *Mademoiselle de Maupin* (1835) that Gautier brings romantic irony to fruition. Gautier's novel is prefaced by a flippant, bourgeois-goading, art-for-art's-sake quasi-manifesto that explicitly enshrines beauty, implicitly favors the ironic temper, and plainly makes no bones about promoting antagonism toward utopian system-builders and old-fashioned virtue-mongers. (The preface, which finds the nineteenth-century dismally non-pagan, is hardly an exemplar of French social romanticism.) Banteringly, yet disdainfully, Gautier declares, in words that Walter Pater and Oscar Wilde would remember, that any attempt to discover in art a useful purpose, a moral aim, or a crusading impulse is quite preposterous. Art exists only for the anarchic enjoyment of its superfluous (hence indispensable) fascination. The notion that art is a sermon (or, in Swinburne's echoing words, a "handmaid of religion, exponent of duty, servant of fact, pioneer of morality"[9]) and the idea that mankind is perfectible are cultural insanities with which utilitarian journalists and hypocritical philistines delude themselves as they solemnly churn out so-called progressive ideas and devices which enable them to master the discomforts of existence. Gautier's aesthetic disaffection from a drably practical age is nicely captured in a comment which today's toileters would find incomprehensible: "Nothing is really beautiful unless it is useless; everything useful is ugly, for it expresses a need, and the needs of man are ignoble and disgusting, like his poor weak nature. The most useful place in a house is the lavatory."[10]

In the novel itself, which is primarily epistolary, romantic irony derives most acutely from the strange experiences and changing attitudes of Mlle de Maupin. Yet the Chevalier d'Albert, whose letters to his intimate friend Silvio take up more space than Mlle de Maupin's correspondence (equally one-way) with her bosom friend Graciosa, is himself a copious, if at first glance dubious, source of romantic irony. D'Albert is a very young, excessively idle, brilliant sophisticate who is often afflicted by the fever, despair, and horrendous tedium of an unfulfilled longing for the ideal – an ideal that is to be embodied in an incredibly beautiful lover. The image of fulfillment he conjures up is not ethereally romantic. Even though d'Albert understands that true love is best revealed when it is unadorned, his vision of love's perfection requires wit, wealth, and a kind of sensuality which is partly ancient Roman and partly modern Turkish. Yet for all its pagan components, d'Albert's (rather passive) quest for supreme physical beauty in love does allow him to reach for the sublime. On the other hand, d'Albert is not devoid of self-mockery, so that from time to time he judges his romance of the ideal to be as nonsensical as it is exalted. In his frequently pessimistic moments, d'Albert's ideal functions as a sanctuary in the midst of what he deems to be universal rot and ennui. But in radically different moods he is ready to believe that reality overflows with poetic fantasticality. The psyche of this seeker of purity and perverse cynic is nothing if not bizarrely labile. D'Albert concludes that he is "the most miserable mass of heterogeneous fragments which has ever existed" (131).

Perfection being scarce, d'Albert's eventual choice of a mistress (Rosette) necessitates shelving the ideal, at least temporarily. Though a prettier, more amusing, more erotically inventive and theatrically resourceful companion would be hard to imagine, d'Albert continues to suffer from the "malady of the impossible" (143), that is, a condition of unappeasable romantic yearning (even if it is oddly qualified by colossal Neronian cravings). D'Albert's contentedly debauched body cannot sedate his restless romantic soul.

When the impossible does materialize before d'Albert's eyes, it takes the shape of a young cavalier, Théodore de Sérannes, to whom he feels irresistibly and, it would seem, unnaturally attracted. D'Albert can only believe that some sort of maleficent sorcery has displaced his ideal of beauty onto a man's body. (It is true that the mentally surfeited d'Albert had once felt a desire for a Teiresian sex-change in order to experience a new species of sensual rapture; nor has the classical image of the hermaphrodite been alien to his imagination. Still, it is Mlle de Maupin's proneness to bisexuality, not d'Albert's, that will ultimately exemplify the novel's exploration of erotic ambiguity and sexual metamorphosis.) Instinct, aided by worried speculation, cries out to d'Albert that his aberrancy must be based on biological truth: Théodore must be a woman in disguise. And so, despite recurrent, tormenting doubts, he becomes convinced that his inner being has at last been liberated by the incarnation of the ideal he has so long brooded over.

Théodore de Sérannes is indeed a woman – Madeleine de Maupin, young, brave, beautiful, and considerably vexed by women's ignorance of men. Driven by urgent curiosity (attended by more than a little anxiety), Mlle de Maupin has decided to test the literature of romance by adopting a masculine garb and mingling at close range with the opposite sex. Only in this manner, she is convinced, will she be able to dissect the nature of the male animal. Her disguise is unusually successful. She becomes a distinguished horseman, swordsman, athlete, drinker, oath-swearer, and (apparent) philanderer. (Gautier has thus, with engaging implausibility, gone far beyond the limits of Elizabethan androgyny.)

Madeleine's preliminary findings are disastrous. Men, she discovers, are horribly gross. They are rude, besotted, and obscene. They exhibit, not genuine gallantry, but rather a repulsively prosaic, disgustingly vain, ignobly contemptuous attitude toward women. After a while, Madeleine will become more tolerant of the male monster, for she will detect in herself a strong affinity with masculine interests and will even acquire a taste for bold patterns of virility. For the time being, however, the betrayal of her romantic reveries (her own awakened carnality is also traitorous) is drastically disturbing. The blue flower of the ideal, she observes, emits only poisoned honey. (For Mlle de Maupin, the ideal is basically moral beauty, as against d'Albert's ideal of physical beauty.)

Mlle de Maupin is not, however, headed toward a tragedy of disillusion, for Gautier has blessed his heroine with a wonderfully modulated sense of comedy. Indeed her comic temper enables Madeleine not only to salve her hurt but to become sagely amused by her own disenchantment. Nor is Madeleine's propensity for comedy evinced so belatedly as to strain our credence. From the very beginning, she has enjoyed the histrionics of her masquerade, even to the point of indulging in dangerous farce. When she joins d'Albert's circle, however, she cultivates a chastened appetite for ironic comedy. It is an appetite that is not foreign, we recall, to d'Albert himself. He is quite capable, without denying the sovereignty of poetic fantasy, of comically trashing his lyrical flights. At one point he hymns a paean to Shakespeare's fusion of comedy and fantasy, a fusion that enables frivolity and unconstraint to convey profound emotions and intimate dreams. The Shakespearean piece that particularly interests d'Albert is *As You Like It,* owing to the fascinating puzzle posed by Théodore, who seems to reflect the sexual doubleness of Rosalind/Ganymede.

When d'Albert and his acquaintances, satiated with conventional entertainment, prepare a performance of Shakespeare's comedy, d'Albert takes the role of Orlando. Théodore inevitably assumes the role of Rosalind, and is astonishingly persuasive in the part. Thrilled by a vision of absolute beauty in the flesh, yet haunted by gender uncertainties, d'Albert can hardly distinguish ecstasy from a plunge into inferno. The being he loves is equipped with the body of a woman and the mind of a man – a man who behaves, moreover, like the most swashbuckling and bloody-minded of heroes. "These are singular qualities for a mistress! Such things happen only to me," d'Albert muses. "I'm laughing," he adds, "but there's certainly nothing to laugh about, because I have never suffered so much" (255). After enduring his anguishing, risible predicament for three months, d'Albert confesses his love to Rosalind/Théodore in a letter that tenders a full account of his perplexities and pain.

The woman who receives d'Albert's letter is of course far more knowledgeable about men than Shakespeare's heroine. Yet the temper of both women is romantic-ironic. Rosalind's romantic irony – she blithely but wisely belittles the poetry of love while simultaneously demonstrating that she is love's delicately exulting advocate – serves as a prelude to marriage. Madeleine's romantic irony, which is certified relatively late in the novel, assuredly will not. Her disillusion with men (this is the most persistent theme in her letters) has severely contracted the visionary charms of love and obliterated the cogency of marriage. Yet her revulsion from male vulgarity and mendacity has somewhat abated. The world, she now recognizes, is little concerned with nobility or refinement, let alone ideal love.

Since she has found – that is, before she gets to appreciate d'Albert – that true love is delusory, Madeleine has toyed with the idea of enjoying merely sensual pleasure. But a unique problem has confronted her: she feels that she belongs exclusively neither to the male nor to the female sex, but rather to a third sex. Because she has "the body and soul of a woman, the spirit and strength of a man," she is persuaded that she will "never be able to love anyone completely, man or woman." The most desirable experience "would be to have each sex in turn . . . man today, woman tomorrow" (330). But this kind of satisfaction of her dual nature has not turned out to be realizable. In any case, d'Albert has begun to affect her as no other man ever has.

When Madeleine takes the full measure of d'Albert, both before and during their Shakespearean adventure, her image of a perfect lover is rekindled, though not, of course, as powerfully as it might once have been. For all d'Albert's show of worldliness and perversity, Madeleine senses that "his heart is far from being as corrupt as his mind" (331). At the same time she is extremely amused by the self-torturing questions he has been raising about his possibly abnormal sexuality. Still, she is no sadist. Because she finds d'Albert relatively noble, she will be kind to him. (Besides, she is pining with sexual curiosity and desire.) And so she tells Graciosa light-heartedly that she will visit, in the costume of Rosalind, both d'Albert and his mistress Rosette, who has also been enraptured by Madeleine. To d'Albert she will offer her love; to Rosette she will present an irrefutable explanation of her evasive behavior. "I have joked throughout this letter," Madeleine writes, "and yet what I'm going to attempt is a serious matter, and I may feel its effects for the rest of my life" (335).

Chapter 16, one of the few non-epistolary sections of the novel, contains the "serious matter": Madeleine gives herself to d'Albert, and then to Rosette. The hitherto inconspicuous narrator prefers to be coy about these love scenes; but at the same time Gautier has permitted his narrator to coarsen his sensibility and wink broadly at the reader. This uniquely crude expression of ambivalence – this juxtaposition of the high and the low, of paradisal fulfillment and universal animality – may not be a ruinous lapse in judgment; but it spoils for the moment the charm of Gautier's novel.

Madeleine spends a perfect night of love with d'Albert – an experience, she decides, which must remain unique. She will not tolerate the clichés of romantic transcendence, especially vows of eternal adoration. In a farewell letter to d'Albert – it is the novel's final chapter[11] – Madeleine explains her decision with tender wit and the kind of Byronic sagacity that accounts, in *Don Juan*, for the necessary brevity of Juan and Haidée's love. Romantic love, Madeleine affirms, can bequeath immortal ardor, but only if it obeys the dictates of fleeting time. It would be foolishly inappropriate, she writes, to disfigure superb moments of romantic passion by stretching them out into a "comical domestic situation" (347) of insipid familiarity. Rather than undergo the death of love through such foreseeable boredom, Madeleine will preserve in her memory the elusive, mysterious element in d'Albert, just as she herself will remain for him an inexhaustible source of wonder. All this she says with good humor, sweetness, grace – and the wisdom of romantic irony.

2.

Mlle de Maupin suggests, moreover (but not wickedly), that d'Albert's probable though temporary heartbreak will likely improve his poetry. She alludes here to the romantic nexus of suffering and song, which is perhaps most memorably expressed in Alfred de Musset's "Nuit de mai" and Shelley's "To a Sky-Lark." The melodiously poignant voice in "To a Sky-Lark" admits that "Our sweetest songs are those that tell of saddest thought." Yet what the poet fervently solicits is the promise of a skylark-taught harmonious "gladness." That achievement would presumably make obsolete the perception that suffering is inherent in the creation of true poetry. (The following lines from Shelley's "Julian and Maddalo" would also become questionable: "Most wretched men / Are cradled into poetry by wrong, / They learn in suffering what they teach in song.")

At the end of the three dialogues between the Muse and the poet in Musset's "Nuit de mai" on the other hand, there remains little ambiguity about the function of pain in the making of poetry. Yet the Muse, the teacher of this truth (she knows a good deal about joy, too), has a hard time persuading the gloomy, recalcitrant poet to accept the message that grief and suffering, far from causing sterility and paralysis, are great fecundating powers for the creative soul. For the poet, certain vexations of the heart are beyond literary expression. The Muse persists. Transmuting cliché into witchery, she argues that suffering is not only a spiritual but a sanctifying force; and she points for evidence to the nourishing wounds of the self-sacrificing pelican.

The Muse reaches the climax of her ecstatic appeal in the lines that correspond to Shelley's: "Les plus désespérés sont les chants les plus beaux, / Et j'en sais d'immortels qui sont de purs sanglots." The poet, however, remains stricken by a martyrdom of despair to which he is incapable of giving a literary voice. He must therefore renounce the Muse's fervent invitation to rise to greatness of soul by breaking his silence. Still, "Nuit de mai" proves the Muse's point; for the poem is the creation of a confirmed romantic familiar with productive agony.

Does this mean that Musset could not successfully combat his romantic impulses, that he could not seek escape from romantic intensities of emotion – that he could not collapse romanticism into a joke? Not at all. The young Musset had as keen an eye as the young Gautier for the absurd extremism, the ballyhooed excesses, of the romantic movement. Such excesses provoked in both writers a jocular antiromanticism that did not, however, destroy their basic allegiance to the romantic temper.

When Arthur O. Lovejoy in his essay "On the Discrimination of Romanticisms" (1924) emphasized the havoc of imprecision wrought by explicators of romanticism who had managed to establish conflicting claims about its origins and significance, he began by wryly alluding to the research undertaken a century earlier by Musset's Dupuis and Cotonet, two fictive, non-Parisian amateur intellectuals who during a dozen alarming years investigated the polymorphous perversities of the romantic epidemic in France.[12] It is in the first of his *Letters of Dupuis and Cotonet* (1836) that Musset traces romanticism's provincial peregrinations, specifically in La Ferté-sous-Jouarre, where his two puzzled bourgeois literary sleuths reside. Dupuis writes up their research; but his friend Cotonet, a notary whose hobby is ornithology, is never able, owing to its exasperatingly elusive nature, to capture romanticism on the wing. The record of their observations and perplexities begins in the mid-1820s, when quarrels break out (as they notoriously did in periodical French publications of the time) over a new phenomenon: a mentally unsettling and socially disturbing hodge-podge of literary oddities, ranging from the cult of the picturesque to the resuscitation of the Middle Ages.

Though Dupuis and Cotonet are in a quandary much of the time, they are not invariably portrayed as dunces; indeed, they can be quite knowledgeable and even astute. Their explorations, however, lead only to befuddlement. They discover, for example, that a single line in a classical poem may represent an invasion of romanticism. Dupuis and Cotonet are rendered sleepless by such revelations. Comparable nightmares emerge from a string of other incomprehensible, rapidly shifting doctrines. Fortunately, Hugo's preface to *Cromwell* (1827) succeeds in tranquilizing the two researchers. For a whole year, Dupuis and Cotonet believe that romanticism is the union of tragedy and comedy, terror and buffoonery. But by 1829-1830, the pair have been led to construe romanticism as the imitation mostly of German and English literature, especially of German ghoulishness and English melancholy.

Since intellectual uncertainties continue to haunt the two scholarly detectives in the next few years, they finally decide to interrogate a certain town clerk, the original, highly provocative local apostle of romanticism. This way, surely, they will be able to solve the mystery of the new literary mode once and for all. Here is the clerk's definition of romanticism:

> Romanticism is the weeping star, the wailing wind, the shivering night, the flower in its flight, and the balmy bird; it is an unanticipated jet, languid ecstasy, the well by the palm trees, rosy hopes and their thousand loves, the angel and the pearl, the white robe of the willows; oh, what a beautiful thing, sir! It is infinity and the starry sky; it is heart, fragmentariness, disintoxication; and yet at the same time it is the full and the round, the diametrical, they pyramidal, the oriental, raw nudity, the embrace, a kiss, the whirlwind; what a new science! It is providential philosophy geometricizing reality, then launching itself into the vagueness of experience to chisel within it secret fibers.[13]

This turgid, incoherent homage suffices to brand romanticism as a lyrical lunacy. A corroborative indictment is obtained from the arch-enemy of romanticism in La Ferté-sous-Jouarre, the magistrate Ducoudray, who maintains that romanticism, largely inspired as it is by cadaverous medievalism, conduces to pathological trivialities, political retrogression, religious anomalies, and sensational immorality.

Musset's coup de grâce is still to come. After listening to the clerk's vaporous derangement and the magistrate's repudiative vehemence, Dupuis and Cotonet come up with an uncomplicated litmus test to determine the presence of literary romanticism. They twice compare two juxtaposed texts which contain more or less the same substance. In each case, the first of the two texts is buried in asphyxiating epithets, while the second is utterly simple. The first text is stigmatized as romantic; the second is honored as classical. Romanticism, Dupuis and Cotonet conclude, is an unrestrained frothiness of language, a thick foam of adjectives.

Musset's burlesque of romanticism was published in 1836, the very year his *Confession of a Child of the Century* – one of the most ardent embodiments of the romantic temper ever penned – also appeared. (The second chapter of the *Confession* had been published independently in 1835.) The novel concerns, for the most part, the anguished relationship between Octave, Musset's turbulent, afflicted protagonist, and the maternally angelic Brigitte Pearson. Octave, like other wounded young idealists, has discovered that the poetry of love can be dishonored, that romantic professions of eternal fidelity – this is precisely what Mlle de Maupin inoculated herself against – can turn to ashes. The result of his disabusement – his sardonic observations do not alleviate his distress – is a pledge to himself (more ineffective than not) to cultivate a mundane, empty-hearted existence. However, his experience of a new devotion, provided by Brigitte, restores within him an image of perfection that elicits his worship, but only intermittently. Whenever this periodically resurgent romantic ideal founders (often through the guilt of sexuality), he suffers agonies of suspicion and commits unpardonable cruelties. Eventually, but only when it is too late, he realizes that the woman whose soul he has been misprizing and crucifying has deserved something other than maltreatment. (Brigitte's love has in fact been unimpeachable.) His only recourse now is to prepare himself for redemptive suffering.

A larger conflict – and a more warrantable scepticism, covering far more than a personal, tormented love affair – pervades the essayistic, impassioned second chapter of the *Confession*, which examines the psychological scars created by a baneful cultural disenchantment. Octave, attempting to effect through his intimate disclosures a self-cure, a purging of destructive disbelief, is convinced that a whole generation of young Frenchmen has been morally enfeebled by the reactionary current of contemporary civilization. According to Octave, the malady of the age – the deprivation of faith and aspiration – began with Napoleon's fall, when the dying powers of Europe were sufficiently reanimated to divide up the continent among themselves. Out of the purple of Caesar, Octave/Musset remarks, sounding very much like Heine, these spidery, nauseating, antiheroic creatures fashioned for themselves the motley of Harlequin, and in the process left the youth of France, with its visions of heroic resolve and purifying peril, stranded and emasculated.[14] A lost generation was condemned to ponder a world in which the grandeur of Napoleonic history had been transformed into farce, a world in which illusion could not survive and in which the natural gaiety of youth too often succumbed to contempt. In the ghostly ruins surrounding this crippled generation, seeds and debris were scarcely distinguishable from each other.

This sense of recent history's grotesque diminution has only been intensified, Octave believes, by the corruptive nature of modern literature. Singling out Goethe, creator of the sufferings of Faust, and Byron, creator of the agony of Manfred, Octave laments the success with which these two colossi of grief and of the innermost darkness of the soul have reinforced the malaise of French youth. German and English ideas have spawned, or at any rate magnified, propensities among young Frenchmen (that is, among those with sensitive, exalted spirits) to surrender to nihilism and disgust.[15]

Despite its febrile, melodramatic basis, what Octave/Musset describes as a historical-literary pestilence illuminates certain recognizable strains of melancholy and despair in French romanticism. What matters here, however, is not so much the validity of Musset's portrait of post-Napoleonic demoralization as the fact that the compulsive romanticism of the *Confession* and the antic antiromanticism of the first of the *Letters of Dupuis and Cotonet* decisively testify to Musset's romantic-ironic ambivalence.

Though it often leans toward caricature, Musset's romantic irony is already apparent in his early verse *Tales of Spain and Italy* (1830). For example, in "Mardoche," the protagonitst's antithetical traits – he bristles with genuine romantic passions but is also loaded with sham romantic obsessions – intermingle in a crazy incongruence of lyricism and rant. The narrator of this tale is himself a major anomaly: he is both remarkably offhand in his treatment of the protagonist and also exceedingly cavalier in his attitude toward the reader. His shamelessly intrusive commentary borrows generously from Byron's digressive license in *Beppo* and *Don Juan*, except that the pupil is considerably more clownish than the master.

The "Ballad to the Moon" is perhaps the crowning comic piece in the *Tales*. The title of the poem seems to signal appreciation of, and perhaps reverence for, a prime symbol of romanticism. But through a series of disingenuous questions which manage to associate the moon's appearance with ludicrously inappropriate objects, Musset quickly demystifies lunar romanticism. The inventory of similitudes in the first part of the poem consists of one gross indignity after another. Is the moon a gloom-launched balloon? An old sundial used in Inferno? A slimly crescent worm-eaten substance? A blinded orb owing to a collision with a pointed tree? A sanctimonious cherub's lorgnette? The dot of an "i" suspended over a faded yellow steeple? (This is a recurrent image.) The mysterious, mystical qualities of the moon seem to be irreparably damaged by such nonsensical, degrading queries.

In the next section of the "Ballad," however, conventional esteem is re-established. The poet abruptly summons a multitude of images and instances of moon-fantasy and moon-worship. Yet now another pendular swing takes place. The last part of the poem, which consists of nine stanzas Musset added to the original version, utterly disintegrates the moon's newly dignified aura. Musset has contrived a scene – seldom has the moon been placed in so compromised a position – in which a virgin bride, shivering in a cold bed, is being roughly deflowered by an overly excited, egregiously laboring philistine. Fumbling, grunting, and sweating, this feckless husband, who has had the bad taste to complain of his wife's sexual ineptness, suddenly becomes aware that the activities of his wedding night, not yet completely botched, are being peeped at, and are now finally balked, by an annoyingly prying moon. To Musset's bourgeois, the moon, that heavenly catalyst of rapture and melancholy among the romantic élite, has become a blasted nuisance, a scandalously nosy interrupter of legitimate (if clumsy) middle-class copulation.

In Byron's contrasting moon stanzas (113-14) in Canto I of *Don Juan*, no single social class is comically vilified for its hostility to, or aversion from, the great romantic icon. Byron makes us suspect, in stanza 113, that the sexually sly moon has probably soaked up a fair share of aristocratic mischief, though of course other elements of English society can hardly be debarred from illicit experience. Byron's point is that the moon, in an antiromantic perspective, is more indictable (so to speak) than any of the social classes on which it shines. Musset, however, does not incriminate the moon's personality. Neither, for that matter, does Heine in the *Harz Journey,* one of the volumes of his *Travel Pictures,* in which two art-intoxicated young romantics open a clothes-closet, assuming it to be a window, and begin rhapsodizing about the moon, which turns out to be a pair of yellow pants. Heine is debunking only student dreamers, pure anti-philistines idiotically ravished by a romantic fetish. (Elsewhere, and often, Heine himself is a moon-cultist.) Musset also mocks moon-fetishists in the "Ballad to the Moon"; but he laughs even harder at the prosaic middle class, of which pants manufacturers obviously are an integral part.

Though "Namouna," another of Musset's early poems, does not entirely dispense with bourgeois ingredients, its romantic ideal collides with comic disgrace in rather exotic circumstances. "Namouna" initially promises to become Musset's version of a Byronic oriental tale, but it surrenders almost immediately to travesty. As in "Mardoche," the narrator maintains a wholly slapdash relationship with the reader; and he often frivolously disrupts the story of his "hero," a wealthy renegade Frenchman named Hassan whose lust, stimulated by a reading of *The Thousand and One Nights,* has driven him to the lavish, if routinized, eroticism of Islam.

According to the analysis proffered by the narrator in section 13 of Canto I, Hassan is endowed with crazily contradictory attributes: he is joyous and ill-tempered, naïve and blasé, terrifically sincere and extremely foxy. On the subject of erotic appetite, however, there appears to be no ambiguity. Hassan equates love with servitude. The narrator protests that a Hassanesque life devoted purely to the senses is degrading. Yet he also casually remarks that he is not sure about what Hassan actually believes.

By the end of Canto I, Hassan has reached the East, turned Muslim, and is now ready to enjoy sultanesque sexual privileges. But his conversion to Islam annoys the narrator, who finds himself stumbling over novel lexical problems; hard new Mohammedan spellings leave him angry, bewildered, and accident-prone. Of course clarity is not the narrator's forte in any case, with or without the nuisance of Islam. Neither is consistency. The narrator refuses to endorse Hassan's antiromantic conduct; on the other hand, he repudiates the kind of literature that encourages illusory romantic dreams. (This does not prevent him from being hopelessly infatuated with Manon Lescaut.)

If Canto I is a medley of daffy inconsistencies and bad taste, Canto II in some ways is even more anomalous. To begin with, the narrator disgustedly rejects the first canto (which he has just reread) as poor, planless stuff, though it does reveal, he is willing to grant, a pretty wit. The theme of Canto II is not, however, the talent of poets but the nature of lovers. We learn that there are two kinds. The first sort of lover is a satanic Narcissus, a heartless, loveless Lovelace. (If Hassan is being targeted here, he does not quite fit the description.) The second type of lover is a compassionately beautiful yet vulnerable soul, the incarnation of a Christlike ideal. This marvelous symbol of aspiring, spiritualized humanity has not, we are told, been captured in any literary portrait, though E. T. A. Hoffmann once caught a glimpse of him. And who is this holy figure? Against all expectation, it turns out to be Don Juan, whom the narrator loves (others have blasphemed him as a ruthless seducer) and whom he can therefore authentically depict. The truth about Don Juan, the narrator avers, is that he wanders throughout the deformed, stupid world in search of a heaven-sent vision of eternal love. Of course he fails to find such love among his (several thousand) mistresses, be they princesses or prostitutes. But this romanticized Don Juan, constantly baffled in his pursuit of the ideal woman, never loses hope in the face of hideous reality. (Musset's narrator either does not notice or refuses to acknowledge that in Hoffmann's interpretation, Don Juan's quest for heavenly love is prompted by the devil.) Nor does Don Juan ever, like Hassan, have recourse to mere sensuality. Hassan, who has been neglected for some time, is dragged back into view at the end of the canto, where we are informed that though he would not mind sharing Don Juan's loves, he is too sceptical to swallow Don Juan's idealistic credo.

Musset himself has of course been giving vent to both his scepticism and his idealism, and has also been yielding to the pleasures of structural chaos, even though his narrator had sworn that he intended to tell a consecutive story. There is, to be sure, a fragment of a plot in "Namouna," which with ludicrous inappositeness gives Musset the title of his poem. Will the Spanish maiden, Namouna, one of Hassan's former slave mistresses, succeed in re-enchanting her owner and establishing a permanent emotional tie? Probably not, for Hassan is fundamentally averse to high intentions and exquisite feelings, and it is certainly hard to think of him as soulfully non-comic. In spite of the narrator's predilection for jaunty commentary and flip interventions, it is equally hard to detect a faint haze of comicality in Don Juan's idealized portrait. Musset's romantic irony is sustained precisely by the interaction of exorbitant lust (rooted in comic scepticism) and romantic aspiration (permeated by grave sublimity).[16]

Musset's ambivalence toward the romantic temper is not always this legible. One may think such ambivalence is entirely absent, for example, in "The White Blackbird" (1842), Musset's contribution (which only adults can fully savor) to a collection of animal stories for children. One may even judge that "The White Blackbird" is expressly designed, in delightfully deflationary ways, to impugn the romantic sensibility as little more than pretentious narcissism. But such a judgment would be wide of the mark.

The diminutive narrator of "The White Blackbird" recounts the sufferings and grandeur of a lonely, misunderstood, beleaguered genius – himself. He begins with the curse of his origins. This avian protagonist has been born white, shockingly white, in a family that is black, wholly black. Though his mother seeks to protect him from prejudice, his irate, suspicious father disowns him with such a show of violence that the white blackbird feels he has only one choice in life: to start out on a wretched pilgrimage in quest of his real identity. This pilgrimage he courageously undertakes. Everywhere, though not at first, he meets with intolerance and scorn. If he is lucky enough to garner scraps of compassion or perceive signs of potential kinship (including a rare hint of love), these are all withdrawn as soon as he inadvertently raises his voice in song; for it is song that betrays his abnormality. The experience of being an ornithological freak is so harrowing that the white blackbird is convinced his odyssey will be marked by unparalleled persecution and pain. Indeed the little outcast soon surmises that he is perhaps the most bedeviled – but also the most sensitive – pariah in the universe.

Nor does it do the white blackbird much good to explore his wounded psyche. He seems doomed to remain an exasperating mystery (rather than a mythological marvel) to himself as well as to others. Yet at the very moment when his failure to find a proper niche in life threatens to consume him in an abyss of disgust, a miracle (apparently) occurs: the trivial, chance (and misunderstood) remarks of a couple of feathered street-cleaners in Paris lead him to believe that there is in fact such a thing – an exceedingly rare thing – as a white blackbird, a creature of extraordinary value. No longer does the protagonist feel degraded ; no longer is he sapped by the anxiety of otherness. Purged of his humiliation, the white blackbird begins alchemizing his base exile into a golden estrangement. From being a fatally handicapped bird, he is determined to develop into a being of unimaginable excellence. Nor is he averse to broadcasting everywhere the news of his uniqueness.

It is at this point that Musset accelerates the transformation of an exceptional individual's alienation and distress into a reductio ad absurdum of the romantic ego. The hero's advertisements for himself, which are intended to astonish the universe, contain a large portion of self-glorifying hokum. Nor are his secret thoughts drenched in naïveté: "I simply must buy Alfieri's memoirs and Lord Byron's poems," this unusual bird reflects. "Such substantial fare will fill me with noble pride to supplement the arrogance with which I have been endowed by nature. I wish, if possible, to increase the prestige which I owe to my birth. Nature has made me a rare bird. I will make myself an enigma . . . .The entire world must learn of my existence. In my verses I shall of course bewail my loneliness, but in such a manner that even the happiest of birds will envy me."[17]

True to his vow, the white blackbird adopts a policy of self-promotional hoopla, while at the same time mining rich veins of literary pathos. With his first poetic work, whose subject, in accordance with romantic fashion, is himself, he challenges all former masterpieces. The response of romantic Europe to the white blackbird's outpourings is overwhelming. Thus encouraged, the white blackbird pours out a formidable spate of poetic works that successfully beat back despair. After a while, however, his solitary triumph begins to feel inadequate. His fame, he realizes, must remain blighted so long as there is no one with whom he can share the secrets of his troubled soul and the vagaries of his creative life. Fortunately, or so it seems, the winged hero is rescued from isolation by a female white blackbird, who flies from London to Paris to join him in his meteoric career. The two birds share romantic enthrallments and produce immortal pages. (While he exudes epics, she knits novels – very much like George Sand.)

The hero's bliss is short-lived, however. Sobbing over one of Madame's literary effusions, the white blackbird happens to shed some tears on his wife's skin. The stain they cause reveals a far greater stain. Our hero discovers with shame and bitterness that his consort, who has always been peculiarly inaccessible in making her toilette, has duped him. She is in reality a blackbird who has been cunningly applying paste and flour to deceive him. The white blackbird's disillusion is ineffaceable. How heartless the world is, after all, he concludes, and how fruitless his poetic mission. (These are not immaculately logical deductions; but then, scrupulous logic is no match for romantic despair.) Like Molière's Alceste, Musset's little hero flees a merciless world.

But as cruel confirmation of the romantic poet's fatality of solitude and sorrow crushes the white blackbird's spirit, Musset's mock-sympathy loses much of its satiric edge. Musset has been extravagantly, if wittily, deriding the genesis and attributes of romantic (that is self-inflationary, exhibitionistic) "genius." Now, however, his submerged romanticism re-asserts itself, though in muted form. This (qualified) revitalization occurs when the errant white blackbird encounters a rapturously vocal nightingale. Once before, during his apprenticeship in misery, he had observed that this very nightingale was the idol of all the other birds. In a deeply self-pitying mood, the white blackbird now congratulates the nightingale on his unfailing harmonious happiness; he even assures him, with up-to-date (and somewhat jarring) comic allusiveness, that Rubini and Rossini are very small beer compared to him.

The nightingale protests that he has not been banally programmed to utter joy. Though he seems to sing with invincible radiance, he is actually translating into song an endless agony engendered by love for a heedless rose, who is quite capable of prostituting herself for a beetle or a bee. The nightingale's utterance derives from the parables of the romantic menagerie (though one romantic's nightingale, to be sure, may not resemble another's) – a menagerie which Musset himself helped to populate. Like the self-destroying yet life-nourishing pelican or the diseased yet pearl-bearing oyster, the melodiously suffering nightingale makes of distress a source of inspiration (in accordance with the Muse's recommendation in "Nuit de mai"). The pathos of the nightingale is rendered somewhat impure, however, for he adds the disconcerting detail that his own wife happens to bore him. The implicit romantic homage to melancholy and sorrow as goads to creative achievement is thereby injured, but not irrecoverably.

Even in reduced circumstances, the romantic temper manages to survive the impact of Musset's subversive comedy. One the whole, "The White Blackbird" is a charmingly sly auscultation of the narcissistic romantic heart and the swollen romantic head. (For Musset himself, the tale is in part a retrospective exercise in self-mockery.) Yet the message with which the tale ends, however comically nibbled at, issues from an unmistakably romantic vortex of art, suffering, and alienation. Musset may relinquish his delicate burlesque of romanticism only at the last moment, and even then not completely. Nevertheless, the dual resonance of that final moment uncovers a well camouflaged romantic-ironic ambivalence.

3.

The amusingly anguished complications of love in the life of Musset's white blackbird might have served, had chronology permitted, as a charming footnote in Stendhal's study of *Love* (1822). But Stendhal's discourse provides enough charms of its own as he examines a variety of amorous beliefs and experiences. His perspective would have gratified both Don Quixote and Machiavelli.[18] The former would have appreciated Stendhal's focus on impulse and the magic of idealism; the latter would have approved of Stendhal's emphasis on cool detachment and realistic stratagems. Officially, Stendhal sanctions only objectivity as his guide. In his "First Attempt at a Preface," he avows that his work is "an exact and scientific description of a brand of madness very rare in France" (a country where fear of ridicule is endemic) and that it has been composed with a "scientific austerity of style."[19]

Stendhal's "scientific" method, presumably aping clinical lucidity, distinguishes between passion-love (which the French would find ridiculously romantic) and several non-romantic kinds, such as physical love and vanity-love, though these are not hermetically sealed off from one another. It becomes clear rather soon that Stendhal, while appearing to categorize passion-love antiseptically as a malady, an insanity of the emotions, or an affliction of the soul, pays extensive tribute to this disease (or madness). For passion-love – here Don Quixote shoves Machiavelli aside – involves, despite certain intermediate periods of pain, the unsurpassable pleasure of transfiguring the beloved. This idealizing process Stendhal somewhat riskily terms "crystallization." It is based on a fascinating, if not utterly reliable, analogy: just as a bare branch tossed into an abandoned salt mine near Salzburg will in time become coated with magic crystals, so the lover's enhanced imaginative powers will create in the beloved certain graces, beauties, and perfections which (at least to the external eye) she does not intrinsically possess. This does not mean that the beloved is initially a blank. It is implied by Stendhal that the imagination of the lover has much more to work with than the actual equivalent of a bare branch, that is, a physically and spiritually commonplace creature. The lover's creation is a gratifying act of discovery, not a tumble into misapprehension and delusion.

Stendhal's pseudo-chemical analogy makes much of certain metamorphic agencies that generate passion-love – especially admiration, hope, jealousy, doubt, and fear. Yet Stendhal's laboratory analysis of these passion-producing elements, so far from derogating the irrationality of the emotion he seeks to explicate, only underscores the (scarcely painless) miracle of romantic love, which is forever denied to the mediocrities of this world. In short, Stendhalian "science" paradoxically validates romantic illusion. Of course Stendhal knows how fallible his presumptive objectivity can be. In the exceedingly brief ninth chapter of Book One, he acknowledges that the success of his expository dryness depends on how well he can tranquilize his heart; perhaps, he concedes, the truths he is attempting to pin down with cool clarity are no more than lyrical sighs (57).

In a late chapter entitled "Werther and Don Juan," Stendhal presents what appears to be a climactic argument on behalf of romantic love. He places himself definitively (or so it seems) on the side of Goethe's Werther, the amorous idealist whose opponent is the cynical seducer, Mozart's Don Juan. The latter, to be sure, has an edge over Werther in several respects: he is daring, resourceful, and witty; he is illustrious on the battlefields of love and war; and, since this Spaniard is never prey to the kind of poetic sensibility that builds castles in Spain, he is extremely entertaining in the drawing rooms of sophisticated society. A Werther type, on the other hand, is at a loss in polite circles, which often regard him as unintelligibly befogged by his emotionalism. He is therefore apt to become the butt of society's mockery. Yet it is Wertherian love, Stendhal insists, whose agitations and anxieties – these hinge on the lover's capacity for suffering constant unrequitedness – open the soul to the influence of art, beauty, and the sublimity of Nature. It is Wertherian love that enriches every moment of consciousness and multiplies the possibilities of joy. Nor does Wertherian love ever diminish or turn sour or cease nourishing the imagination: "Everything is new, alive, and pulsating with the most passionate interest" (209).

Don Juan's predatory sexuality, in contrast, murders love and assassinates joy. "Instead of losing himself in the bewitching reveries of crystallization his attitude is that of a general to the success of his tactics" (206). Worse, Don Juan's sensuality and heartless inconstancy doom him in the end to satiety, boredom, and disgust. Werther, however, is never disabled by jadedness or ennui. Granted, unconsummated passion may breed despair and may even, abetted by subsidiary social frustrations, lead to suicide. Yet defeat and despair may produce an ecstasy that transcends mundane happiness.

So far as ethical issues are concerned, moreover, there is no contest. Werther is a virtuous man, like Rousseau's Saint-Preux (though the latter strikes Stendhal at times as somewhat dull). Don Juan, on the other hand, is a virtuoso of vanity and immorality. (Stendhal never suggests that Goethe might have conceived of Werther, whose unabating but impossible love helps precipitate his self-destruction, as a figure it would be madness to emulate.)

The case against Don Juan is not closed, however, inasmuch as erotic exploits supply more than a minimal interest in *Love*. Indeed the narratives of aborted or successful love affairs in Stendhal's study depend on stratagems that are by no means always in support of transcendent passion. One may deduce therefore that Stendhal would not quickly jettison, even if he did not officially endorse, a composite ideal: a Don Juanesque Wertherism, a happy brew of sensibility and worldliness, of pure emotion and martial opportunism, of idealizing love and energetic, tactical amorousness. Romantic passion, that is to say, would remain pure; but its poetry would be clinched by erotic conquest. In *The Life of Henry Brulard,* Stendhal tells us that as a youngster in Paris he believed himself to be "a mixture of Saint-Preux and Valmont,"[20] a mixture which is loosely convertible into a blend of Werther and Don Juan.

This belief cannot be discounted as an adolescent fantasy. It is the mature Stendhal who favors a coalescence of the heavenly and the lighthearted in love and who in *Brulard* maintains that "a man ought to be a passionate lover, and at the same time he ought to carry life and animation into every company where he happens to be." Indeed the passionate lover ought to be a carrier of "universal gaiety" (309). (Nor is gaiety, in Stendhal's view, of less importance in the making of literature.) "Life," "animation," and "gaiety" are obviously not the exclusive property of Don Juan, but they are surely not fostered by the increasingly doleful Werther. Stendhal reports that his own lively romantic propensities "extended to love, to courage, to everything" (373). It is likely that Werther achieves compensatory prominence in "Werther and Don Juan" precisely because Stendhal was more familiar with French erotic pursuit than with German soulfulness.

Victor Brombert believes that in *Love* "it is the tender and musical element that predominates" and that Stendhalian analysis ultimately serves not only as a counterpoint to, but "as a protective facade" for, the Rousseauistic, incommunicable reveries of love.[21] Yet the social self stakes out an impressive position in *Love,* so much so that a Don Juanesque-Wertherian amalgam becomes inevitable. Though Stendhal may be indirectly rebuking his own Don Juanesque ventures, he does not consign Don Juan to paralysis and perdition without some regret. He even wonders whether Don Juan cannot be reclaimed. Instead of running the risk of becoming old and sated, perhaps he can be reformed in time by his own intelligence and the help of a sensitive woman. Stendhal also suggests, but only in passing, that romantic lovers often lose their wits through excessive sensibility. This suggestion is rather dangerous, since one might go on to discern in Wertherian love a self-undermining neurosis desperately in need of a saving component of Don Juanesque scepticism.

The romantic-ironic interplay of Wertherism and Don Juanism – these are terms that require a loose fit – shapes some of Stendhal's most brilliant comic scenes in *Red and Black*[22] (Robert M. Adams' translation of the title). These involve the two great love affairs of Stendhal's hero, Julien Sorel, the first with Mme de Rênal, who is immune to romantic irony, the second with Mathilde de la Mole, who might have become an authority on the subject. Julien often stumbles ludicrously, or is obliged to maneuver acrobatically, between lyrical emotions and dispassionate decisions and devices. But Wertherism and Don Juanism are part of a larger duality in Julien that encompasses romantic energy, spontaneity, and aspiration, on the one hand, and counter-romantic lucidity, restraint, and cunning, on the other. Thus there reigns in Julien a psychic civil war between the heart's sincerity and the mind's swift retractions. These opposing forces produce romantic ironies that are far more intricate than Byron's in *Don Juan.*

There are six quotations from *Don Juan* (one is repeated) among the chapter epigraphs in Stendhal's novel. Whether genuine or bogus, these epigraphs are often nimbly perceptive; nor do they lack a strong element of cynical mockery. Yet none of Stendhal's quotations from *Don Juan* (most are from Canto I, the others from Canto XIII)[23] illustrate Byron's romantic irony. There are no selections, for example, from Cantos III and IV, which consistently reveal Byron's contradictory attitudes toward the love of Juan and Haidée. Such selections might have served as a parallel of sorts to the alternately frenetic and frigid relationship between Julien and Mathilde de la Mole. (The love between Julien and Mme de Rênal may be primary, but it is much less strenuous.)

Romantic irony prevails in both of Julien's love affairs, though hardly in the same manner. Romantic irony in Julien's love affair with Mme de Rênal is conveyed by Julien's intermixture of innocence and experience – and by Stendhal's commentary. Though Stendhal does not project himself into his text in quite the jouncing manner of Byron in *Don Juan,* there are a good many fragmentary and conflicting editorial insertions in the novel. Toward his protagonist, who is a student of deceit but who is exalted in temper and fired by indignation (only seldom histrionically) at social injustice, Stendhal may be affectionate, avuncular, teasing, severe, caustic, or ambiguously ironic. His interventions in the text are therefore hermeneutically tricky, especially since Stendhal habitually "denigrates his hero at the very moment he enjoys him most," that is, when he is "at his romantic best."[24]

The romantic irony in Julien's love affair in Paris with Mme de Rênal's apparent antitype, Mathilde de la Mole, derives not only from Julien's dualistic attitudes but, even more impressively, from Mathilde's. Moreover, the conflict between true feeling and pure tactics in Julien and the collision between exalted passion and its ferocious repudiation in Mathilde provide astonishing moments of romantic-ironic ecstasy and iciness that surpass those generated in the first half of the novel.

Stendhal, who notes in *Brulard* that fidelity in love, like heroism, has been leached out of Parisian society, consistently, if somewhat implausibly and in defiance of his more positive verdicts, suggests that the romantic quality in the relationship between Julien and Mathilde is mostly a delusion, a bad dream, a pathological irritation of the nerves. In this view, the Julien-Mme de Rênal bond is absolutely genuine, whereas the Julien-Mathilde connection is basically fictive. F. W. J. Hemmings, for example, claims that Mathilde, a "secondary heroine, as is made clear by Julien's rejection of her at the end" may "mutatis mutandis . . . be considered the Molly Seagrim to Julien's Tom Jones."[25] But this is hardly the case. The "secondary" love affair between Julien and Mathilde creates desires and tensions, thirsts and humiliations, rhapsodies and hurts that make Julien's love affair with Mme de Rênal seem almost reasonably restrained. (This is not to deny that Julien's lost edenic love for Mme de Rênal becomes his principal salve at the end of the novel, and then his very salvation.)

Between the moment when Mathilde, dying of elegant ennui while wittily assassinating the morally conformist, intellectually feeble members of the aristocracy, realizes that Julien "wasn't born on his knees"[26] and the moment when she chooses this rebellious young man as a lover, there lies a tortuously troubling but also hilarious history of attraction and repulsion. After avowals of love have presumably solidified it, that history becomes even more feverish in its passion and more fantastic in its comedy. So recurrently, remarkably ambivalent is this love affair that Stendhal can scarcely enhance his language sufficiently to make it tally with new heights of passion and new (often comic) shocks of jeopardy. Thus the perception that reconciliation between Julien and Mathilde (after periods of violently real or occasionally histrionic hostility) elicits an even more intense resurgence of romantic feeling is underscored by Stendhal through a single stylistic device: a slight adverbial refashioning of the observation that Julien (less often, Mathilde) has finally, genuinely, unshakably, definitively, unquestionably, irrevocably fallen in love. However altered the circumstances, the language of miraculously renewed passion remains much the same. (Of course, Stendhal's energetic but rather monotonous reiterations of virtually identical phrases may also be taken to signify a refusal of artful embellishment.)

The process of Stendhalian crystallization, whatever the language in which it is described, and however desperately it is disguised by the lovers – Julien learns how to hide volcanic emotions beneath an agonizingly feigned indifference, while Mathilde is capable of unleashing disdainful rebukes even when her heart is in a turmoil of adoration – is so potently stimulated by bouts of jealousy, doubt, fear, hope, and adoration that it seems insusceptible of ever being minimized. Yet Stendhal repeatedly endeavors to dissuade the reader from believing this.

He wastes little time in announcing that intellect so clearly rules in Mathilde's psyche that she is capable of inducing in herself only "love-in-the-head." In spite of this reiterated assessment, however, Stendhal often indicates that fiery feeling, which in Mathilde's social circle has become an outmoded if not disgraceful phenomenon, lies simmering beneath her aristocratic skin. Indeed her reflections on Julien's insurrectionary animus at the ball in the Hôtel de Retz are testimony to a nobility of spirit (somewhat skewed toward perversity) that is likely to engender inflammatory emotions.

Nor is Mathilde immune to Stendhalian crystallization, which affects her as profoundly, if more slowly and more erratically, as it does Julien. Crystallization, moreover, is not divorced, either for Mathilde or for Julien, from lucidity. Julien knows how morbid, how cruelly mercurial, even how mad Mathilde can be, just as Mathilde is painfully, horribly aware of Julien's familial and social shortcomings. Yet their lucidity cannot conquer raging jealousy, humiliation, and torment; nor can it question repeated surges of hope, admiration, and dizzying enthrallment.

Because Mathilde refuses to play the role of dependent, let alone victim, in the contest of power that underlies social and personal relations, Mathilde's attraction to Julien is expressed chiefly through hostility; crystallization takes on the lineaments of a savage conflict, both internal and external. A good many pages of *Red and Black* are concerned with the merciless game of tit-for-tat that Mathilde plays with Julien, a game wherein superiority in maintaining an insolent, freezing remoteness is a major means of victory, as effective as ruthless aggressiveness. Nor does Julien's fascination with her elicit a scrap of maidenly gratitude. In Mathilde's eyes, Julien's homage translates into an advertisement of servility. If he wears his heart on his sleeve for this beautiful, brilliant, haughty woman, he will suffer only contemptuous dismissal.

Eventually Julien and Mathilde become friendly and even quietly intimate. Forgetting "to play the depressing part of a resentful plebeian" (245) whose poverty obliges him to forge a career based on mendacity, Julien shows himself to be genuinely sensitive and frank, just as the lofty, apparently demonic Mathilde reveals herself to be gentle, candid, enthusiastic, and intellectually delightful. Nevertheless, their friendship is an "armed truce" (246) which has to be daily re-established.

When Mathilde senses that she is in love with Julien, she does not shrink prudentially from a "grand passion" (252) – no other kind could possibly be tolerated – which requires the transcendence of obstacles, impediments, dangers. Mathilde's passion is intellectually reinforced, not cerebrally induced, by literary images of love. In one respect, it is true, she cannot conceal imitativeness, though it is of a chivalrous nature: the most dynamic irrationality that licenses her vision of a grand passion derives from her ancestor, Boniface de la Mole, and his beloved Marguerite de Navarre. Mathilde feels bound to emulate the lovely Marguerite, whom the epigraph to Book 2, ch. 12 describes as possessed of a "need to gamble" with "the most precious thing she owns: her reputation" (252). Mathilde's own need to gamble extravagantly with her life may be locked into a neurotic fabulation, but it is not reducible to insincerity, or to a facile rejection of dullness.

If this last comment is valid, the narrator's insistence that Mlle de la Mole "decides" that she loves Julien – on a single page of the novel, Stendhal uses the word "decision" three times, as in "every day she congratulated herself on her decision to indulge in a grand passion" (255) – has to be interpreted with a good deal of semantic flexibility. It may even be argued that Stendhal emphasizes mental deliberation precisely because Mathilde's emotionalism is so tindery. But even if we grant that Mathilde's love is generated to some extent by an appetite for the dramatic – elements of egoism, calculation, and vanity infect Mathilde's conduct as well as Julien's – in the course of time that appetite is transformed into a supremely authentic passion.

What follows Mathilde's confession of love in Stendhal's text is a one-hundred-page propagation of romantic irony, wherein lyrical soaring and frosty revulsion vertiginously, unremittingly – and comically – contend with each other. The heady affirmations and comic countermandings of romantic irony come particularly into play when Julien and Mathilde finally convert the literary paradigm of passionate love into a reality – or, rather, a reality that is no longer repressed. But ineffable peace is not available, for Mathilde's pride continues to make for harrowing difficulties. Racked by the notion that she has given herself to a master with a potentially vindictive hold over her, she blisters Julien with a venom that soon transforms them once more into mutual enemies. Were it not for the antic effect produced by virtually unarrested oscillations between emotional extremes, one might cite comparable love-hate intensities in Strindberg or D. H. Lawrence.[27]

Consider the astonishing shifts of feeling exhibited by Mathilde and Julien when, finding it impossible to achieve some pacifying degree of wisdom from their turmoil, they assent to a "declaration of perpetual hatred" (280). Immediately afterwards, Julien discovers that his passion for Mlle de la Mole is as powerful as ever. Faced by the threat of madness, Julien commits the worst of diplomatic mistakes: he timidly solicits a renewal of Mathilde's love. Such folly can have only one result: Mathilde's enmity explodes into outrage, for she can interpret Julien's "sentimental" entreaty only as proof of contemptible weakness. " 'I'm horrified at having given myself to the first comer,' said Mathilde, weeping with fury at herself." Julien, whom the slightest suggestion of insult has always galvanized into a heroic response (for the most part, such responses are variously, and fortunately, balked), snatches an old sword hanging on the wall and appears poised to transform into physical strife what has up to now been a psychological duel. But though "he would have been the happiest of men had it been in his power to kill her" (281), he cannot, after all, simply extinguish the Marquis de la Mole's daughter; and so he quietly, though not without some trouble, puts the sword back in its sheath, wondering all the while whether Mathilde will now mock the melodramatic commotion she has witnessed. In fact, Mathilde is enchanted by this lightning restoration of sixteenth-century manliness and considers it matter for rejoicing that she has been on the verge of being killed by her lover. But even this ecstasy does not forestall subsequent outbreaks of unnerving antagonism.

Though there are many deeply moving passages in the novel which convince us that a permanent sealing of the bond between the two lovers is inevitable, the comedy of reciprocal misconceptions and seemingly ineradicable ambivalence perversely prospers. When, for example, Mathilde, after demonstrating murderous scorn for Julien's emotional fragility, reinterprets his confession of love as a natural expression of passion and respect on the part of a great future revolutionary (with whom, moreover, she will be able to play an original, distinguished role), she recants her hostility so completely that, at the Italian opera, her reveries about Julien lead to "the keenest transports of passion." The only audible irony in this episode belongs to the narrative voice, which is quick to emphasize once more the (apparently) cerebral quality of Mathilde's emotions: "Thanks to her love of music, she was for that one evening what Mme de Rênal always was when she thought of Julien. Doubtless the love born in the head is more witty than real love, but it experiences only instants of enthusiasm; it knows itself too well; it is built only on a frame of thought" (288).

This analysis is far from accurate. Mathilde's "frame of thought" is usually shattered by devastating emotional pressures which are neither headed off by acute self-knowledge nor governed by a regard for rational advantages or a fear of adverse social consequences. Thus the day after the opera, the comedy of tumultuous ambivalence reasserts itself. Mathilde repudiates her passion for Julien, which she now views as insane. This does not look like evidence of a cool mentality, a keen self-judgment, or a constitutional stability of attitude. Mathilde's bewildering, havoc-wreaking duality is revealed once again when Julien, after contemplating and then renouncing suicide, launches his second heroic climb into Mathilde's room to give her one last kiss. His daring is rewarded by Mathilde's penitential, irrevocable surrender (presumably genuine this time). She prostrates herself before the man she now welcomes as master, and later recklessly tosses a (disfiguring) lock of hair to Julien as a symbol of her eternal obedience.

Eternal obedience lasts less than forty-eight hours. In a blatant reversal of attitude, but with a familiar, if accelerated, wildness of inconsistency that keeps nourishing the reader's sense of manic comedy, Mathilde reproaches herself for having genuflected before a man she now deems insufficiently unordinary. Once again, she absolutely rejects Julien; once again, she conclusively humiliates him. She spews out such clever scorn that Julien's often weakened self-esteem is crushed. Such scorn does not, however, destroy his idealizing passion. On the contrary: the "frightful doubt, amazement, and despair" (294) which his love has been repeatedly subjected to function as potent agents of hyper-crystallization, to the point where thinking of "something unrelated to Mlle de le Mole was beyond his powers" (316).

To offset his maddening, seemingly futile obsession with Mathilde, the distressed Julien accepts Prince Korasoff's advice, which is in fact a regurgitation of French amorous savoir-faire. In the Prince's scheme, Julien is to re-attract Mathilde by courting another woman – the beautiful but notoriously prudish, pseudo-religious Mme de Fervaques will be chosen for this purpose – with whom he will engage in totally dispassionate conversation but to whom he will write a stream of hotly passionate love letters copied from a set of fifty-three letters written by a Russian to an English Quakeress. Julien's feverish romantic adulation of Mathilde is to be fulfilled only by paradoxically resorting to a blend of Don Juanesque artifice and Machiavellian deceit.

This strategy, more obviously than Julien's previous suppressions of vital emotion, makes for a merger of romantic irony and circumstantial irony; that is, appearance glaringly clashes with reality in a sustained comedy of ambivalence. Julien must take care to avoid the slightest hint of wounded devotion; he must treat Mathilde with chilly, unrelenting indifference. Unobserved and alone, Julien tearfully fosters his Wertherian feelings. In society, however, this otherwise silent sufferer spends hour after hour mechanically simulating fascinated interest in the starchily patrician ideas of Mme de Fervaques. He thus ruins Mathilde's expectation of seeing a grieving lover. He also astonishes her with the deftness of his political playacting. (She is, after all, familiar with his subversive mentality.) When curiosity induces Mathilde, no longer intransigently armed with snubs and vituperations, to draw nearer to

Julien and Mme de Fervaques, Julien manages to transform his inner apathy into incomprehensibly animated talk.

As it turns out, Mme de Fervaques fails to show contempt for the boringly preposterous letters Julien methodically prepares for her. She appears to be immune not only to amorous epistolary nonsense but to grotesque copying errors. Her impercipience invigorates Julien's sense of the ludicrous; but the psychic relief granted by an occasional bit of fun is no more than a minor grace. In the long run, Julien feels spiritually drained by his protracted stage performance.

Yet the epistolary scheme is successful. Though she is at first only intellectually impressed by Julien's clever duplicities, Mathilde ends by virtually collapsing in Julien's arms, not without bitterly protesting what she claims has been his appalling neglect of her. Julien is of course overjoyed, but he has learned enough about Mathilde's personality to realize that his rapture must be instantly immobilized. Even a trivial token of his passion-love, which, according to the narrator, has been reaching ever greater depths and generating ever more burning intensities, might wreck everything by reviving Mathilde's disdain. Her obvious grief, her supplicant tone, her avowal that she can no longer live without Julien's love – all must be frigidly, Napoleonically disregarded. It is clear to Julien that candor would be the death of consummation, that only a desperate politics of camouflage can preserve his romantic passion.

But in fact Julien has misperceived the situation. When, in an unguarded moment, he communicates his Wertherian bliss to Mathilde and then sees love (or so he imagines) quickly vanishing from her eyes, Julien feels instantly, maliciously compelled to inform her that he has just lied to her, that he is virtually addicted to telling lies. The truth, though he has not grasped it, is that his inflamed imagination has finally been liberated, that he no longer has to play lunatic games of self-extinction. Mathilde, her ambivalence purged, is completely won over. The oscillations of romantic irony, anomalously associated with a master-servant complex, have definitively ceased, though not without an expectable reminder from the narrator that Mathilde's "arid soul felt everything in passion that is possible for a person raised amid the excess of civilization which Paris admires" (359). But there is little that is spuriously Parisian in Mathilde's self-conquest. Nevermore will she scorn Julien, nevermore renounce him, nevermore cease dedicating herself to him. "For the first time," the narrator announces, as though he had not already availed himself, on numerous occasions, of precisely the same language, "Mathilde was in love" (346). This tigress will no longer need taming while being secretly worshipped as a goddess.

But betrayal by a misguided Mme de Rênal falls like a thunderbolt. And once the "Spanish" commandment that requires Julien to retaliate against the staining of his honor (this is an overly simple account) lands him in prison, a sea-change takes place in Julien's psyche. In non-incriminating circumstances, Julien would presumably feel too young, too vital, too driven by irrepressible energy and the frenzy of aspiration to settle for everlasting tranquility. But complexities of the heart evaporate in his imprisonment, where Julien yearns only for the charms of his purer impure days with Mme de Rênal.

Having spent, before his death, some redemptively idyllic moments with Mme de Rênal, he tells her with heartfelt sincerity yet questionable accuracy, "You must know that I've always loved you, I never loved anyone but you" (394). Stendhal confirms Julien's state of heart with the kind of phrasing he has repeatedly deployed in referring to Julien's love for Mathilde de la Mole: "Never had he been so delirious with love" (394). The narrator's skill, moreover – this too has often been the case in his presentation of Julien's love for Mathilde – "cannot describe the excess and madness of Julien's devotion" (404), without resorting, that is, to meretricious verbal enhancements. What is plain is that Julien's love will no longer be subject to comic fluctuations of Wertherism and Don Juanism (or Wertherism and histrionic pretense), for romantic irony has now been wholly superseded.

It is by no means a critical commonplace that romantic irony is a paramount force in *Red and Black,* either in explicit or implicit authorial leanings toward both romantic sensibility and comically disengaged scepticism. Dominick La Capra believes that there are "two interacting modes of irony" in the novel, "one a rather stable or 'monological' form in which the narrator masters or dominates the story and the other involving the narrator in 'dialogically participatory' and self-questioning movements that contest the status of novelistic narration itself as an adequate answer to the problems it treats."[28] The first ironic mode is Boothian (traditional). The second is indebted to Bakhtinian and deconstructive criticism. Whether, or how, these ironic modes may be related to comedy is not La Capra's concern, though obviously Boothian stable irony, a Bakhtinian multi-voiced structure, and deconstructive self-contestation are all capable of feeding comic impulses.

Victor Brombert, accentuating Stendhal's "subversive delight" in springing "ironic disclaimers" and in "denigrating his hero at the very moment he enjoys him most,"[29] sees Stendhal's interventional irony as a protean, teasing ambiguity; at its sharpest, it becomes a sly dialectical perspective whose mockery paradoxically protects enthusiasm and integrity. (This is something of a halfway approach to romantic irony.) Robert M. Adams, discussing Stendhal's psychological instability, comes closer to the idea of European romantic irony: "His gifts for irony and sentiment," Adams remarks, "were equal . . . . Stendhal was not really an ironist with an overlay of sentiment, nor a sentimentalist lurking beneath a surface of irony; he was not even committed consistently to the opposition of these two principles."[30] Though a more or less even balance of irony and sentiment (if "sentiment" is construed upwards as "romantic sensibility") is essential to romantic irony, along with the impact of comedy, Adams's comment on the inconsistency of such opposition in Stendhal may serve as a reminder that romantic ironists are not predictably pendular, that they do not always choose to match idealizing fervor with a de-idealizing critique, or confront magnificent passion with the laughter of dispassion.

Stendhal's fluid responsiveness to experience elicits this further observation by Adams: "He sees a situation as sublime, he sees it as ridiculous; the sublime may override the irony, the irony undercut the sublime, or the contrast may remain, troublesome and unresolved."[31] This observation is accurate enough, though a change in diction would help. The sublime and the ridiculous, as has been pointed out more than once in this study, are terms that correspond poorly to the ambivalence of romantic irony. And though unresolved contrasts are indeed characteristic of romantic irony, they lose much of their troublesomeness in the pleasures of comedy.

If Adams does not mention romantic irony as such, perhaps that is because at the time his book on Stendhal was published (1959), romantic irony had not yet raised much of a critical fuss. In Anglo-American criticism (before the apotheosis of Friedrich Schlegel), romantic irony was generally held to be simply a conflation of conflicting moods, notably exemplified in Byron's *Don Juan,* where pathos was often checked by mockery. This duality, though provocative, was not viewed as especially noble. Satire valuably derogated the warped aspects of society's precious idols and esteemed values. Romantic irony, on the other hand, seemed to express an erratic, derisive, near-pathological self-division. Thus Raymond Giraud, apparently having in mind strong affinities between Byron and Stendhal, once described the latter as a romantic ironist who "laughs bitterly at what he respects most."[32] Yet the bitter laughter Giraud ascribes to Stendhal (whose energy and urbanity sufficiently muffle such bitterness) would better suit a romantic like Lermontov, as we shall see in the next chapter.

Chapter 6

Laughter and Laceration: Lermontov, Pushkin, Dostoevsky

1.

In the chapter devoted to "Pushkin, Lermontov, Gogol: Ironic Modes in Russian Romanticism" in *Romantic Irony* (1988), Roman S. Struc concludes that in his three romantics "irony appears as something incidental and gratuitous and does not appear to constitute an integral part of their poetics."[1] The irony Struc virtually dismisses signifies, it would seem, not only Schlegelian self-critical attitudes, Schlegelian hovering over the world's contradictions, and the Tieckian destruction of artistic illusion but also the Byronic practice of playful, irreverent intrusiveness, as well as Byronic combinations of empathy and detachment, sublimity and triviality, gravity and mockery.

The "incidental and gratuitous" role of irony may not, however, be as thin as Struc suggests, for he concedes that "in Pushkin's lyrical poetry dealing with the poet's role, and in his narrative poetry and prose, one can legitimately speak of Romantic irony, at times in the sense formulated by Schlegel" (247). Nevertheless, at the very end of his essay, Struc concludes (once more) that "the Russian literature of the Romantic age does not seem to include irony as one of the firm constituents of its poetics" (249). There are no Byrons or Heines, he adds, among the Russian romantics. Thus whatever irony Lermontov, for example, deploys, according to Struc, is of the "tragic" sort; that is to say, it is permeated by "bitterness, sarcasm, and a generous dose of *Weltschmerz*" (249). It does not resemble the "lightness and playfulness" typical of Pushkin (247).

It may be claimed, however, that both Lermontov and Pushkin, in their respective masterworks, are European romantic ironists. It is true that Lermontov's *A Hero of Our Time* (1840) is preceded by, and is to some extent dependent on, Pushkin's *Eugene Onegin* (1833); but because Lermontov's novel presents a simpler illustration of romantic-ironic dichotomies, let us look at this work first.

Pechorin, the protagonist of *A Hero of Our Time,* views himself mainly as a destructive victim of ennui, long fed up with worldly pleasures, fashionable love affairs, and profitless studies. Exaltation is not his psychic style. Certainly Pechorin feels only contempt for the banality of magical emotions. Nevertheless, this seemingly impenitent cynic cannot wholly disengage himself from the wounded romanticism of a failed idealist. Pechorin apparently drifts through life without much hope; yet he retains memories of certain transcendent experiences and at times feels possessed of an "insatiable heart."[2] However smothered by disillusionment and boredom Pechorin may be, it is impossible for him to claim unconditional fealty to a disenchanted, antiromantic view of the world. (The anonymous narrator of some of the shorter tales in *A Hero of Our Time* – he happens to be a fledgling writer – himself betrays a romantic streak, for example, when he contemplates the mountains of the Caucasus; but his romanticism is properly chastened by an air of worldliness.)

Pechorin can still find the anticipation of romantic adventure irresistible, though not if it begins to resemble an endurance test. In "Bela," the first section of *A Hero of Our Time* (but not chronologically a prelude to the rest of the novel), Pechorin looks forward to the thrill of danger in facing hostile tribes in the Caucasus; and in the midst of that danger, he demonstrates incredible courage. Yet this kind of thrill quickly dissipates. Even Pechorin's love for the beautiful Circassian girl Bela, whom he had at first regarded as an angel sent by "compassionate fate" (40) to purge him of his weariness and near-hopelessness, soon palls. If need be, he is ready to die for Bela, so unabatingly fierce is his pride, and so daunting is his impulsive heroism. Elsewhere in the novel, however, Pechorin is prompt to ridicule a romantic taste for the heroic; indeed he is an adept at scorning anything that smacks of romantic excess. Yet the romanticism he punishes by his laughter is never utterly defeated in his inner being. Even the ultimate remedy Pechorin conceives of to nullify his apathy – exotic travel, enhanced by the possibility of death – is essentially a romantic resolution (and rather dubious as a cure).

By itself, "Bela" does not carry enough substance or attain sufficient perspective to point up the distinguishing marks of the romantic ironist in Pechorin. The tale's narrator, the simple, frank, kind-hearted Capt. Maksim Maksimitch, is astonished by Pechorin's contradictory traits, but he can describe only their external manifestations. Pechorin, this bluff officer observes, is both robust and fragile, heroic and withdrawn, hilariously loquacious and gloomily taciturn. But we do not understand why.

In "Princess Mary," a first-person tale which chronologically precedes "Bela" – it is the longest and psychologically the most intricate of the novel's five interrelated tales – the incompatible elements in Pechorin's temper are abundantly, if never entirely satisfactorily, disclosed. His primary insight into his own nature is based on the compulsions of contradiction. Certainly his response to others appears to be intensely and habitually oppositional, apparently in reaction to the fact that his "entire life has been nothing but a chain of sad and frustrating contradictions to heart or reason" (89). This elucidation of psychic injury – of feelings crippled by a pedestrian world's misprision of his gifted nature – is made for the benefit of Princess Mary. But Pechorin's depiction of himself, to some extent at least, is a pose, adopted as part of a time-killing jest directed against a transparently naive princess and her nauseatingly pseudo-romantic worshiper Grushnitski. Yet even if this account of his Byronic alienation is theatrically touched up, Pechorin's self-dissection is not basically false. He may seem to be mockingly, invincibly nonchalant; but he is at times almost as emotionally vulnerable as Julien Sorel.

Pechorin's hidden romantic sensibility is capable of being swiftly revitalized. The unexpected arrival of his former lover Vera at Pyatigorski, the spa where Princess Mary, Pechorin, and many others are idling away their time, elicits a remarkable confession from a supposed master of disillusion and indifference: "there is no man in the world over whom the past gains such power as it does over me. Every reminder of a past sorrow or joy painfully strikes my soul and extracts from it the same old sounds . . . . I am stupidly made, and I forget nothing . . . nothing!" (97) If this is true, beneath Pechorin's practice of detachment and professions of boredom there are still embers of a romantic temper that may be stirred, perhaps violently, into flame. Nevertheless, in his social relations Pechorin remains as contemptuous of obtrusive emotionality as he is of factitious civility. He is often dismissive and even predatory in his lack of social generosity. And not the least of his disconcerting traits is a flair for demonic comedy. Yet evidence of ambivalence is incontrovertible. As Nabokov points out in his introduction to the novel, Pechorin's head may be cool, but his blood is hot. Pechorin can be tender as well as brutal; he can exemplify "romantic dash" as well as cynicism (xvii).

Pechorin's reunion with Vera – she is "the only woman on earth he could not bear to deceive" and her memory is "inviolable" (106) – precipitates a recovery of unattenuated romantic energy: "at last our lips came close together and merged in an ardent rapturous kiss." After this triumph of lyrical emotion, a conversation ensues which makes "no sense on paper, which cannot be repeated and which one cannot even retain in one's mind: the meaning of sounds replaces and enhances the meaning of words, as in the Italian opera" (104). This summary statement cannot easily be disambiguated. Pechorin may be intent on emphasizing the indistinct, unformulatable surge of poetic rapture; but he may also be insinuating (perhaps not wholly consciously) that romantic passion is a tumultuously opaque, operatic muddle.

At the end of "Princess Mary," Vera bids him farewell in a letter that unmistakably, if reluctantly, reveals her reverence for his extraordinary qualities of pride, mystery, and power. Acknowledging Pechorin's profound unhappiness, Vera claims, with some authority, that he is fascinated by evil yet hungers for love; she adds that she herself has known little bliss. Having sacrificed everything for Pechorin, she is left with only one hope: to be at least remembered by him. The letter causes an emotional upheaval in Pechorin: "nothing can express my anxiety, my despair! Faced by the possibility of losing Vera forever, I felt she had become dearer to me than anything in the world – dearer than life, honor, happiness! God knows what strange, mad plans swarmed in my heart" (175).

Pechorin's immediate move is both commendable and thoroughly irrational: he gallops after her in so great a frenzy that he rides his horse to death. He then continues on foot until he collapses, exhausted not only by the strain of the chase but by the insomniac agitations of a mortal duel fought with Grushnitski only hours before the reception of Vera's letter. Pechorin, who has been accustomed to regarding himself as "hard and cold as iron" after buying his early idealism and emotional susceptibility, and who claims to be alive "only out of curiosity" (159), sinks to the ground and sobs his heart out. Yet not much later, the cool rationalist in Pechorin – the rationalist who defines infinite passion as merely the product of balked desire – repudiates the folly of his re-ignited romantic temper. His lunatic ride becomes a joke. He explains away his tears as perhaps due only "to upset nerves, to a sleepless night, to a couple of minutes spent facing the muzzle of a pistol, and to an empty stomach" (176). His mocking conclusion is that his hectic ride and long walk will make for some much needed sound sleep. Thus Pechorin succeeds in transmogrifying his desperate renewal of romantic fervor into a laughably cretinous, though healthful, diversion.

Until her letter of farewell reaches Pechorin and feverishly quickens his pulse, Vera has had a clearly diminishing, even minimal, role. It is Princess Mary Logovskoy who has almost completely supplanted Vera in Pechorin's thoughts. Pechorin is apparently able to sense intuitively when women will fall in love with him; and Princess Mary, who is beautiful, tender, sensitive, vivacious and proud (she also has a bit of youthful vanity and coquetry; and she has not entirely snuffed out an element of aristocratic presumption) betrays the right symptoms. The game Pechorin plays with her is marked by calculatedly cruel cat-and-mouse tactics which profoundly confuse her. The tales of his adventures make him a remarkable person in her eyes, but his temperament, unlike Othello's, has a certain disturbing, even forbidding quality. The Princess is shocked and alarmed, in particular, by Pechorin's laughter "at everything in the world, especially at feelings" (121). Yet feelings, together with passions and ideas, constitute a major theme in Pechorin's journal, whose pages might conceivably have been designed as a catch-all for cynical (and often comically oriented) ruminations. Pechorin regards passions as perturbations belonging exclusively to youth; the calm of maturity, in contrast, requires "the plenitude and depth of feelings and thoughts" (124). This sounds (conventionally) wise enough. The trouble is that the journal does not lend itself to consistency, for Pechorin also believes that the soul needs storms in order not to dry up. And Pechorin tends to be, more often than not, a seeker of storms, some of which he helps to engender.

Thus he sets in motion a major storm when he contrives to fascinate Princess Mary. To begin with, he encourages her to associate with the sentimentally ecstatic Grushnitski while he himself deliberately stretches out his absences from her. In this way Princess Mary is bound to become properly bored with Grushnitski's stale, parodic postures of romance.[3] In examining his reasons for toying with the princess in this fashion,

Pechorin finds three dominant, if overlapping, motives: the urge to destroy sweet delusions, the delight in possessing and then discarding a virginal soul, and the need to nourish his pride through the exercise of power. But though he is bent on corrupting innocence and at the same time feels a satanic zest in foiling his enemies, Pechorin is hardly the devil incarnate. The pensive, vulnerable princess, who has fallen ill after a somewhat spidery amorous maneuver on Pechorin's part, has in fact stirred within him a supposedly defunct tenderness and a presumably discarded susceptibility to illusion. Of course he does not welcome this inner commotion. "Can it be," he asks himself, "that I have really fallen in love? . . . What nonsense!" (137)

One might well imagine that questions concerning women and love in Pechorin's journal would be the source of more than one deflationary comment, for Pechorin hardly believes in women as magically veiled angels or as models of absolute morality. Yet at one point he ascribes to the love of women virtually the whole meaning of his existence: "I, who love nothing in the world save them – I, who have always been ready to sacrifice to them peace of mind, ambition, life . . . women ought to desire that all men know them as well as I do, because I love them a hundred times better, ever since I stopped fearing them and comprehended their little weaknesses" (142). But this passage in his journal scarcely tells the whole truth. There is no mention here of his egoistic exploitation of women, or his thirst for power, or his role as executioner (at times reluctantly) in human relationships. In a later passage, Pechorin's love of women takes on precisely this complexion: "My love brought happiness to none, because I never gave up anything for the sake of those whom I loved. I loved for myself, for my proper pleasure. I merely satisfied a bizarre need of my heart, avidly consuming their sentiments, their joys and sufferings" (159). Of course few journals are devoid of mixed views and even incompatible attitudes; but Pechorin's discrepant self-analyses are particularly striking.

On the whole, the journal passages that record shifts in the relationship between the princess and Pechorin lean toward the gratifications of subtle erotic villainy. The thought of the princess's sufferings even provokes in Pechorin a vampiric pleasure. When the princess tearfully demands to know whether Pechorin despises her or loves her, he maintains a frigidly experimental silence; when she offers to confess her own love, Pechorin indicates that the offer fails to interest him; and when, pleading with him, she says she is ready to make any sacrifices for his love, Pechorin flatly disavows any passion for her. Not surprisingly, Princess Mary sinks into a feverish condition.

Pechorin's uncommunicated rationale for rejecting the princess is that he is incapable of behaving "nobly" (honorably, hence laughably) toward her. This is so partly because he scorns the silly pieties of romantic love and partly because the idea of marriage, of giving up his freedom, however pointless that freedom may be, is repellent to him. (Besides, a fortune-teller once predicted that marriage would ruin him.) Yet Pechorin's journal is not bereft of a sense of guilt. However far beneath the surface it may lie, and however grotesquely deformed it may be, the feeling for Princess Mary that Pechorin has experienced approximates the condition of romantic love.

We may be revolted by Pechorin's chilly profanation of Princess Mary's soul, but we are also aware that Pechorin's confession to his friend Werner that for a long time he has "been living not with the heart, but with the head" (162) is (creditably) inexact. Shortly before Pechorin makes that comment, on the unexpectedly lovely morning of the disastrous duel with Grushnitski, he realizes anew his profound love of Nature; and during the sleepless night preceding the duel he is "carried away by the magic fantasy" (160) of Scott's *Old Mortality*.[4] It is of course easier for Pechorin to succumb to romantic Nature and romantic literature than to yield to the immediate exigencies of romantic love.

Before his last interview with Princess Mary – she is now more drastically ill – Pechorin's heart beats violently, though his mind, through long practice, remains tranquil. "No matter how hard I searched my breast for one spark of love for the charming Mary," he assures himself, "my efforts were in vain" (179). Yet his search has not been thorough enough. Even as he assures her that she can only despise him for having laughed at her all along, and even as the princess pitifully absorbs this betrayal, Pechorin senses that his habitual aloofness is on the verge of deserting him: "This was becoming unbearable: another minute, and I would have fallen at her feet" (179). Emotional dishevelment does not, however, conquer his art of restraint. Pechorin remains much too aware that romantic love pitched at the high social level occupied by the princess would make marriage obligatory; and he is not prepared to settle for domestic peace and contentment. In his own mind he remains a kind of pirate, though the reader knows that this enemy of solid virtues is capable of nobler self-images.

Paul Foote's description of Pechorin's psyche is not unlike Nabokov's. Pechorin, Foote writes, is a "dual character, in conflict with himself, torn between good and evil, between idealism and cynicism, between a full-blooded desire to live and a negation of all that life has to offer."[5] But this comment needs to be supplemented by the recognition that Pechorin's sense of comedy, which in "Princess Mary" is generally mordant, is for him a significant means of survival and control.

Pechorin's reliance on the power of comedy to escape, or at least significantly reduce, the heart's tumult is conspicuously tested in the tale entitled "Taman," the action of which takes place sometime before the events recounted in "Princess Mary." Taman, an enchanting girl who happens to be a member of a small band of smugglers, is intent on warding off any suspicions of irregularity that might be forming in Pechorin's mind. She doesn't have to work hard to do so. She has only to gaze at Pechorin with a Tatyana-like, "wondrously tender" look (75) to kindle within him (he is, it seems, not yet a fully Byronic, world-weary figure) an "ineffable confusion" (76). But he is not blind to what is going on. When Pechorin recalls that, as an army officer, he represents the authority of the law, he threatens to expose the smuggling operation. The threat is purely playful, for Pechorin is convinced that he himself possesses the moral imagination of a buccaneer. Taman's response is to assume an even more fetchingly seductive (yet somewhat worried) look. Pechorin, no longer speculating about lawlessness, is transfixed by the girl. Since, however, Taman's prolonged magnetic gaze seems endless, Pechorin retrieves something of his independence and soon becomes uncomfortably aware that his fascination is in danger of dissolving. If only Taman's adoring look were reinforced by some sort of verbal magic, his heart, he is certain, would be hers. But this sort of enchantment never materializes.

The girl's troubled silence lasts so long that Pechorin's incipient romance with an undine mutates into a comedy of ennui – a comedy which is brusquely canceled by what seems to be, finally, a decisive emotional commitment on the girl's part: Taman gives him an overwhelming (and utterly treacherous) kiss. Instantly Pechorin reverts to a blindingly romantic intensity of feeling: "Everything turned dark before my eyes, my head swam, I crushed her in my embrace with all the force of youthful passion" (76). The girl's whispered suggestion of a nocturnal tryst by the shore turns out, however, to be a preface to war rather than a prelude to further ecstasy. Taman attempts to drown Pechorin, who has to wrestle for his life with this supple, 18-year-old sprite. He succeeds, but Taman manages to escape him. And that is the end of the story.

Pechorin's mature conviction that he is impervious to human joys and sorrows evidently has not always tyrannized his consciousness. "Taman" suggests that the (somewhat) younger Pechorin has developed into an ironist in whom romantic passion, so far from being extinct, can exert almost instantaneous sovereignty. The (somewhat) older Pechorin is usually saved from such romantic intoxication by deeper reserves of dispassion, analysis, and mockery (including self-mockery). But even the mature Pechorin is scarcely a stranger to the kind of ambivalence posited in the lines he himself quotes from Pushkin's dedication of *Eugene Onegin* to Peter Alexandrovich Pletnev: "The mind's cold observations. / The mournful comments of the heart." Indeed Pechorin and Onegin, as John Mersereau remarks, "have much in common, especially a spiritual frigidity which manifests itself in intellectual control of emotions, a surfeit with the joys of life which engenders a contemptuous attitude towards everything, a boredom which they seek to relieve by travel and love affairs." Mersereau points out, however, that "there are also vital differences, for Onegin is essentially apathetic while Pechorin is energetic, thriving on conflict."[6]

2.

A major distinction between *A Hero of Our Time* and *Eugene Onegin* is that while Pechorin exhibits undeniable romantic-ironic traits, it is the all-important narrator of *Eugene Onegin,* not Onegin himself, who is marked by the ambivalence of romantic irony. But the narrator, who has an ample capacity for laughter, is also given to other modes of comedy, for example, amiable humor and stinging satire. André Sinyavsky has observed, not unlike Struc, that "lightness is the first thing – the most general and immediate feeling – we get out of [Pushkin's] works. Lightness in relation to life was the basis of Pushkin's worldview."[7] What makes the lightness of spirit in *Eugene Onegin* often identifiable as romantic irony is that Pushkin's narrator defends, either vigorously or wistfully, the virtues of romantic sensibility while also smiling sophisticatedly at the madly romantic predilections and anxieties of youth.

Both the narrator and his friend Onegin are products of worldliness; but while Onegin is wrapped up in a barren, scornful urbanity, the narrator, despite his witty deprecations of lyrical propensities, has retained certain saving romantic graces. He avows, for example, that he was born to enjoy the kind of rural beauty and tranquility that gives birth to, or sustains, poetic dreams. Onegin, in contrast, is alienated by country life, which he would translate proleptically, without sharing an iota of ideology with Marx and Engels, as rural idiocy. Onegin has passed from poetic dreams and tempestuous passions to Ovidian amours, and then to an apparently permanent state of disenchantment, ennui, and derision. The narrator, on the other hand, as familiar as his friend Onegin with the trivialization and destruction of illusion, still believes, even if only intermittently, in the magic of emotion. Moreover, he remains nimbly sociable, tolerant, humane. He does not cultivate, like Onegin, an insouciant, flippant, derivatively demonic detachment. The romantic irony he embraces serves as a provisional cure for the supreme romantic malady: a youthful overdose of idealism. (The cure is necessarily provisional, inasmuch as romantic irony's Voltairean purgatives are susceptible of being voided by renewals of Rousseauistic ardor.)

The narrator may profess to have a withered heart; but that his heart can be readily regenerated is well illustrated by his empathy with Tatyana, whose sensibility is only minimally ironized. The narrator is never caustic, for example, in noting the tyranny of literature in Tatyana's life, a tyranny which intensifies when her largely self-induced love for Onegin begins to obsess her. And when Tatyana's yearning for love receives a polite dismissal, the narrator delicately describes her hopeless passion for Onegin. He not only defends her unsubdued desire but regards her letter to Onegin as a sacred treasure.

The letter (in French) that Tatyana sends to Onegin transcends many of the banalities of literary romanticism by which she has been nourished (and somewhat poisoned). Onegin's disinclination to accept the letter's poignant offer of love (it is essentially love for a stranger) is conveyed by expectable sentiments: he is (infernally) armored against domesticity and enduring love; he must not corrupt an innocent soul; he is saving her from disaster, and so on. Onegin's diplomatic shunting aside of Tatyana is initially assessed by the narrator as a thoughtful, civilized act. Later, however, he implies that the motives and conduct of this Russian Childe Harold were not perfectly admirable. (That Onegin is not precisely a model of nobility is perceived well enough by Tatyana herself after his departure.)

If the narrator's regard for Tatyana is untinged by romantic irony, the same can hardly be said of his treatment of Onegin's friend, the poet Lensky. We are informed that Lensky is fire, Onegin ice. We soon surmise, however, with the narrator's help, that in singing of love, grief, freedom, and death, the young poet may be as foggily exalted as he is nobly stirred. Onegin's opinion (he indulgently suspends his customary cynicism) is that Lensky's infection with poetry will be brief, though blissful. The narrator's own attitude – and he is never less than agreeable – fluctuates. When he views the poet, not as a victim of immaturity, but as a symbol of "sacred poesy" and of youth's generous aspirations, he boosts Lensky's talents. On the other hand, he does not scant the weaknesses stemming from Lensky's Schillerian fervor. Idealistic poetry, it is implied, may recklessly, and on occasion laughably, court unreality; and it remains true that Lensky's gentle feelings are not unaccompanied by hackneyed verse.

The narrator's apparent neutrality in judging Lensky's poetry is maintained (imperfectly) up to the moment when Lensky's poetizing ambitions are lethally abbreviated in a duel prompted by the young poet's incendiary jealousy: he has watched Onegin, who is moved by vindictive boredom at Tatyana's nameday party, and seen him dance provocatively and uninterruptedly with Olga, Tatyana's younger, prettier sister, to whom Lensky has abundantly devoted dreams and verses glowing with love's purity. (Olga will not be in mourning very long.) Before killing him off, the narrator suggests, again with utter amiability, that Lensky's virginal, German-influenced lyricism may reveal a limp idealism, though he equivocates by hinting that romantic poetry as a species cannot be reliably pinned down. In their more agitated, self-intoxicating moods, however, Lensky's poems are unambiguously described as "compact of amorous trash and worse."[8]

Though Lensky's poetry appears thus to have been gently deflated down to a fine-yet-foolish sort of adolescent romanticism, the final verdict is not yet in. After Lensky's death, the narrator allows that the youthful poet was perhaps endowed with authentic gifts that might one day have gloriously served the world and brought him immortal fame. But there is a less promising scenario: Lensky might perhaps have subsided into normality, sacked his Muse, and settled for a complacent, mindless, humdrum family life,[9] so that "at forty he'd have got the gout, / drunk, eaten, yawned, grown weak and stout" and died in bed (6.38-9). The narrator, who a moment ago honored the splendid potential of the romantic style of being and creating, is not simply jeering. The pleasures of comfort and mundanity, it is understood, are hard to escape. But the narrator is not exactly unsmiling, either. In pointing to Lensky's possibly philistine future, he is in all likelihood implying, somewhat mockingly, that romanticism may be discredited as a seedbed of illusions that are not likely to survive the stage of impassioned youth. The impression we are inevitably left with is that romanticism is both valuable and spurious.

The narrator's double attitude toward Lensky's poetic prospects parallels his earlier perspective on Lensky's elation at his impending marriage with Olga. On the one hand, the narrator pities those who are too soberly realistic not to be immune to rapture. On the other hand, he likens believers in romantic fictions to reeling drunkards or insects drowning in nectar (4.51). Pushkin's own ambivalence in all this is difficult to miss. Richard Freeborn puts the matter somewhat tentatively: Lensky is "chiefly victim of his own romantic illusions and perhaps also of Pushkin's part-regretful, part-sceptical abandonment of youthful idealism."[10]

Toward the end of *Eugene Onegin,* Pushkin's lightness is suspended, though not ultimately displaced, by a stunning, woeful circumstantial irony. Onegin had responded to Tatyana's love letter by politely, professorially, therapeutically pushing aside this young woman's idolization of him. A complete reversal occurs when Onegin, still unfailingly disabused, returns from his travels and falls in love with Tatyana. He tells her so in a letter that reveals a genuine descent from arid pride to loving humility. (Neither of the two love letters, however, is wholly untouched by romantic literary clichés.) Tatyana is now married, honorably, if also dully, and has self-protectively assumed an air that is dignified and remote but by no means disdainful. Her rejection of Onegin's suit is informed by a noble, though still unrepentant, pathos; for Tatyana does not, finally, deny her love for Onegin, who is now overcome by despair. Yet *Eugene Onegin* does not maintain a tonality of grief for very long. Pushkin's lightness can be counted on to supersede somberness, erase melancholy, and negate a sense of futility. We are assured by the narrator, echoing an earlier prognosis, that neither madness nor suicide – nor even poetizing – is destined to do away with Eugene Onegin.

Among the critics it is inevitably German romantic irony that is cited (when it is cited at all) in connection with *Eugene Onegin.* Consider Monika Greenleaf's interpretation of Pushkin's verse novel – an interpretation much indebted to critics like Gary Handwerk, Paul de Man, and Kathleen M. Wheeler. Greenleaf's remarks are extensive, learned, and considerably nuanced in their theoretical formulations. Yet her commentary is dominated by a single paradoxical absolute: the infinite elasticity of German romantic irony. This largely translates, in critical analysis, into undecidablity: *Eugene Onegin,* "that classic work of 'undecidable' modern irony,"[11] perfectly exemplifies, Greenleaf claims, the all-inclusive "spiritual mobility" of German romantic irony. No other figure in European romanticism, according to Greenleaf, comes closer than Pushkin to embodying F. Schlegel's "poetics of modernity" (17).

Greenleaf vigorously rehearses a litany of Schlegelian virtues. Thus Schlegelian mobility, which "fights the reader's tendency to seek closure, whether of plot, meaning, or tone" (17), is an exhilarating embrace of multiple worlds and manifold possibilities. Such mobility is based on the perception that all utterances or texts (or selves, viewed at a particular moment) are partial, fragmentary, restricted; all articulated perspectives and "truths" exist by muffling alternative perspectives and "truths" (22). Hence "finer illuminations" are always possible in Schlegelian romantic irony's liberation from finality – from the distortion of unified views, accepted meanings, and well-worn insights (40).

Ironic mobility in *Onegin,* Greenleaf maintains, is evidenced chiefly by authorial self-scattering and authorial dissemination of conflicting ideas. Pushkin, Greenleaf writes, "is engaged in precisely the act of ironic self-representation described by de Man: by fragmenting rather than hypostasizing his subjectivity, he locates it in the hovering, now narrowing, now widening gap between various parts of characters, or counterpointed perspectives" (237). Of course, such fragmentation may get channeled into ambivalence. Greenleaf observes, for example, that Lensky, whose inane poetic idealism and derivative language have not passed unnoticed by the narrator, is accorded a "variegated feast" of elegies (280) after his fatal duel with Onegin, so that the question of what Lensky might have become had he continued to live is not simply tossed in for ironic depreciation. Irony itself, that is, is ironized (for awhile) in favor of a re-established "lost glamor" (282).

The ambivalence of romantic antiromanticism turns out, after all, to be quite important to Greenleaf's understanding of romantic irony, though she does not regard comedy as the indispensable vehicle of such ambivalence. Comedy, it seems, has little voice even when Greenleaf associates Pushkin with Byron. She speaks of their "jumps from style to style" as marking "the movements of a mercurial subjectivity," then adds that "this was Schlegel's idea of Romantic irony in the flesh" (45). Ambivalence at least persists, though not quite magisterially, among the three elements – it is the second that counts – Greenleaf thinks Byron and Pushkin shared: (1) an appreciation of the fragment, connoting approximation, provisionality; (2) a disorienting "oscillation between lyricism and irony" (19); and (3) a creative, interpretive partnership between writer and reader. Greenleaf cites three other elements, three (questionable) ways in which German romantic irony escapes from "the conceptual prison of accepted meanings" (40): (1) inspirational *Witz*; (2) ecstatic lyric; and (3) allegory. Presumably comedy has a function here, at least in the element of *Witz*. But *Witz* is a troubling Schlegelian signifier (it is much less fuzzy in Freud) that can hardly be honored as the pure, if miniaturized, essence of comedy.

3.

Greenleaf might be hard put to it to apply her generous estimate of Schlegelian irony to *A Hero of Our Time,* if only because authorial self-scattering is consistently confined to Pechorin's dualistic temper. One may also wonder how Greenleaf would apply Schlegelian doctrine to Dostoevsky's *Notes from Underground* (1864), where an even more extreme case of psychic dualism blocks a proliferation of perspectives.

Though Lermontov's Pechorin and Dostoevsky's Underground Man seem to be polar opposites, certain aspects of Pechorin's character and background may remind us more than faintly of the Underground Man's acrid nature and pathological experiences. Indeed, Lermontov's "concern with the problem of evil and the complexities of the human personality" constitutes a powerful preface to Dostoevsky's themes.[12] Pechorin's somewhat histrionic autobiographical discourse to Princess Mary on how he became a "moral cripple," owing to early psychological bruising and subsequent self-withdrawal, might, for example, have been pronounced, with few modifications, by the Underground Man: "I was gloomy – other children were merry and talkative. I felt myself superior to them – but was considered inferior: I became envious. I was ready to love the whole world – none understood me: and I learned to hate. My colorless youth was spent in a struggle with myself and with the world. Fearing mockery, I buried my best feelings at the bottom of my heart; there they died."[13]

Pechorin may remind us of the Underground Man even more vividly when he ruminates on the will to power, or occasionally lapses into self-contempt, or yields (more often) to a wild impulsiveness, or surrenders to his "innate passion" for antithetical postures (though the Underground Man's miasmic, "hysterical craving for contradictions"[14] makes Pechorin seem almost a model of mental stability), or bristles at ridicule, or indicates that he is constantly on the alert to thwart his enemies.

Far more intensely than Pechorin, however, and with a much greater dosage of (morbid) comedy, Dostoevsky's Underground Man is a veteran of romantic irony: he is obsessively involved with, and furiously, funnily detached from, romantic idealism. This creature of exaltation and spite undergoes seizures of romanticism that are due partly to an ambivalent glorification of the irrational (erratically expounded in Part I of *Notes*) and partly to bookishly inspired dreams of redemptive love and brotherhood (perversely illustrated in Part II).

In Part I, the confessedly hyper-neurotic Underground Man underscores the value of irrationality in providing a salvational escape from stifling Western theories of rational progress. Such theories, he argues, cunningly intertwine enlightened self-interest and social betterment in such a way as to relegate man to the level of utilitarian anthood. Only the irrational, the Underground Man is convinced, can preserve man's indispensable, irreducible freedom of imagination and impulse. This kind of freedom spurns merely reasonable advantages: neither money, nor honor, nor peace, nor dignity, nor any other artful trap can seduce the genuine nonconformist, the authentic immoralist. Yet one of the Underground Man's chief sources of vanity is the cogency of his reasoning powers. This professed irrationalist, who insists that formulaic thinking (like twice two makes four) is an impertinence, and that the laws of Nature are intolerable, deems himself cleverer than others and scorns, in the very accents of a devotee of rationalism, thoughtless men of action (whom at the same time he tormentedly envies). Yet if he inveighs against healthy mindlessness, he also mocks the malady of consciousness.

However indispensable irrationality may be, the Underground Man is too knowledgeable to extol it as a thing of beauty. The irrational and the terrifyingly abnormal, he is aware, have been wedded throughout history: "one may say anything about the history of the world – anything that might enter the most disordered imagination," he notes. "The only thing one cannot say is that it is rational" (27). Despite history's appalling evidence of the failure of reason, however, the Underground Man feverishly claims that if the threat of rational, "advantageous," scientifically advanced social control presses upon man too tightly, his bent toward independence, his inextinguishable freedom of will, his dedication to irrationality construed as both the generator and safeguard of his autonomous ego, may necessitate nothing less than an eruption of chaos, to the point of self-destructive madness. Freedom of choice is thus ultimately served by a "fatal fantastic element" (27) in human nature. We are left, then, with two models of action: the utilitarian who seeks pleasure and profit while plumping for humanity's allegedly "most advantageous advantage" (that is, rational gain and ordered communality) and the capricious, anarchic, bizarre individualist, embodied by the Underground

Man, who is ready to save himself by means of a self-annihilating insanity.

In the Underground Man's sour assessment, human beings are ungrateful, perpetually immoral, viciously unsensible, comical bipeds whom civilization has only rendered "more abominably, more loathsomely bloodthirsty" (21). Of course the Underground Man himself exemplifies much that is pettily nasty or funnily grotesque in human nature. He is a failed virtuoso of malice, a bumbling connoisseur of vindictiveness, a self-damaging practitioner of humiliation. Yet in his recurring romantic reveries (which tend to spill over into caricature) he is generous, heroic, triumphant, forgiving, compassionate, and self-sacrificing.

The aberrant psychology illustrated in Part II of *Notes* – the incidents recounted there predate by a number of years the nervous reflections in Part I – scarcely succeeds in glamorizing, let alone authenticating, the dream of romantic benevolence. Rather, Part II corroborates the Underground Man's intimation in Part I that the self is the inevitable object of irrationality's destructive drive. Moreover, the personal disgraces the Underground Man records in Part II – these are filtered through the bitter but often hilarious comedy of a compulsively self-lacerating consciousness – regularly violate his redemption-seeking, visionary idealism.

Joseph Frank writes that Part II of *Notes from Underground* finally brings into relief the true target of Dostoevsky's satire: "the romantic dreamer," who is "manhandled very harshly indeed. Nor is he any longer a purely literary Romantic lost in exotic fantasies or erotic gratification and artistic glory; he has become a Social Romantic filled with grandiose plans for transforming the world."[15] But if the Underground Man is a target of satire, it must be recognized that he himself wittily satirizes the romantic temper. He makes a sharp distinction, however, between European romantics, whom he ridicules as foolish transcendentalists inhumanly armored against the turmoil and ordinariness of life, and Russian, non-transcendental romantics, whom he derides more devastatingly, though he pretends to be captivated and comforted by their versatility.

The Russian romantics – epigones presumably at a great remove from the likes of a Pushkin or a Lermontov – may be forever blessed by the spirit of "the sublime and the beautiful," yet oddly enough they manage to be both positivistic in their mentality and opportunistic in their conduct: "there are so many 'broad natures' among us who never lose their ideal even in the depths of degradation; and though they never lift a finger for their ideal, though they are arrant thieves and robbers, yet they tearfully cherish their first ideal and are extraordinarily honest at heart" (41).

Dostoevsky may very well be parodying himself here, in large part proleptically, for the alternation between (or simultaneity of) a lust for degradation and a thirst for idealism is a notorious theme in his fiction, especially in later works like *A Raw Youth* and *The Brothers Karamazov.* But though the Underground Man himself is an egoistic, self-inflationary, self-indulgent dreamer-idealist (or a farcical version thereof), he can hardly be accused of being positivistic; nor does he ever thrive opportunistically by means of combined idealism and perfidy.

Still, the violent fevers spawned by the Underground Man's sense of his own degradation do have a way of "sincerely" (that is, delusorily) engendering idyllic visions. Consider the following episode: a preposterously arrogant officer shoves the Underground Man aside as though he were an inanimate object. The Underground Man of course chokes with resentment at this rude dismissal; nor is his psychic suffocation merely transitory. His abjection festers ridiculously for years, until the moment he is inspired to write a letter to the officer – only to thank God later that he has never seen fit to send it. This is a nice bit of illogic: the letter could not possibly have been delivered, since the Underground Man knew neither the uniformed ruffian's name nor his address. Nevertheless, the unsent letter reflects the Underground Man's symbiosis of debasement and dream, for though it hints at a duel, the letter is composed in such a splendidly sensitive and fraternal manner (that is, fawningly) that "if the officer had had the least understanding of the 'sublime and the beautiful' he would certainly have rushed to me to fling himself on my neck and offer me his friendship" (45). In the meantime, the Underground Man concocts retaliatory projects. After many complex rehearsals and many aborted attempts, he at last succeeds in colliding with the overbearing officer. The latter scarcely notices that someone has brushed against him; but the Underground Man, believing he has escaped once and for all from the role of perpetual victim, is filled with such triumphant delight that he cannot resist singing Italian arias. Shortly afterwards, however, Italian arias give way to the agonizing realization that throughout this entire episode he has remained a downtrodden, laughable, disgusting worm.

Since his shame and guilt breed paradisal yearnings, the Underground Man is not always reminded of his prolonged seasons in hell. Visions of "the sublime and the beautiful," he declares, "were particularly sweet and vivid after a little vice; they came with remorse and tears, with curses and transports. There were moments of such positive intoxication, of such happiness, that there was not the faintest trace of irony within me, on my honor. I had faith, hope, love" (49). This intermittent exaltation is largely sustained by the literature of romanticism. The shape of his romantic dreams, the Underground Man acknowledges, has been "violently stolen from the poets and novelists" (50-51). With the help of such thefts, the Underground Man can imagine himself as a figure greatly loving, colossally heroic, and profoundly artistic. In his reveries he even becomes universally worshipped as a religiously and politically regenerative force. Yet such fictions cannot succor the Underground Man's depressed spirits for very long; and self-derision infallibly follows the "cheap mirage" of his fantasies. The Underground Man's romantic irony is hard to distinguish from pathology.

At times the cumulative pressure of the Underground Man's visions of universal love becomes so potent that he can no longer imprison them in familiar literary forms; come what may, he must find an outlet for them in real life. Since, however, his social personality is rather exiguous, and since he is far more abrasive than suave, the landscape of his real life is terribly limited. He is obliged to settle for a visit to his only genuine acquaintance, his bureaucratic superior, Anton Antonich Syetochkin. Unfortunately, the latter's at-home day is Tuesday; hence the Underground Man "always had to adjust [his] passionate desire to embrace humanity so that it might fall on a Tuesday." This poignantly ludicrous artifice, needless to say, is not fulfilling; the Underground Man is bored stiff in Anton Antonich's apartment. After one such typically disastrous visit, the Underground Man remarks that "on returning home, I deferred for a time my desire to embrace all mankind" (52).

In one crucial episode, the "yellow stain" of reality (the stain is on his clothing and in his soul) threatens to dissolve beyond repair the dictates of transcendent fraternity. After the Underground Man forces himself on several former classmates during a farewell celebration (in a small hotel room) for Zverkov, their favorite, a series of ugly, risible clashes of temper culminates in that characteristically torturous mode of Dostoevskian comedy – the buffoonery of humiliation. While the others, engaged in besotted conviviality, scornfully disregard him, the Underground Man keeps pacing back and forth – for three hours – without uttering a syllable. This anguished farce becomes in his mind an ingenious exhibition of unyielding dignity. However, when the others disperse, no Italian arias issue from the Underground Man's throat; his behavior, he knows perfectly well, has been unforgivably, nauseatingly absurd.

Feeling the need to recoup his honor (another borrowing from the literary imagination), he desperately proposes to himself a duel with Zverkov, which the latter will of course contemptuously reject. The Underground Man intends nevertheless to stick to his plan, even if he has to bite the braggart to get results. Afterwards, he will accept arrest, dismissal from the bureaucratic service, and Siberian exile: "Never mind! In fifteen years when they let me out of prison I will trudge off to him, a beggar in rags, I shall find him in some provincial city. He will be married and happy. He will have a grown-up daughter . . . I will say to him: 'Look, monster, at my hollow cheeks and rags! I've lost everything – my career, my happiness, art, science, *the woman I loved,* and all through you. Here are pistols. I have come to discharge my pistol and – and I . . . forgive you.' Then I will fire into the air and he will hear nothing more of me." The Underground Man's rhetoric is constructed of several levels of fabrication. To begin with, neither tangible happiness nor an extraordinary career is remotely conceivable at any period in the Underground Man's life. Attainments in art and science also have to be ruled out. Finally, his italicized love affair encroaches upon the absolutely impossible. In any event, the whole passage is indebted to his reading in the romantics: "I was actually on the point of tears, though I knew perfectly well at that very moment that all this was out of Pushkin's *Silvio* ['The Shot'] and Lermontov's *Masquerade*" (74).

The collision between dreamy immersion in romantic purity and benevolence and a mordantly mocking recognition of mendacious romantic nonsense is illustrated with particular perversity after the Underground Man, wildly agitated, follows Zverkov and his retinue all the way to a brothel. Here the Underground Man's self-loathing and self-lashing are shunted onto a more available victim, an innocent prostitute names Liza. Relishing the compensation of (re-routed) vindictiveness, the Underground Man begins lecturing her, evoking harrowing images (especially that of a drunken, bruised, bloodied, howling whore with a fish in her hand) that make Liza feel the shame and horror of selling her body and soul (but her soul remains unpolluted) instead of nurturing the "holy love" of married life, with a babe at her breast. The Underground Man almost hypnotizes himself with his own eloquence, which, though heavily padded with trite expressions of the feeling heart, is by no means negligible. The Underground Man's cunning, relentless sentimentalization of life ends by inducing in Liza a state of convulsive despair.

The inspiring success of the Underground Man's half-bogus, half-sincere proselytizing is of brief duration. For days he is harassed by the thought that Liza, whom he has urged to come to him as her savior, will bear witness to his beggarly rooms and his sordidly unheroic existence. This astonishingly hybrid creature, hopping between theatricality and sincerity, frenzy and lucidity, romantic reverie and rough reality, nihilistic scorn for others and burlesque self-abasement, will be forced to put on a "dishonest lying mask again" (97). At moments he convinces himself, though falteringly, that he has spoken to Liza with genuine concern, that he has been true to the incorruptible sensibility of the heart. But what prevails in his mind is dismay. His panic at being sought out by Liza and exposed as a pitiful nonentity who commands no one's respect and lacks even an iota of dignity tips the scales against the reputed sanctity of "real feeling," which he then proceeds to equate with intellectual deficiency: "The damnable romanticism of these pure hearts! Oh, the vileness – oh, the silliness – oh, the stupidity of these 'wretched sentimental souls' " (97-98).

When Liza fails to appear, the Underground Man is soothed once more into "damnable romanticism," which inspires him to choreograph another redemptive idyll: he now becomes the salvation of Liza, whose love for him is returned with inordinate delicacy in a union of beautiful souls. But even as this romantic fiction takes wing – "I launch off at that point into European, inexplicably lofty subtleties à la George Sand" (98) – it is wrecked by an antiromantic spasm of self-consciousness that jeeringly demeans subtleties of spiritual elevation as a vulgar sham.

That he is incapable of romantic love, despite his compulsive lyrical-heroic imaginings, the Underground Man makes dreadfully clear in a venomous confession to Liza, who unwittingly puts him to shame simply by appearing in his shabby rooms. He has plied Liza with "fine sentiments," he maliciously assures her, but only to laugh at her. There has never been any question of "love," which, so far as he is concerned, signifies an exercise of power, not a noble display of unselfishness. Yes, he has romantic dreams, but they are spun out of words, out of his total dependence on books. The truth – his vindictiveness now becomes entirely self-punitive – is that he is an egoistic scoundrel who would send the world to hell, or sell it for a farthing, in order to maintain his own comfort. In short, he is the "nastiest, stupidest, pettiest, absurdest, and most envious of all worms on earth" (108-09). This revelation of ignominy, which he mistakenly assumes will make him hideously unworthy in Liza's eyes, is reinforced by a spiteful release of sexual passion, made even uglier by the Underground Man's subsequent attempt to reduce to a commercial transaction the lovely impulses he has awakened in Liza. Traumatized, she rushes out.

The Underground Man's urge to beg Liza's forgiveness for this deliberate desecration of "holy love" collapses under the weight of a twisted rationalization which paradoxically elevates him to the status of benefactor: surely Liza will be strengthened, even purified, in her future ordeals by an enduring sense of outrage (his contribution). Perhaps, he reflects, hesitatingly (he is unwilling to peer too deeply into his duplicitous illogic), Liza will be fortified by a conjunction of hatred and forgiveness. To make his repulsive conduct bearable, the Underground Man then flings a flimsy, fraudulent challenge to the world (that is, to himself, his only audience): "Which is better – cheap happiness or exalted suffering? Well, which is better?" (114) Though exalted suffering is often a supreme value in Dostoevsky, the Underground Man's own agony has hardly been transfigured into edifying energy; nor has his pain ever ratified the need for forgiveness. The Underground Man remains a squirming, self-boosting, self-ridiculing, brilliantly but pathologically devious antihero who is indispensably inspired by, and moved irresistibly to nihilistic laughter at, romantic idealism and rapturous emotion. A literary character more singularly swayed by the rhythm of romantic irony would be difficult to find.

Chapter 7

Epilogue: Baudelaire and Flaubert

1.

An absorption in pain, impurity, and mockery would suffice to link Dostoevsky with Baudelaire, though the parallels often drawn between these two writers include much else. Donald Fanger, for example, notes that Dostoevsky and Baudelaire are both fascinated by the perverse; both share a belief in a dualistic psyche which simultaneously espouses the sublime and caters to the abominable; both urgently press toward, but are insecurely possessed of, religious convictions; and both deny that civilization is definable as the product of material progress. Fanger concludes that "there is . . . no European writer who displays a more striking thematic affinity with the mature Dostoevsky than Baudelaire."[1]

Similarly, Alex de Jonge, probing thematic affinities between Baudelaire and Dostoevsky, discerns "profound resemblances in the patterns of views and values that lie at the very heart of their respective creative impulses, and from which their whole work is to be derived."[2] However, de Jonge repeatedly exaggerates what he considers to be the key resemblance between the two writers: a "self-destructive escapism" (41) – an "intoxication by intensity" (42) played out in a culturally vacant, money-driven world.[3] But if de Jonge overemphasizes the self-destructive inebriation of spiritual failure in Dostoevsky and Baudelaire, he does allude, at least occasionally, to the role that comedy plays in connection with Dostoevskian spiritual lapses. On Baudelairean comedy, de Jonge is silent. Yet the moral abyss in Baudelaire's poetry is hardly alien to comedy. In both Baudelaire and Dostoevsky, analytical disenchantment applied to spells of exaltation is apt to produce a morbid species of romantic-ironic comedy. (As we have seen more than once, romantic irony is not a definitive exorcism of bewitchment. Disillusion in both writers, though this process is more native to Dostoevsky than to Baudelaire, entails the potential recrudescence of the romantic temper.)

It would scarcely be eccentric to assume, on the basis of Baudelaire's prefatory poem, that comedy in *The Flowers of Evil* is likely to be saturnine in character. "To the Reader" ("Au lecteur") is so charged with mockingly damnationist convictions about the nature of man that one expects more than a few of Baudelaire's poems to be marked by a note of savage railing or harsh demonic laughter. That is not quite the case, as it turns out, though D. J. Mossop is persuaded that "the subject matter of *Les Fleurs du Mal* is filled with the satanic laughter of Melmoth."[4] The relevant question here concerns the degree to which Baudelaire's comedy (whatever there is of it) takes on the accents (however somber) of romantic irony. This would not appear to be a baffling issue inasmuch as the title of the first, and by far the longest, section of *The Flowers of Evil* is "Spleen and Ideal." Baudelaire, one is led to speculate, must be signalizing fluctuations between malodorous realism and romantic transcendence – surely at times in a comic key. But can Baudelaire's duality be securely identified as representing the dichotomy of romantic irony? Do "spleen" and "ideal" correspond, respectively, to antiromantic and romantic perspectives?

"Spleen" is a capacious term whose connotations range from acedia to world-weariness, from disgust to despair.[5] Nevertheless, it is possible to regard Baudelaire's spleen, at least in part, as the product of romanticism's lost illusions. The sense of spleen as the soul's blight caused by romanticism's collapsed urges may conceivably be detected – one can hardly be pontifical about this – in a letter Baudelaire wrote to his mother shortly after the publication of *The Flowers of Evil*. Baudelaire explains to her that spleen is really "a sort of metaphysical malady, a complete paralysis of the mind and emotions, a feeling of discouragement and unbelievable isolation, a total lack of desires."[6]

If Baudelaire's "spleen" need not automatically be identified with antiromantic attitudes, Baudelaire's "ideal" does not necessarily evoke the romantic imagination. According to Jonathan Culler, the "ideal" may be viewed as "whatever provokes effort and aspiration, including the world of ideal forms and beauty itself."[7] In *The Salon of 1846,* Baudelaire defined romanticism as "intimacy, spirituality, colour, aspiration towards the infinite."[8] But beauty, ideal forms, spirituality, and aspiration towards the infinite are often highly idiosyncratic, anomalous, or subversive in *The Flowers of Evil.* (The title of Baudelaire's collection – "mal" translates as "evil," though it also means pain or anguish – is of course sufficient warrant for such peculiarities.) Mossop thinks that the ideal follows a clear-cut pattern of devolution, betraying a "more and more degraded" career through the various sections of *The Flowers of Evil.* Baudelaire's poet-hero, he asserts, "seeks his ideal in God, art, beauty, woman, Paris, drugs, evil, the author of evil, before turning to death and the beyond."[9] Perhaps, but the point to retain here is that the Baudelairean ideal often violently upsets standard romantic expectations. Certainly high romanticism does not favor the artificial over the natural, or the voluptuously morbid over the radiantly innocent; nor does high romanticism, with some interesting exceptions, tend to prize beauty generated by infernal impurities.[10]

Though Baudelaire cultivates, if not in equal measure, both the natural and the artificial, both morbidity and innocence, both supernal and infernal sources of beauty, his theorizing can be startlingly unambiguous. For example, the need to improve on Nature, perhaps the least enigmatic of Baudelaire's scandalous divergences from inherited high romantic themes, is underscored almost brutally in an essay entitled "In Praise of Cosmetics," in *The Painter of Modern Life.* Baudelaire maintains that "fashion should . . . be regarded as a symptom of that attachment to the ideal which is superimposed in the human brain upon all coarse, terrestrial and foul accumulations of natural life." "Who," he goes on to ask, "would dare assign to art the sterile task of imitating nature?"[11] Yet supplanting Nature with a (more or less) aristocratic fantasy of artifice is difficult to sustain and is often disregarded in *Les Fleurs du Mal.* (Besides, there are traces of an unfallen world in Nature that, as M. H. Abrams suggests, the artist is uniquely able to discern.)[12] In "Invitation to the Voyage" the speaker, who proposes love in a milieu of "order . . . elegance, / pleasure, peace, and opulence,"[13] is not averse to having Nature's (heightened) attractions complement his idealization of the artificial. In the landscape he has in mind – it would resemble his beloved – the rarest of flowers, tranquil canals, and sunset gold would match gleaming furniture, richly encrusted ceilings, and an atmosphere of oriental splendor (58-59).

Though it is not usually an imprisoning or otherwise odious presence in *The Flowers of Evil,* it is true that in certain poems Nature is figured as vulgarly fecund or as terrifyingly aggressive. In "Obsession" ("Spleen and Ideal"), Nature is thoroughly demonized – but only because it seems to reflect the narrator's spiritual agony: the forest howls with reminders of damnation; the ocean's surges multiply the bitter laughter of defeat; even the starry night brands the speaker's soul with its lacerating language of light.

It is probably fair to say that Baudelaire more tantalizingly violates romantic tradition when he turns his attention to women and beauty. The one poem in *The Flowers of Evil* that is entitled "The Ideal" ("Spleen and Ideal") has nothing whatever to do with the noble enchantment women may exercise, or with the ravishment that springs from pure loveliness. The poem does extol the most desirable kind of woman; but far from being a pale, placid flower, she turns out to be a creature endowed with the criminal aptitudes of a Lady Macbeth (25). This is a "red ideal" which refuses to fake romantic rituals of awe at the feet of the (anemic) eternal feminine.

Yet among the early poems of *The Flowers of Evil,* the Baudelairean ideal is not predominantly "red," whatever the poet's subject may be. In "Consecration" ("Bénédiction"), the ideal is rooted in the salvation of the poet, redeemed by his terrible suffering in a callous, uncomprehending world. In "Elevation" the ideal is attached to the capacity for exultant, self-purifying spirituality. In "I Prize the Memory" ("J'aime le souvenir de ces époques nues . . ."), the ideal is the golden age of youth (whether in antiquity or in the present). In "Association" ("Parfum exotique") and "The Head of Hair" ("La Chevelure"), the ideal is an exotic, paradisal state, induced by the oasis of the beloved's body. All in all, however, the poems celebrating such (relatively) non-aberrant ideals seem paltry in number; and in the latter part of "Spleen and Ideal," poems of spleen – of depletion, sin, and remorse – pile up with such devastating force that they almost completely usurp the prior impact of the ideal.

When "ideal" and "spleen" are represented with comparable vigor, and with more than a marginal investment in comedy, the result may very well be romantic-ironic. But Baudelaire's romantic irony is seldom conveyed with Byron's buoyancy or Heine's lightness. Baudelaire's grotesque inversions of conventional romantic themes and images produce a more complexly comic shock than the antinomian impulses expressed by earlier romantic ironists, few of whom transmute the pleasures of perversity into lyrical magic.

The Flowers of Evil may even strike some readers as so somber a work that it chokes off the possibility of levity. Indeed, if "spleen" signifies varieties of apathy, demoralization, and revulsion; if the "ideal" tends to assimilate non-romantic and even antiromantic ingredients; and if one is prone to credit a description of *The Flowers of Evil* such as Eric Auerbach's – "It is a book of gruesome hopelessness, of futile and absurd attempts to escape by inebriation and narcosis"14 – one may be disposed to exclude Baudelaire not only from the company of romantic ironists but from the wider realm of literary comedy.

It is true that Baudelaire's "voracious" ironic consciousness often seems unrelievedly grim, yet lightness has a way of creeping in. In "Hymn to Beauty" the confounding perception that beauty is both supernal and infernal in its genesis[15] instantly crumples the romantic sentimentalist's notion of beauty as the embodiment of an exquisite dream. (Baudelaire's title, *The Flowers of Evil,* of course suggests that romantic confidence in regenerative Nature is going to be roughly, indeed insidiously, handled.) The poet's imagery, also, focuses compellingly on beauty's sinister, rather than celestial, aspects: "You walk on corpses, Beauty, undismayed, / and Horror coruscates among your gems" (29). Moreover, the hellish contribution to beauty's twofold nature evokes no moral anxiety. On the contrary, the poet savors the emancipatory, amoral power of beauty with almost religious fervor; for such power, even if only temporarily, is capable of metamorphosing "this hideous universe" by opening the door to "the Infinite I love and have never known" (29). (Liberation into the unknown, or the unknown infinite, ranks as perhaps the most seductive of Baudelaire's themes.)

The poem appears, then, to be stripped of comic attributes. Yet the scandal of duality in "Hymn to Beauty," is not devoid of a bizarre levity; for the poem is implicitly engaged in debunking beauty's clichéd associations with grace, awe, delicacy, splendor, and holiness. It is true that when Mario Praz described Baudelaire in *The Romantic Agony* as "the poet in whom the Romantic Muse distilled her most subtle poisons,"[16] he was not concerned with the power of comedy either to dilute or to intensify romanticism's subtle intoxications. Indeed Praz twice implicitly defines romantic irony as a macabre entity that arises from abnormal or horrible circumstances.[17]

Baudelaire's "Carrion" ("Une Charogne") would presumably be a suitable illustration of Praz's (implied) definition. Yet the poem's meld of lugubriousness and jest invites a more cogent conception of romantic irony. "Carrion" both exalts and smilingly (even leeringly) disfigures beauty, love, poetry, and the yearning for immortality. The poet recalls, for the benefit of his beloved, the sight of a "hideous carrion" they came across on a lovely summer day. His densely figurative reminder becomes, it would seem, a paean to fascinating loathsomeness. What the two lovers saw was a roasted putrescence, its whorish legs in the air, its flowering belly "swollen with foul gas" and heaving with a tide of musical maggots (35). The narrator insists on a parallel likely to be ill appreciated by his beloved: "– Yet you will come to this offence, / this horrible decay, / you, the light of my life, the sun / and moon and stars of my love!" (36) Disgusting images of decay presumably enhance, yet also ironize, the poet's passion for his beloved.[18] It is not surprising that Baudelaire's blend of beatific love and ordurous decomposition evoked Sainte-Beuve's description of the poet as "Petrarchising on the horrible."[19] Petrarch, however, was not a dark comedian.

The ultimate target of Baudelaire's sardonic desecration in "Carrion" is the long-standing idealizing tradition that certifies the beloved's enshrinement, after death, in the poet's verse. The following lines adhere to, but also risibly, cynically derail, that tradition: "But as their kisses eat you up, / my beauty, tell the worms / I've kept the sacred essence, saved / the form, of my rotted loves!" (36) The strong tincture of black comedy in this poem has not always been recognized. "Carrion" has been construed by one critic as both a complex expression of extreme tenderness and devotion and a sober sermon (all mockery eclipsed) on the vanity of the flesh and the consolation of art.[20]

A less blithely sinister comedy may be tracked in "Against Her Levity" ("À Celle qui est trop gaie"). The beloved in this poem is inclined to innocent laughter, which, the speaker initially suggests, is so little objectionable that it resembles a beautiful pastoral breeze; indeed, such laughter betokens the radiant health of the beloved's body. So far, so good. Yet the speaker's tone begins to shift, to invite ambiguity. Soon, it becomes conspicuously edgy, to the point where hostility indelicately supplants homage. Everything about the beloved is now degraded. Her clothing, for example, may be a veritable dance of flowers; but really, the speaker insists, it brilliance is much too blatant. By the fourth stanza, the speaker's rancor is wholly undisguised. The beloved's mind, he unchivalrously declares, is as motley, and as hatefully foolish, as her clothing – and indeed as Nature herself, whose seemingly innocuous beauty the speaker had at first appeared to esteem. In the last five stanzas, the dispraise which has been threatening to tumble the romantic mythos of Nature and love into trash becomes an unequivocal repudiation.

The outrage which the speaker no longer dissembles mutates into a pathological comedy of revulsion from the ideal incarnated by Nature.

The speaker admits that the physical and psychological enervation he is betraying is not a novelty, that he has more than once chastised the humiliating, ironic insolence of sun and spring and greenery by brutally despoiling any number of flowers. Now, once again, the devitalized (yet verbally energetic) speaker will retaliate against the colorful, insulting exuberance of Nature. Nor will his vulgarized companion be exempted from pain. What he has in mind for the repellently lovely, odiously joyous flesh of the beloved is a vindictiveness far more shocking than his relatively infantile mauling of Nature: she will endure a new, profoundly original carnal connection, one that will destroy both the ludicrous pieties of romantic love and the awful triteness of "natural," physical sex. This he will achieve through a daringly decadent act of surgery, an act that will license more imaginative lusts than those afforded by Nature's banal orifices: "in a final ecstasy / between those lovelier / new lips, my sister," the speaker announces, "I'll inject my venom into you!" (49). He sounds dead serious.

That is one reason why romantic irony in "Against Her Levity" may be more speculative than assured. If the poem's switch from love to hate, from radiance to debasement, seems much too wayward; and if a demonic smile annexed to the poem's final, dreadfully amorous lines seems to be lacking, the presence of romantic irony may have to be discounted. Indeed the speaker's planned addition to the inlets and outlets of original sin may strike the reader as only sadistically chilling. Certainly the passage in Baudelaire's *Intimate Journals* where the poet states that "love greatly resembles the application of torture or a surgical operation"[21] is not intended to raise a laugh, though Baudelaire adds that this idea may be ironically developed (as is perhaps the case in "Against Her Levity").

Nor is Baudelaire's reference, in "My Heart Laid Bare," to the "shameful tragedy," the "insane ferocity," the frightful, delirious decomposition of the human face and body in the throes of sexual passion other than searingly solemn, like his comment that "the sole and supreme pleasure in love lies in the absolute knowledge of doing evil" (5). A later passage in "My Heart Laid Bare," however, welcomes the comedy of Providence, which Baudelaire claims has exercised a "malicious and satirical intent . . . against Love" by obliging our immortal souls to dwell before birth "for nine months amidst excrement and urine" (35). (Of course, the divine merger of excretory organs with love and reproduction does not always prove to be joke material. Voltaire may regard this fusion as a celestial jest; Yeats, in contrast, thinks it is a gravely wonderful phenomenon.)

Certain other comments in *The Intimate Journals* bear directly on the question of romantic-ironic dissonance, particularly Baudelaire's assumption that there are "two fundamental literary qualities," which he designates as "supernaturalism and irony" (12). The first of these qualities ("supernaturalism") signifies either spiritual transcendence or a sense of enhanced reality; the second ("irony") presumably involves devaluational mockery, which may be defensive, or retaliatory, or willfully transgressive. Other passages in the *Journals,* like the description of the male psyche (but not the female's) as harboring "two simultaneous allegiances, one to God, the other to Satan" (30), or the sentences that allude to Baudelaire's enduring sense of "the horror of life and the ecstasy of life" (50), may be linked at least peripherally to romantic irony, though they seem to relate more compellingly to the cleavages of Christian consciousness.

Duality is the common denominator of these passages; and it is duality that has been construed by most critics as "the principle that dominates and explains" most of Baudelaire's work.[22] There are other critics, however, for whom this dualistic explanation of the Baudelairean psyche has become wearisomely monotonous and regrettably constraining. Leo Bersani maintains that Baudelaire's own professions of duality are discredited by his finest poetic practice. Such professions, Bersani thinks, constitute a rigid, escapist stabilizing of his "psychic mobility"; they betray an anxiety-engendered conventionalizing of the "disruptive . . . fragmented desire" that reveals the poet's genuine "scattered self."[23] It is provisionality, or "indeterminacy of being," Bersani affirms, that "is dramatized in Baudelaire's greatest poems."[24] Bersani's position is in line with contemporary suspicion of fixities, boundaries, and closure. It may be argued, nonetheless, that there is ample room for Baudelaire to float his various selves, minor or major, experimental or seasoned, on the extensive fields of force situated between "spleen" and "ideal," and that the poet's psychic nuances are not blunted by the play of polarity.

James R. Lawlor believes that between "Au lecteur" and "Le Voyage" (the first and last poems in *The Flowers of Evil,*) Baudelaire "followed a well-designated, dialectically structured course that embraces unending self-contradiction." Indeed, "the Baudelairean persona makes of contradiction his moral and esthetic discipline."[25] But invariable, reliable self-contradiction may or may not assimilate extraordinarily diverse attitudes. Baudelaire's love poems, for example, are hardly limited to one or two definable tensions between ideal and spleen. "By turn tender, reverent, vicious, suppliant, declamatory, mocking, and insinuating, these poems often shift abruptly from one tone to another, enacting the instability of fantasy so central to passion."[26] And even if the struggle between the ideal (however artificial or deviant) and its liquidation (perhaps comic, perhaps harrowing, perhaps satanic) is fairly recognizable, that does not mean that duality undiscriminatingly impoverishes Baudelaire's power of fantasy or lessens the complexity of his dissonances.

In any event, "psychic mobility" presumably does not disallow thematic coherence. Consider the fate of mobility (psychic and geographical) in "Travelers" ("Le Voyage"), the most extended example of romantic-ironic ambivalence – of magical illusion intertwined with (blackly) comic disenchantment – in *The Flowers of Evil.* The theme of this final poem of the book's last segment ("Death") may be interpreted as the necessary purging of "indeterminacy of being," of random, "disruptive desire," under the influence of an ultimate fixity of purpose – a purpose that is nevertheless scarcely bereft of mystery and risk.

In the first of the poem's eight sections, two kinds of travelers are contrasted. Most travelers belong to the first, inauthentic sort. Made rancorous by ugly circumstances, disgusting memories, and a hopeless future, they are bitterly, desperately propelled to disenslave themselves under exotic skies. True travelers, however, are those who are inebriated in advance by a pure sense of buoyancy and by dreams of still undiscovered pleasures and wonders. (The poem does not steadily distinguish between these two types.) Section 2 casts a savagely absurd light on ordinary travelers (that is, most of us) who are tormented and grotesquely whirled about by unsatisfiable curiosity and lunatic fancies. Our overheated imaginations chase after undiscoverable Americas and descry non-existent Eldorados which invariably offer only shipwreck. (Almost incidentally, the speaker who tells us we are crazily, self-destructively seduced by one mirage after another also claims that in our mad mobility we are actually searching for peace.)

Section 3 erases, or at least momentarily disregards, the delusions that have just been stamped on the brows of most voyagers, in recognition, it would seem, of an irrepressible human commandment: myth must prevail over detestable reality. Thus merely mental travelers (the speaker does not disassociate himself from them) seek to break out of the prison of boredom by sharing the mythic pleasures of illusion, the "noble chronicles" of real yet seemingly fabulous voyagers. However, in section 4 the real travelers' response to such dreamy inclination conveys little that is heartening or therapeutic. Not only have they incurred many jolting disasters, but they too have suffered immense boredom. They are the victims of insatiable but always defeated desire. In spite of their disappointment, however, they have brought back some objects for (compensatory) domestic consumption: sketches of idols, thrones, palaces, and so on. These will fill the albums of the stay-at-homes who remain infatuated with the notion that distance breeds enchantment.

"Yes, and what else?" persists the ingeniously avid (plural) speaker in section 5, which contains only this urgent question. The reply in section 6 is harshly disconsolatory: the truth is that the "boring pageant of immortal sin" (155) is ubiquitous. Everywhere men and women are vile. Everywhere one sees victims and executioners, barbaric despots and masochistic masses, drug-crazed addicts, sick saints, and despairing maligners of God. Such is the eternally disenchanting message of the tedious, demented globe.[27]

The negative news from abroad is summed up early in section 7 in an elegantly absurdist aphorism: the life of man is an "oasis of horror in a desert of ennui." (In Richard Howard's version, the image of man evokes "oases of fear in the wasteland of ennui" ([155].) And whether we stay put or rove about, our infamous, "tireless adversary, Time" (156) can be cheated only temporarily. ("We" again includes the poet, who now becomes more intimate with the reader, addressed as "tu.") But at this point the poet peremptorily casts despair aside. In the last four stanzas of the section, he conjures up a radically new ideal: we can purge ourselves of earthly illusion, age, and ennui if we sail hopefully, heroically, elatedly toward death.

Yet this visionary drive toward the great unexplored region of death is for a while not so much sidetracked as becalmed by ancient mythical resolutions of harried lives. Those of us who will be passengers on this ultimate voyage will hear charmingly funereal Greek voices offering us the appeal of a perpetually entrancing lotus-land or the reassumption of precious relationships and the celebration of dear reunions. But these comforting, reassuring images of a future state tricked out in Grecian guise – they are somewhat similar to the goal of tranquility inserted in section 2 – are glamorously irrelevant. They cannot heighten the poet's revelation of a great, suddenly unfolding possibility: the renovation of the adventurous human will.

The eighth and final section of the poem purifies the death-travelers' enthusiasm by discarding Hellenic vestiges of static immortality. (Their dubious balm would have constituted only a pseudo-extinction robbed of the promise of the unknown.) Briefly and boldly, the last lines of the poem, summoning Death in a spirit of incandescent commitment, herald the thrill of mortality's introduction to absolute, ennui-shattering novelty: "we can plunge to Hell or Heaven – any abyss will do – / deep in the Unknown to find the *new!*" (157) The poem's romantic irony, which has been counterpointing exorbitant aspiration and drastic disavowal, the pursuit of the ideal and its darkly comic repudiation, ends on an upswing, in a burst of re-enchantment, uncancelable and unmockable by mere rationality. The poison of the ideal has mysteriously metamorphosed into a magic elixir. (Yet there is room for incertitude here. Sensing that death in its infinity will surely open up a wondrous world may be unconsciously, if heroically, camouflaging a self-destructive urge.)[28]

Though romantic irony is a distinctive presence in Baudelaire, it must be acknowledged that the words "irony" and "ironic" in *The Flowers of Evil* usually accentuate disharmony, aberration, abandonment, destruction. Nor is irony easily separable from a sense of damnation. Thus in "Heauton Timoroumenos" irony, neither a proof of cosmic ignominy nor a sign of the world's faceless hostility, is an utterly subjective wretchedness. The speaker, consumed by some peculiar need for self-torture, condemns himself as a "dissonance / in the divine accord, / because of the greedy Irony / which infiltrates my soul" (80). A nihilistic ironic temper has produced within the speaker the kind of laughter that signifies moral corruption rather than intellectual detachment; and this laughing impurity endlessly dissociates him from the smiles of the innocent.

In "The Irremediable," irony and a sense of damnation are again interlinked, though the nexus between them is powerfully altered. The speaker, intimately familiar with irrevocable spiritual soilure, feels no remorse and delivers no adverse self-judgment. Without any display of cheap bravado or theatrical vanity, he maintains that the "ironic, infernal beacon" shining in his heart is the "graceful torch of the Devil" (82); he insists, moreover, that "consciousness in Evil" is both a solace and a glory. In his pride the speaker is candidly, even valorously perverse in refusing to weigh irreparable soul damage against the benefits of discipleship to the devil: psychic ease, absolute lucidity, and an aura of splendor. (The speaker's fealty to the devil seems to transcend any hint of self-mockery.) Irony in Baudelaire is seldom advanced as a victory of the spirit.

In "The Seven Old Men" ("Les Sept Vieillards"), "the ironic" returns to more conventional usage. In this poem the speaker betrays, not collusion with, but rather panicky fear of, the devil, who has been manufacturing nauseating, nerve-shattering phantoms – seven identical, grotesque old men emerging, one after the other, from a hellish abyss. The speaker's dread at witnessing this infernal parade becomes so intense that he does not wait for an eighth "ironic," and perhaps fatal, apparition. "Indignant as a drunk who sees the world / double, I staggered home and locked my door, / scared and sick at heart and scandalized / that so much mystery could be absurd!" (93) Yet the speaker is not entirely a prey to gothic terror, since he is aware that some readers may find more laughable than fearful what he believes to be an insult perpetrated by the absurd. (Their laughter would presumably derive from a balefully Bergsonian mechanical repetitiveness.)

In *The Flowers of Evil,* the comedy of the absurd may be the product of a satanic joke, an insoluble mystery, a collapsed ideal, or a sense of the inescapable calamity of being. The prose poems in *Paris Spleen* offer corroborative evidence of absurdist comedy.[29] Lightness of touch, for example, characterizes "The Bad Glazier," where the interplay of the ideal and its comic disembowelment reaches a point of complexity and perversity that recalls the psychic predispositions of Dostoevsky's Underground Man. According to the narrator of "The Bad Glazier," there are times when a malicious demon "gets into us, forcing us, in spite of ourselves, to carry out his most absurd whims" (13). When this happens, souls ordinarily indolent and dreamy are charged with crazy energy and become capable of performing dangerous actions or outrageous pranks. So it is that one day, when he is feeling out of sorts, an unaccountable impulse compels the narrator to summon a glazier up six flights of stairs. The idea of the burdened man's difficult ascent fills the narrator with hilarious anticipation. The glazier having finally arrived, the narrator accuses him of being a scoundrel because he has not brought with him any colored, magical window panes, the kind, the narrator emphasizes, that are necessary to make life beautiful, especially in poor neighborhoods. But this narrator is no sociologist of sentiment, no professor of compassion. After roughly dismissing the glazier, the narrator waits for his reappearance down below, only to drop a flower pot on him that knocks him over and shatters his wares. "And drunk with my madness, I shouted down at him furiously: 'Make life beautiful! Make life beautiful!' " (14)

Is a histrionically disposed Imp of the Perverse (not quite Poe's agent of self-ruin) really pulling the strings in "The Bad Glazier," stirring up damnable comic mayhem? Or do purely mundane fantasies of sadistic cruelty account for the poem's farcical irrationality? In either case, it seems that the craving for beautiful, consolatory dreams (a monstrous overvaluation of the ideal, diminished here to the level of childish illusion) somehow contributes to the making of a warped temper. At the end of "The Bad Glazier," the narrator exalts what most readers would deem a deficiency of responsibility and sensitivity, a desertion of humaneness and moral balance. Buoyed up not only by an indecent hedonistic euphoria but also by a kind of pseudo-metaphysical hysteria, the narrator justifies himself by insisting that "an infinity of pleasure in a single second" is worth an "infinity of damnation" (14). The narrator's wild, clownish, unholy fit of excitement is invested with so startling an intensity (and so lunatic an arithmetical assessment of the future) that one may be tempted to assume his soul has indeed been trapped in the coils of a satanic delusion.[30]

Buffoonery and perversity are differently intertwined in "A Heroic Death," for in this prose poem a passionate, if doomed, respect for humanity and social justice is an important, though not primary, theme. The gifted clown Fancioulle is aware that he has been condemned by a sadistic, art-loving, Neronian prince to be hanged for political conspiracy in the cause of freedom, though Fancioulle's theatrical magic is probably more dangerous to political power than his commitment to freedom.[31] Fancioulle is commanded to play one of his most dazzling roles in a fairy pantomime. Though he is about to become a martyr of the absurd – of unjust, peremptory death – Fancioulle performs his antics to perfection. In the judgment of the narrator, who would probably have applauded Nietzsche's comments on the redemptive power of art in *The Birth of Tragedy,* Fancioulle proves conclusively "that the intoxication of Art is more apt than any other to veil the terrors of the eternal abyss; and that genius can play a part, lost, as it is, in a paradise that shuts out all thought of death and destruction" (56). However, this fine conception of art and genius as conquerors of the terrors of extinction is conceivably invalidated by what follows. A calculatedly ugly hiss in the midst of the enchanted audience suddenly destroys Fancioulle's miraculous self-absorption in his role. The intrusion of this disgusting reality, carrying with it the stench of death, is so great a shock that it kills him.

Is the power of artistic metamorphosis, then, severely limited? Is it only a fiction? Is genius scarcely a foolproof means of subverting the tyranny of unexpected, drastic misfortune? In his reading of "A Heroic Death," Edward K. Kaplan stresses the inadequacy of the narrator's interpretation. Kaplan's point is that the artist's inebriating gift of veiling "the terrors of the abyss" is deadly in its delusoriness, since ultimately "material power" can wreck the heroism of "spiritual autonomy."[32] One might, of course, make a simple, if not overly satisfying, distinction between art, which by its very production demonstrates that it is capable of withstanding the terrors of the abyss, and the more or less frail flesh-and-blood artist, who may be physically jolted out of his creative magic by unforeseen disaster. But perhaps the clown role in "A Heroic Death" suggests only that the art of buffoonery, though skilled in temporarily easing and even erasing psychic infirmities and social perils, cannot pit its brief joy against the random, incurable traumas of the absurd.

2.

In his astute review of *Madame Bovary,* Baudelaire suggested that Flaubert had muted his powers of lyricism and irony, at least in comparison with the way those powers had been unleashed in *The Temptation of Saint Anthony.*[33] Yet *Madame Bovary* is the one nineteenth-century literary work whose interlocking of lyricism (whether pristine or hackneyed) and irony is so notorious that it would seem to be irrefutably illustrative of romantic irony. Nevertheless, the fact that Emma Bovary, like Don Quixote, swallows an overdose of romantic illusion does not in itself guarantee that Flaubert's novel is an exemplary work of romantic irony.[34]

It is true, however, that Flaubert's ambivalence toward the romantic ethos is both incontrovertible and amply documented. His letter to Louise Colet, dated March 20-21, 1852 makes it clear that in his novel in the making (*Madame Bovary*), he is balancing romantic and antiromantic urges: "the entire value of my book, if it has any," he writes, "will consist of my having known how to walk straight ahead on a hair, balanced between the two abysses of lyricism and vulgarity which I seek to fuse in analytical narrative."[35]

Nor is comedy alien to Flaubert's conflicting impulses. In an earlier letter of January, 1852, Flaubert clearly signals an interest in, and even a relish for, the comic maneuvres of a disabused mind. In a brief self-analysis, Flaubert refers to "two distinct persons" in his inner being.[36] The first is infatuated with eagle flights of lyricism, while the second is in love with truth, fact, and laughter. In *Madame Bovary,* the second person, a comedian-demoralizer, strikes out at both the mean world of antiromanticism and the delusory world of lyrical emotion.[37]

The antiromantic way of life in *Madame Bovary* is callously opportunistic, heartlessly prosaic, and contemptibly treacherous. On the other hand, Emma Bovary's provincially constricted soul is engulfed in the shoddy idealism of a "bastard Romanticism."[38] At times Flaubert exhibits an almost perfect parity of revulsion. Romantic and antiromantic attitudes are both ingloriously displayed, for example, when the Bovarys first arrive at Yonville, where Emma immediately discovers a soul mate: Emma and Léon see eye to eye on the power of Nature to induce dreams of the infinite and the ideal; and they share the view that the reveries furnished by literature provide compensatory value in a commonplace, disenchanted world. While this duet of harmonious interests is being performed, Charles is discovering a different, unmistakably antiromantic kind of compatibility as he soaks up the presumably practical wisdom of the vigorously self-important pharmacist Homais, who, along with local gossip and helpful recommendations, ceaselessly disgorges facts and statistics (that is, "scientific" information). In this scene, tired romanticism (whether sincere or sincerely faked) brushes against tiresome bourgeois reality. Neither much outdoes the other in the charmless delinquencies of banality.

As has often been noted, the pages devoted to the agricultural fair ingeniously sustain these clashing perspectives – at both a higher and a lower level. Rodolphe's lofty claptrap about elective affinities and Emma's attunement to his words are struck off against the crude economic (or portentously patriotic) preoccupations of government bureaucrats, shopkeepers, well-to-do farmers, and illiterate peasants. Yet the two performances creating this comic discordance are not quite balanced. Though far from being honorable or illustrious, vulgarity below seems less tainted by duplicity than the fancy dialogue above. Prize hogs and prized manure are not simply deflationary correlatives of Rodolphe's platitudes. They are less delusory than poetic phoniness. The scene is salvageable for romantic irony, however, mainly because of Emma's fluttering receptivity to Rodolphe's trumpery phrases. However drenched in second-hand lyricism Emma may be, her response to an impossible romantic ideal achieves value, if only by default, when matched against Rodolphe's cynical, corrupt, rote manipulativeness.[39]

In his study of Flaubert's fiction, Victor Brombert entitles his chapter on *Madame Bovary* "The Tragedy of Dreams," though he subsequently describes the novel as "a tragic-comedy of lies, ersatz and illusion."[40] If this description suggests a rather negative estimate of the romantic world caught in the novel's overlapping of tragic tension and comic zest (71), note what Brombert has to say about Flaubert's ambivalence: "Flaubert's pity blends with his caricature of Romantic dreams, and nothing would be more difficult than to draw a line separating the two" (77). If we elevate "pity" to a more generous level of interpretation, we may regard it as a limited sanctification of romantic illusion.

A blessing (forthright or reluctant) of the romantic imagination is seldom directly expressed in *Madame Bovary*. However, "pity" viewed as a compassionate comprehension of the romantic ideal does appear to dominate caricature at certain crucial moments. Consider the scene in which Emma, her repressed desires on the verge of metamorphosing into insurrectionary adulterous passion, seeks spiritual consolation from Bournisien, the local priest. Emma is not delineated here merely as a dupe of shopworn romanticism who foolishly continues to think of love as a hurricane force or a splendid exoticism. She does not, for the moment, bear the burden of Flaubert's early, reiterated depreciations. This does not mean that Flaubert is now manifesting undiluted sympathy for his protagonist. But some kind of sympathy, and possibly even empathy – readers disagree considerably here – seems to be at work as Emma solicits, more delicately than artfully, spiritual support from Bournisien. Though Emma is in a febrile state and is in danger of moral shipwreck, Bournisien, self-declared doctor of the soul, has too roughened a sensibility to recognize the nature of her ailment. (Flaubert is presumably not displeased, however, to temper his empathy with a mischievously grotesque analogy when he makes the priest equate Emma's sorrows with the grievous condition of a swollen cow that has been cast under a spell.) Had Bournisien been worldly enough to intuit the source of Emma's anguish, he would perhaps have attempted to solace her (if a bit archly) by ascribing her suffering to an indigestion of noxious romantic yearnings for the unattainable and the insubstantial. As it is, Emma can only wilt beneath the priest's incomprehension of her repeated efforts to make him grasp her heart's torment.[41]

The most potently oblique (if always partial) exoneration of Emma's misbegotten lyricism is transmitted through Flaubert's mordantly comic portraits of such self-satisfied, predatory bourgeois specimens as the pharmacist Homais, the notary Guillaumin, the tax collector Binet, and especially the dry-goods merchant Lheureux, all of whom are bound to consider the romanticization of life as a preposterous impracticality, a disastrously non-commercial transaction. (Gushing, pedantic, antic Homais is often amiable enough; and his verbal energy and rationalist posturing are from some time more amusing than repulsive. But by the end of the novel, his hypocrisy, self-serving schemes, and conscienceless betrayals have turned positively sinister.) Emma's romantic temper, however derivative, and however ruinous and ultimately corrupt, can hardly be viewed as more revolting than the loathsomely cunning tactics of the novel's bourgeois realists, though Flaubert's rage at bourgeois realism is usually well filtered through his stance of impersonality. A comment by Harry Levin is pertinent here: "Emma's dreams are destined, at the touch of reality, to wither into lies. Is that a critique of her or of reality? If she suffers for her mistakes, shall we infer that those who prosper are being rewarded for their merits?"[42]

What is missing in Emma's life is what she is unwilling to accept as the distinctive (and perhaps unique) gratification of art: a stirring of the emotions, an enrichment of consciousness, a revitalizing discovery of adventurous potentialities. Emma's inability to abide by the fictiveness of the romantic life is precisely what dooms her. While watching a performance of *Lucia di Lammermoor* in Rouen, Emma bitterly recognizes that the dream of combining valor, virtue, and voluptuousness in a great love is a lie invented by art. Yet shortly thereafter she succumbs once again (and even more intensely) to artistic illusion: she sees, not an opera, not the theatrical trickery she has just smilingly scorned in her newfound critical detachment, but incarnate love upon the stage – and off, for she also envisions herself as the companion of the great singer Lagardy in his world tours. The chance encounter with Léon at the opera re-ignites her former amorous, if discreetly repressed, interest in him. The result is a liaison that graduates (or descends) from discretion to operatic extravagance.

Emma's erotic-operatic turbulence will intensify almost to the very end, at which point she is far from being the woman whose sincere but trite language of passion once warranted Flaubert's defense against Rodolphe's insentience. Emma's romantic ideal has become increasingly contaminated by feral sensuality, not to mention obsessive lies and catastrophic indebtedness. Even her reading plummets from visions of perfect love to scenes of violence and orgiastic sexuality. Emma's degradation recalls D. H. Lawrence's contention that lyricism (though not the frank sort) and pornography are two sides of the same coin: lyricism replaces reality with emotional ideals that are impossible to achieve, while pornography degrades healthy eroticism into a base appetite.[43]

That a failed romantic paradise has led to an inferno of sexuality is a more ravaging irony than that "Emma found again in adultery all the platitudes of marriage" (211). But if one can scarcely argue, against Lawrence, that unholy sexuality may be an alternative consummation of the romantic spirit, one can at least argue that Léon's defection from lyricism is more repulsive than Emma's surrender to a vitiated sensibility. Flaubert remarks that poetic feeling in the life of a bougeois like Léon is only a fugitive, youthful malady. Emma's passion, on the other hand, is a perilous but permanent fixation. Even in the abyss of perversion, she can still dream of a princely, godlike lover who will make her heart "beat wildly in awe and admiration" (211). The "vague ecstasies of imaginary love" exhaust Emma Bovary "more than the wildest orgies" (212).

Though the romantic imagination accumulates a good many deficits in *Madame Bovary,* Flaubert insisted that, far from being a realist, he was a "rabid old Romantic – or a fossilized one ... whichever you prefer."[44] Whether he was also a (dark) romantic ironist, like Dostoevsky and Baudelaire, is more difficult to judge. Grim events and (muted) disgust increasingly characterize the last sections of the novel. Even the extensive mockery of the priest Bournisien and the freethinker Homais, who smugly encircle and thickly smudge Emma's death with their stale polemics, does not sufficiently counterbalance the sense of hopelessness (smoothly, not biliously, presented) in the final pages of *Madame Bovary.*

Critics who comment on the presence or absence of romantic irony in *Madame Bovary* seldom suffer the minor anguish of having to decide whether the novel is basically a comic enterprise. Lillian Furst, for example, in *Fictions of Romantic Irony* (1984) excludes *Madame Bovary* from the world of romantic irony, not because Flaubert is a failed comedian but because his sense of values is closer to Jane Austen's (Austen is not a romantic ironist, either) than to Byron's. Furst argues, that is to say, that irony in *Madame Bovary,* as in *Pride and Prejudice*, subserves reconstructible discourse (she is relying here on Booth's language in *A Rhetoric of Irony*), thus insuring that discordances will be resolvable and values correctly reconstituted. The "fictions of Romantic irony," on the other hand, reveal "irreconcilable paradoxes" and "lasting, elemental disruptions."[45] (Nowhere does Furst postulate that comedy is central to, or inherent in, paradoxical, disruptive romantic irony.) Furst concedes, however, that Flaubert's irony is "more devious and far more complex" (75) than that of Jane Austen, and that it is also more "persuasive and menacing in the long run" (76) – menacing because there is no longer a confident communion between narrator and reader; the latter is much less sure of being able to penetrate uncertainties and contradictions, especially when they appear to underline destructive rather than restorative attitudes.

In an earlier study, *Flaubert: The Uses of Uncertainty* (1974), Jonathan Culler asserts that   Flaubert's novelistic irony is indeed a "version" of romantic irony and that this Flaubertian romantic irony, which is more evident, Culler claims, in *Bouvard and Pécuchet* than in *Madame Bovary,* is the key to the novelist's strategies of indeterminacy (which apparently add up to a Kierkegaardian "infinite absolute negativity"). What, then, is romantic irony? Culler defines it as "the posture of a work which contains within itself an awareness of the fact that while pretending to give a true account of reality it is in fact fiction and that one must view with an ironic smile the act of writing a novel in the first place."[46] (We have seen that this definition, which accepts a rough synonymity between German romantic irony and playfully self-conscious fiction, is not uncommon among literary critics. Thus Erich Auerbach suggests in *Mimesis* that a literary work which contains an interwoven account of its own genesis is written "in the ironic vein of the romanticists.")[47] Furst thinks that Culler's definition has a limited validity. She agrees that Flaubert's text makes definitive conclusions about Emma Bovary, and even Charles Bovary, impossible; but she contends that such indefiniteness is dominated by a generally firm perspective, based on negation and mockery (comedy is not being exiled, then), a perspective that "is closer to the certitudes of Jane Austen than to the relativism of the Romantic ironists."[48]

It is the opinion of Lloyd Bishop, in *Romantic Irony in French Literature* (1989), that Furst mistakenly de-emphasizes, even while pointing to, the ways in which Flaubert deprives his reader of assurance and certitude in relation to Emma. Indeed Flaubert's ambivalence toward his protagonist, Bishop remarks, is "one of the chief sources of his romantic irony."[49] But this major source of romantic irony is not, according to Bishop, the core of romantic irony. (Nor is comedy essential.) Bishop prefers a broader view of the subject, one that would include "the radical indeterminacy of meaning such an ambivalent irony deliberately produces" (122-23). Why ambivalence must generate "radical indeterminacy of meaning" – why self-division must be the cause of multiple elusiveness – is not explained.

What one can finally maintain is that in *Madame Bovary* Flaubert repudiates, quite unequivocally, the antiromantic view of life, and that though he also impugns the romantic temper, Flaubert does so with some equivocation. The result might, with some exaggeration, be described as a variable stand-off between counter-romantic and romantic impulses. The question of comedy is less easy to resolve. All readers are aware that Flaubert exercises his sense of the comic more than intermittently. Indeed *Madame Bovary* is at times suffused with devastating mockery. But it is also true that Flaubert tends to make his levity almost suffocatingly somber and bleak. Flaubert has produced, one may conclude, a work of dark, almost strangled romantic irony.

Appendix: *Don Juan*, Romantic Irony, and the Critics

1.

In 1957, the year Leslie A. Marchand's 3-volume biography of Byron amply recorded the interplay (or intershock) of romantic idealism and realistic disenchantment in the poet, Ernest J. Lovell, in his essay "Irony and Image in *Don Juan*," undertook to shield Byron from the regressive impertinence of romantic irony, which he assumed was a commonplace concept. (This was the case primarily in Germanistic studies.) At the same time, Lovell advanced the idea that Byron's irony had been strangely neglected by the New Critics, inasmuch as it accorded handsomely with New Critical tenets. Byron's irony in *Don Juan*, Lovell claimed, was powerfully modern and needed to be recognized as such, though not in the deprecatory way in which Ivor Winters had spoken of Byron – as standing "at the head of that long line of masters of the double mood and the conversational-ironic manner which comes down through Laforgue, Pound, and Eliot."[1]

The romantic irony Lovell scorns as an insidious entity appears to be partly his own invention. Lovell tells us that Byron's irony is "neither shallow, cynical, insincere, incidental, nor typically romantic, whether the latter type be understood as self-irony, self-pitying disillusion, or the willful destruction of the dramatic illusion" (132). The first alleged category of romantic irony ("self-irony") is in fact highly characteristic of *Don Juan*, whose narrator tends to make fun not only of the world's follies and fallibilities but also his own. The second alleged category of romantic irony ("self-pitying disillusion") is extremely wide of the mark.

Romantic irony may be significantly indebted to disillusion, but it is alien to mournful emotion, and especially to the kind of plangency that accompanies self-pity. When the narrator's disenchantment in *Don Juan* borders on teary self-regard (this happens only occasionally), lamentation is quickly expunged by self-mockery.

Although Lovell cites no German sources – he never makes clear what authorizes his threefold definition – the third alleged category of romantic irony ("the willful destruction of the dramatic illusion") echoes the regrettably restrictive definition of romantic irony which derives mostly from Tieck's theatrical mischief. As it happens, however, one of the comic glories of *Don Juan* is Byron's nonchalant shattering of both epic and narrative conventions. If we expand the scope of "dramatic illusion" to include other genres, Lovell's dismissal of romantic irony in *Don Juan* may be seen, once more, as misguided.

Lovell's attempt to make Byron an icon of irony for the New Criticism is bolstered by the proper vocabulary. He emphasizes "Byron's use of ironic qualification within a lyrical context, to achieve the illusion of increased comprehensiveness and complexity" (134). Byron's practice thus presumably corresponds to the New Critics' rejection of single, especially emotional, vision. Lovell's further comment that *Don Juan* "combines and reconciles within itself the extremes of the love poem and of the satire" (138) is familiar but debatable. In *Don Juan* this kind of duality is more usefully described as a bold, tantalizing disequilibrium than as a Coleridgean reconciliation of antithetical forces – or as a New Critical merger of opposed impulses rendered homeopathically invulnerable to irony. Lovell, mistakenly claiming that Byron's irony "is not any sense the self-contradictory attitude of romantic irony," is certain that "the romance" in *Don Juan* "is not canceled out but intensified" (138) by satire. That the romance is not canceled out by satire may be granted. In the early cantos, romance often recovers from damage caused by antiromantic mockery. But recuperation is not the same as intensification. Byron's satiric comedy does not serve mainly as a foil to enhance his lyricism.

Lovell's essay was included in the first edition of *English Romantic Poets: Modern Essays in Criticism* (1960), edited by M. H. Abrams. In the second edition of Abrams' critical anthology (1975), "Irony and Image in *Don Juan*" was superseded by other essays, most relevantly by W. W. Robson's "Byron and Sincerity," a slightly revised version of an essay on Byron published in 1958.[2] The difference in the two critics' tolerance of romantic irony is startling. Where Lovell shuns attributing romantic irony to *Don Juan,* Robson sees romantic irony as a major factor in Bryon's comedy. Romantic irony is defined by Robson as a mingling of the romantic, feeling self with its cynical counterpart (expressed as Restoration rakishness or Augustan reasonableness).

Yet Robson's further analysis of the Byronic blend of "man-of-the-world" realism (287) and romanticism is somewhat murky. The trouble begins after Robson sensibly acknowledges that Byron's romantic irony is not unique in European romanticism, that "neither the Romanticism, nor the irony, nor their coming together from the same poet, is specifically Byronic. There is such a thing as Romantic irony, as in Heine or Musset." (No illustrations are provided for what is apparently a familiar, unproblematic literary phenomenon.) Robson's next sentence is puzzling, however. "What *is* highly personal to Byron," he remarks, "is the temporary stabilization of conflicting emotions, in a manner which is neither Romantic nor ironical" (292). By "conflicting emotions" Robson presumably does not mean something like love combatting hate or ecstasy struggling with despair, but rather a clash between romantic sensibility and antiromantic matter-of-factness. But why Byron's romantic irony is segregated from Heine's or Musset's is not made clear.

Though Robson is convinced that "the success of *Don Juan* is mainly a matter of Byron's success in effecting a positive relation" (289) between his romantic and antiromantic selves (a "positive relation" apparently signifies the momentary condition of "resolution," "reconciliation," or "stabilization"), Byron's romantic and antiromantic selves usually wrestle towards a state of radical instability rather than toward reciprocal accommodation. In any event, it turns out that Robson is unwilling to celebrate the temporary stabilization of antagonistic forces he has underlined in Byron's comedy. His ultimate verdict is that *Don Juan* "cannot . . . rank very high among the creative works of literature" primarily because it is not possessed of an "integral vision" (302). "Integral vision" means an Arnoldian self-respect, as well as a respect for one's art. Byron's failure in this regard is measured, according to Robson, by the unusual stress he places on both self-boredom and boredom with his subject matter in the final cantos, "though they are the finest and most mature parts of the poem" (33). "Integral vision" also connotes a super-mature ability to accept the past, however painful, "as a condition of the present." This, Robson says, Byron cannot do; he cannot, unlike Stendhal, recreate "the follies of youth . . . from within . . . always under the eyes of maturity." He is impotent to do this – "except in the early cantos" (300). Since Byron's romantic irony is at its peak in the early cantos, it would seem, if we follow Robson's line of thought, that romantic irony must have some (positive) relationship to integral vision. But of course romantic irony is inherently disintegrative, however neatly bundled its antithetical materials appear to be.

Unlike Lovell and Robson, Truman Guy Steffan in *The Making of a Masterpiece* (1957), the first volume of the 4-volume edition of *Don Juan* edited by Steffan and Willis W. Pratt, makes no mention of romantic irony (nor is there any in the second edition [1971].) He has much to say about satire, however. Steffan sees in Byron's epic a world which satire (whose great, basic weapon is irony) cannot purge, but which Byron cannot resist satirizing. The endless "futility of human endeavor . . . and the hypocrisy of men and women"[3] elicit from Byron almost incessant Ecclesiastian, destructive authorial observations. On the other hand, omnipresent hypocrisy and stupidity stimulate a forceful appetite for truth and lead to a devastating Byronic ridicule of sham.

There is no room in *The Making of a Masterpiece* for a concept like European romantic irony primarily because Steffan perceives in *Don Juan* a huge disparity between antiromantic disillusion, which is immense, and romantic idealism, which is feeble. He notes, for example, that a great many of Byron's revisions are "negative, skeptical, destructive" (85). Though he does not deny that Byron's idealism is temperamentally ingrained in him, Steffan's fundamental argument is that such idealism is only an impulsive, emotional concession to the tiny possibilities of human goodness; at best, it is "a warming speck in a universe of cold things" (289).

Even in the early cantos of *Don Juan*, where Byron most abundantly nourishes and demolishes illusion, Steffan detects no more than a collision between a mite of idealism and a mountain of disenchantment. Although Byron is later described as "at times disillusioned, at times eagerly leaping to idealized and sentimental extremes" (291), Steffan never intimates that lapses into negation and leaps into illusion may achieve equal rank. Oscillations between romanticism and antiromanticism merely illustrate "the variety of [Byron's] epic carnival" (130).

Byron remains, in Steffan's view, essentially an irreverent satirist. But since *Don Juan* also smacks of the carnivalistic, Byron's satire may for some readers be indistinguishable from buffoonery. Paul West, who makes much of Byron's chameleonic nature in *Byron and the Spoiler's Art* (1960), finds that Byronic buffoonery – the poet's predilection for irreverent antic maneuvers – is the key to the comedy of *Don Juan*. What

Hazlitt decries as satanic malice in *Don Juan* is viewed by West as Byron's peculiar repudiative excellence, "his most impressive displays" being "those in which he grafts a grotesquely inappropriate item on to a revered growth."[4] According to West, the defilement of the "serious" or the ideal in *Don Juan* is performed by a master of riotously destructive farce who relishes irresponsibility and a talent for hoaxing.

Byron's satire, one might think, cannot be submerged that easily beneath a tempest of nothing-is-sacred clowning. West contends, however, that Byron's refusal to spell out his allegiances wobbles his satiric stance. If there are no overt, hardy satiric principles, he assumes, then multiple inconsistencies in *Don Juan* must be driven by a great lawless energy. Romantic aspiration and romantic melancholy, West believes, are especially subjected to Byron's derisive buffoonery. The only way West can account for the romantic impulse that generates "many lyrical passages" (27) in *Don Juan*, most remarkably in Julia's letter and in the entire Haidée episode, is by interpreting that romantic impulse as an anomaly in the farce puppeteer's nonchalant or contemptuous disposition. (Hence the concept of romantic irony does not surface in West's book.) Though at one point he admits that Byron lets his characters "behave naturally" (27), West thinks that character in farce is, on the whole, necessarily inhuman: "in farce there is no considerateness, no sensitivity and no response" (13). Farce is a protection against the liabilities of human emotion.

West so tenaciously conceives of Byron's comic temper as an armored flippancy which permits him to deprecate "what might not otherwise be bearable" (68) that he is bound to reduce the dangerous "tenderness of the Haidée idyll" to a minor ripple in Byron's busy travesties: "Some days he wrote things idyllic or compassionate," but "most days he made pugnacious fun" (123). Yet if Byron's work, as West concedes, actually "flourished in tensions between . . . romance and farce" (37), we should be able to discover more romantic sensitivity in Byron than West allows. And if it is true that "in terms of our times, [Byron] can be said to vacillate between Camus's man of stone in *L'Etranger* and Malraux's Garine, the fierce seeker after commitment in *Les Conquérants*" (123), then passionate engagement in Byron may be more certifiable than West is willing to admit.

Strangely enough, after repeatedly emphasizing Byron's burlesque shufflings and vertiginous paradoxes in *Don Juan*, West finds fault with the absence of emotional consistency in the Haidée episode. He claims that "Don Juan lacks not moments of true tenderness but a maintained unity of atmosphere. It is a mixture, not a compound. It gives life's incongruities without art's integration" (123-24). But if farce is meant to emasculate potent feelings and to "tweak anguish by the nose" (127), how can an emotional "unity of atmosphere" be maintained? Since West hails Byron's farce for its marvelous, tonic disintegrativeness, it seems perverse to accuse *Don Juan* of being an artistic failure, of lacking, as Robson put it earlier, "integral vision." It is also disquieting to observe that West finally translates the "clattering chaos" of *Don Juan* into a "poem of intelligent despair – an inspired gibbering in the lazar-house of the human condition. It inspires, surely, a tremor of horror in every reader" (127). Surely it does not. If such were the case, farce would be (at its best), not a great saturnalian comic power but a thin mask for anxiety and despair, a poorly disguised sinking feeling in the bowels.

West is effective as well as spirited when he deals with Byron as a farceur of language – a madcap mauler of rhymes, a clowning transgressor of lexical decorum. Byron's "knack of zany conjunctions" (40) creates "choppy absurdities which are the essence of the poem" (49). This is an interesting point, but it invites a misperception; for as *Don Juan* develops, Byron's exhilarating unruliness becomes more and more conspicuously modified by (very lively) satiric motives. The satire in the English cantos – satire need not, as West thinks, explicitly advertise a reformist bias – clearly dominates verbal giddiness; in these cantos, anarchic linguistic disruption is not enjoyed merely for its own sake. It is therefore difficult to agree with West when he says that from the first to last " 'anything goes' is the method of *Don Juan.* The poet remains uncommitted" (107).[5]

Unlike West, George Ridenour in *The Style of "Don Juan"* (1960) invokes the genre of satire, held to derive mainly from Pope, Horace, and Juvenal, over and over again to describe the nature of Byron's comedy. Because he trusts the diagnostic, truth-telling, ridiculing impulse in Byron's "epic satire," he puts little value on the poem's early announcement that *Don Juan* is meant to provide a cornucopia of carefree giggles.[6] Ridenour is also much preoccupied with the Christian myth of the Fall in *Don Juan,* so much so that despite his desire "not to minimize the comic" (151), he consistently scants Byron's disruptive levities. In particular, the conflict between the ideal and its comic disavowal gets short shrift in Ridenour's pages. In his second chapter, he briefly weighs the claims of certain earlier critics – Richter, Calvert, Porta (he does not mention Marchand in this connection) – that Byron may be viewed as "a classic-romantic paradox" or a "Rousseau-Voltaire" (21); but this kind of duality is subordinated by Ridenour to what he regards as the more comprehensive Byronic doubleness of harmony and corruption, salvation and damnation.

Ridenour touches on Byron's (unspecified) romantic irony in a single, late allusive comment: "Byron (like Spenser in the Bowre of Bliss) normally works by building up and tearing down his values" (141). It is doubtful, however, that Spenser is being Byronic in depicting the Bower of Bliss in Canto II.12 of *The Faerie Queene.* Ambivalence seems to reign, it is true. Acrasia's corrupt paradise, which will be cleansed by Sir Guyon and the Palmer, is a thing of exquisite beauty, Art and Nature having competed with each other to create its singular loveliness. Spenser's description obviously gives a certain license to aesthetic and erotic lusciousness. (Even Sir Guyon's virtue is temporarily rendered assailable by two ravishing nudes.) But if ambivalence complicates Spenser's moral vision for a while, it does not engender a recurrent building up and tearing down of values. Spenser is by no means humorless, but he does not cultivate his duality, such as it is, in a persistently comic vein.

It is not Spenser but his Italian antecedents who are usually cited as having attracted Byron, directly or indirectly, to the seriocomic style he exploits in *Beppo* and *Don Juan,* though David V. Erdman rightly points out that "as for the art of sinking in burlesque poetry, the efforts of Frere and the Italians appear quite puerile alongside the Byronic."[7] The greatest of the Italians, Ariosto, has often, like Byron, been described as both tender and ironic.[8] His tender, expansive lyricism is carefully cultivated, however; for Ariosto has too sceptically sophisticated a sensibility to surrender to genuine, blindly romantic urges. Certain romance motifs he can bring to hyperbolic perfection: pure chivalry, sublime passion, awesome exoticism, superhuman heroism, fabulous sorcery, endlessly gory combats. But if he indulges extravagantly in the magical, the marvelous, and the monstrous, he cannot resist from time to time making fun of his epic-amorous material.

Consider the episode in Canto X of *Orlando Furioso* in which Ruggiero, potently and also notoriously enamored of the thrillingly brave and faithful Bradamant, rescues the beautiful, naked Angelica from a sea monster, and does so with magnificent chivalry – only to find himself overpowered by lust. The transition from Canto X to Canto XI portrays a vigorously opportunistic Ruggiero fumbling feverishly with his knightly gear in an effort to liberate his instrument of erotic conquest. Before he has a chance, however, to wrestle much further with his armor, Angelica magically vanishes. Though all of the details are recounted apparently with the full approval of the narrator, certain heroic indecencies obviously impugn the chivalric ethos; indeed, the whole episode is drenched in sly mockery. Ariosto honors the heroic ideal, embedded in incredible, fantastic contexts, in a spirit of vivid but basically suave detachment. Compared to *Orlando Furioso,* where romantic illusion is merely a marvelous game and the ideal is splendidly theatrical, *Don Juan* is virtually a Bible of romantic sincerity.

If Ridenour singles out Spenser's perspective on the Bower of Bliss as a prototype of Byronic duality, Brian Wilkie in his chapter on "Byron and the Epic of Negation" in *Romantic Poets and the Epic Tradition* (1965) finds the closest analogue to Byron's temper in Montaigne. "In its combination of seriousness with radical inconsistency of tone," Wilkie asserts, "no work seems to be more like *Don Juan* than Montaigne's *Apology for Raimond Sebond.*"[9]

Wilkie describes *Don Juan* as an all-embracing, inconclusive poem informed by a temper of "philosophic nihilism" (189), elsewhere identified as a "generally tolerant" skepticism (211). Such skepticism, generating "radical disorder" (190) in Byron's "comprehensively aimless" poem (191), is itself subjected to mockery. But if Byron ironizes his own Pyrrhonism by means of an idealism described as fundamentally flimsy, he does so, according to Wilkie, because he is aware that without certain illusions "nations and individuals cannot flourish" (219). This is as close as Wilkie gets to bearing witness to the frequent intersection of romanticism and antiromanticism in the early part of *Don Juan.* Since Wilkie considers Byron's romanticism to be a necessary falsity, a concession to human and cultural weakness, he is of course far from recognizing, let alone endorsing, the presence of romantic irony in *Don Juan.*

Is Wilkie at least justified in associating *Don Juan* with the *Apology for Raimond Sebond?* One can understand Wilkie's statement that "Byron is very close to preaching – and in *Don Juan* exemplifying – the Negative Capability that Keats had once urged" (223). Reaching for certitude, after all, is not a Byronic compulsion. But it is less easy to grasp the relevance of Wilkie's allusion to Montaigne's longest essay, where "seriousness" allegedly combines with "radical inconsistency of tone." The core of the *Apology* is a Pyrrhonic rejection of conclusions drawn from man's presumptuous but defective reason, though Montaigne at times finds Pyrrhonisim itself as amusingly hollow as other pagan philosophies. Nevertheless, he does not communicate his acceptance of universal incertitude in radically inconsistent ways, and certainly not in a Byronic, jocoserious manner. Moreover, Montaigne insists over and over again (even if somewhat mechanically), that though profound skepticism saves us from a host of preposterous vanities, it must be buttressed by faith – not by the horrors of Christian zeal, but by reverence for God (that is, true reason), without which man is nothingness and knowledge is a mere plague. Such reiterated affirmations, whether perfunctory or not, are scarcely germane to Byron's "epic of negation." Montaigne's blend of Pyrrhonism and faith paradoxically makes for unity of mind. Byron's mix of romanticism and counter-romanticism, however, nourishes a provocative disunity of spirit.

In *Byron the Poet* (1964), which is largely concerned with *Don Juan,* M. K. Joseph does not suggest, like Wilkie, that Byron cultivates a factitious fineness of feeling for the sake of individual well-being and social survival. Nor does he consider romantic irony an invisible or forbidden topic. Joseph is one of the very few Byron critics who are prepared to cite Babbitt's strictures on romantic irony in *Rousseau and Romanticism.* He specifically quotes Babbitt on the romantic ironist's tendency to harbor both dream and disenchantment, and to flee irresponsibly from an ethical center. Joseph then answers this charge by arguing that "for Byron, there *is* a centre, in the sense that there is a moral point of view implied throughout the dialectical interplay, not only of 'sentiment' and 'irony' [he is alluding to Babbitt's quotation from Jean Paul], but of all the varied forms of discourse the poem contains."[10] The narrator of *Don Juan,* Joseph claims, preserves "a moral normality while at the same time expressing his mocking and ironic despair of a world that he sees as morally abnormal" (209). But perhaps "moral normality" is too hygienic a concept to apply to Byron's buoyant refusal to shrink from political and social anomalies.

Be that as it may, Joseph's observations on the comedy of *Don Juan* rarely err by being squeezed into a one-sided position, as in his isolated, misleading statement that "the poem is a satire on the romantic cult of passion" (278). Joseph in fact frequently underlines his conviction that, for all Byron's sighing about the metamorphosis of what was once romantic into burlesque, the poet often sees to it that a mood of comic antiromanticism acts as a prelude to the resurrection of romantic passion. Joseph's comment that "the first ten cantos simultaneously maintain and satirize the world of romance" (320) is too generous by far in its arithmetic, but at least it may be seen as corroborating the Cervantesque basis of romantic irony.

The corroboration is at best oblique, however, for the phrase "romantic irony," which crops up in Joseph's quotations from Babbitt, is never adopted by Joseph himself. Nor does he, like Babbitt or Robson, find nineteenth-century European parallels to Byron. He prefers, like G. Wilson Knight in *Byron and Shakespeare* (1966),[11] to link Byron to Shakespearean polarities – thus Byron "has Falstaff in him as well as Hamlet" (267) – or to associate *Don Juan* with *The Canterbury Tales.* "One has to turn back to Chaucer," Joseph remarks, "to find, in English poetry, the same movement between romance and burlesque, chivalry and bawdry, ideal and real" (266).

In his last chapter, "Green Tea and Cognac: The Irony of *Don Juan,*" Joseph quotes a passage from Lovell's *Byron: The Record of a Quest: Studies in a Poet's Concept and Treatment of Nature* (1949). Byron's irony, Lovell declares, stems from the fact that "the diverse elements of experience gathered together . . . defy the poet's powers of reconciliation" (quoted, 318). Joseph reverses this conclusion, insisting that "the irony *is* the reconciliation, for it enables [Byron] to maintain a consistent attitude towards a world where inconsistencies make all systems unreal" (318). (Had Joseph also referred to Lovell's later essay "Irony and Image in *Don Juan*" [1957], he might have pointed to a considerable argumentative shift, since Lovell, we remember, claims in that essay that Byron's irony signifies, not the impossibility of harmony, but rather a reconciliation of discordances.)

The "consistent attitude" Joseph attributes to Byron is "sympathetic detachment" (321). This oxymoronic phrase does not quite coincide with romantic irony; yet Joseph observes that Byron's mobility – the poet's version of "negative capability" (Wilkie uses the same analogy) – "enables him to identify himself, fully for the moment, with both the romantic and the ironic" (320). (Nowhere in his discussion, incidentally, does Joseph refer to F. Schlegel or to "German romantic irony." The one German writer he does have recourse to is Brecht. "Don Juanism," Joseph writes, "has a good deal in common with Brechtian 'Verfremdung,' which likewise distances the spectator from the action and provokes his reaction to it by a calculated use of the strange, the unexpected or the discordant" [323].) Byron's comic temper is ultimately certified by Joseph to be a compound of "detachment without indifference" and "humorous calm" (326).

In his lengthy discussion of *Don Juan* in *The Plot of Satire* (1965), Alvin B. Kernan comes up with rather different analytical categories. Kernan is of the opinion that the contradictions in *Don Juan* "resolve ultimately into three senses of life, comic, satiric, and tragic."[12] Kernan thus sanctions the widely held but disabling theory that comedy and satire, if not mutually alien entities, are at the very least radically dissimilar. The distinction Kernan adheres to is that comedy is wholesomely celebratory, while satire is usefully denigratory.[13] But this distinction rather glibly robs comedy of mind. Since, according to Kernan, comedy is the unsystematic expression of the life spirit, comedy apparently does not have to reason about, or worry about, such things as unsustainable beliefs or an incomprehensible universe. Indeed comedy need not consort with ideas at all. Since the comic sense in *Don Juan* is "a natural, unthinking instinct for what is good and a freedom in moving with the full stream of life" (191), one may deduce, furthermore, that the less Juan thinks (or speaks), the more satisfying he becomes as a representative of comedy's naturalness and beneficence.

Satire is another story. It is represented in *Don Juan*, Kernan tells us, by the cynical narrator, who finds it impossible to accept existence in the innocent, youthful, healthy, spontaneous, zestful, unthinking fashion of comedy. In the face of life's bitter constraints and nauseating shams, comedy's appetitive, bubbling naïveté is at a great disadvantage. Satire, however, is wise in the ways of the world. It is intensely, probingly rational; it is realistic; it is objective. It aims, Kernan asserts, to expose the gap between appearance (virtue) and reality (vice); it seeks to unmask the world's corruption and stupidity. In other words, satire, in the hands of Byron's narrator, inevitably corrects the exuberant romanticism of comedy. Yet Kernan argues that the narrator is not merely satiric; he is also estranged, caught in a "tragic situation" (219) because he finds only provisional truth in a meaningless universe.

Because the narrator's playful zest and conspicuous surges of idealism (in the early cantos) are completely passed over by Kernan, nothing resembling romantic irony is given a voice in his chapter. In the early sections of his book, it is true, Kernan does tackle the question of irony – in a thoroughly conventional way. His major point (unsurprisingly) is that ironic techniques hone the cutting edge of satire, whose purpose is to reduce what is wickedly serious to the level of the ridiculous. Irony, "the master trope of satire" (90), is "the perfect device" for uncovering sham and hypocrisy. Yet circumstantial irony is not a negligible element in Kernan's thinking. He remarks, for example, that the "appearance-reality conflict is at the heart of irony" (87).

After Joseph's study, a dozen years elapsed before the next sizable, perceptive, thoroughgoing analysis of *Don Juan* appeared. This was

Jerome J. McGann's *"Don Juan" in Context* (1976). In an earlier book, *Fiery Dust: Byron's Poetic Development* (1968), McGann had begun by disagreeing with the position taken by Robert F. Gleckner in *Byron and the Ruins of Paradise* (1967). McGann had rejected Gleckner's "controlling idea that Byron's is a poetry of radical despair." Gleckner, McGann maintained, had disregarded the poet's frequent "alternative insights and possibilities in his later work."[14]

In *Byron and the Ruins of Paradise*, Gleckner's main argument in regard to *Don Juan* (to which he devotes comparatively few pages) is that the poem offers the same "journey into nothingness and despair" presented by *Childe Harold,* along with the same remarkable "feat of mental strength and endurance." In *Don Juan* "the tack [is] different,"[15] but Gleckner believes that alienation, horror, and damnation are not themes which can be erased or diminished by shifts in tone. He insists that "by accepting varieties of tone as automatically indicative of variety of aim, it is plain we have overlooked the fundamental sameness of the voice's message, befouling ourselves in silly arguments about whether [Byron] is a satiric or a romantic poet" (301). This bizarre dismissal of tone as a superficial quality incapable of modifying substance or theme – as though attitudes were simply to be fetched from a closet of flimsy disguises – permits Gleckner to describe the laughter in *Beppo* as "the mask of despair" (302) and to assert that Byron's comedy "is but a mask for the prophetic voice of doom which underlies the whole" (305).[16]

Whatever assuaging, healing, or reintegrative powers comedy possesses are brushed aside as Gleckner fastens on the formula Byron himself invokes: I laugh that I may not weep. Gleckner makes of this limited aperçu (already a cliché when Byron was composing *Don Juan*) the key to all of Byron's comedy, so that the poet's laughter is never the product of exuberance or free-floating gaiety. A joke is an evasion of darkness; flippancy is a shield for protecting a vulnerable heart; laughter is an artificial stay against insanity. In comic theory, such claims exist cheek by jowl with many other, contrary commonplaces; and of course those Gleckner favors are defensible in specific cases. The trouble is that in Gleckner's view, Byron's gloom is an ineffaceable reality: the wounded heart's bleeding remains visibly unstaunched; the threat of madness is ubiquitously acute. Gleckner's dismissal of comedy's potentially palliative or even therapeutic properties is decisively evidenced in his treatment of *Don Juan,* the totality of which, he declares, is informed by "the horror of the vision of doom" (311). The "so-called gaiety and fun of *Don Juan*" (311) cannot hide ultimate depression and cannot cancel out Byron's "vision of a fragmented and meaningless universe" (312).

Gleckner regards Byron's emotional (romantic) and rational (satiric) proclivities as essentially similar reactions to "the world's waste and the unending self-destruction and corruption of man" (329). If Byron's cynical mockery melts from time to time into a resuscitated romantic dream, that is only because the poet's intense nostalgia for paradise lost – Gleckener acknowledges the influence of Ridenour here – cannot help desperately conjuring up a celestial vision. Nevertheless, "the judgment of the Augustan satirist," which reveals universal nightmare (though not precisely in Augustan fashion), is finally more telling than "the indomitable idealism of the Romantic poet" (335). Byron remains a heroic nihilist whose comedy is "analogous to the laughter of a death's head" (339).

In *Fiery Dust: Byron's Poetic Development,* McGann agrees that Byron's poetry "is indeed built upon a vision of the world's horror and absurdity"; but he is convinced that Byron "attempts to show how man achieves a Godlike sovereignty (or a childish innocence) even in a 'waste and icy clime' " (65). Though the quotation is from *Don Juan* (VII.2), the longest chapter in *Fiery Dust* focuses on *Childe Harold. Don Juan* receives only scattered comments, as when McGann states that "Jaques, Hamlet, Sterne and the Byron of *Don Juan* are all famous for their ability to hold mockery and melancholy in a delicate – and significant – equipoise" (61). Shifting ground slightly, McGann later translates Byron's self-division into "pessimism" and "mocking humor" (74).

McGann mentions (Schlegelian) romantic irony only once in *Fiery Dust,* in connection with the "moral ambiguities" and "moral contradictions" – "activity and futility, achievement and vanity, pleasure and pain, good and evil, life and death" – that produce instability and melancholy in the early cantos of *Childe Harold.* McGann comments on this "threatening duality" as follows: "*Childe Harold's Pilgrimage* does not seek to eliminate or negate this duality but, in a way similar to Schlegel when he formulated his concept of Romantic irony, to establish [the] sense of division as a value rather than a liability" (77). Nevertheless, McGann concludes, double perception does in fact constitute a liability in the early cantos of *Childe Harold.*

If McGann's single reference to Schlegel in *Fiery Dust* seems skimpy, one has to remember that in 1968 neither Schlegel nor romantic irony had yet been deified in Anglo-American criticism. Consider Northrop Frye's *A Study of English Romanticism,* which also appeared in 1968. In a comment that derives from Mario Praz, Frye claims that "Romantic irony revolves around de Sade and the so-called 'Romantic agony,' the sense of interpenetration of pleasure and pain, beauty and evil, intensity and destructiveness."[17] (Byron's *Don Juan,* Shelley's *The Cenci,* and Mary Shelley's *Frankenstein* are identified by Frye as works of romantic irony.) But Germanistic studies in 1968 would hardly have accepted F. Schlegel and the Marquis de Sade as romantic-ironic blood brothers.

In *"Don Juan" in Context* (1976), where the relevance of Schlegel's views on irony would seem to be more pointed, McGann makes no reference to Schlegel at all. But then, McGann has no need of German theory. English, Latin, and Italian sources supply him with a sufficiency of models. The English influence on *Don Juan* is "Pope's witty mock-heroic style," whose obverse is Byron's "denunciation of Romantic mannerisms,"[18] though Byron "was to incorporate his [purified] Romantic Style . . . into his 'conversational' poetry" (56). The Italian influence is the seriocomic *ottava rima* poetry of the Romance Epic (to a large extent mediated by Merivale, Frere, and Rose). The Latin influence is Horace, who serves as a purgative for romantic trashiness. As a conversational (plain) stylist, Horace also merges with Pulci, who "is slightly more arch and intimate than Horace" (73).

McGann's prefatory description of *Don Juan* as "both a critique and an apotheosis of High Romanticism" (ix) seems to augur well for European romantic irony; and McGann persuasively fills in the background of this dualistic development. Both early and late in his poetry, Byron evinces problematic, irresolvable dualities. Even in *Hours of Idleness,* the young aristocratic poet both "mocks at" and "gushes over" Love (8). (In the matter of mockery, it should be noted that McGann habitually speaks of Byron's "comic and satiric" verse without bothering to differentiate between the two qualifiers. Presumably, as in Kernan, "comedy" is good-humoredly acceptant, while "satire" is punitively corrective.)

Appropriately enough, McGann points out that though the "basic style of *Don Juan* is chatty and conversational, the tone of the poem has always been recognized as extremely various" (79). This distinction between style and tone is not always heeded in McGann's text. Distinctions seem impeccably presented when McGann signalizes the fluctuations in *Don Juan* between Horatian plainness (the colloquial-moderate) and Juvenalian elevation (the less conspicuous formal-sublime). But a certain confusion of terms occurs when McGann, after reminding us of Byron's "equivocal serio-comic tonality" (82), spells out once more (but not quite in the same way) the two major styles/tones/modes in *Don Juan*: the elusive "elegiac mode" and the "Horatian style of good sense and liberal jests" (83).

According to McGann, romantic irony is generated when these modes/styles/tones collide. "As has been frequently noted," he declares, "the conflicts between the poem's two most important styles (they are variously described) is the basis for the 'Don Juan' effect, Byron's Romantic Irony, properly so-called" (83). Apparently the "Don Juan" effect – that is, romantic irony – is also being referred to a moment or two later when McGann remarks that the collision between the elegiac mode and the plain Horatian mode "produces the serio-comic tone for which *Don Juan* is famous" (85). Yet Byron's plain style alone is perfectly capable of creating a mixed, serio-comic tonality. McGann himself acknowledges at one point that Byron's "theoretically normative style" can veer between any extremes (98).

McGann's second (and last) reference to romantic irony in *"Don Juan" in Context* deals more suitably with attitudes rather than with styles. The method of romantic irony, he writes, is a "two-edged sword." That is, romantic irony tends "to laugh at . . . Romantic attitudes" (124); but at the same time, unworthy antiromantic attitudes also require mockery. This is an acceptable account of (European) romantic irony. But McGann is not always consistent in his definitions. In an essay on the function of criticism, also published in 1976, McGann refers once again to "Byron's romantic irony, properly so-called,"[19] except that this time it appears to signify a sense of the adversities of mortality and the limitations of human power.

Several years earlier, M. C. Cooke in *The Blind Man Traces the Circle: On the Patterns and Philosophy of Byron's Poetry* (1969) had made three interesting references to romantic irony. The first occurs in his chapter on the third canto of *Childe Harold*. After citing the narrator's paean to the intensified life of the creative artist in the sixth stanza, Cooke calls attention to the self-conscious, cooling qualification visible at the beginning of the seventh: "Yet I must think less wildly." "This acknowledgement," Cooke declares, is "a sort of foretaste of romantic irony in Byron."[20] The real thing occurs, however, only in *Don Juan*, where ambivalence – the poet ceaselessly soars yet constantly cancels his flight – is skillfully managed by Byron's "paradoxical art" (56). Byron's passion and reflection, though indissolubly opposed in a skeptical disequilibrium, are equally fostered and equally valid in the poet's "gospel of uncertainty" (139).

Cooke's second (somewhat overseasoned) reference emphasizes the "Mephistophelean extreme of romantic irony and skepticism" (174), a mind-set that dampens romantic optimism and weakens even the courage of positive assertion. Cooke's third and last reference to romantic irony appears almost immediately after the second: "Byron, the romantic ironist, continually entices us with the apple of vision, only at the peak of aspiration or faith to spin into prominence the dismaying worm of 'reality' " (175). But this observation, which resembles early nineteenth-century criticism of *Don Juan* (Hazlitt's, for example), fails to be an adequate description of romantic irony not only because it neglects the resurgence of the ideal but because it ignores the role of comedy. "Dismaying worm," which sounds rather dispiriting, scarcely suggests Byron's amusing dismissal of his romantic impulses.

In broaching the question of romantic irony, Cooke does not invoke the name of F. Schlegel. He does, however, mention a number of influences on *Don Juan* usually neglected by critics. He dilates, for instance, on the partial coloring of *Don Juan* by Restoration comedy (Robson had briefly brought up this point). He also judges that the poet who most strikingly anticipates Byron – recall Ridenour voting for Spenser, and Wilkie for Montaigne – is Marvell, especially in "An Horation Ode," "with its pervasive and unfaltering dualism" (102). On the other hand, Harold E. Toliver has nothing to say about Byron in *Marvell's Ironic Vision* (1965).

The year Cooke's study appeared (1969), Schlegel did figure importantly in D. C. Muecke's chapter on romantic irony in *The Compass of Irony*. (Among Germanists, of course, the Schlegel industry had never halted.) Muecke's study, which highlights the theoretical significance of "German romantic irony" while exhibiting its actual poverty of expression during the romantic period, helped to re-invigorate the question of romanticism's relation to irony. This intrinsically unsettling question assumed great importance when M. H. Abrams memorably served notice, in *Natural Supernaturalism* (1971), that the bond between irony and romanticism might be usefully and honorably underplayed, though it could not go unrecorded. In his preface, Abrams writes that Keats figures only marginally in his study of "the secularization of inherited theological ideas and ways of thinking,"[21] while Byron is omitted altogether, "not because I think him a lesser poet than the others but because in his greatest work he speaks with an ironic counter-voice and deliberately opens a satirical perspective on the vatic stance of his Romantic contemporaries."[22] In noting the "satirical perspective" of Byron's "ironic counter-voice," Abrams is not underscoring a dualistic consciousness; he is not implying that Byron can be idealistic and even visionary (if not quite vatic) in *Don Juan* while at the same time retaining a comically oriented skepticism and cynicism.

Abrams later admitted that a different historical view of the romantic movement might be based precisely on the ironic stance; and this "valid alternative history" of romanticism he would "ungrudgingly accept."[23] "This imaginary history," he remarks, "will focus on what several reviewers chided me for omitting, the ironic perspective in general and the theory and practice of 'Romantic irony' in particular. It will claim, rightly, that the very concept of Romantic irony was developed by German writers of that era, and also that the theory and practice of the ironic mode is not only a primary Romantic achievement, but the most important and forward-looking one, since it anticipated what is most characteristic in our present temper and established the basic models which are being exploited by the best and most representative writers of our own era." Abrams could scarcely have made a more resonant confession of his sins of omission. He goes on: "the history will bring to the forefront German writers such as Friedrich Schlegel, whom I hardly mention, as well as others, such as Tieck, Richter, Heine, and Büchner (the author of *Woyzeck*), whom I did not mention at all. In this plot, the hero among the English Romantics will be Byron . . . . Keats will rank high; and Blake, Shelley, and even Coleridge, despite their vatic pretensions, will readily be shown to sing an ironic counterpoint to their own visionary claims. But Wordsworth, because he is 'the egotistical sublime' – self-absorbed, complacent, and inflexibly solemn and un-ironic in his pronouncements – will inevitably drop to the bottom of the scale as the weakest and least representative of the prominent poets in this central mode of the Romantic imagination and achievement."[24] In a later essay, Abrams, backtracking from his very generous concessions, declares that however admirable Byron's irreverent irony may be, Wordsworth's solemnity is much more interestingly complex: "It is easy to show that in many passages in *Don Juan,* Byron can be construed as deliberately subverting not only the poem's own narrative premises, but also major concepts and oppositions in Western metaphysics – so easy, in fact, that it doesn't present much of a challenge. Wordsworth, in his seriousness of asseveration, presents a much more inviting challenge."[25]

In any event, an alternative contemporary history of romanticism could hardly fail to acknowledge that European romanticism is inherently discordant and ambivalent, that it thrives on disharmony as well as unity, that it is energized by alienation as well as a need for transcendence, and that it has a significant relationship with comedy. Charles Rosen takes up precisely these points: Abrams "omits as irrelevant all mention of the explicitly ironic Romantics like Byron and E. T. A. Hoffmann; but their comic sense is not an aberration from the Romantic tradition but an illumination of patterns implicit in Hölderlin and Wordsworth." "In the ironic movement necessary to Romantic art," he goes on, "it is not unity and reintegration, not the return to the lost paradise that is sought, but division and estrangement."[26]

Two years after the appearance of *Natural Supernaturalism,* Stuart M. Sperry took up the task of defining English romantic irony. In *Keats the Poet* (1973), Sperry locates romantic irony in Shelley, Keats, and Byron; but he distinguishes the English poets' romantic irony from that of "their more philosophically oriented German counterparts." According to Sperry, the new English conception of irony, which "develops more individually and spontaneously"[27] and emphasizes a "sense of failure, irrelevance, or human and artistic limitation" (246), is exemplified by Shelley's wavering between skepticism and faith, Byron's mobility, and Keats's Negative Capability (or "perpetual indeterminacy"). In his chapter on romantic irony in Keats, Sperry interprets the poet's great odes as, for the most part, crystallizations of paradox, of "ultimate inconclusiveness" (259).

A year later (1974), Sperry delivered a lecture, "Toward a Definition of Romantic Irony in English Literature," which was subsequently included, with inevitable changes, in *Romantic and Modern: Revaluations of Literary Tradition* (1977), edited by George Bornstein. Sperry begins by admitting that the phrase "Romantic irony" is liable to be "unfamiliar and . . . puzzling" even to "some specialists in the period of English Romanticism . . . though the expression is beginning to be used increasingly by students of British and American literature."[28] He defines romantic irony, once more, as a state of irresolution or "a sense of indeterminacy" (5) produced by "openness to experience" – the kind of experience that offers a mixture of "potentiality" and "unfathomability" (6). Reversing the significance of Morse Peckham's "Positive Romanticism" and "Negative Romanticism," Sperry affirms that Byron's Negative Romanticism supplies release from hopelessly unsatisfactory visions of organic, cosmic harmony. Byron, that is to say, has transcended a Wordsworthian "need for certainty, or at least security" (20). Indeed, "no major work of the nineteenth century better illustrates Romantic irony – the quality of indeterminacy – than *Don Juan.*" Though the poem has obvious satiric elements, "throughout Byron plays one mood or attitude off against another. What we have is a work in which each position, philosophic or emotional, ironizes every other. What emerges as its final value is the spirit of mobility or irony itself, seen as a governing principle of life" (21).

Sperry distinguishes between unconscious romantic irony in Shelley and Keats and deliberate romantic irony in Byron. (In neither case, Sperry intimates, does the genesis of romantic irony in England require German romantic theorizing for its proper elucidation.) Yet Sperry pays insufficient attention to tonal distinctions among the three poets. Since, moreover, Sperry considers Wordsworth's "Resolution and Independence" to be illustrative of romantic irony (25n3), one hardly carries away the impression that romantic irony may have a special affiliation with the world of comedy. Nor, in speaking of Byron's mobility, does Sperry indicate that playing off contrary moods and attitudes becomes particularly significant when Byron counterpoints romantic idealism and antiromantic scepticism. Finally, Sperry does not distinguish between the role of indeterminacy and the function of ambivalence.[29] Indeterminacy is not only a current critical mantra. It is also the core of Pyrrhonic irony, which views efforts to pin down truth and certitude as amusingly absurd. A comically slanted ambivalence toward the ideal, however, is basic to European romantic irony.

2.

The years 1978-1980 signal a turning point in Anglo-American critics' receptivity to romantic irony. Three books attest to the emergence of critical attitudes that not only welcome but honor and even exalt romantic irony as an invaluable key (among very few others) to the discourse of romanticism: Peter Conrad's *Shandyism: The Character of Romantic Irony* (1978), David Simpson's *Irony and Authority in Romantic Poetry* (1979), and Anne K. Mellor's *English Romantic Irony* (1980).

Peter Conrad's *Shandyism: The Character of Romantic Irony* (1978), a book "less about than around *Tristram Shandy*,"[30] intricately insinuates that romantic irony long ago won its indispensable place in the sun. Conrad's prose in this critical extravaganza teems with complex allusions (which can be enlightening), bold aphorisms (which can be stimulating), and vertiginous pronouncements (which can be exasperating). *Shandyism* cannot easily be stripped down to its essentials; but one of the book's basic themes is clearly stated in Conrad's preface and is subsequently renewed in many serpentine variations: "Romanticism discovers its source in Shakespeare, and Sterne's romantic originality consists in his rearrangement of the vexed Shakespearean relation of tragedy and comedy, which for him are no longer literary forms but reflexes of moods, paradoxically interchangeable. From this similitude between tragedy and comedy comes irony, the visionary composite expounded by Sterne's German critics" (vii). Romantic irony, then, is a hybrid, a recomposed Shakespearean fusion of tragic and comic moods, ideally incarnated in *Tristram Shandy,* a "sacred text of romanticism" (viii).

The most important of "Sterne's German critics" is of course Friedrich Schlegel. Though Conrad makes abundant references to Jean Paul and Coleridge, among others interested in irony (or in humor, conceived as a sort of inverted sublime), F. Schlegel's ideas about irony and chaos, and his conviction that a merging of opposites is at the core of paradoxical, heteroclite, progressive romanticism remain the chief, recurrent guide to Conrad's commentary on Sterne and on romantic irony's double vision. The importance of such a guide is discernible, for example, in Conrad's remark that "the romantic ironist . . . is possessed, as Schlegel says, by a disorderly spiritual rage to overcome himself" (105). Sterne's "witty chaos" is thus "a spiritual imperative" (106).

Peter Conrad both enriches and obscures his definition of romantic irony – he has his own disorderly spiritual rages – by pursuing what turns out to be the main project of his book: an examination of libertinism in the arts, the idea being that a Shandean freedom of irregularity – a movement from moral to aesthetic libertinism – is vital to romantic individuality. Conrad believes that the mutual assimilation of "artistic license and moral licentiousness" (50) leads to the comic wisdom of ironic chaos, which asserts that "living is a readiness to abandon consistency" (68) and that existence is "exhilaratingly contingent" (73). The libertine "closest to Sterne, and the most interestingly complicated," Conrad maintains, "is Mozart's Don Giovanni." Like Tristram, "Don Giovanni is alternately tragic and comic . . . he may, like Tristram, be seen as a paradoxical fusion of the spirits of Hamlet and Falstaff" (50). According to Conrad, both Tristram Shandy and Don Giovanni are among literature's most dangerously subversive comic rebels. Yet dangerous rebels, Conrad is convinced, become ironic sages.

A baffling mind-body duality is much involved in the transmutation of subversive comedy into ironic wisdom. Though Conrad affirms at one point that comedy is self-delightedly spiritual in nature, it is comedy's corporeal compulsions and deficiencies that are especially noteworthy in his comments on romantic irony. Comedy for the romantic ironist signifies both constriction (the shaming body, which Conrad unpersuasively claims is the equivalent of constricting literary form) and subversive liberation (or pleasurable consciousness). Tristram Shandy himself is a composite of "mental freedom and bodily necessity" (22). If the downside of romantic irony (bodily incapacity) is its association with ineffectiveness, disorganization, failure – well, such weakness is a very acceptable price to pay for what is provisional and inconclusive in the unconfined romantic imagination. Moreover, such weakness can be surmounted by being paradoxically celebrated, at which point it coheres with the positive side of romantic imbalance, that is, emancipation from restraint within a rich chaos, a musical madness. "Inconsequence and inefficiency" become "the comic hero's salvation" (189), inasmuch as these apparent disvalues metamorphose into the defiant absurdity of antic irresponsibility.

Some of Peter Conrad's observations stem from a luxuriant glibness. Thus in tracing the Don Juan theme in European literature from Molière to Shaw, Conrad offers a facile, misleading interpretation of Byron's *Don Juan*. Establishing once again an equivalence between libertinism and narrative/stylistic heterodoxy, Conrad states that "for Byron the picaresque is the promiscuous: Juan's malleable eagerness to slide into any erotic attachment which presents itself answers to Byron's own gleeful irresponsibility with narrative and style" (57). But describing Byron's Don Juan as a slithery womanizer, or a Mozartian Cherubino, or, worse, as an "homme moyen sensuel" (60) not only falsifies Juan's capacity for romantic relationships but disregards Byron's predilections, in the early cantos, for counterpointing genuine romantic impulses and authentic counter-romantic urges.

Like Peter Conrad, David Simpson sides with mobility against authority. Unlike Conrad, however, Simpson is an attentive expositor of texts. In his preface to *Irony and Authority in Romantic Poetry* (1979), Simpson announces that he will be concerned with the hermeneutic aspects of the romantic ego's "radical instability."[31] And in fact hermeneutics at the level of diction, syntax, and metaphor, but also in matters of structure, does overwhelmingly preoccupy Simpson. His thesis, which reveals deconstructive leanings as well as the profit and peril of reader-response theory, is essentially that of Stuart Sperry, who, we recall, defined romantic irony as "a sense of perpetual indeterminacy" (quoted, 238n34).

Time and again Simpson points to illusions of fixity, underlines the tyranny of precise cognition, detects the suspension of determinate pointers, notes the absence of confident overviews, and reveals the unsettling of customary perceptions and habitual values. Simpson's dethronement of the romantic text as a self-assured entity becomes, however, something of an absolute. If the reader finds epiphanies in romantic poetry rather than evasive or partial meanings, that is because, Simpson insists, he has chosen to read them into the text. Grand revelations and harmonious significances simply do not characterize romantic poems, which favor "tonal confusion" (115), "incompatible perspectives" (103), and ubiquitous openness. Thus Shelley's poetry is rife with indecisiveness: his multitudinous metaphors so "interfere" with one another that "the inmost meaning is unachieved" (163) – in accordance, Simpson states, with Shelley's own view of poetry. Hence the reader must inventively provide coherence among many options; he is responsible for the "meaning" of the knots, vacancies, and enigmas in romantic poetry.

In a book devoted to romantic instability and self-division, where "the voice of assertion, insistence and achievement is almost always undermined" (139), it is astonishing that Byron alone receives no critical attention. Except for two fugitive footnotes, the only time Byron's poetry is (very briefly) mentioned – this mention symptomatically does not show up in the index – is when Simpson ties it to a discussion of Diderot's *Rameau's Nephew,* a work which "is very close to the nerve of what I want to call 'Romantic irony' " (182). When Simpson quotes an early nineteenth-century reviewer's complaint about Byron's destructive yoking together of contradictory tendencies, he does so not because the quotation will serve to launch a probe into Byron's romantic irony (which is never referred to) but because Simpson wishes to indicate that the intelligence of Rameau's nephew, like Byron's, is "anarchistic," though "much less confidently" (183). After this comment, Byron passes out of the picture.

In Simpson's view, the supremely uncommitted version of Rameau's nephew is Shakespeare, who "produced the infinitely writeable text, ever productive of new meanings." In fact, "Shakespeare is the most successful romantic ironist" (185). With the help of F. Schlegel and Kierkegaard, Simpson also affirms that Socrates and Jesus, like Rameau's nephew and Shakespeare, are possessed of "lives and meanings" that "constitute the infinitely writeable text" (187); that is, "like Rameau's nephew, Christ and Socrates are all things to all men" (186). (Barthesian writeability could hardly be more expansively stretched.) Goethe's indirections in a complicated historical situation also make of him "a Romantic ironist" (188). Shakespeare, Rameau's nephew. Socrates, Jesus, and Goethe are all romantic ironists. Byron apparently is not.

Goethe does not remain an isolated representative of German culture in *Irony and Authority*. Simpson often invokes Kant and Hegel – more often than F. Schlegel, though the latter receives pertinent treatment. Toward the end of his chapter on "Romantic Irony," Simpson briefly remarks that while German romanticism alone has explicitly fostered the kind of irony he has been writing about, and while there is no question of direct influence on English romanticism, it remains true that there are "extraordinary correspondences" (189) between the two romantic literatures. His summing up follows shortly thereafter: "English Romantic irony, broadly put, consists in the studious avoidance on the artist's part of determinate meanings" (190).

A more substantial work than Conrad's or Simpson's was published in 1980: Anne K. Mellor's *English Romantic Irony*. In her preface, Mellor contrasts the perspective of romantic irony with the "secularized Judaeo-Christian" version of romanticism which M. H. Abrams proffers in *Natural Supernaturalism*. Both perspectives, however, are held to be valid. Balancing historical turmoil and literary gains, Mellor indicates that romantic irony "grows out of philosophical scepticism and the social turbulence of the French Revolution and the American War of Independence." Nevertheless, romantic irony is not confined to the romantic period. Sterne, Mellor intimates, can "easily" be read as a romantic ironist, as can Yeats, Woolf, and Joyce. However, the real pioneer of romantic irony, which "posits a universe founded in chaos and incomprehensibility" (these are not words to be shuddered at) is F. Schlegel.[32]

But in England, F. Schlegel's ideas could not have counted for very much. In England, Mellor declares, "by far the most direct and pervasive source of romantic irony as a mode of consciousness . . . was the native eighteenth-century Deist 'higher criticism' of the Bible, as Elinor Shaffer has shown in *'Kubla Khan' and the Fate of Jerusalem: The Mythological School in Biblical Criticism and Secular Literature, 1770-1880"* (viii).[33] This "most direct and pervasive source of romantic irony as a mode of consciousness" in England is never explored in Mellor's text; nor are the French and American Revolutions ever resuscitated.

Toward the end of her preface, Mellor enlarges the historical scope of romantic-ironic scepticism: "Romantic irony was a significant part of the nineteenth-century English 'spirit of the age,' a recurrent skeptical reaction to the egotistical sublime of Christian fundamentalism, apocalyptical poetry, and Victorian myths of progress and imperialism" (viii). Mellor is no slouch, however, in transforming presumptive negatives into resounding positives: romantic-ironic scepticism is essentially life-affirming, even celebratory. Indeed, in reviewing Schlegel's theory of irony (constantly rephrased as "romantic irony") in her initial chapter, Mellor so much modifies the connotations of scepticism that it becomes an adjunct of holiness; at the very least, scepticism is viewed as a guarantor of valuable change, of beneficial becoming.

To exemplify the point that Schlegelian romantic irony "embraces change and process for their own sake" (4), Mellor quotes parts of two letters by Byron ("the finest literary exponent of romantic irony") to Annabella Milbanke. The Byronic selections do not serve Mellor's purpose very well, however, since they emphasize not the sanctity of process and change but rather a drive for "sensation" in the form of "intemperate but keenly felt pursuits of every description" (quoted, 4), such as gambling, warfare, and travel. What these ventures provide, Byron says, is the kind of "agitation" (this is the heart of the matter) that banishes stagnation and proves that one really exists, whether in pleasure or pain. (Curiously, these unhelpful epistolary fragments are cited three times in Mellor's book.)

In her initial chapter ("The Paradigm of Romantic Irony"), Mellor thoroughly explores Schlegel's "abundantly fertile," energizing chaos. The promise of such chaos is not boundless, however, since the Schlegelian blend of "enthusiastic self-creation and skeptical self-destruction" (16) makes for inconclusiveness. Because the romantic ironist's "sacred participation in the process of life" (6) – his eternal, joyous, liberating, divine sense of becoming – is bonded to a critical counterforce, a sense of finiteness and inadequacy limits his art. Still, the Schlegelian dialectic between the infinite and the finite, the free and the conditioned, creation and destruction, chaos and order – a dialectic which "allows for no genuine resolution or synthesis" (11) – is nobly challenging. At the same time it enables the ironic artist to engage in a kind of Socratic self-parody or "transcendental buffoonery," whose witty zest, Mellor assures us, need not literally be an indulgence in self-mockery. Schlegelian "transcendental buffoonery," Mellor suggests, may signify only "conflicting ontological systems" (18), as in "The Rime of the Ancient Mariner," or may simply involve (laughterless) antithetical voices and themes. The point is that in Schlegel's vision of art, a fictional world "must be both sincerely presented and sincerely undermined" (14).

In Mellor's study of Byron, a near-ecstatic explication of Schlegel's irony is constantly applied to *Don Juan*. Nor is it missing in her discussion of *Childe Harold,* which ultimately voices "the magnanimous spirit of generosity and commitment to all the contradictions, sufferings, limitations, and glories of the human condition" (34). After citing Childe Harold's "concluding image for the chaotic abundance of life," the ocean, Mellor declares that Byron celebrates the "monsters of the deep" as "destructive forces which prepare the way for new creations" (35). The fact that Byron in the passage Mellor cites (*Childe Harold* IV. 179-84) describes man as a troubling, impure element best forgotten, and that the poet pays loving homage to the ocean's contemptuous immunity to the ruin caused by mankind – the fact, in short, that Byron defines man as a corrupt creature whom ocean scorns and spurns, along with his spoiling, crumbling civilizations – is totally disregarded by Mellor.

This kind of slanted reading is often detectable in Mellor's discussion of *Don Juan,* a work which is held to embrace "philosophical irony as a mode of openness and comic freedom" (35). Mellor so intently cherishes the infinite, incomprehensible, yet "merrily multiplying" chaos of endless destructive-creative energies in *Don Juan* (44) that she often forgoes nuances and even plain particulars for the sake of theoretical consistency. Thus she claims that "in a world that so clearly moves in and out of chaos, human relationships are no more stable than physical objects. Juan's love-affairs with Julia, Haidée, Dudù, Gulbeyaz, and Catherine all end. Yet every lost relationship is followed by a new one . . . . Haidée, the child of nature, is abundantly recompensed by Aurora Raby, the child of nurture. Even Don Juan is replaceable" (43), Mellor adds, since his mother Donna Inez informs him in Canto X that in her second marriage she has given birth to another son.

There is a certain amount of nonsense in these remarks. How can the "love-affair" with Gulbeyaz (which is no love-affair; it is a one-sided, overwhelmingly sensual non-relationship which lasts perhaps a half-hour, though it is true that Juan, before being whisked away, finally begins to melt at the sight of the balked Sultana's tears) be compared with the unique, protracted love idyll with Haidée? And how can Haidée be "abundantly recompensed" by a psychologically detached, physically unclasped Aurora Raby, who allegedly (this must be news to both narrator and protagonist) shares a "passionate love" (54) with Juan? As for Dudù, she offers little more than a single night's partly giggly, partly orgasmic warmth, while Catherine commands an ardor which is at best semi-compulsory. As for Juan's replaceability by a baby brother, born of a mother who is the starchy antithesis of the world's merry multipliers, one can only suggest that there may be a large gap between population growth and literary significance.

In Mellor's frequent, not necessarily concordant definitions of Schlegelian romantic irony, comedy is more often extraneous than not. And though comedy can hardly be treated perfunctorily in the case of Byron, there are substantial instances of Mellor's failure to capture Byron's comic inflections (and even some of his most obvious bits of clowning). For example, in concluding that Byron cherishes the spirit-expanding, divine desirability of constant inconstant love, Mellor completely misses Byron's tongue-in-cheek approach to amorous inconstancy, which he pretends to justify as a paradoxically Platonic, reproachless absorption in the worship of female beauty. Juan himself is described by Mellor as an incarnation of erotic desire, as a lover ever-growing "through his love-experiences" and "always striving to transcend his single self, to experience the infinite" (51). If always striving to experience the infinite is what characterizes Juan in the arms of Dudù in the harem, or of Catherine at the Russian court, or of Lady Fitz-Fulke in one of Britain's great country houses, Byron seems perfectly unaware at such times that he has placed in the Spanish body of his young protagonist an erotic deity deepened by a German romantic soul.

Consider three short, tonally interlinked passages that are designed, according to Mellor, to show that the mind of Byron's narrator "never stagnates" in "creating and decreating his fictive world. Exuberantly it asserts the object of its consciousness" (73). Mellor's proof of this, to begin with, is a passage in which the narrator admits he may have gotten a bit lost: "The coast – I think it was the coast that I / Was just describing – Yes, it *was* the coast –" (II.181). Far from exemplifying an exuberant play of consciousness, these lines exhibit only the narrator's idiosyncratic nonchalance, which readily deranges memory, if only momentarily, and thus disrupts continuity. Mellor, convinced that the narrator's mind "arbitrarily changes its intentions" in accordance with the principles of resilient creation and decreation, adduces these corroborative lines: "I feel this tediousness will never do – / 'Tis being too epic, and I must cut down / (In copying) this long canto into two" (III.111). The narrator is indeed being arbitrary, and he is certainly rejecting stagnation; but his shifting intentions have little to do with a Schlegelian theory of creation and decreation and much to do with satirizing boring epics. Undeterred,

Mellor further states that the narrator's mind is so spiritedly non-stagnant that it "even forgets what it was going to do." Her illustration: "Oh, ye great Authors! – 'Apropos des bottes' – / I have forgotten what I meant to say" (IX.36). Immediately after quoting these lines, which disclose a Byronic aplomb of staggering carelessness, Mellor writes, incredibly: "Thus the ongoing creation of the poem reflects the narrator's ever-changing, ever-expanding consciousness" (73).

Mellor's commentary on Keats, her next "quintessential" romantic ironist, is useful, but only if one accepts her implied premise that romantic irony may be defined in several related ways, all valid, and that none is guided primarily by a comic impulse. Thus romantic irony is "negative capability"; it is the balancing of antithetical ideas and attitudes; it is indeterminacy, open-endedness; it is "a process of soul-making" before the mystery and chaos of life. Definitional pliancy does not end there. Keats's poetic "hovering between . . . celebration of the beauty of life and a recognition of the certainty of death" (78) is presented as still another variation on Schlegelian romantic irony. Of course, one may wonder which poetic worshiper of beauty is not conscious of the mutable, even ephemeral, nature of things. Innumerable poets, after all, have expressed a yearning for beauty, have suffered disillusion, and have been haunted by a recognition of inevitable death. But they do not constitute an army of romantic ironists.

So long as Mellor can corral various versions of romantic irony within such rubrics as abundant chaos, she seems to view the question of tone as a matter of minor importance. Mellor is even willing to accept pathos and poignance, as in "Ode to a Nightingale," as proper ingredients of romantic irony so long as they help to convey a Schlegelian-Socratic, romantic-ironic stress – for example, on the indissoluble opposition between the absolute and the relative, the infinite and the finite. "La Belle Dame sans Merci" is presented as another specimen of romantic irony. It may have a "plaintive tone, a melancholic coloring, and a ritualistically repeated, grim ending" (94); but it belongs to romantic irony through its "ironic-skeptical" orientation (95).

What Mellor finds in "The Eve of St. Agnes," a poem which is at times distinctly comic, is another of Schlegel's requirements for romantic irony: "transcendental buffoonery." This concept, Mellor had earlier (and conveniently) suggested, need not relate to comedy as such. But comedy, she is now pleased to point out, flourishes in "The Eve of St. Agnes." "Like Schlegel's ideal romantic poem," Mellor says, " 'this artfully ordered confusion, this charming symmetry of contradictions, this wonderfully perennial alternation of enthusiasm and irony which lives even in the smallest part of the whole' . . . is infused with a 'transcendental buffoonery' that graces every moment with the lightest comedy" (90). But in the quoted passage ("this artfully ordered confusion . . ."), Schlegel is thinking primarily of *Don Quixote*. In effect, then, Mellor is drawing a parallel between two incommensurable works, *Don Quixote* and "The Eve of St. Agnes." Keats's poem does intermittently mix comic, sceptical, even clownish insinuations into its gorgeous solemnity; but it is not characterized by an incessant alternation of enthusiasm and irony. Nor is every moment in the poem graced with the lightest comedy.

On the other hand, "transcendental buffoonery," Mellor admits, is not characteristic of "The Fall of Hyperion." "Its romantic irony," she persists, "is sung in a darker key" (98). How dark? The face of Moneta, uniting suffering and beauty, is "an icon of romantic irony." It is also "Keats's closest approximation to the existentialist tragedy of *King Lear*" (103). That is dark indeed. Romantic irony is apparently not hobbled by pathos, melancholy, grimness, or tragedy.

In Mellor's book, any romantic work that substantially explores life's dualities can hardly escape being lassoed into the flexible precincts of romantic irony. A phrase like "creation and decreation," which basically has to do with spontaneous artistic creativity disciplined by critical self-consciousness, has been made by Mellor to embrace any vital clash of opposites, any significant union of irreconcilables, any "hovering" between two great irresolvable contraries. In Mellor's Schlegelian study, "a willed acceptance of the contradictions of human experience" (107) amid the eternal flux of a non-teleological but by no means disheartening universe in effect becomes the core of romantic irony.

Why is "To Autumn" judged to be Keats's "most completely romantic ironic poem"? Because "in truly ironic fashion," Mellor affirms, "the poem holds together both contradictory extremes – the beauty of becoming and the sorrow of ending, the ecstatic apprehension of perfect pleasure and the certainty that such pleasure is but momentary" (107). But if this is so – if this dualistic perspective of gain and loss, beauty and sorrow, ecstasy and melancholy, is held to be typical of romantic irony – then most of the world's poets and sages, who are profoundly aware that "harmonious fulfillment" may intervene or fail to intervene between summery life and wintry death, who know that pleasure is impermanent, that beginnings are often promising, that fruition is often beautiful, that endings are often sad, and that the temporal and the eternal are strangely intertwined, may have to be recognized as romantic ironists too.

In her last, Johnsonian chapter, "A Conclusion in Which Nothing is Concluded," Mellor repeats, with a few changes (e.g., the Industrial Revolution replaces the American Revolution), the weak historical comments she expresses in her preface but subsequently drops: "Historically . . . romantic irony was born from the upheavals of the French and Industrial Revolutions, flourished during the early nineteenth century and was seriously weakened by the violence of World War I" (186-87), after which the absurd, angst, despair, etc., set in. The "legacy of the Great War . . . sabotaged the romantic ironist's sense of exuberant freedom in an infinitely various and infinitely possible world" (187). Pre-World War I doubt, disillusion, and disgust are not alluded to in this jumpy historical survey. In any event, "nothing" is not exactly what is concluded in this chapter, since we are left with the therapeutic message that "a genuine participation in romantic irony . . . could bring us pleasure, psychic health, and intellectual freedom"; indeed, "romantic irony . . . can potentially free individuals and even entire cultures from totalitarian modes of thought and behavior" (188).

The nucleus of Lilian R. Furst's *Fictions of Romantic Irony* (1984), the next important work on the subject, is an essay entitled "Romantic Irony and Narrative Stance," which became the second chapter in Furst's *Contours of European Romanticism* (1979) and was later included in *Romantic Irony* (1988). Two of Furst's ideas in this essay are of particular interest. The first establishes romantic irony as an archetypal phenomenon (and therefore not a unique expression of the romantic period). The second suggests that romantic irony turned out to be more of a failure than an enhancement of romantic aspirations of transcendence. (This idea is abandoned in *Fictions of Romantic Irony*, though not without multiple signs of struggle.)

Furst points out that in the German romantic movement, the narratorial self-consciousness of romantic irony was heralded as an assertion of Promethean creative freedom – a demonstration, in Schlegelian terms, of the artist's "divine superiority,"[34] of his "transcendence even of his own creation" (27). This potent freedom was expressed in disruptive tactics, ranging from illusion-breaking and authorial intrusions to the jumbling of plot strands and temporal disjointedness. Why, then, was romantic irony not an aesthetic and philosophic success? According to Furst, the reason for this is probably that readers of unstable romantic-ironic narratives were on the receiving end of too many bewildering "ambiguities, doubts, and paradoxes" (36). Since the narrator of a romantic-ironic work abdicates authorial control and therefore "has no clear and firm position," readers get "conflicting and confusing signals." Such irresolution leads them "progressively into a dizzying hall of mirrors" (28). The riddling narrative dislocations in *Jacques the Fatalist* are a good illustration of such romantic-ironic chaos.

Furst concludes that godlike "supremacy over his universe as well as over his narrative is not within the reach of the romantic ironist. Though he still grasps for it, he is *de facto* resigned to its loss" (31); the romantic ironist's attempt to embody paradox, the world's quintessential condition, by means of artful disorientation and equivocation, collapses. The disastrous cleavage between promising theory and unfortunate practice is again emphasized in Furst's comment that romantic irony "led not to transcendence and progression, but to reduction and dishevelment" (37). But any inference the reader of Furst's essay may be tempted to make about a negative developmental process in literary history during the romantic period is undermined by Furst's chronologically mixed selection of (presumably) romantic-ironic works. In Furst's view, the relationship between romantic irony and literary history is fluid rather than fixed. She contends that romantic irony is "not primarily a historical phenomenon" limited to the romantic epoch (35). Romantic irony is basically "archetypal" in nature and arises in periods of increased self-consciousness, for example, in the late eighteenth and early nineteenth centuries and in the early Freudian years of the twentieth century. This risky contention becomes an important theme in Furst's subsequently published book-length study.

In *Fictions of Romantic Irony* Furst carefully lays out her critical nomenclature. To begin with, she separates genial comedy from acerbic satire. She then distinguishes between satire and irony. Satire, Furst believes, is based on firm ethical convictions: the satirist is a judge-moralist filled with "absolute certainty" as to the proper values of mankind.[35] (Most critics are convinced that satire flourishes in stable societies where values are conspicuously shared. But one may wonder whether absolute certainty is not a dreadful virtue, even for a satirist.) The ironist, more given to doubt, questions basic assumptions. He is "always ambivalent" (9), Furst remarks, for his vision is governed by "contingencies, incongruities and relativities" (12), and also by a sense of "indefinity" which he expresses in ambiguities. (There is a certain muddle here with respect to ambivalence and ambiguity.) Whereas the satirist has entrenched commitments, the ironist's perceptions of the universe derive from a "perspectivistic multiplicity" (11).

Furst then turns to F. Schlegel's aphorisms on poetic irony's "capacity to confront, and ideally, to transcend the contradictions of the finite world" (26). Furst is comprehensively perceptive in discussing Schlegel's ideas on self-creation and self-destruction, on hovering, on chaos, on the significance of paradox as a "spur" to "dynamic evolutionary progression" (27), on the "roguish appearance" and "lofty purpose" (28) of "transcendental buffoonery," and on the negativity wrought by a failure of transcendence. Furst also looks "spatially and temporally beyond Friedrich Schlegel and German Romantic literary theory" (x) to get at the core of romantic irony. Furst observes that Schlegel "derived his theory from the practical models he acknowledged in Socrates, Petrarch, Dante, Cervantes, Shakespeare, Sterne, and Diderot," and that he did not describe his theory of irony as "romantic" in "any of the writings that appeared during his lifetime" (29). She also calls attention to the fact that neither Tieck, nor A. W. Schlegel, nor Solger, nor Adam Müller, nor Hegel, nor Kierkegaard referred to "romantic irony," a misleading phrase which was first used in 1850 by a German critic named Hermann Hettner, and which was destined thereafter "to haunt literary criticism" (30). Not that the polarity of feeling and irony is inappropriate to the romantic temper. Furst considers such a polarity to be a productive agent of romanticism's mobility and sense of boundlessness.

After this substantial introduction, Furst is ready to tackle the distinction between traditional irony in fiction, represented by Jane Austen (*Pride and Prejudice*) and Flaubert (*Madame Bovary*), and romantic irony, represented, in reverse chronological order, by Byron (*Don Juan*), Jean Paul (*Flegeljahre*), Diderot (*Jacques le fataliste et son maître*), and Sterne (*Tristram Shandy*). Jane Austen's ironic comedy in *Pride and Prejudice* is traditional because it hinges on a world which is regarded as "fundamentally intelligible," stable and sound (51). Though major truths may be questioned, and though folly and misapprehension may be unavoidable, discords and disturbances finally yield to "harmonious resolutions" (61) in a basically "well ordered society" (63).

In Furst's judgment, this is not true of *Madame Bovary*. Though Flaubert's irony, Furst notes, is not always insidious and may even be sympathetic (or at least ambiguous), it does tend to victimize characters and erode certainties: "its essentially destructive impact is in contrast to the restorative function of irony in *Pride and Prejudice*" (83). Yet despite its demonstrations of triviality, ignominy, and failure, and despite its problematic, "pervasive ambivalence," Flaubert's irony is regarded by Furst as by and large "traditional and amenable to reasonably confident reconstruction" (84). Hence Flaubert's irony, like Austen's, is not basically akin to romantic irony.

How is one to define romantic irony reliably? The answer, in Furst's view, has a lot to do with the metaphysics of paradoxicality and the aesthetics of randomness. When multiple perspectives, uncertainties and indeterminacies prevail, when, above all, a fiction's narrator queries or mocks or otherwise subverts his own authority as narrator by persistently playing fast and loose with the content or shape of his own text – when, in brief, the quirky freedom of story-telling *per se* preempts the significance of the story itself and becomes its own focus of irony – then, Furst maintains, we have the makings of romantic irony. But Furst rejects the notion that self-conscious fiction, abounding in whimsical or droll caprices of self-annihilation, is alone capable of conveying the essence of romantic irony. It is her conviction (at times only obliquely expressed) that consciousness of a disordered, haphazard, paradox-ridden world is also indispensable.

The first work of romantic irony Furst takes up in detail is Byron's *Don Juan,* which, she declares, is a failure as a work of satire but a success as a work of irony. The satire in *Don Juan* is impotent, Furst claims, because "the corrective impulse fundamental to satire is not uppermost in Byron" (101); no "restorative vision that would create some positive values to replace the falsehoods and hypocrisies that are exposed and rejected . . . is ever implied." Indeed, Byron "can champion nothing other than incoherent freedom" (102). Moreover, unlike Gulliver, Juan is too lacking in ethical fiber and intellectual solidity to serve as an effective carrier of satiric intention. (But hadn't Gulliver been pushed opportunistically by Swift into juggling contrary moral positions?) The narrator himself, deprived of a judgmental pedestal and "world-improving" faculties, offers only a simulacrum of satire, not the real thing.

But a countervailing position may be borrowed from Furst herself. Early in her book, she claims that *Don Juan* is "strongly satirical in thrust, aiming sharp attacks against specific, clearly visible targets and harnessing irony as a means to an end" (8). Why she should later entertain so complete a reversal of opinion on the power and priority of satire in Byron must remain a mystery. In any event, it may be argued that if, as Furst indicates, "falsehoods and hypocrisies" are not only exposed but are also clearly rejected in *Don Juan,* then satire must be achieving its aim rather handily. (Explicit blueprints are not indispensable to satire.)

Besides, Furst acknowledges that Byron's "questioning, exposing, debunking irony . . . holds together the multiple facets of *Don Juan*" (103). If so, if the poet's irony is unifyingly "debunking," *Don Juan* is perhaps, after all, marked by a coherent satiric animus, however diverse its targets may be. This is not to deny, of course, that there is "a deep substratum of . . . uncertainty in Byron's irony" (102).

Irresolutions and uncertainties abound in Furst's analysis of Byron's self-fracturing epic. Byron's jolting narrative discontinuities not only "testify to the uncertainty of all things" (116) but register "the fundamental instability of . . . the universe" (115). Furst's propensity to see narrative self-disruption as a clue to profound ontological malaise does not, to be sure, deny Byron's "exhilarating awareness of freedom" (116). Yet Furst stresses an "undertone of anxiety" (111) in Byron's jocular temper, and even sees in the poet's "intellectual fun" evidence of "intellectual torture" (115).

At the beginning of her chapter on Byron, Furst declares, as has been noted, that Byron presents no "restorative vision," no signpost to positive values; "no such alternative," she insists, "is ever offered" (102). In the last few pages of the chapter, however, she reverses her position by suggesting that Byron's demolitional, nihilistic irony in *Don Juan* has been transformed into Schlegelian "transcendental buffoonery" (119), and that the destruction wrought by infinite doubt and universal contingency in *Don Juan* still "leaves space for further buoyant reconstruction" (120). Byron's irony, in short, is now empowered to climb salvationally out of its own "abyss of negativity" (118) and act "as a force of reconciliation" (120). The buffoonery of Jean-Paul, Diderot, and Sterne, in whose works the metafictional and philosophical components of romantic irony reach even more extraordinary proportions, also manages to subdue, while thoroughly incorporating, the dissonances, instabilities, and contingencies of a precarious, mystifying world.

That wildly eccentric self-reflexiveness is the (non-defeatist) corollary of an incoherent universe is not the most compelling idea in Furst's book. In the last chapter of *Fictions of Romantic Irony* ("In Search of a Theory"), Furst challenges the validity (or, rather, the use) of the term she has been interpreting throughout her book. (Her reverse chronological scheme has been strongly hinting at a definitional crisis.) She now claims (echoing a major idea in her earlier essay) that so-called "romantic irony," having achieved its preeminent incarnation before romanticism emerged as a historical period, is an "unfortunate misnomer" (238).[36] (Yet Furst weakens this assertion by conceding, with a good deal of exaggeration, that "at a particular phase in history, roughly contemporaneous with its cognitive formulation . . . this kind of irony became widespread and prominent in fiction" [236].)

The historical periodization of romantic irony is further invalidated, according to Furst, by the fact that themes and processes in twentieth-century irony – uncertainties, dialectical tensions, tactics of artistic self-consciousness – strongly parallel those of nineteenth- and pre-nineteenth century romantic irony. (Furst is much too ready to identify as romantic-ironic certain twentieth-century works that interestingly deviate from traditional modes of narration and inherited consolatory certitudes. Thus Svevo's *Confessions of Zeno,* Joyce's *Ulysses,* Beckett's *Molloy,* Bellow's *Herzog,* Borges's fictions, and Delmore Schwartz's short story "In Dreams Begin Responsibilities" are all described as romantic-ironic.) In light of these literary parallels, Furst argues, romantic irony "must be accorded archetypal as well as historical status. It encompasses a typological approach to the manipulation of fictional illusion together with an open-ended querying epistemology and an ontology that embraces an order of disorder quite distinct from orderliness" (237).

Furst's disapprobation of "romantic irony" as a concept (and practice) limited to the romantic period seems almost revolutionary in its boldness. Yet she offers no alternative term for the combined metaphysics and metafiction she has been analyzing. Romantic irony remains "the instrument for registering the obdurate paradoxicality of a universe in eternal flux" (229). It is romantic irony, whether in the eighteenth, nineteenth, or twentieth century, that expresses pervasive uncertainty and infinite doubt. It is romantic irony that conveys a chaos of contradictions, contingencies, and relativistic perspectives that yield no clear perception, no reliable knowledge, no determinate position, no firm truth, no sure interpretation, no resolution, no final comprehension, and no faith in reason. Nihilism is not, however, the consequence of such disorientation; for disorientation is assimilated, exploited, and mastered by the self-conscious ironic artist, who exuberantly (but with more than occasional tremors of darkness) arranges and re-arranges his endlessly tricky narrative games. Furst's last word, however, is far from being an optimist's dream. Romantic irony, she suggests, "ends in an alienating derangement of the text and of the world" (239).[37]

Romantic irony is scarcely viewed as an invalid term in Frederick Garber's *Self, Text, and Romantic Irony: The Example of Byron* (1988). What interests Garber is the concept of romantic irony as a Schlegelian marriage/divorce of chaos and continuity, a concept which Garber finds indispensable to an understanding of Byron. Garber's argument was initiated in his earlier *Autonomy of the Self from Richardson to Huysmans* (1982). In a chapter entitled "Egotism, Empathy, Irony," romantic irony is defined as "the dialectical alternation of chaos and order, breakup and renewal."[38] F. Schlegel is presented as romantic irony's principal theorist, Byron as its prime exemplar. Though Garber points out that chaos is distinctly less pregnant with benign possibilities for Byron than for Schlegel, he contends that Byron as well as Schlegel "affirmed the dialectic of dissolution and regeneration" (116). *Don Juan* in particular entertains omnipresent chaos, yet the epic "affirms the genuine, if impermanent sovereignty of consciousness" (117). The power of sovereign consciousness over chaos is not, however, reducible to the banal observation that while life is anarchic, art is shapely. The romantic ironist, Garber writes, constantly plays a risky game of self-recovery in the midst of disruptive forces. He is, fortunately, "a consummate manager of antitheses" (119); nor is he averse to exhibiting his mastery of such antitheses by mocking his own apparent triumph over disorder – or, for that matter, order.

In *Self, Text, and Romantic Irony,* there is some shifting of emphasis. Garber now contrasts the romantic organicist, "the poet of incessant copula," with the romantic ironist, "the poet of incessant disjunction."[39] The romantic ironist, for whom any tendency toward enclosure, wholeness, fixedness, completeness, totalization is bound to be unveracious, believes that truth resides in instability, in a chaos that can be productively, if warily, cooperated with. Indeed, chaos can have a "fertilizing role in an encompassing scheme" (163).

In highlighting romantic irony's disjunctiveness, Garber examines much of the Byron canon for evidence of "the recoil of consciousness," which "seems to be the essential movement in Byron's work" (5). The poet's unsurpassed specimen of self-recoil, Garber states, is *Don Juan,* which exhibits the warfare of Byron's opposing selves, one working towards order, the other luxuriating in disruption. Garber adds that a higher authorial consciousness superintends this warfare and sees to it that dizzy disorder is matched, or more than matched, by a mending of narrative fractures – by an art of salutary, even salvific, rebuilding. The romantic ironist in Byron transcends antagonistic forces through the progressive, if limiting, quality of Schlegelian self-restraint. This does not mean, however, that he seeks a Coleridgean reconciliation of warring impulses, that is, a return to organic unity. He sustains, rather, a dialectic wherein skepticism is indispensable.

Though he reiterates the point made in *Autonomy of the Self* that Byronic chaos does not brim over with Schlegelian fecundity – he concedes that "chaos in Byron is a threat, not a promise" (164) – Garber slides way from (or at least considerably modifies) this important qualification by suggesting that the threat of chaos in *Don Juan* is creatively conquered, even if only tentatively. Though Garber ascribes "beneficence and bane" (190) to both continuity and chaos, it is continuity, not dislocation, that endorses error and entrapment. On the other hand, the poet's acts of fracture are surrounded by Garber with an aura of nobility: they are essentially "acts of redemption" which "assert the strength of the mind and the will" (182). Whereas continuum and closure, unlike difference and indeterminacy, may breed claustrophobia and dishonesty, Byron's disruptions represent, in part, "a busy seeking for safety and health" (189). Lest all kinds of virtues (psychic health, intellectual power, moral grace) and no weaknesses be ascribed to romantic irony, Garber notes that Byron and Hoffmann "made careers out of showing us" (258) that the cornucopia of possibilities proffered by Schlegelian romantic irony might contain quite acrid ingredients. Still, Garber's commentary regularly returns to the idea that romantic irony is "a way of being in the world" (167) that represents productive, redemptive power.

So impressed is Garber by this productive, redemptive power that he finally identifies romantic irony with the "inclusive mode of satire" (295) in *Don Juan.* Following Robert C. Elliott and Francis M. Cornford, Garber esteems satire (and now romantic irony) as a life-promoting force that "cleanses and redeems the tribe" (290). Satire (and now romantic irony) negates in the cause of ultimate potency. There remains a theoretical difference, Garber acknowledges, between satire and romantic irony: satire reaches a fixed vantage point from which it attempts to restore a fallen world, while in romantic irony, "the world is . . . in a perpetual state of falling"(310). ("Incessant disjunction" and "a perpetual state of falling" are extremist metaphors, but they are hardly synonymous.) Nevertheless, Garber insists that "the romantic ironist is a satirist because part of his business is to arraign our foolishness about all sorts of order – cosmic, personal, and literary. He exposes our smugness in order to reform us." Reformatory romantic irony "unmakes for the sake of another and better making" (294).

But endowing romantic irony's disintegrativeness with a purifying energy and handing it over, not partly but wholesale, to satire (which is by no means all-inclusive in *Don Juan*) does a disservice to the diversity of

Byron's comic energies. Byron's lightness of temper is scarcely unrecognized by Garber; yet he offers very few illustrations of Byronic comedy. Indeed, specific episodes in *Don Juan* are at times treated as though comedy had to be filtered out of them. Thus the "primary purpose" of the idyll of Juan and Haidée, according to Garber, "is to enact the nostalgia [for Edenic innocence] that infects us all and then to purge the nostalgia by the pity and fear generated by a hard look at its object" (187). But purgative Aristotelian tragic emotions (a dubious currency in this context) have been potently forestalled: Byron's romantic idyll has been recurrently, ambivalently, comically subjected to antiromantic jolts, and has in the end been ungallantly punctured by a turn toward farcical dismissal. (Byron's last word, however, is given to elegiac pathos.) Though the comedy of romantic irony is thus undervalued by Garber, who also finds Byron's explosive shifts in tonality somewhat mechanical, his definition of romantic irony as the "perpetuation of the process of demolition and renewal" (310) ultimately pays the kind of homage to romantic irony's therapeutic, salvational powers that we have seen in Anne K. Mellor's commentary.

For a while, Peter W. Graham's critical perspective in *"Don Juan" and Regency England* (1990) resembles the Schlegelian orientation of Garber and Mellor. Indeed Graham affirms that Schlegel's "theory of romantic poetry, brilliantly dispersed and dispensed in fragmentary utterances, goes as far as any system is likely to go in accounting for the self-consciously antisystematic vision of the world presented in *Don Juan*."[40] Graham also notes that "Mellor speaks of *Don Juan's* intellectual method of proceeding as the 'associative arabesque,' a phrase in which Schlegel attempts to capture the seemingly chaotic yet actually and intricately patterned intellectual phenomenon that is romantic irony" (199n6).

Yet Graham's effort to make Schlegel pertinent to his key chapter ("All Things – But a Show?") appears to be superfluous, inasmuch as he is intent in this chapter on providing evidence of how "English and Italian spectacular theater – especially pantomime . . . – offers subjects, vehicles, roles, and a supply of tricks that could prove useful to Byron in the composition of *Don Juan*." "Why not embrace," Graham asks (assuming the role of Byron), "Fancy and the fanciful device of transformation? Why not have a joke on the fickle, provincial English public by constructing, as Grimaldi's Clown might, an English epic out of the least promising, most outrageous materials?" (76) At the same time, the chapter's principle of associative flexibility invites Schlegel back in; for

Graham has no difficulty stretching the English pantomime's device of "transformation" to accommodate Schlegel's view that irony is a "permanent parabasis," constantly suspending action and shattering dramatic illusion (129). The result is that pantomime's transformation, Schlegel's permanent parabasis, and Byron's digressions become virtually indivisible kin.[41]

Though it was by now a familiar term usually linked to F. Schlegel's ideas, romantic irony in the late 1980s was still too hazy a notion to be uncontroversially pinned down as a definitive concept in Anglo-American critical discourse. Frederick W. Shilstone nevertheless takes it for granted, in the preface to *Byron and the Myth of Tradition* (1988), that "the doctrine of romantic irony" is universally and unambiguously recognized as "one of the nineteenth century's most original (and lasting) contributions to the history of ideas."[42] According to Shilstone, this original, enduring "doctrine" – F. Schlegel's name is not invoked, and it is for some time not clear who (or what) is the prime propagator of this major contribution to the history of ideas – signifies a state of ambivalence stemming from a "transitional consciousness" (xiii). In Byron's case, which Shilstone believes is perfectly representative of the romantic period's wandering between two worlds, transitional consciousness involves a struggle between "the imperative of the past" and "an ethic of the self" (xii). The latter, while recognizing the value of tradition, rejects the disvalues of its superannuated dogmas. The struggle is resolved in a compromise (or synthesis): Byron's "romantically ironic perspective" is "the only true peace that can be forged between his past and his future" (xiii) – a peace that is nevertheless "aware of its own tentativeness" (xiv).

Shilstone's final pages reaffirm his prefatory remarks: Byron's "movement from a sense of antagonism between the individual present and the universal past toward a merger of the two that sees the past living only in its current adaptations" – in literary terms, Byron embraces Pope's satire but also supersedes it – "is in fact the development of the attitude defined as romantic irony" (242). The authority for defining romantic irony as the consciousness of a (resolvable) conflict between the claims of tradition and the demands of the autonomous self may not be Anne K. Mellor; but Mellor is the only critic Shilstone cites as having aptly described the romantic-ironic attitude in art. (There is also an endnote bow to Lilian Furst.) Shilstone quotes a passage from *English Romantic Irony* on the theme of "simultaneous creation and decreation" (quoted, 242), a passage that presumably establishes the ground which is common to both Shilstone's ideas and the nature of romantic irony. But "creation and decreation" makes for an exceedingly loose, baggy rubric. Resorting to a Schlegelian all-purpose vocabulary (mediated by Mellor) to describe the "dialectical interplay of traditionalism and iconoclasm" (246) in a transitional age is much too facile; so is adducing romantic irony to formulate the conflict between Enlightenment universality and existentialist autonomy. These suspect equations are hardly propped up by Shilstone's claim that the meaning of romantic irony is officially established and wholly secure.

That claim is not quite corroborated in Frank Jordan's introduction to the Modern Language Association's *English Romantic Poets: A Review of Research and Criticism* (4th ed., 1985). In "Natural Supernaturalism and Romantic Irony," the initial thematic segment of the introduction, Jordan indicates that romantic irony rather than Abrams's natural supernaturalism "became the watchword of the 1970s"[43] (and, he implies, romantic irony has not yet ceded its dominance). His account of the difference between these two perspectives on romanticism is plain enough: natural supernaturalism is organic, unitary, "apocalyptic, redemptive, explanatory"; romantic irony is open-ended, fragmentary, irresolvable, "anti-redemptive, anti-explanatory" (32).

But this interpretation of romantic irony is not universally supported in the works Jordan discusses – or in post-1985 criticism. (Neither Mellor nor Garber nor Furst, for example, would agree that romantic irony is antiredemptive.) A reader hungering for insight into the reputedly arcane subject of romantic irony would discover, with Jordan's help, that Mellor's major theme is change and process, creation and decreation, under the beneficent sway of philosophic skepticism; that Tilottama Rajan (*Dark Interpreter*) balances transcendent affirmation and dark deconstructive doubt; that Simpson has his eye on indeterminacy, engendered by conflicting forces of self-assertion and self-sabotage; that Peter Conrad focuses on the Shandean union of comedy and tragedy; and that critics like Ernst Behler and Raymond Immerwahr (among others following Schlegel's lead) also underscore the importance of *Tristram Shandy* (not to mention Cervantes, Shakespeare, and eighteenth-century comic fiction) for an understanding of romantic irony. The reader would also learn that a chaotic universe is nearly indispensable in alluding to romantic irony, that Schlegel is widely accepted as the only begetter of fecund ideas concerning the ironic temper in the Romantic period, and that Byron is not always thought to be romantic irony's practitioner par excellence. The reader would also probably become aware that comedy is not generally considered to be essential in the making of romantic irony.

Schlegelian ironic lore continues to excite ardor here and there in Anglo-American criticism. (We have only to recall Monika Greenleaf's assertion, published in 1994, that Pushkin's *Eugene Onegin* is the supreme, peerless embodiment of Schlegel's concept of irony.) Yet tepidness may be replacing frissons of exhilaration. For one thing, critics at the turn of the 1990s did not automatically link Schlegelian romantic irony to the spirit and strategies of *Don Juan*. Thus Ann Barton's *Byron: Don Juan* (Cambridge: Cambridge UP, 1992) is devoid of any allusion to romantic irony; nor do her suggestions for further reading supply compensatory references. Barton is of course compelled to note Byron's dualistic practices. Thus in commenting on the love of Juan and Haidée, she shows how Byron counterpoints unrestrained ecstasies of passion and "sobering reminders" of what love and marriage ordinarily entail. Byron's "reminders" are often not so sober, however, and Barton concedes that the island episode is "by no means lacking in humour."[44] Though Caroline Franklin, in *Byron's Heroines* (Oxford: Clarendon, 1992), appears to view romantic irony as fundamental to Byron's art, she translates it into Bakhtinian currency. "At the centre of Byron's Romantic irony," she writes, "are what Bakhtin terms 'dialogics,' or the competing discourses of libertinism and libertarianism" (133-34). The competing discourses in *Don Juan* turn out basically to be (1) sympathy with sentiment and romantic love; and (2) satirical, deflationary cynicism.[45]

Malcolm Kelsall would not agree with this assessment. It is his contention, in "Byron and the Romantic Heroine" (1990), that modern criticism has succumbed repeatedly to an over-emphasis on the dualistic element in *Don Juan*. Kelsall is convinced that the ideals of love and freedom in the Juan-Haidée episode have purely destructive effects. Such ideals are "set up only to be subverted"[46]; "the romantic vision is offered only to be shown as wanting, and disappears" (57). Nor is Kelsall ravished by the presumption of ambivalence in the Juan-Julia section of *Don Juan*. Kelsall leans toward the notion that Julia's celebrated letter, like her bedroom tirade, is primarily manipulative. "The aim is to create a sense of guilt in the man so that he may be controlled. His conscience is her means to power" (54-55).

In the *Cambridge Companion to British Romanticism* (1993), there are chapters on romantic Hellenism, romantic fiction, romantic poetry, romantic criticism and theory, romanticism and the Enlightenment, romanticism and revolution, romanticism and the sister arts, romanticism and language, and so on; but none of the work's eleven chapters is assigned to romantic irony. In his essay for the *Companion,* "Romanticism, Criticism, and Theory," David Simpson writes that "irony, the literary trope of skepticism . . . was addressed by the Germans and Kierkegaard, but was largely unnoticed in Britain, as indeed it remains to this day." Romantic writing, Simpson continues, "is full of references to God, nature, truth, beauty, and the soul"; yet romantic writing is "also replete with irony," and with instances of "hermeneutic instability".[47]

Although such repletion does not receive special attention in the *Companion,* two other essays in this work also take up the question of romantic irony. In "German Romantic Idealism," Peter Thorslev believes that the repudiation of Schlegelian irony by Hegel and Kierkegaard was justified, for "irony pursued as an end in itself, or as a means for vacuous freedom from all intellectual and ethical imperatives, leads only to . . . aestheticism and ennui" (92). Byron's irony, however, like his predecessor Bayle's, is something else: it "is the sign of the disinterested mind," though in creating "a stance of disillusioned or unillusioned commmon sense" (92), Byron's irony in *Don Juan* does not inhibit moral imperatives. Indeed, Byron's irony is an agent of satire: *"Don Juan . . .* is an ironic exposure, sometimes caustic, sometimes half-indulgent, of the follies of his age" (92).

The only other chapter in the *Cambridge Companion* that takes a look at romantic irony (unanalytically) is Gary Kelly's "Romantic Fiction." Kelly simply states, in passing, that central to a number of early nineteenth-century novels, for example, Germaine de Staël's *Corinne* (1807), Mary Shelley's *Frankenstein* (1818), Maturin's *Melmoth the Wanderer* (1820), Hazlitt's *Liber Amoris* (1823), James Hogg's *Private Memoirs and Confessions of a Justified Sinner* (1824), and Disraeli's *Vivian Grey* (1826-27) is "a Romantic irony of excessive selfhood thwarted by social convention, oppressive institutions, or cosmic indifference" (208). But romantic irony is not dedicated to depicting the defeat of the romantic ego's rebellious or transgressive or narcissistic energies in an antiromantic society and a non-romantic universe. The frustration Kelly cites is a particular instance of either circumstantial or cosmic irony (by which, of course, both romantic and non-romantic temperaments can be damaged).

The dynamics of desire and frustration are an important motif in Stuart Curran's chapter ("Romantic Poetry: Why and Wherefore") in the *Cambridge Companion.* Though he does not directly broach the subject of romantic irony, Curran postulates that the clash of opposites, the dialectic of contradictory elements, is the key to British romanticism. Blake's axiom ("Without contraries is no progression") "stands almost as a defining concept for the Romantic impulse in poetry. It even justifies self-contradictory or ambivalent stances as being stations in a progression yet to be worked out" (234). Curran's postulation is more than tangential to European romantic irony; but the latter's ambivalences must be viewed not as tentative expressions of an ultimately transformative experience but rather as indices of a permanent polarity.

A number of slim studies of romanticism in the 1990s – for example, Nicholas V. Riasonovsky's *The Emergence of Romanticism* (1992), Maurice Cranston's *The Romantic Movement* (1994), and Aidan Day's *Romanticism* (1996) – reveal neither hostility toward nor approval of the idea of romantic irony; they merely disregard it. Thick anthologies of critical essays on romanticism are not much more helpful. Thus the fifty-two essays and more than five hundred pages devoted to romanticism in *A Companion to Romanticism*, ed. Ducan Wu (1998) manage to squeeze out half a dozen lines on romantic irony.[48] One might conclude, in perusing this text, that romantic irony is no longer an issue in need of investigation or debate, or that it is considered too enigmatic or too multiplex to be captured (and perhaps trivialized) by lucidity.

An interesting (and early) exception is *Revolution and English Romanticism: Politics and Rhetoric,* ed. Keith Hanley and Raman Seldan (1990). One of the two relevant essays in this book, Josie Dixon's "Revolutionary Ideals and Romantic Irony: The Godwinian Inheritance in Literature," does not in fact deal with romantic irony as such. What Dixon has in mind is the circumstantial irony of wholly unintended or contrasting consequences: Godwinian ideals of justice, freedom, benevolence, and happiness proved barren in their visionary rationality and provoked an "inverse influence"[49] which stimulated finer insights into the requirements of the romantic imagination and the individual romantic psyche.

On the other hand, Greg Kucick's essay "Ironic Apocalypse in Romanticism and the French Revolution" is overtly affiliated with recent scholarship on romantic irony, although Kucick chooses to concentrate on the dark side of the subject. His theme is revolutionary idealism and its perverted ironic outcome. If Dixon traces beneficial counter-movements to Godwin's ideas, Kucick stresses the ruin of the French Revolution's regenerative impulses (romantic apocalypticism). Critics ranging from Mellor to Garber all (somehow) nourish Kucick's conclusions about the romantic irony that emerges from such ruin. But his obligatory deference to F. Schlegel is more of a hindrance than a help. Kucick remarks that the "dashing of millenarian hopes by the abortive apocalypse of the French Revolution drove many of the period's writers and painters toward a habitual mode of trenchant irony in their thought and their creative productions – 'transcendental buffoonery' in Schlegel's happy phrase."[50] Perhaps not so happy, inasmuch as "trenchant irony" hardly conveys the radiant implications (there are others to be sure) of Schlegel's difficult phrase. (Later, Kucick cites "creative buffoonery" and "tragic art" [71] as the two contrary scenarios wrought by revolutionary dislocations.)

Kucick's major thesis is that the rhetoric of "the Revolution's millenarianism was fundamentally ambivalent" (72), and that it contributed to the fashioning of romantic-ironic duality by imaging both the New Jerusalem and its dreadful collapse. Post-revolutionary disillusion reinforced the negative element of such millenarian ambivalence and thus bitterly intensified the (dark) duality of romantic irony. Yet Kucick, not unlike other critics, appears to be underscoring mainly a ghastly sort of circumstantial irony, the irony brought about by the monstrous reversal of apocalyptic expectations in the 1790s. Given his concentration on ruined, if still potentially regenerative, aspirations, Kucick obviously discovers far more dire gravity than lightness in romantic irony.

The "striking moments of irony in British Romantic poetry" (76) that Kucick points to, especially in Blake and Shelley, embody indeterminacy and contrariety, the tone of which is peculiarly summed up in Kucick's comment that "it should not be surprising to find the horrific forms of that rhetoric [the rhetoric of the perverse ironization of the revolutionary temper] often conditioning Romantic irony to assume the attitude of vexation" (78). Vexation of spirit is a rather mild offshoot of the appalling historical scourge Kucick has been discussing. It is the hovering presence of Schlegel that accounts for this relatively gentle phrasing. Schlegel's fecund, "beautiful confusion," Kucick remarks, also influences the temper of the romantic ironists. Nevertheless, such "beautiful confusion" serves as a foil for the gloomier side of romantic irony, which "grew increasingly sinister" (85) in an industrialized, war-contaminated Europe.

Jerome McGann is one of the few critics who do not reverently embrace Schlegelian fecund chaos before initiating any comments on romantic irony. McGann's view of romantic irony is not always luminous, however. In the final chapter ("Conclusion: Imaginative Belief and Critical Commitment") of *The Beauty of Inflections: Literary Investigations in Historical Method and Theory* (1985), McGann writes that in a "purely critical or negative sense, Romantic poetry can be shown to re-enact the internal contradictions of its own expressed ideal attachments. Romantic melancholy and Romantic irony are the manifestations of the presence of such re-enactments, the felt truths of those longed-for lies which the poets were sometimes compelled to defend."[51] (If romantic melancholy mourns, through re-enactment or even enactment, the mendacities of idealism, romantic irony presumably expresses, or re-enacts, romanticism's self-criticism with more gusto.)

But in his penultimate chapter, "Rome and Its Romantic Significance," McGann, discussing Stendhal's *Rome, Naples, and Florence,* writes as follows: "From the first, Stendhal's Romanticism had been tied up with his irony, just as Byron's Romanticism reached its culmination and apotheosis in irony" (328). (The deified state of Byron's ironized romanticism is a bit hard to swallow.) McGann continues: "But Stendhal moves past the final form of Byronic (and Stendhalian) Romanticism by de-subliming that mode of Romantic irony – specifically by reducing the size and pretensions of his most cherished illusions, the ideal of Romantic Irony. This event comes at the end of his book when Romantic Irony is revealed in its true significance and its purest form. Stendhal's entry for 10 October is an enthusiastic report of an evening spent in the company of the marionettes of the *Palazzo Fiano;* as such, it is also a literal representation of the importance, as well as the triviality, of his Romantic irony – indeed of the importance *of* that triviality" (328). It is possible to extract from McGann's commentary the notion that romantic irony properly deflates the illusions of romantic idealism. It also seems possible, illogical though this may be, to read into McGann's sentences the notion that romantic irony itself is a carrier of the romantic ideal. At the end, we are left with the idea (apparently) that romantic irony is an important trivialization of romanticism.

In a number of McGann's subsequent essays on Byron, romantic irony continues to be a somewhat indistinct concept. In "Byron's Twin Opposites of Truth," published in *Towards a Literature of Knowledge* (1989), McGann declares that the "integrity and stability" of *Don Juan* "lie in the work's flaunting of its own contradictions . . . in . . . romantic irony." These contradictions are viewed by McGann as non-dialectical. McGann's next sentence, however, indicates that romantic irony in *Don Juan* is invoked to "expose and transcend its own contradictions."[52] He adds that "Romantic irony is not the work's ground of truth either" (55). A page later he remarks that "the terms of all [Byron's] contradictions are neither idealistically transcended nor nihilistically canceled out. They simply remain in contradiction" (56). Romantic irony is thus a force that transcends contradictions but also does not transcend contradictions. As for romantic irony's not being the foundation of truth in *Don Juan*, McGann adds that "it is through its many forms of contradiction that the poem declares its truth-fiction to consist in the setting of problems and not the presentation of solutions" (56). Romantic irony is thus a force that does not constitute basic truth in *Don Juan* but also does constitute basic truth.

In "Byron and the Anonymous Lyric" (originally published in 1993), the only essay in *Romanticism: A Critical Reader*, ed. Duncan Wu (1995), that shows some interest in romantic irony, McGann writes that "Byron adopts the conventions of romanticism he inherited – spontaneous overflow, internal colloquy – in order to break them apart."[53] "Byron's lyric style, in effect, is a satire upon a normative mode of romantic writing" (246). (Can one distinguish between lyric-satiric subversion of romantic conventions and romantic-ironic ambivalence?) McGann, to be sure, never suggests that Byron's adoption of romantic perspectives is merely insincere. Yet his remarks about Byron's romantic irony remain puzzling. He states that "Byron's significance as a lyric poet lies in the range of ironizing and critical techniques that he brought to the new lyrical forms of romantic sincerity. These techniques extend from the most sentimental kinds of 'romantic irony' . . . to corrosive and nakedly self-imploding forms." But what are "the most sentimental kinds of 'romantic irony' "? Are they feeble, flabby demolitions of romantic lyricism? Or perhaps displays of residual tenderness in the negation of romantic illusion? Equally unspecified are the corrosively "self-imploding forms" of Romantic irony. In any event, Byron's "originality – and hence his importance for Heine and Baudelaire – must be located in his critical exploration of romanticism and the inheritance of sentimentality" (250).

After alluding, in the second part of his essay, to "certain conventional styles of romantic irony" (whose essence is once again unaddressed), McGann introduces Schiller's distinction between "the naive" and "the sentimental." The latter term now signifies, not some aspect of emotionality, but rather critical self-consciousness; and this, McGann holds, is a mode of romantic irony. But critical self-consciousness is also assigned by McGann to the Wordsworthian art of recollective, reflective composition (though it builds on potent spontaneous feelings). Byron's poetry, of course, does not cultivate Wordsworthian regenerative tranquility. On the contrary. Yet however satanic its "posture of aloofness" may appear to be, Byron's poetry, McGann claims, is bent on "restoring a commitment to elemental passion" (253). Thus Byron's romantic irony (both the weak and the strong species) is able to subvert romantic conventions of feeling while at the same time his most vital poetry authentically nourishes tumultuous romantic passion.[54]

Since a number of critics have been pointing out that necessary alternatives to, limitations of, uncertainties about, or rejections of, imperious romantic lyricism and idealism are supplied by the skeptical element in romantic irony, one would think that a significant position would be allotted to this topic in a critical anthology entitled *Questioning Romanticism*, ed. John Beer (1995). Two essays, Drummond Bone's "The Question of a European Romanticism" and John Beer's "Fragmentations and Ironies" do in fact address the issue of romantic irony, the first marginally, the second somewhat less so. Bone distinguishes between Schlegel's universalizing, "totalizing" romantic irony and the more radical "secular ironic relativism" of late Byron and late Goethe.[55] As against "the actual ironies of Byron and Goethe," which are "happily . . . plural" (130), romantic irony (this is put somewhat hazily) "is the possibility of infinite expression behind one form" (131); in other words, the "Romantic theory of irony foregrounds the retreat of particular meaning" (130). Bone necessarily excludes Byron, the secular ironic relativist, from romantic irony (that is, Schlegelian irony).

In "Fragmentations and Ironies," John Beer, like Kathleen Wheeler in *Romanticism, Pragmatism and Deconstruction* (1993), recites some fairly old news: British (that is, Swiftian) notions of irony are unlike German (metaphysical) irony. Nevertheless, Beer observes, some British romantic ironists can be identified. Unlike Muecke, whose candidate is Byron, and unlike Wheeler, who endorses Coleridge, Beer prefers a compromise: "if . . . one attends to the metaphysical preoccupations of ironists – as in Germany – Coleridge is likely to emerge as its chief British exponent"; but "if English Romantic irony is viewed against the perspective of Pope and Swift, Byron readily assumes a central position" (249-50). Perhaps this concessive formula should not be slighted too quickly, but it is worth remarking that it is Byron's satire, not his romantic irony, that becomes distinctive when the perspective of Pope and Swift is presumed to be all-important.

It is probable that few readers of these pages are on the verge of conjecturing that sticky definitional problems with regard to romantic irony are bound to be resolved sooner rather than later. Some comments on romantic irony by Eric Gans, the last critic we shall cite in this appendix, will likely not accelerate such a conjecture. In *Signs of*

Paradox: Irony, Resentment, and Other Mimetic Structures (1997), Gans first tells us that romantic irony is "an attitude toward life that consists . . . in a knowing superiority to the ironies of fate that await us in the real world."[56] (The burnt romantic, that is, knows the score. Presumably his disabused but resilient temper transcends a merely smirking stoicism.) Next we learn that "the ironist is an atheist who condemns God for his failure to exist. Raised to the status of a life principle, this atheism becomes 'romantic irony' " (69). Romantic irony, then, according to Gans, is a species of condemnatory yet knowingly superior atheism. The genesis of romantic irony involves more than the shocks of fate and a lapsed divinity, however; for Gans, sounding very much like Irving Babbitt, declares that romantic irony is a late phenomenon that "in France corresponds to the disillusionment of the failed romantic revolution of 1848" (69). The disenchantments engendered by fate, godlessness, and reactionary history have had a hand, then, in creating romantic irony, which, incidentally, also "plays on the contrast between material triviality and spiritual importance" (70). It is improbable that Schlegel, who is not mentioned, would applaud Gans's commentary.[57]

Endnotes

Preface

[1] Søren Kierkegaard, *The Concept of Irony, with Constant Reference to Socrates,* trans. and ed. Lee M. Capel (New York: Harper, 1965) 236n.

[2] Vladimir Jankélévitch, *L'Ironie ou la bonne conscience,* 2nd ed. (Paris: Presses Universitaires, 1950) 129.

[3] Louis Mackey, *Kierkegaard: A Kind of Poet* (Philadelphia: U of Pennsylvania P, 1971) 31.

[4] Søren Kierkegaard, *The Concept of Irony with Continual Reference to Socrates,* trans. and ed. Howard Hong and Edna H. Hong (Princeton: Princeton UP, 1989) xvii.

[5] George J. Stack, *Kierkegaard's Existential Ethics* (Tuscaloosa: U of Alabama P, 1977) 33.

[6] Anthony Winner, *Culture and Irony: Studies in Joseph Conrad's Major Novels* (Charlottesville: U of Virginia P, 1988) 70.

[7] Winner, *Culture and Irony,* 9.

[8] Candace C. Lang, *Irony/Humor: Critical Paradigms* (Baltimore: Johns Hopkins UP, 1988) 14, 271, 95, 195.

[9] D. J. Enright, *The Alluring Problem: An Essay on Irony* (New York: Oxford UP, 1986) 2.

[10] Ernst Behler, *Irony and the Discourse of Modernity* (Seattle: U of Washington P, 1990) 73, 75.

Chapter 1

[1] Carl Dawson, "Peacock's Comedy: A Retrospective Glance," *The Keats-Shelley Memorial Bulletin* 36 (1985): 107. The extraordinarily diverse writings of the romantic epoch prompt David B. Pirie to remark that this period "was also an age of comedy, not only in the wit of its more humorous novels but also in verse. Shelley himself, Blake, Wordsworth, Coleridge, Keats – and supremely, of course,

Byron – all wrote comic poems that succeed in being funny." Introduction,*The Romantic Period,* ed. David B. Pirie (Harmondsworth: Penguin, 1994), xv.

[2]Marilyn Butler, "Satire and the Images of Self inthe Romantic Period: The Long Tradition of Hazlitt's *Liber Amoris," English Satire and the Satiric Tradition,* ed. Claude Rawson (Oxford: Blackwell, 1984) 209.

[3]Jerome J. McGann notes in his introduction to *The New Oxford Book of Romantic Period Verse,* ed. Jerome J. McGann (New York: Oxford UP, 1993), that romanticism is generated out of contradictions, that Hazlitt's*The Spirit of the Age* reveals the romantic epoch's self-division (xxii), and that satire flourished from Burns to Byron (xxi). But romantic diversity and romantic contradiction, especially between idealism and scepticism, do not prompt McGann to allude to the comedy of romantic irony. Twenty years earlier, David Thorburn and Geoffrey Hartman, editors of *Romanticism: Vistas, Instances, Continuities* (Ithaca: Cornell UP, 1973) remarked in their preface that romantics "could be at once visionary and sceptical" (8); But they too fail to use this perception as a prelude to a discussion of comedy in romanticism. Nevertheless, in this same 1973 collection of essays, comedy did not remain unmentioned. Frederick A. Pottle ("Wordsworth in the Present Day") writes that Wordsworth, avoiding metaphysical cold-hearted wit, engages from time to time in "waggish and earthy" humor that Wordsworth himself called "drollery" (117); and Harold Bloom ("Emerson: the Glory and Sorrows of American Romanticism") describes Blake as an "apocalyptic, Rabelaisian satirist" (163).

[4]Wordsworth's sense of the comic often appears muffled in neutrality and even gravity of tone. George Watson states that Coleridge is "almost uncharitably funny about his old friend's endless solemnity," that is to say, about Wordsworth's excessively reverential cast of mind. *The Literary Critics* (Baltimore: Penguin, 1962), 129. In chapter 22 of the *Biographia Literaria,* Coleridge notes that "the feelings with which, as Christians, we contemplate a mixed congregation rising or kneeling before their maker" are those which "Mr. Wordsworth would have us entertain at *all* times as men, and as readers." *The Collected Works of Samuel Taylor Coleridge,* vol. 7, ed. James Engell and W. Jackson Bate (Princeton: Princeton UP, 1983), 130. Coleridge is far less charitable in reducing to occasionally hilarious nonsense Wordsworth's ascription of blessed seerdom to the six-year-old philosopher in "Ode: Intimations of Immortality" (138-139). Recent critics tend to view Wordsworth as both endowed with good humor and armed with satiric power. M. H. Abrams, citing the critical work of John F. Danby, claims that "Wordsworth is an accomplished comic poet." "Two Roads to Wordsworth," *The Correspondent Breeze: Essays on English Romanticism* (New York: Norton, 1984), 150. In an essay on "Wordsworth as Satirist of His Age," Stephen M. Parrish, corroborating the judgment of other critics, writes that "some of the most powerful and brilliant strains" in Wordsworth's writing, whether in verse or prose, are fired by a sardonic satiric animus. *The Age of William Wordsworth: Critical Essays on the Romantic Tradition,* ed. Kenneth R. Johnston and Gene W. Ruoff (New Brunswick: Rutgers UP, 1987), 22.

[5]Thomas Love Peacock, *Memoirs of Shelley, and Other Essays and Reviews,* ed. Howard Mills (New York: New York UP, 1970), 45-46.

[6]Quoted in *Shelley's Poetry and Prose,* ed. Donald H. Reiman and Sharon B. Powers (New York: Norton, 1977), 322. Steven E. Jones asserts that though Shelley was all too aware of the oppressive, resentful aspects of the literary tradition of satire, he himself exercised a "satiric sense of humor" that was "bound up with, and represented the other side of, his moral earnestness."*Shelley's Satire: Violence, Exhortation, and Authority* (De Kalb: Northern Illinois UP, 1994), 166n2.

[7]As he challenges the reader to examine this major, but not respectable, incident in his life, Rousseau not surprisingly repudiates the perversions of decorum. *Les Confessions, Oeuvres Complètes,* vol. 1, ed. Bernard Gagnebin and Marcel Raymond (Paris: Gallimard, 1962), 320.

[8]In *Rousseau's Venetian Story* (Baltimore: Johns Hopkins UP, 1966), Madeleine B. Ellis magnifies whatever affinity Rousseau may have felt for Zulietta. She suggests that Rousseau must have realized that both he and Zulietta had prostituted their talents and that both were outcasts, degraded victims of an evil society (138-39).

[9]Jean-Jacques Rousseau, *La Nouvelle Héloïse: Julie, or The New Héloïse,* trans. and abridged by Judith H. McDowell (University Park: Penn State UP, 1968) 159.

[10]George R. Havens remarks that "this very serious Rousseau prizes the healing power of laughter."*Jean-Jacques Rousseau* (Boston: Twayne, 1978), 78. Yet laughter does not penetrate to the core of his sense of uniqueness. Rousseau, incidentally, has a strong gift for caricature, though he insists in the*Confessions* that he has too little malice in his heart to make use of his talent for satire (162).

[11]Quoted in Gerald Graff, *Poetic Statement and Critical Dogma* (Evanston: Northwestern UP, 1970), 103. Irony is more often associated with ice than with fire. But there are interesting exceptions. A character in a long short story by Henry James, "The Papers," reflects on the "inextinguishable flame ... of the ironic passion." *Complete Stories 1898-1910* (New York: Library of America, n. d.), 620. Irony in this instance signifies the frequently injurious power of critical observation.

[12]Stendhal, *The Life of Henri Brulard,* trans. Catherine Allison Phillips (New York: Vintage, 1955). The "Spanish" influence is pointedly discussed on pp. 59, 65-6, 110, 166, and 282.

[13]Stendhal, *Racine and Shakespeare,* trans. Guy Daniels, introd. André Maurois (New York: Crowell-Collier, 1962) 38.

[14]*Racine and Shakespeare,* 130.

[15]*The Romantic School. Heinrich Heine: Selected Works,* ed. and trans. Helen M. Mustard (New York: Vintage, 1973), 151. German madness, Heine adds, is more methodical than the French sort: "The Germans cultivated that madness [of medievalism] with unequaled pedantry, with horrifying conscientiousness, with a thoroughness which a superficial French mad man cannot even conceive of" (152).

[16]Heinrich Heine, *Religion and Philosophy in Germany: A Fragment*, trans. John Snodgrass (Boston: Beacon, 1959) 153.

[17]Quoted from "Discorso di un itialiano intorno alla poesia romantica," trans. V. H. B., in "Leopardi Versus the Romantic,"*Yale French Studies* 13 (1954): 119.

[18]This selection from *Zibaldone*, along with a number of others, is included in Giacomo Leopardi, *Pensieri*, trans. and introd. W. S. Di Piero (New York: Oxford UP, 1984), 171n20.

[19]Giacomo Leopardi, *Selected Prose and Poetry*, ed. and trans. Iris Origo and John Heath-Stubbs (New York: NAL, 1967), 253. The prose includes selections from the *Zibaldone* and the *Operette Morali*.

[20]*Selected Prose and Poetry*, 145-46.

[21]A. Walton Litz, *Jane Austen: A Study of Her Artistic Development* (New York: Oxford UP, 1965) 78-79. Marvin Mudrick puts the case more devastatingly. He asserts that Jane Austen finally buries Marianne "in the coffin of convention. Against her own will and conscious artistic purpose, the creator makes her creature wholly sympathetic – because, one must conclude, Marianne represents an unacknowledged depth of her author's spirit." Nevertheless, "Marianne, the life and center of the novel, has been betrayed" by Jane Austen.*Jane Austen: Irony as Defense and Discovery* (Princeton: Princeton UP 1952), 91, 93. Julia Prewitt Brown remarks that "one has only to think of the conclusion of *Sense and Sensibility* ... to see that Austen was fully aware of the potential sickness of consciousness, of the silent, ferocious irony of life without passion." Yet, "like so many of Jane Austen's heroines, Marianne has learned that the self flows into the world, that the self is not free."*Jane Austen's Novels: Social Change and Literary Form* (Harvard UP, 1979), 15, 64. Jean H. Hagstrum also observes that "Austen is ... not opposed to feeling, only to the excess of it, only to lack of control, only to the abandonment of the whole being to its dominance." In a word, Austen remains "unsentimentally loyal to right reason, which is never allowed to extinguish the fires of feeling." *Sex and Sensibility: Ideal and Erotic Love from Milton to Mozart* (Chicago: U of Chicago P, 1980), 272-73. Hagstrum has it both ways when he declares that "paradoxically" the "finest quality" of sense "is that it possesses feeling – even deep feeling" (271).

[22]Henry Hatfield, *Goethe: A Critical Introduction* (Cambridge, Harvard UP, 1964) 178. In his introduction to Alice Raphael's translation of *Faust: A Tragedy, Part I* (New York: Holt, Rinehart and Winston, 1955), Jacques Barzun, without mentioning romantic irony as such, notes that "Faust and Mephistopheles mutually debunk each other," the temper of each being subjected to an enduring ironic critique (xxii). In his *Classic, Romantic, and Modern* (Garden City: Doubleday-Anchor, 1961), Barzun applies "the principle of Sweeney and the Nightingales," to sudden juxtapositions of contrary moods. This technique he calls "an old satirical device" that "helps make Byron's*Don Juan* the masterpiece it is" (120). German romantic irony, which he does not identify with "the principle of Sweeney and the Nightingales" is defined by Barzun as "the ability to stand above oneself and the universe and look quizzically at the scene" (120). In the introduction to his own translation of *Faust* (Garden City: Doubleday-Anchor,

1961), Walter Kaufmann states that "the function of Mephistopheles resembles that of Heine's sarcasms: romantic reverie is felt to be too glib, too near the cliché, too far from honesty – hence must be exposed" (27). John Geary's view of *Faust I* suggests a cross between European romantic irony and Schlegelian irony: "Mephistopheles pits his cynical humor not only against the idealism ... of Faust, but ... against the seriousness of the work itself. That is romantic irony, which is the turning of art back on itself and upon life." *Goethe's Faust: The Making of Part I* (New Haven: Yale UP, 1981), 155.

²³ Irving Babbitt, *The Masters of Modern French Criticism* (1912; rpt. New York: Farrar, 1963) 129.

²⁴Irving Babbitt, *Rousseau and Romanticism* (1919; rpt. New York: Meridian, 1955) 133.

²⁵Friedrich Schlegel, *Dialogue on Poetry and Literary Aphorisms,* trans. and introd. Ernst Behler and Roman Struc (University Park: Pennsylvania UP, 1968) 126.

²⁶George Brandes, *The Romantic School in Germany* (London: Heinemann, 1906) 40.

²⁷*The Romantic School in Germany,* 72.

²⁸George Brandes, *Naturalism in Nineteenth-Century English Literature* (New York: Russell, 1957) 275.

²⁹*Naturalism in Nineteenth-Century English Literature,* 324.

³⁰Babbitt borrows the phrase "gypsy laughter from the bushes" from Stuart P. Sherman, who applies it to J. M. Synge in *On Contemporary Literature* (New York: Holt, 1917), 206.

³¹*Jean Paul: A Reader,* trans. Erika Casey, ed. Timothy J. Casey (Baltimore: Johns Hopkins UP, 1992) 50.

³²This mistaken formulation about tonal shifts is unfortunately persistent. Donald Sutherland, for example, writes that "what is called Romantic Irony, the interruption of a serious passage by an absurdity, more or less in self-mockery, is ... simple juxtaposition of the sublime and the ridiculous, with little or no use of the infinity of tones between these two poles." *On, Romanticism* (New York: New York UP, 1971), 175. Similarly, Walter Redfern asserts that "'Romantic irony' sets up serious lines followed by afterthoughts which deflate or modify the preceding pretentiousness." *Puns* (London: Blackwell, 1984), 96. Not much more illuminating is the commentary by H. G. Schenk, who in *The Mind of the European Romantics* (New York: Ungar, 1966) squeezes romantic irony into a single footnote (although elsewhere he makes a number of pertinent remarks on dissonance and duality in romanticism): "At times ... a shadow of doubt arose about the genuineness of some feeling or other, or else the paradoxical coexistence of two irreconcilable sentiments made itself felt too strongly. In such cases, the Romantics, especially in Germany, sometimes took refuge in a literary device which they themselves described as 'Romantic Irony'" (253n17).

Herman Broch's thoughts on this issue are much more compelling. In his view, the artist-soul is, above all, subject to inner fissures, and self-irony is at the very core of poetry's inevitable self-doubts. Hence romantic irony has an ancient background: "just because the element of irony is definitely a function as well as a result of a [psychic] split, we must assume it reaches back to the beginnings of poetry, perhaps back to the laughter of the gods, and cannot be confined to the Romanticists, in spite of the eminent place they gave it in their instrumentarium." Introduction to Hugo von Hofmannsthal, *Selected Prose,* trans. Mary Hottinger and Tania and James Stern (New York: Pantheon, 1952), xvii. Hofmannsthal himself wrote an essay on "The Irony of Things." More interesting, however, is his "Letter to Lord Chandos," in which an Elizabethan nobleman apologizes to his friend and mentor, Francis Bacon, for abandoning all literary activity. He is grateful for Bacon's solicitude, which is seasoned with "the expression of lightness and jest which only great men, convinced of the perilousness of life yet not discouraged by it, can master" (129). Such mastery is not unrelated to the ironic temper, which of course may be lacking in sufficient greatness.

[33]According to Suetonius, as paraphrased by Will Durant, many Romans mourned for Nero, "for he had been as generous to the poor as he had been recklessly cruel to the great ... and when they reconciled themselves to his passing they came for many months to strew flowers before his tomb."*Caesar and Christ* (New York: Simon, 1972), 284.

[34]Quotations from *Don Juan* are from Jerome J. McGann's edition of Lord Byron, *The Complete Poetical Works,* vol. 5 (Oxford: Clarendon, 1986).

[35]*Byron: The Critical Heritage,* ed. Andrew Rutherford (New York: Barnes, 1970) 296. Macaulay, who at the beginning of his essay ("Moore's Life of Lord Byron") excoriates the British public for its "periodical fits of morality," claims toward the essay's end that Byron's characterization of Don Juan, "in the first and best cantos," is "a feeble copy of the page [Cherubino] in *The Marriage of Figaro.*" Thomas Babington Macaulay, *Critical and Historical Essays* (New York: Dutton, 1951) vol. II: 616, 635.

[36]"Of Glory," *The Complete Essays of Montaigne,* 3 vols., trans. Donald M. Frame (Garden City: Doubleday-Anchor, 1960) II:324.

[37]Michael Neill's excellent brief discussion of the theme of self-as-flux traces a line of indebtedness from Plutarch to Montaigne to Shakespeare in the introduction to *Anthony and Cleopatra,* ed. Michael Neill (New York: Oxford UP, 1994), 81-82.

[38]Hiram Haydn, *The Counter-Renaissance* (New York: Harcourt, 1950) 11. Norman Rabkin borrows from physics, and methodically applies to Shakespeare, the idea of complementarity, "which signifies that two logically self-canceling truths must nevertheless both be accepted as true (thus light is both waves and particles.)" Contradictory interpretations of Shakespeare's universe exist, Rabkin believes, because it harbors irreconcilable ideals. Absolute values ("mighty opposites") are opposed to other absolutes, both being equally compelling. In *King Lear,* the gods may be viewed, with equal validity, as both malicious and benevolent. *Hamlet* embodies the ideal of reason but also subverts it, for "only destructive and self-destructive impulsiveness can make [Hamlet] capable of performing his divinely sanctioned mission." *Shakespeare and the Common Understanding* (New York: Free Press, 1967), 5.

The most persuasive parallel to romantic irony in Shakespearean comedy occurs in *As You Like It.* C. L. Barber, in "The Use of Comedy in *As You Like It,*" notes that in this play "love has been made independent of illusions without becoming any the less intense." Similarly, Harold Jenkins, in *"As You Like It,"* writes that ideals in this comedy, "though always on the point of dissolving, are forever recreating themselves. They do not delude the eye or reason, yet faith in them is not extinguished in spite of all that reason can do." *Twentieth-Century Interpretations of "As You Like It,"* ed. Jay L. Halio (Englewood Cliffs: Prentice, 1968), 24, 43. T. S. Eliot, whose assertion that Baudelaire was "the first counter-romantic in poetry" ("Baudelaire," *Selected Essays* [New York: Harcourt, 1950], 376) was chronologically amiss, might conceivably have staked a claim for proto-romantic irony, of a sort, in the wit/passion of seventeenth century metaphysical poetry. A kind of extra-literary romantic irony is manifested in Quidam's diary, in Kierkegaard's *Stages on Life's Way,* trans. Walter Lowrie (New York: Schocken, 1967): "in our age there is only one way of being an enthusiast and preserving the soul's romanticism in the midst of the laughing hard-headedness of the nineteenth century, and that is by being just as cold externally as one is inwardly hot" (216). Flaubert, for one, would have enjoyed this comment.

[39]The selections from Hugo's preface are taken from *European Romanticism: Self-Definition,* ed. Lilian R. Furst (London: Methuen, 1980), 122, 129.

[40]The juxtaposition of contrary impulses is usually not related to romantic irony. Certainly romantic irony does not seem to be targeted in Roma A. King's comment that typically "idealism and cynicism" in Browning "meet in one man or one situation ... [Browning's] awareness of the co-existence of good and evil and beauty and ugliness in all life and his struggle to reconcile them makes him inevitably an ironist on the cosmic scale." *The Bow and the Lyre: The Art of Robert Browning* (Ann Arbor: U of Michigan P, 1957), 97. In *The Democratic Vista: A Dialogue on Life and Letters in Contemporary America* (Garden City: Doubleday-Anchor, 1958), Richard Chase notes that Henry Adams, unlike Whitman, allowed himself to be "reduced to a futile irony by his galling sense of polarity" (40-41). Chase's point is that contradictions enliven a healthy spirit, while neurotic spirit is neutralized by them. In any case, "irony, wit, dialectic, drama, finally intelligence itself – are all impossible without a sense of contraries and oppositions" (147-48).

Chapter 2

[1]Leslie A. Marchand, in the preface to his *Byron: A Biography,* 3 vols. (New York: Knopf, 1957), writes that "the key to the paradox of Byron's personality" is furnished by the "balance the poet strikes between idealistic aspiration and realistic disillusionment" (I: xii-xiii). Although this insight is amply prepared for in nineteenth-century criticism, Marchand credits it specifically to Hoxie Neale Fairchild, who in *The Romantic Quest* (New York: Columbia UP, 1931) states that

Byron is "too idealistic to refrain from blowing bubbles, and too realistic to refrain from pricking them" (370).

[2]In his chapter on "The Anti-Romantics" in *The Victorian Temper: A Study in Literary Culture* (Cambridge: Harvard UP, 1951), Jerome Hamilton Buckley points out that early Victorian enemies of romanticism denounced it as an isolationist flight from practical social commitment.

[3]Marilyn Butler suggests that the character whom Scythrop "most resembles is perhaps the hero of Shelley's Alastor, another young writer at the outset of his career, and in the grip of a wrong idea about how to be a poet. But where Shelley's hero in 1815 is implicitly misled by the example and teaching of Wordsworth, Peacock's Scythrop is unmistakably a Coleridgean. He is a thorough-going Germanist." *Peacock Displayed: A Satirist in His Context* (London: Routledge, 1979), 124.

[4]Thomas Love Peacock, *Nightmare Abbey and Crotchet Castle,* introd. J. B. Priestley (London: Hamish Hamilton, 1947) 10.

[5]But Byron never cancels his comments on the Lakers. With superb unfairness, he pitches more than once into a triumvirate of tedium (and much worse: mystification, vulgarization, and hypocrisy) made up of Southey, Wordsworth, and Coleridge. In Canto I, Byron specifies, in decalogue form (while making fun of his own Mosaic injunctions) that it is Pope, along with Milton and Dryden, who must be worshiped – certainly not that other, more recent trio.

[6]Byron's response, in a letter to John Murray (Aug. 12, 1819), to Francis Cohen's objections to "the quick succession of fun and gravity" in *Don Juan* deals with what is startlingly seriocomic rather than romantic-ironic. "[Cohen's] metaphor," Byron writes, "is that 'we are never scorched and drowned at the same time!' Did he never play at Cricket or walk a mile in hot weather? – did he never spill a dish of tea over his testicles in handing the cup to his charmer to the great shame of his nankeen breeches? – did he never swim in the sea at Noonday with Sun in his eyes and in his head – which all the foam of the ocean could not cool?" The barrage of Byronic evidence goes on, at times more outrageously than pertinently. At this early stage of the composition of *Don Juan,* Byron is still claiming the privileges of untrammeled fun, buffoonery, giggling; he intends a "playful" rather than a serious satire. In the same letter to Murray, Byron indicates that the point of his gravity in *Don Juan* is precisely to "heighten the fun." *Byron's Letters and Journals,* ed. Leslie Marchand (Cambridge: Harvard UP, 1976) VI: 207. The year before, in a letter to Thomas Moore (Sept. 19, 1818), Byron, without this time having any reason for combative buoyancy or for underscoring his license with dualities, had described *Don Juan* (the first canto, actually) as "meant to be a little quietly facetious upon everything" (VI: 67). But some years earlier, writing to Lady Melbourne (July 1, 1813), he had revealed his "natural love of contradiction and paradox," which Byron's comic poetry and his correspondence easily corroborate. *Byron's Letters and Journals,* ed. Leslie A. Marchand (Cambridge: Harvard UP, 1974)III: 70. It is clear to most of Byron's critics that his comments on Burns's "antithetical mind" – delicate and coarse, emotional and sensual, "soaring and groveling" between "deity" and "dirt" (III:

239) – apply perfectly to Byron's own self-division. David D. Erdman differs from such critics. "Since it is possible," he writes, "to consider the life of an individual as a consistent whole, I reject those formulas that rest on a psychological dualism, such as the views that maintain a paradox, recognizing the conflict of Classic and Romantic sympathies, of eighteenth- and nineteenth-century ideals, or symptoms of classicist, romanticist, and realist in various expression of Byron's life. I see *one* Byron, playing complicated roles." "Byron's Flirtation with his Muses," *Rereading Byron: Essays Selected from Hofstra University's Byron Bicentennial,* ed. Alice Levine and Robert N. Keane (New York: Garland, 1993), 126.

[7]Byron intended "to have displayed him gradually gâté and blasé as he grew older – as is natural." Letter to Murray (Feb. 16, 1820). *Byron's Letters and Journals,* ed. Leslie A. Marchand (Cambridge: Harvard UP, 1978) VIII: 78. Candace Tate believes that by the close of Canto XII, "the reader can see that Juan has developed a social cunning that makes the most of any occasion, and the defenseless man-child of the first canto has developed at last into the libertine after whom he is named." "Myth as Psychodrama," *Lord Byron's "Don Juan",* ed. and introd. Harold Bloom (New York: Chelsea House, 1987), 99.

[8]There is an excellent discussion of these roles in Leslie A. Marchand, *Byron's Poetry: A Critical Introduction* (Boston: Houghton, 1965), 167-89.

[9]Candace Tate (see n.7, above) may think that Juan finally achieves the predatory savoir-faire of the original Don Juan. Moyra Haslett, however, in *Byron's "Don Juan" and the Don Juan Legend* (Oxford: Clarendon, 1997), is convinced that no alteration in Juan's character actually takes place, that from the very beginning Juan is inescapably delineated as the legendary Don Juan. Hence the on-and-off realization of amorous idealism in the early cantos of *Don Juan* is rigorously blotted out in Haslett's study. Such intermittent romantic impulses would be hopelessly contaminated, in Haslett's view, by Byron's relentlessly sexual innuendoes – by his slyly sustained invitation to the reader to enjoy the pleasures of libertinism. Though the affirmative aspects of romantic irony (this term is not part of Haslett's vocabulary) recurrently purge Byron's fondness for antiromantic eroticism, Haslett is certain that the rhetoric of duplicity is unredeemably pervasive in Byron's text.

[10]Several critics, apparently engulfed by Julia's unrestrained mendacity in the bedroom farce, distrust her subsequent epistolary devotion to Juan. Paul Elledge, for example, writes that "[Julia's] valedictory…clutches the subject to which it bids farewell; a textual imposture, it quietly reprises the brazen linguistic deceptions of her bedroom harangue." "Parting Shots: Byron Ending *Don Juan I,*" *Studies in Romanticism* 27 (Winter 1988), 564.

[11]Truman Guy Steffan, in *The Making of a Masterpiece,* the initial volume of the 4-volume variorum edition of *Don Juan,* ed. Truman Guy Steffan and Stuart Pratt, 2nd ed. (Austin: U of Texas P, 1971), carefully analyzes Byron's accretions to his text. These accretions, which often establish clashes of tone, reveal, in Steffan's judgment, striking evidence of growing disillusion and cynicism. See especially pp. 74 and 85.

[12]In the English cantos, Aurora Raby's partly mocking attraction to Juan promises little of the lyricism that characterizes Haidée's love. For a decidedly adverse view of Aurora's romantic potentialities, see Cecil Y. Lang, "Narcissus Jilted: Byron, *Don Juan,* and the Biographic Imperative,"*Historical Studies and Literary Criticism,* ed. Jerome J. McGann (Madison: U of Wisconsin P, 1985), 143-79.

[13]Malcolm Kelsall, *Byron's Politics* (Sussex: Harvester, 1987) 158. Caroline Franklin also points out that the ironic refrain of "The Isles of Greece" ("Fill high the cup with Samian wine") "simultaneously reproaches both the islanders' hedonistic festivity and their political apathy: for Samos was the adopted home of Anacreon, whose poetry celebrated pleasure and ridiculed heroic and military values. Furthermore, the decisive battle of the Persian wars was lost by the treachery of Samos, a wine-producing area." *Byron's Heroines* (Oxford: Clarendon, 1991), 140.

[14]Jerome McGann, *The Beauty of Inflections: Literary Investigations in Historical Method and Theory* (Oxford: Clarendon, 1985) 285.

[15]Bernard Beatty has quite a different view. He thinks that "Aurora Raby and the Duchess of Fitz-Fulke take the poem in a new direction altogether while, miraculously, restoring Don Juan's long-lost confidence in life and love. This moment is, perhaps, the most remarkable one in *Don Juan.*" *"Don Juan" and Other Poems* (Harmondsworth: Penguin, 1987), 101. It is, moreover, Aurora, Beatty declares, who allows Byron's poem to end with a religious reading of life. Aurora "is a religiously conceived figure who knows all about the Fall and seems to be in touch with something like divine grace rather than with Nature. Yet Aurora Raby functions as a heroine in the poem, even, so it seems, as a potential wife for Juan" (130). Indeed, Beatty believes that Aurora's emergence "out of what appears to be the unshakable grip of satire in the last cantos is...the most surprising and the finest thing in English romantic poetry" (105).

[16]In "The Editor and the Controlling Voice in*Sartor,*" the third chapter of*The Rhetorical Form of Carlyle's "Sartor Resartus"* (Berkeley: U of California P, 1972), Gerry H. Brookes states that the voices of the Editor and the Professor are "fully coordinated" (60) and that the two men are essentially "reflexes of the same mind" (67). Brookes insists, overmuch, that Carlyle "is no skeptic and brooks no real disagreements in *Sartor"* (56n4). Rosemary Ashton reformulates a more subtle critical position: in *Sartor,* Carlyle's solution to the problem of conveying his convictions was to "allow himself full reign with the rhapsodic visionary Teufelsdröckh, while cannily retrieving a common-sense, deflationary presence in the form of the English editor." *The German Idea: Four English Writers and the Reception of German Thought 1800-1866*(Cambridge: Cambridge UP, 1980), 75. But the consequence, she adds, of using "the ironic device of a doubting editor who constantly undermines the rhapsodist" is that "finally it is difficult for the reader to assess Teufelsdröckh's 'philosophy.'" Nevertheless, Carlyle's defensive irony "was a useful rhetorical bracket to put around subversive material (a device well known to Carlyle from Swift's*Tale of a Tub*.) More than that, Carlyle could here give vent to his own doubts" (101).

[17]Thomas Carlyle, *Sartor Resartus: The Life and Opinions of Herr Teufelsdröckh*, ed. Charles Frederick Harrold (New York: Odyssey, 1937) 7.

[18]Albert J. La Valley is not alone in pointing out that "Carlyle's ambivalent attitude toward Voltaire is testimony of an ambivalence within himself – the need for belief and the need for skepticism." *Carlyle and the Idea of the Modern* (New Haven: Yale UP, 1968), 41-42.

[19]One of the conversations in Imre Salusinszky, *Criticism in Society* (New York: Methuen, 1987) contains the following pertinent comment by Geoffrey Hartman: "There is a way that ideology enters all our thinking. The question is whether one can have ideology and irony together...If you can have both ideology and irony, fine. Neither, by itself, will do. Irony by itself will simply strike most people as sterile" (90). Carlyle's "ideology" and "irony" are of course not meant to play an unremitting duet.

[20]"The conflict [in Carlyle] between the apocalyptic vision he aspired to (in Teufelsdröckh) and the critical intelligence he could not escape (in the Editor)," as George Levine puts it in *The Boundaries of Fiction: Carlyle, Macaulay, Newman* (Princeton: Princeton UP, 1968), 57, is transmitted in a number of ways. Obviously these cannot all be categorically reduced to the patterns of romantic irony. Chris V. Vanden Bossche makes a single reference to romantic irony in *Carlyle and the Search for Authority* (Columbus: Ohio State UP, 1991): "while Carlyle employs something like Romantic irony in *Sartor Resartus,* he does not intend to destabilize meaning completely. In this respect I concur with those critics who insist that Carlyle intends his irony to be limited by his insistence on an ultimate ground of meaning" (185). But Schlegelian irony, which is what Vanden Bossche is apparently alluding to, is supposed to promote dialectical suppleness, not intransigent destabilizations.

Justin Kaplan was presumably not thinking of Schlegel when he wrote the following passage in his biography of Whitman: "In this 'rapt,' 'weird' and 'grotesque' book, as Whitman described *Sartor Resartus,* Carlyle had written his spiritual autobiography and a secular gospel on the pattern of Rousseau, Goethe and Nietzsche, but it was impossible to tell where the skylarking left off and the seriousness began – the romantic irony of the Europeans had been carried over wholesale into English." *Walt Whitman: A Life* (New York: Simon, 1980), 173. From these remarks, one might gather that romantic irony is seamlessly jocoserious, that it runs rampant in European romanticism, and that Carlyle's exalted sobriety in *Sartor Resartus* is absolutely inextricable from his hilarity.

[21]G. B. Tennyson, *Sartor Called Resartus* (Princeton: Princeton UP, 1965) 276-77. A. Abbot Ikeler, writing about comedy and dualism in *Sartor,* suggests that "the manner of *Sartor* displays the playful, even amoral aspect of parody and satire as much as the matter of it chronicles the growth of spiritual conviction in the author." *Puritan Temper and Transcendental Faith: Carlyle's Literary Vision* (Columbus: Ohio State UP, 1972), 100. Like Ikeler, Philip Rosenberg does not use the phrase "romantic irony" in discussing Carlyle. Rosenberg does, however, call sharp attention to Carlyle's Manichean stress on "the presence of the divine and the diabolical in human affairs" – and also in Teufelsdröckh's prose. The

consistent promotion and persistent mockery of Teufelsdröckh's ideas and style are described by Rosenberg as a "somewhat schizophrenictechnique apparently derived from a habit in the Carlyle household of speaking with mocking irony about what was taken most seriously."*The Seventh Hero: Thomas Carlyle and the Theory of Radical Activism* (Cambridge: Harvard UP, 1974), 47, 45-46. Nietzsche, incidentally, claimed that "Jean Paul had been responsible for destroying Carlyle and making him England's 'worst writer.' " Adrian del Caro, *Nietzsche Contra Nietzsche: Creativity and the Anti-Romantic* (Baton Rouge: Louisiana State UP, 1988) 70. Caro adds that "Nietzsche had nothing positive to say about Carlyle, whom he considered to be a confused, pathetic Christian and romanticist" (70).

²²Thomas Carlyle, "Jean Paul Friedrich Richter,"*Critical and Miscellaneous Essays* (New York: Scribner's, n.d.) I:16-17. Elsewhere, in a discussion of Jean Paul, Carlyle describes humor as "the balm which a generous spirit pours over the wounds of life...Such humor is compatible with tenderest and sublimest feelings." *German Romance* (London: Chapman and Hall, 1898) II:123. Later critics usually "define" Jean Paul as a Sternean-Saturnalian humorist, or a romantic ironist who creates and destroys illusions or who hops from sentimentality to realism. See, for example, Dorothea Berger, *Jean Paul Friedrich Richter* (New York: Twayne, 1972) especially pp. 8, 46, 54, and 102.

²³Thomas Carlyle, "Jean Paul Friedrich Richter Again," *Critical and Miscellaneous Essays,* II:218. Jean Paul's concept of humor and Friedrich Schlegel's idea of irony have often been viewed as similar in nature. Timothy J. Casey agrees that Jean Paul's humor, that "converse sublime," in Jean Paul's words, is "at once destructive and liberating." But he does not equate humor's destructive-liberatingtendency with the creative-destructive rhythm of Schlegelian irony. Referring to Jean Paul's *Vorschule der Esthetik (Preschool for Aesthetics),* Casey writes that "we play for real, not for play, is the gist of his argument in *Preschool's* final *cantate* lecture, with its implied criticism of Schlegel irony and Schiller play." *Jean Paul: A Reader,* 30, 77.

²⁴Thomas Carlyle, "Schiller," *Critical and Miscellaneous Essays,* II:200.

²⁵Elizabeth M. Vida, *Romantic Affinities: German Authors and Carlyle* (Toronto: U of Toronto P, 1993.) Of particular interest are the chapters "Jean Paul's Theory of Humour" (33-40) and "Teufelsdröckh's Romance and Jean Paul's Concept of Love" (57-61).

²⁶*Carlyle and the Idea of the Modern,* 40. La Valley offers the following overview of the idea of humor in Richter and Carlyle: "Humor allows [Richter] to treat the universe as a plaything, yet to regard it not with anarchy but with a purpose: to...feel pathos and pity for his living beings, and to transform his aversion into a form of love...Humor is the measure of insight and flexibility; as the embodiment of fire and the central imaginative force, it molds opposites and unlike things together, producing, in its style and vision, a new means of looking at existence. With Teufelsdröckh the utilitarian 'clothes' will lead through humor to the transcendental vision which will return the reader to a new awareness of the

everyday. Humor embraces the cosmos, through sensibility melting it into one unity" (39).

[27]Karl Miller, *Doubles: Studies in Literary History* (London: Oxford UP, 1985) 19.

[28]Margaret Kirkham has made a strong contrast between *Northanger Abbey* and *The Heroine* that lends no aid to Miller's thesis. *The Heroine*, she observes, is one of those burlesques that "deny value to the novel, especially the novel of female authorship; the heroine's delusions are unambiguously corrected by the superior wisdom of the hero and she herself is simply a figure to be mocked. *Northanger Abbey* differs in important ways: the value of the novel, especially as written by women, is pointedly affirmed...the deluded Catherine is never so far deluded as to abuse or disobey her genuinely affectionate(if rather dim) parents [Cherubina, Barrett's heroine, confines her tender-hearted old father to a lunatic asylum] and a balance, characteristic of Austen, is set up between the hero and heroine so that his superiority of age, education, and sex does not get unqualified validation." "Jane Austen: Questions of Context," *The Romantic Period,* ed. David Pirie (Harmondsworth: Penguin, 1994), 96.

Chapter 3

[1]D. C. Muecke, *The Compass of Irony* (London: Methuen, 1969) 185.

[2]Gary J. Handwerk in *Irony and Ethics in Narrative: From Schlegel to Lacan* (New Haven: Yale UP, 1985) studies irony's ethical, socializing potential. This is an unusual topic inasmuch as the ironic temper does not ordinarily crave (perhaps not even unconsciously) to be fulfilled and supplanted by intersubjective communion. In Handwerk's view, ethical irony implies "a possible reintegration beyond incompatibles"; it forces "the isolated subject beyond its internal inconsistencies" (3-4). Locating specific confirmation of this view in Schlegel's philosophic writings, Handwerk claims that ethical irony in Schlegel serves to "reintegrate the individual and society, to pass beyond the isolated creative consciousness and regain the sense of speaking to kindred spirits" (30). That is why Handwerk takes exception to critics who limit their discussion of Schlegel's irony to its aesthetic impact, to its "self-reflexiveness and parabatic quality" (226n4).

[3]Hans Eichner, *Friedrich Schlegel* (New York: Twayne, 1970) 51.

[4]In his chapter on F. Schlegel in *The Romantic Age,* vol. 2 of *A History of Modern Criticism 1750-1950* (New Haven: Yale UP, 1955), René Wellek domesticates "transcendental buffoonery" by putting ironic smiles and farcical laughter in the same box. He explains that "the ironic author always smiles at his imperfect medium just as the buffo laughs at his comic role" (15).

[5]Peter Conrad, *Shandyism: The Character of Romantic Irony* (New York: Barnes, 1978) 184.

[6]Siegbert Prawer, Introduction,*The Romantic Period in Germany,* ed. Siegbert Prawer (New York: Schocken, 1970) 7. Eudo C. Mason, contributing a chapter

on "The Aphorism" in the same volume, extols the youthful Schlegel's Wildean, paradoxical roguery. The "sublime impudence" (216) of this "great mocker" is also directed, Mason writes, against "his own most cherished convictions" (211). Yet Schlegel's Fragments, compared to Novalis's, reveal "a certain strain and exertion, a certain ponderousness in the use of language, and a chronic quarrelsomeness" (217).

In his preface to *European Romanticism: Literary Cross-Currents, Modes, and Models,* ed. Gerhart Hoffmeister (Detroit: Wayne State UP, 1990), the editor declares that through the term "romantic irony," Schlegel "could transfer the principle of political freedom to the sphere of poetics" (13). Fortified by*Lyceum* Fragment 42 (the poet's irony enables him to rise infinitely above all conditions, even above his own "art, virtue, or genius") and*Lyceum* Fragment 37 (through poetic reflection, the author, in Hoffmeister's words, "liberates himself from the thralls of subject matter as well as from the chains of instinctive enthusiasm to regain complete control over himself and his art" [14]), Hoffmeister sees romantic irony as an internalized "political" insurrection against repressive, tyrannical rule. Certain contributors to *European Romanticism* do not quite align themselves with the editor on this point. In his essay "New Harmony: The Quest for Synthesis in West European Romanticism," Henry H. H. Remak asks this question: "How much reality is there in the intellectually beguiling paradigm of F. Schlegel, which elevates irony to the common denominator of a romantic literature whose claim to revolutionary universality supersedes that of politics?" (334) Presumably, not a great deal. The volume's first essay, John Francis Fetzer's "Romantic Irony," certainly does not accord with the editor's preface. Fetzer describes romantic irony as a "twilight zone" (21) or a "halfway house" (26), wherein both writer and reader are "compelled to straddle a middle ground of ambivalence between dichotomous or contrastive opinions" (22). It seems evident that liberation is not Fetzer's theme. After referring to Strohschneider-Kohrs's judgment that*Puss-in-Boots* (1797) and "Princess Brambilla" (1821) best exemplify*German romantic irony (in which art mirrors itself), Fetzer states that the "deliberate destruction of the illusion" is "an intrinsic symbol of the artist's acknowledgment of the indissoluble dichotomy between aim and accomplishment"; and this signifies an eternal preclusion of "aesthetic fulfillment," which in turn may engender a "sense of inadequacy or imperfection," a "nagging doubt" and even traces of despair (25). Irony may become a "quagmire ... of ambiguity," act like a viral infection (29), and instill a spiritual malaise" (30). Heine, for example, was captured by the "Byronic disease," that is, a "perpetually unresolved tension between coexistent polarities" (30). Although he does not especially emphasize comedy (which would perhaps be interpreted as another expression of malady), Fetzer's further comment on Heine leads directly to the concept of European romantic irony: "The irony of the *Book of Songs* is 'romantic' to the extent that archmotifs of romanticism together with their debunking antipodes are both regarded as integral and reciprocal parts of the scheme of things. In this work, Heine may no longer believe in the existence of a romantic world, but he cannot deny its essence; on the other hand, he rejects the essence of its philistine counterpart, but he cannot deny its existence" (31).

[7]*Friedrich Schlegel's "Lucinde" and the "Fragments,"* trans. and introd. Peter Firchow (Minneapolis: U of Minnesota P, 1971) 27-29.

[8]Quoted in Muecke, *The Compass of Irony,* 200.

[9]*Friedrich Schlegel's "Lucinde,"* 47.

[10]Søren Kierkegaard, *The Concept of Irony with Constant Reference to Socrates,* trans. and introd. Lee M. Capel (New York: Harper, 1965) 305.

[11]Muecke believes that a dedication to romantic idealism counterpointed by a mockingly dissolvent impulse "is only one aspect" of Schlegelian irony. *The Compass of Irony,* 186.

[12]Erich Heller, *Thomas Mann: The Ironic German* (Cleveland: Meridian, 1961) 166-209. Heller observes, however (though not in the terminology used in the present work), that Mann's thinking comes close to Pyrrhonic irony's emancipatory refusal of resolution. As Mann himself puts it, "the really fruitful principle, the principle of art, is ... that irony which plays subtly and undecidedly ... among opposites and is in no great hurry to join issue" (quoted, 168).

[13]*The Ironic German,* 185.

[14]Paul de Man, "The Rhetoric of Temporality," *Interpretation: Theory and Practice,* ed. Charles S. Singleton (Baltimore: Johns Hopkins UP, 1969) 193.

[15]In *Irony/Humor: Critical Paradigms* (Baltimore: Johns Hopkins UP, 1988), Candace D. Lang makes some perceptive comments on de Man's misuse of Baudelaire. See especially pp. 54-55. Other critics have also noted the misapplication of de Man's thesis. See, for example, Dominick La Capra, *Soundings in Critical Theory* (Ithaca: Cornell UP, 1991), 101-32, and Joseph A. Dane, *The Critical Mythology of Irony* (Athens: U of Georgia P, 1991), 172-82.

[16]*The Ironic German,* 176.

[17]Here and there Tieck still receives substantial recognition as a co-progenitor of romantic irony. He is accorded high honors, for instance, in Gerald Gillespie's lengthy and learned introduction to his edition (and translation) of *Der gestiefelte Kater* (Austin: U of Texas P, 1974). Though Gillespie links Tieck to Pirandello (Tieck, like Schlegel, was apparently destined to exert his influence mainly in the twentieth century), Eric A. Blackall points rather to Brecht as Tieck's heir. Tieck wrote "some highly innovative dramas in which irony and alienation foreshadow the theater of Bertold Brecht." *The Novels of the German Romantics* (Ithaca: Cornell UP, 1983), 151. In his introduction to his translation of Tieck's *Die Verkehrte Welt,* or *The Land of Upside Down* (Rutherford: Fairleigh Dickinson UP, 1978), Oscar Mandel situates Tieck between Aristophanes and Brecht: "All this exuberant art of playing with art naturally precludes what we call 'identification' by the spectator or reader with the characters and events of the play. As Tieck is detached from his materials, so, very pleasantly, are we. It is the Olympian approach of the god toying with his puppets below. This 'Romantic irony,' as it is called in Germany, this literary consciousness of itself, this theater which exhibits its greasepaint, timber, and sound effects, had been extolled by F. Schlegel in his work on Aristophanes. Tieck probably conceived and wrote his

theatrical jests before any such theories struck him, but afterward he readily acceded to the formulations of the Schlegel brothers ... While the *Sturm und Drang* writers had sought to draw the spectator into a maelstrom of passion, Tieck and the Schlegel brothers, anticipating the 'alienation' practices of Brecht, were sacrificing total immersion in favor of smiling control."

[18]Victor Terras, *A Karamazov Companion* (Madison: U of Wisconsin P, 1981) 113. In "Romantic Irony, Spatial Form, and Joyce's *Ulysses,*" Ann D. and J. J. Johnson define romantic irony as the deliberate, jesting "destruction of the illusion that the art work is a self-contained reality system."*Spatial Form in Narrative*, ed. Jeffrey R. Smitten and Ann Daghistany (Ithaca: Cornell UP, 1981), 49. Dorrit Cohn suggests that in her appeal in the final section of*Ulysses* – "O Jamesy, let me up out of this" – Molly is "perhaps calling on her creator-author in a spirit of romantic irony." *Transparent Minds: Narrative Modes for Presenting Consciousness in Fiction* (Princeton: Princeton UP, 1978), 232.

[19]Anthony Winner, *Culture and Irony: Studies in Joseph Conrad's Major Novels* (Charlottesville: UP of Virginia, 1988) 69. In*Mythology as Metaphor: Romantic Irony, Critical Theory, and Wagner's "Ring"* (Westport: Greenwood, 1998), Mary A. Cicora identifies romantic irony as "a kind of play with the fictionality of the text" (24). Wagner's*Ring* is basically romantic-ironic because "a modern mythical drama will inevitably be a self-conscious product" (4).

[20]*The Bedford Glossary of Critical and Literary Terms,* ed. Ross Murfin and Supryia M. Ray (Boston: Bedford, 1997) 181.

[21]Frederick Garber, "Coda: Ironies Domestic and Cosmopolitan,"*Romantic Irony,* Ed. Frederick Garber (Akadémiai Kiadó: Budapest, 1988) 369.

[22]René Wellek, *A History of Modern Criticism 1750-1950,* II:15.

[23]Ted Emery, "Introduction: Carlo Gozzi in Context,"*Five Tales for the Theater,* by Carlo Gozzi, ed. and trans. Albert Bermel and Ted Emery (Chicago: Chicago UP, 1989) 1.

[24]Raymond M. Immerwahr affirms that "Gozzi probably exerted a greater influence upon Tieck's comedies than any other single precursor."*The Esthetic Intent of Tieck's Fantastic Comedy* (Saint Louis: Washington UP, 1953), 27.

[25]Lloyd Bishop, *Romantic Irony in French Literature from Diderot to Beckett* (Nashville: Vanderbilt UP, 1989) xi.

[26]*Romantic Irony in French Literature,* 19.

[27]Clyde de L. Ryals, *A World of Possibilities: Romantic Irony in Victorian Literature* (Columbus: Ohio UP, 1990) 4.

[28]Peter Gay, *Pleasure Wars* (New York: Norton, 1998) 47.

[29]"Editor's Preface," *Romantic Irony* (1988), 8.

[30]Stuart Curran, *Poetic Form and British Romanticism* (New York: Oxford UP, 1986) 251n8. René Wellek and Austin Warren pointed out some time ago that "the strong integration between philosophy and literature, even during the German Romantic movement, can be achieved only by arguing from fragments and theoretical disquisitions of Novalis and Friedrich Schlegel, avowedly Fichte's disciples, whose speculations, frequently unpublished in their time, had little to do with the production of concrete works of literature."*Theory of Literature,* 3rd

ed. (New York: Harcourt, 1977), 121. Wellek and Warren's single reference to romantic irony links it primarily to self-conscious fiction: the romantic-ironic writer "deliberately magnifies the role of the narrator," and he "delights in violating any possible illusion that this is 'life' and not 'art' " (223).

[31]Joseph A. Dane, *The Critical Mythology of Irony* (Athens: U of Georgia P, 1991) 73, 118.

[32]Kathleen Wheeler, *Romanticism, Pragmatism and Deconstruction* (Oxford: Blackwell, 1993) 36.

[33]Kathleen Wheeler, "Coleridge's Friendship with Ludwig Tieck," *New Approaches to Coleridge: Biographical and Critical Essays,* ed. D. Sultana (Totowa: Barnes, 1981) 106.

[34]*New Approaches to Coleridge,* 102, 111.

[35]*Romanticism, Pragmatism and Deconstruction,* 11.

[36]Wheeler's treatment of German romantic irony recycles ideas contained in her introduction and headnotes to *German Aesthetic and Literary Criticism: The Romantic Ironists and Goethe* (Cambridge: Cambridge UP, 1984). In Wheeler's discussion, the romantic aesthetic merges indistinguishably with romantic irony; and romantic-ironic ideas are described as often "coincident with many of the most exciting concepts of modern criticism today," though these ideas also constitute a "a principle essential to all art" (viii). Socratic irony, however, remains "the precondition for the concept of romantic irony" (20). Wheeler's commentary on romantic irony forms a web of apparently synchronic affiliations, so that Karl Solger, for example, is not less prominent than Friedrich Schlegel, and is so often referred to that Schlegel almost figures as his St. John. All in all, one derives from Wheeler the idea that creatively destructive art and criticism, fragmentariness, self-contradiction, paradox, illusion-destruction, parody, wit, intuition, imagination, intelligence, and mysticism all function energetically in the matrix of German romantic irony.

[37]This judgment is reiterated in many of Behler's other works, for example in *Irony and the Discourse of Modernity* (Seattle: U of Washington P, 1990): "When Schlegel decided to term the mood which permeates certain works by Boccaccio, Cervantes, Sterne, and Goethe ironic, he caused indeed a fundamental change in Western critical thought" (75). Socrates remains indispensable, however: "In varying forumulations, Schlegel attempted to rescue the Socratic-Platonic irony of a configurative, indeterminable, self-transcending process of thinking and writing and to integrate it with the modern style of self-reflection and self-consciousness as the decisive mark of literary modernity" (82).

[38]Ernst Behler, *German Romantic Literary Theory* (Cambridge: Cambridge UP, 1993) 8.

[39]Does Behler provide an avenue between Schlegelian theory and European romantic irony? In his essay "Techniques of Irony in the Light of the Romantic Theory" (*Rice University Studies,* vol. 57 [Fall 1971]), he advances the idea that such an avenue not only exists but is broadly accessible. Behler begins by defining Schlegelian irony as a constant alternation between "poetic enthusiasm" and "corrective scepticism" (2), after which he remarks that this "theory of irony had

strong repercussions and came to be considered the core of that mental attitude labeled by later critics Romantic irony" (3). Yet this "mental attitude" – a blend of creative effervescence and counterbalancing scepticism – immediately metamorphoses in Behler's essay into a "device," which is then held to be prominently on display in German romantic literature (3). The "device" is illustrated in two widely separated works, Grabbe's play *Comedy, Satire, Irony, and Deeper Meaning* (1827) and Brentano's novel *Godwi* (1801). Grabbe's play bears the stamp of Tieck's zany theater pieces, while Brentano's novel shows the influence of Goethe's *Wilhelm Meister.* Both works, Behler indicates, exhibit a tendency to derail the artistic process of make-believe by playfully, capriciously violating artistic illusion. (In fact, it is only at the very end of Grabbe's chaotic farce – it begins with the freezing of the devil on earth and virtually concludes with the devil's departure for hell, newly subjected to spring cleaning, in the company of his lovely, fur-clad grandmother – that one comes across obvious illusion-destruction, sense having already been long destroyed. Two characters, Baron Mordax and Verdant, jump into the orchestra pit in defiance of the threat of punishment by the righteous Baron von Huldingen, who is then scornfully identified as a mere actor in a play. A moment later, the Schoolmaster, an aficionado of drunkenness, curses out Grabbe as the stupid, worthless, vacuous author of the play now being presented. After retaliating, invisibly, by calling the Shoolmaster a monster of mendacity, Grabbe enters on stage with a lighted lantern, thereby terminating the play. Brentano's *Godwi* provides a number of astonishing structural obliquities and self-demolitions in its second volume.)

At the very beginning of his essay, however, Behler had declared that Tieck's fantastic, illusion-destroying plays were not a significant factor in the making of German romantic irony. Indeed Schlegel's *Lyceum* aphorisms, Behler observes, "had no demonstrable influence on Tieck and indeed go considerably beyond his intentions" (2). We are thus faced by a contradiction: the device of disruption which, suddenly melted down from a dualistic mental attitude, is supposed to characterize German romantic irony is also declared to be irrelevant to the genesis of German romantic irony.

There is a more damaging bit of illogic to contend with. The meaning of illusion – not illusion as non-factual belief, hope, or dream, but theatrical or fictional illusion – takes a curious turn in the essay. Right after discussing Brentano's deliberately whimsical, outrageous sabotage of artistic continuity and coherence in *Godwi*, Behler states that "this ironic counterpoint of illusionary poetry and empirical reality" (4) is a customary romantic practice. Behler's shift in terminology and emphasis is accomplished without the slightest hint of strain. Illusion-destruction turns into illusionary poetry; and illusionary poetry becomes the poetry of illusion, pitted against "empirical reality." Illusion is then given an even more generous frame of reference in its opposition to pedestrian reality. Behler also views illusion as including the fantastic. And so we have Hoffmann's antithesis of the fantastic and the prosaic. Illusion also comprises dreamy, idealizing visions. And so we have Heine's play of discrepancies between the "poetic" and the "empirical" (4).

By associating the "illusionary" with the fantastic and the rhapsodical, and the "empirical" with the disenchantingly realistic, Behler appears to have dropped the technique of theatrical or fictional illusion-disruption to a secondary or even tertiary level of interest. His position now is that sharply conflicting attitudes and feelings are the hallmark of German romantic irony. Moreover, irony of this sort, Behler maintains, is not limited to German romanticism. Thus in *Don Juan* Byron mixes enthusiasm and illusion (aspects of youth) with scepticism and self-distrust (aspects of maturity). Stendhal similarly highlights the illusions of youth in *The Red and the Black,* illusions which he exposes primarily by pulling away "the masks formed by habit" (5-6). If clarity is not well served in this remark about Stendhal, that is because "illusion" in Behler's essay has from the outset straddled dissimilar meanings. These are further tangled when Behler writes that "Stendhalian irony is at its best when in crucial moments the original nature of the hero breaks through and destroys the illusion of imaginary duties" (6). In later writers like Dostoevsky and Nietzsche, Behler continues, the Stendhalian irony of outer, pragmatic rationality struggling with inner, sincere feeling continues to operate powerfully.

Behler concedes that "the Romantic doctrine of irony was by no means thought to delineate something new, but rather intended to give an essential feature of modern literature, long in existence, its name" (7-8). This "essential feature," however, has by now attached to itself several connotations, chief of which are self-reflexiveness (variations on the "device") and conflicted dualisms. Shakespeare is cited as a masterly romantic-ironic intermingler of contradictory voices, Cervantes as the magisterial romantic ironist of authorial interventions and self-criticism. Yet it is Socrates in particular, Behler claims, who closes the gap between past and present; for the difficulties of modern literary communication are best surmounted through Socratically cunning yet noble interdiction, understatement, and self-criticism. Socrates, therefore, becomes modern literature's liberator: "Socratic irony became the force by which means [the modern writer] could – in Schlegel's terms – 'infinitely rise above himself' " (12). Since Socratic irony does not illustrate psychic ambivalence, Behler reaches the end of his essay with a large problem of transition.

Having managed in the meantime to expand the range of contradictory spheres in romantic irony to the point where it also embraces the lofty and the trivial, as well as mirth and sadness, Behler now projects romantic-ironic dualities into the increasingly haunting ambivalences of the later nineteenth century, ambivalences exemplified, for example, by the clash of reason and will in *Notes from Underground,* or the antagonism of "vitality and decadence, intellect and life" in Nietzsche (13). But while it would be idle to quarrel with the idea that nineteenth-century ambivalence links Schlegelian paradoxicality to the irony of European romantics like Byron, Stendhal, and Heine, it needs to be reiterated that no specific Schlegelian influence can be adduced to underscore this linkage.

Nor is the comedy of European romantic irony to be accounted for by viewing Byron, Stendhal, and Heine as the (oblique) heirs of Friedrich Schlegel's sense of humor. (In truth, Behler does not suggest such a relationship.) Close readers of Heine, to take the most likely candidate for such an heirship, do not usually assimilate his poetry to the Schlegelian concept of irony. S. S. Prawer observes, in *Heine: Buch der Lieder* (Great Neck, NY: Barron's, 1960) that Heine introduced in *Das Buch der Lieder* "a new and disturbing note into [German] poetry: a play of wit and irony which had hardly any antecedent and was to have hardly any issue in the poetic tradition of Germany. Germany never had its Metaphysicals, never had its Dryden or its Pope, and the Byron it enthusiastically adopted was the Byron of *Manfred* and *Childe Harold,* rather than the Byron of ... *Don Juan.* This is one of many reasons Heine has always seemed such an alien body in the poetic tradition of his own country and why his work has been accepted so much more readily in England and France" (42). Prawer's description of what Heine achieved in German poetry is applicable to Byron, who may be regarded as having initiated a "new and disturbing" (and delightful) note of irony – the kind in which genuine idealism is contested by de-idealizing comedy – in European romanticism.

[40]*The Oxford Companion to the English Language*, ed. Tom McArthur (Oxford: Oxford UP, 1992) 532.

[41]*The Cambridge Guide to Literature in English,* ed. Ian Ousby (Cambridge: Cambridge UP, 1993) 475. Readers seeking further clarification in *The Johns Hopkins Guide to Literary Theory and Criticism,* ed. Michael Groden and Martin Kreisworth (Baltimore: Johns Hopkins UP, 1994), will learn from one contributor (Russell A. Berman) about "the progressive infinity of Romantic irony" (345), and from another (Steven Gillies) that irony in Schlegel's view is not only a form of paradox but "a combination of wit and allegory" (342). Gillies suggests that Jean Paul's idea of humor "comes very close to the Romantic conception of irony ... as a procedure ... that provides insight into the contradictory nature of existence" (343). This is a frequently held correlation, but Timothy J. Casey remarks that Jean Paul can more especially "be called romantic if we are using the term as René Wellek and Austin Warren use it in their distinction between the objective mode of narration and the 'romantic-ironic' mode, with a narrator who plays up his own presence and parades his artistry and, indeed, the artificiality of the work. If the extreme example of this in English is Laurence Sterne, in German it is Jean Paul." *Jean Paul: A Reader* (Baltimore: Johns Hopkins UP, 1992), 6. Jean Paul's unfailing humor/irony may of course, whatever its denotation, strike some readers as tedious. In her essay "German Wit: Heinrich Heine" *(Westminster Review,* Jan. 1856), George Eliot notes, as Rosemary Ashton comments, that Jean Paul, " 'the greatest of German humorists,' (beloved by Carlyle and De Quincey) is unendurable to many readers, and frequently tiresome to all, in his prolixity and lack of measure and tact." *The German Idea: Four English Writers and the Reception of German Thought 1800-1860* (Cambridge: Cambridge UP, 1980), 174. In his essay "Romantic Irony," in *Romanticism* (2000), ed. Marshall Brown, vol. 5 of the *Cambridge History of Literary Criticism,* Gary Handwerk states that "romantic irony," however sharply contested its meaning, is a suitable term for romantic and postromantic literary experimentalism. Such experimentalism emphasizes diverse modes of structural disruption.

Chapter 4

[1]Ingrid Strohschneider-Kohrs, *Die romantische Ironie in Theorie und Gestaltung,* 2nd ed. (Tübingen: Niemeyer, 1977) 130. Friedrich Schlegel dominates the "Theorie" section, while Hoffmann is pre-eminent in the "Gestaltung" part of the book. (Tieck is not far behind, however.) It should be mentioned that Anglo-American criticism long ago associated Hoffmann with Tieck as a practitioner of German romantic irony. Harvey W. Hewitt-Thayer wrote that "in the use of Romantic Irony Hoffmann was unquestionably following Tieck's Märchen comedies: the characters step out of their roles and speak *in propria persona,* as in *Der gestiefelte Kater* and *Die verkehrte Welt* .... But of course neither Tieck nor Hoffmann confined the Romantic conception of irony to an external formula that is calculated to startle the reader. This was merely an exuberant form of irony by which the author demonstrated his superiority to the work of his imagination by destroying the illusion he had created. In the writings of the Romanticists, irony was a subtly pervasive spirit informing the work of the poet. It was a kind of intellectual exaltation, or rather the evidence of it. The author was in his work but stood above it, and through irony he expressed his release from the bondage under which most men live and think." *Hoffmann: Author of the Tales* (Princeton: Princeton UP, 1948), 145, 161.

[2]Charles Baudelaire, "The Essence of Laughter,"*The Essence of Laughter and Other Essays, Journals, and Letters,* ed. and introd. Peter Quennell (New York: Meridian, 1956) 122.

[3]This is Horst S. Daemmrich's perspective in *The Shattered Self: E. T. A. Hoffmann's Tragic Vision* (Detroit: Wayne State UP, 1973). Heine once described Hoffmann's work as "a frightening scream of fear in twenty volumes." Cited in James Trainer, "The Märchen," *The Romantic Period in Germany,* ed. Siegbert Prawer (New York: Schocken, 1970), 114.

[4]Eric A. Blackall, *The Novels of the German Romantics* (Ithaca: Cornell UP, 1983) 19.

[5]*Kater Murr, Selected Writings of E. T. A. Hoffmann,* 2 vols., trans. and introd. Leonard J. Kent and Elizabeth C. Knight (Chicago: U of Chicago P, 1969) II:30.

[6]In his introduction to *The Life and Opinions of the Tomcat Murr* (Harmondsworth:Penguin, 1999), Jeremy Adler writes that Hoffmann's "narrative polarity corresponds to what Friedrich Schlegel called 'romantic irony': a variety of dialectic by which we are tossed between opposing viewpoints, each time returning to the previous one at a higher level, until eventually, we become free to 'float' or 'soar' " (xxv). Such theorizing will not be sanctioned by readers who remain obstinately earthbound. Adler himself cannot float above certain semantic difficulties. After indicating that Hoffmann preferred the term "humor" to "romantic irony," he goes on to state that "humour and irony themselves engage in a dialectic. Irony – the novel's constant weapon – exposes the negative. Humour reveals the positive, and entails the acceptance of, and thereby the elevation above, negativity. Hoffmann's 'humour,' therefore, subsumes 'romantic

irony' "(xxvi). But Schlegelian irony is meant to embody both the positive and the negative.

[7]See Ritchie Robertson, "Shakespearean Comedy and Romantic Psychology in Hoffmann's *Kater Murr,*" *Studies in Romanticism* 24 (1985): 201-22.

[8]"Princess Brambilla," *Three Märchen of E. T. A. Hoffmann,* trans. and introd. Charles E. Passage (Columbia: U of South Carolina P, 1971) 113.

[9]Introduction, *Three Märchen of E. T. A. Hoffmann,* xxii.

[10]G. T. Hughes observes that Hoffmann's "interpolated or interwoven Märchen" in "Princess Brambilla," as well as in "The Golden Poet," "derive from G. H. Schubert, and present the disruption of a golden age (a paradisal garden) by the intrusion of reflective consciousness." Nevertheless, "the poetic imagination, the inner world of dreams, provides a link between reality and the supersensual world, even if only a tentative one." *Romantic German Literature* (New York: Holmes, 1979), 119.

[11]Tieck's evaluation of his own comedy resembles such "humor": "My kind of irony is not mockery, derision, persiflage . . . . Rather it is the deepest earnestness bound together with true merriment." Quoted in the introduction to *The Land of Upside Down,* by Ludwig Tieck, trans. and introd. Oscar Mandel (Rutherford: Fairleigh Dickinson UP, 1978), 14.

[12]Marshall Brown makes an interesting comment on the "disease" of this "chronic dualism." According to him, Jean Starobinski, who in his essay "Ironie et Mélancholie (II): La 'Princesse Brambilla' de E. T. A. Hoffmann" believes that psychic wholeness is restored in Hoffmann's tale, and Paul de Man, who in his essay "The Rhetoric of Temporality" is convinced that ironic non-reconciliation marks the story's finale, "both agree in seeing duality in exclusively negative terms. In doing so, they overlook the double meaning of the crucial phrase ... The disease of chronic *dualism* is in fact cured, but the cure is none other than *chronic* dualism ... [The hero] does not overcome his split personality, but he learns to conduct life on two planes at once: ideal and real, in the imagination and in the senses, in allegory (utopian myth) and in ironic, demystified self-awareness."*The Shape of German Romanticism* (Ithaca: Cornell UP, 1979), 205.

[13]Jocelyn Kolb, " 'Die Puppenspiele meines Humor's: Heine and Romantic Irony," *Studies in Romanticism* 26 (1987): 400. Kolb defends her thesis by referring to the company of romantic ironists, especially Cervantes, Shakespeare, and Sterne, whom Schlegel celebrates and whom Heine strongly resembles. She declares that "the essence of Heine's poetry and thoughts lies in an ambivalence that is unresolvable" (401), and that Heine's ambivalence toward romanticism is only one of many dualisms expressed by a simultaneity of the sublime and the ridiculous (408). Without specifying that any influence is involved, Kolb finds in Heine (or, more accurately, perhaps, Heine-as-Sterne) ample evidence of Schlegel's ideas and tonalities, for example, permanent parabasis, transcendental buffoonery, the alternation of enthusiasm and irony, the dissolution of generic boundaries, wit and humor, and artfully cultivated confusion. In*The Ambiguity of Taste: Freedom and Food in European Romanticism* (Ann Arbor: U of Michigan P, 1995), Kolb writes that "the fusion of serious and humorous, of

lyrical and commonplace in writers like Shakespeare, Cervantes, and Sterne" forms the basis for what Schlegel calls 'romantic irony' " (6). This is a notable simplification of her earlier commentary.

[14]Max Brod, *Heinrich Heine: The Artist in Revolt*, trans. Joseph Witriol (New York: New York UP, 1957) 201-02. Though Brod grants Heine an "innate love of leg-pulling" (205), he also suggests, rather like Irving Babbitt, that Heine's irony functioned as an alternative to the madness, suffocation, or suicide which a forthright plunge into insuperable seriousness might conceivably have occasioned (203-04).

[15]Laura Hofrichter, *Heinrich Heine*, trans. Barker Fairley (Oxford: Clarendon, 1963) 27.

[16]Hanna Spencer, *Heine* (Boston: Twayne, 1982) 23. Spencer later repeats this assertion: Heine's is "not an irony which dissolves reality as does the so-called [German] romantic irony but, on the contrary, an irony which destroys illusion and exposes reality" (42). Without alluding to romantic irony in his brief study*Heine* (New York: Grove, 1988), Ritchie Robertson cites the poet's intense "love-hate relationship" with romanticism (1) and notes that "much of the *Book of Songs* simultaneously exploits and questions the language of romanticism" (9).

[17]Jeffrey L. Sammons, *Heinrich Heine: A Modern Biography* (Princeton: Princeton UP, 1979) 178. In *Heinrich Heine: Poetry in Context: A Study of "Buch der Lieder"* (Oxford: Berg, 1989), Michael Perraudin on several occasions brings up the question of Heine's self-contradictoriness, of his conflicting dispositions. Perraudin does not, however, mention romantic irony (of any sort).

[18]Muecke, *The Compass of Irony*, 206.

[19]Translations of Heine's poetry are taken from *The Complete Poems of Heinrich Heine: A Modern English Version*, ed. and trans. Hal Draper (Boston: Suhrkamp, 1982).

[20]*The Romantic School, Heinrich Heine: Selected Works*, ed. and trans. Helen M. Mustard (New York: Vintage, 1973) 150. The mixed nature of Heine's mockery was recognized in 1835 by *Blackwood's Magazine*, which "coupled Heine with Börne and with Joel Jacoby as the chief representatives of the modern German School of Irony, whose founder was Jean Paul. All three possessed playful fancy, passionate enthusiasm, deep feeling, wild wit, but they fell short of their prototype in literary quality, in brilliance, and raciness." Sol Liptzin, *The English Legend of Heinrich Heine* (New York: Bloch, 1954) 20.

[21]Jerome J. McGann, in *The Romantic Ideology: A Critical Investigation* (Chicago: U of Chicago P, 1983), has a high regard for Heine's cultural-political lines of reference in dealing with German romanticism. He notes the interplay of sympathy and severe critique in *The Romantic School* (11), though he does not especially delve into Heine's flippant, often sardonic distortions of elements of German romanticism: (Lillian R. Furst, in *Counterparts: The Dynamics of Franco-German Literary Relationships 1770-1895* [Detroit: Wayne State UP, 1977], deems Heine's book to be a hatchet job, "the product of calculated malice" [117].) McGann sees Heine's critical method as a desirable corrective to romanticism's self-honoring perpetuation in critical works on the subject (11-13,

33). McGann also quotes Heine's purported comments on the capacity of "Romantic Irony" to sidestep censorship (28-29). But in fact Heine refers only to "humorous irony" or "humor and irony," and he names Goethe and Cervantes (he later changed his mind about Cervantes) as the chief practitioners of this censorship-circumventing, evasionary mode of comedy. The existence of such humorous irony, Heine observes, is "only a sign of our lack of political freedom" (quoted, 39). McGann, incidentally, finds fault with Anne K. Mellor's*English Romantic Irony.* "In Mellor's view," McGann writes, "the emergence of either guilt or fear signals the termination of Romantic Irony and the beginning of 'something else' " (22). He concludes that Mellor will not accept dark or nihilistic elements in romanticism. Mellor points out McGann's error (as well as other questionable matters) in a review of *The Romantic Ideology* in *Studies in Romanticism* 25 (1986): 285. In the same article she asserts, rather dubiously, that Heine's *Romantic School* is itself an example of romantic irony because if "moves … through … rhythms of commitment and detachment," "enthusiastic creation … and sceptical decreation" (285).

²²*Heine's Prose and Poetry,* introd. Ernest Rhys (New York: Dutton, 1966) 321.

²³Kurt Weinberg in *Heinrich Heine, 'romantique défroqué,' hérault du symbolisme français* (New Haven: Yale UP, 1954) constructs a tortuous path from German romantic irony to Heinesque mockery. According to Weinberg, Heine's point of departure in the domain of irony is the early collection of poems entitled *Youthful Sorrows (Junge Leiden).* These, he says, are marked by demonic irony and fantastic imagery characteristic of writers like Hoffmann, Arnim, Brentano, and La Motte-Fouqué, who in turn inherited Schlegel's theory of irony. The basic urge of Schlegel's irony, in Weinberg's opinion, is the impulse to prove the freedom of the human spirit in all its powers of originality and revolt. By reading into this impulse the desire to transcend the laws of nature and to destroy the conventions of society, Weinberg is able to account for all the strange mockeries, monstrous visions, and artificial universes brewed in the German romantic cauldron. Weinberg's further pursuit of the sources of Heine's irony gets more complicated. In the first *Travel Pictures (Reisebilder),* Weinberg claims, Heine exchanged his early macabre delirium (part of the German romantic flair for the grotesque) for an almost ethereal levity, which nevertheless soon yielded to an increasingly pessimistic disenchantment (100). Heine next fell under the sway of the aesthetics propounded by Solger, for whom irony has a semi-mystic significance (123). Finally, though merely in passing, Weinberg indicates that the young Heine adopted the mordant irony of the rebellious Byron (137).

²⁴Friedrich Schlegel, *Dialogue on Poetry and Literary Aphorisms,* 86.

²⁵"Don Quixote," *Heine's Prose and Poetry,* 301. In *The Baths of Lucca,* as Ritchie Robertson points out, Heine "suggests that one cannot do without profound beliefs, even if, like Don Quixote's, they are delusions and lead to humiliation." *Heine* (New York: Grove, 1988), 91.

²⁶*Heine's Prose and Poetry,* 346-47.

[27]*The Baths of Lucca, The Sword and the Flame: Selections from Heinrich Heine's Prose,* ed. and introd. Alfred Werner (New York: Yoseloff, 1960) 367. Heine's self-division has been seen at times as a severe limitation. Thus Gerhard Thrums writes in *Der Typ des Zerrissenen* (1931): "That inner powerlessness to lend continuity to an idea or sentiment, to exercise control over one's heart or mind, that constant medley of thoughts and feelings which are at once infinitely delicate and coarsely sensual, longing and mocking, romantically dream-like and crudely realistic, – that is the Heine 'Zerrissenheit.' " Quoted in Israel Tabak, *Judaic Lore in Heine* (Baltimore: Johns Hopkins, 1948), 187. Kurt Weinberg, on the other hand, recognizes that the cultivation of such psychic duality releases creative power; he also recognizes that the bitter, pessimistic element in Heine's irony effectively separates his irony from that of the Schlegels. *Heinrich Heine, "romantique défroqué,"* 33, 100. Nigel Reeves sees "Zerrissenheit" as "Heine's version of A. W. Schlegel's 'innere Entzweiung.' Schlegel saw modern man suspended between memories of a past Golden Age and a yearning for the true existence after death. For Heine the yearning is for a new Golden Age on earth and it is man's intellect that forever seems to balk a satisfying union with our earthly surroundings. Heine's values ... are the exact opposite of Schlegel's. But for both men this inner dissonance is the product of a specific historical situation; it is the malaise of the age, not just the state of mind of some lovesick poet." *Heinrich Heine: Poetry and Politics* (London: Oxford UP, 1974), 28. In J. P. Stern's judgment, Heine's "Zerrissenheit" is often a matter of moral integrity in the face of insoluble conflicts: "Unlike Nietzsche (whom he resembles in many other ways), [Heine] had no stomach for 'positive' solutions. His predicament is the predicament of modernity: it lies precisely in his refusal to allow his critical, sardonic consciousness to be appeased and arrested by assent . . . . No sooner has Heine put an object of value before us – the love of a woman, of Germany, of Nature or of God – than his critical consciousness overtakes it." *Idylls and Realities: Studies in Nineteenth-Century German Literature* (New York: Ungar, 1971), 70-71.

[28]*Ideas: Book Le Grand, Heinrich Heine: Selected Works,* 72-73.

[29]*Ideas: Book Le Grand, Heinrich Heine: Selected Works,* 73.

[30]Edmund Burke, *Reflections on the Revolution in France,* introd. Russell Kirk (Chicago: Regnery, 1955) 21.

[31]*Friedrich Schlegel's Lucinde and the Fragments,* 233.

[32]Quoted in S. S. Prawer, *Heine: The Tragic Satirist: A Study of the Later Poetry 1827-1856* (Cambridge: Cambridge UP, 1961) 170-71.

[33]*The Complete Poems of Heinrich Heine,* 480.

[34]Jeffrey Sammons portrays them as muses "in that they symbolize elements of Heine's poetic inspiration, and their imperfections are part of the dynamics of his restless spirit." Sammons goes on to speak of Heine's "permanently ambiguous relationship to the aesthetic heritages of Classical antiquity, Romanticism, and the Bible." *Heinrich Heine: The Elusive Poet* (New Haven: Yale UP, 1969), 286.

[35]*Heinrich Heine: The Tragic Satirist,* 33.

[36]Sammons describes "the sudden turn from the sublime to the ridiculous" as a manner "central to Heine's style."*Heinrich Heine: The Elusive Poet,* 162. But we have seen that this would make for a misleading definition of European romantic irony. In a subsequent essay, which constitutes the foreword to a collection of Heine's poems entitled *Songs of Love and Grief,* trans. Walter W. Arndt (Evanston: Northwestern UP, 1995), Sammons makes an indispensable addition to his earlier comment (though it would still make for an inadequate grasp of European romantic irony): often in Heine's poetry, "feeling is broken up and undercut by irony, but, once dismissed as delusion, returns nevertheless as imperishably genuine" (xix). Barker Fairley provides a first-rate discussion of Heine's ambivalent clown-complex in *Heinrich Heine: An Interpretation* (London: Oxford UP, 1954), 138-41. Roger F. Cook makes no mention of romantic irony or of F. Schlegel's ideas on irony in *By the Rivers of Babylon: Heinrich Heine's Late Songs and Reflections* (Detroit: Wayne State UP, 1998); but he reminds the reader often enough that Heine was a "poet whose Romantic vision of beauty and desire was always fractured by dissonant voices" (39), including the very active voice of self-mockery.

[37]S. S. Prawer, *Heine's Jewish Comedy* (Oxford: Clarendon, 1983) 541. "While speaking of a true nostalgia," Prawer adds, "a true feeling of loss and self-division, Heine seems to be parodying all that appeared too easy and melodious in his own poetry" (541). Henry Hatfield, who finds "something tawdry in Apollo's language," believes that the music of the poem "is closer to Offenbach than to Gluck." *Clashing Myths in German Literature* (Cambridge: Harvard UP, 1974), 38. Responding to an earlier opinion of Prawer's, Hatfield states, "I cannot agree with Prawer that the poem represents 'undeniable beauty' but find poignancy in the fate of the nun and of Apollo' " (38). Cook writes that "Der Apollogott" "offers a self-critical perspective on [Heine's] apotheosization of Romantic longing as well as on the self-styled Hellenic paradise he felt he could establish for himself in the middle of nineteenth-century Europe. The last part of the poem parodies these illusions he has harbored in a burlesque manner."*By the Rivers of Babylon,* 197.

Chapter 5

[1]Philippe Van Tieghem, *Musset: l'homme et l'ouevre* (Paris: Hatier-Boivin, 1944) 20.

[2]Paul Bourget, *Sociologie et littérature,* quoted in Lloyd Bishop, *The Poetry of Alfred de Musset: Styles and Genres* (New York: Lang, 1987) 90.

[3]P. E. Tennant, *Théophile Gautier* (London: Athlone, 1975) 102.

[4]Jacques Barzun, "Stendhal on Love," *The Energies of Art* (New York: Vintage, 1962) 105.

[5]Victor Brombert, *Stendhal: Fiction and the Themes of Freedom* (New York: Random, 1968) 3.

⁶Théophile Gautier, *Les Jeunes-France: romans goguenards* (Paris: Charpentier, 1883) ii-iii.

⁷Théophile Gautier, *A History of Romanticism, The Works of Théophile Gautier,* ed. and trans. F. C. Sumichrast (New York: Sproul, 1905) XVI: 153.

⁸*A History of Romanticism,* XVI: 49-50.

9Algernon Charles Swinburne, *William Blake* (1866), quoted in Carl Woodring, *Nature into Art: Cultural Transformations in Nineteenth-Century Britain* (Cambridge: Harvard UP, 1989), 148.

¹⁰Théophile Gautier, *Mademoiselle de Maupin,* trans. and introd. Joanna Richardson (Harmondsworth: Penguin, 1981) 39.

¹¹Richard B. Grant believes this final chapter "clumsily undid Madeleine's evolution [toward utterly free self-development] and desperately reversed the direction of the story." *Théophile Gautier* (Boston: Twayne, 1975), 42. But there is nothing in Madeleine's luminously witty letter which suggests that she will henceforth lead a significantly inhibited life.

¹²Arthur O. Lovejoy, "On the Discrimination of Romanticisms,"*Essays in the History of Ideas* (New York: Capricorn, 1960) 228.

¹³Alfred de Musset,*Lettres de Dupuis et Cotonet, Oeuvres Complètes,* (Paris: Editions du Seuil, 1963) 877.

¹⁴Alfred de Musset,*La Confession d'un enfant du siècle, Oeuvres Complètes,* 555.

¹⁵*La Confession,* 558.

¹⁶Though Lloyd Bishop underlines Musset's idealistic-cynical ambivalence in "Namouna," his emphasis on impermanence and instability in Musset's poetry makes for an extremely broad definition of romantic irony: "This view of a universe governed by chance and change is reflected in Musset's style: the quickly changing tonalities, the contradictory moods, the sudden switching of themes, the mixing of registers, the shifting perspectives, the tendency to juxtapose fragments – in two words, romantic irony." *Romantic Irony in French Literature, from Diderot to Beckett* (Nashville: Vanderbilt UP, 1989), 57.

¹⁷Alfred de Musset, *The White Blackbird,* trans. Julian Jacobs (London: Rodale, 1955) 41.

¹⁸Harry Levin describes Stendhal's outlook as "an unexpected combination of Machiavellism and Quixotry, an opportunism which makes a point of missing its opportunities." Levin observes that "while Europe moved from revolution to realpolitik, Stendhal was moving from*Don Quixote* to *The Prince.* This transition is not so abrupt as it may seem to us, for both books – uniquely and unforgettably – had embodied the Renaissance perception of the incongruities between romance and reality . . . . One satirizes the code of chivalry, the other codifies the tactics of the unchivalrous; one expresses the mood of undeception, the other expounds the technique of deception." *The Gates of Horn: A Study of Five French Realists* (New York: Oxford UP, 1963), 99.

¹⁹Stendhal,*Love,* trans. Gilbert and Suzanne Sale, introd. Jean Stewart and B. C. J. G. Knight (Harmondsworth: Penguin, 1975) 25. Jonathan Keates points out that in *Love* Stendhal attempts "to convince himself that his enquiring spirit can

effectively detach him from the rawness and vulnerability of passion," but discovers "simultaneously that it cannot." *Stendhal* (New York: Carroll and Graf, 1997), 244. He adds that Stendhal's reliance on systems and categories shows he is "trying frantically to hang on, by way of codifying and analysis, to an essentially uncontrollable emotion that both embarrasses him with the absurdities he perpetrates under its incalculable influence, and at the same time reassures him that, unlike most of his countrymen, he is at least capable of spontaneous feeling à l'italienne" (244).

[20]Stendhal, *The Life of Henry Brulard,* trans. Catherine Allison Phillips (New York: Vintage, 1955) 308.

[21]Victor Brombert, *Stendhal: Fiction and the Themes of Freedom* (New York: Random, 1968) 45. For all its surface ideology, Brombert declares,*Love* is "in fact simultaneously a sentimental justification, a self-administered therapeutic treatment, and a Stendhalian *Vita Nuova"* (42).

[22]Robert Alter states that "the plots . . . of [Stendhal's] two greatest novels are a kind of derailing of Don Juanism and the discovery of a Wertherian dénouement: the protagonist in each case is made to abandon a boldly manipulative attitude toward the world at large in favor of a Romantic withdrawal from the world."*A Lion for Love: A Critical Biography of Stendhal* (New York: Basic, 1979), 153. But Julien's intense relationship with Mathilde de la Mole in *Red and Black* constantly fluctuates between Wertherism and Don Juanism; to a lesser extent, this is also true of Julien's relationship with Mme de Rênal.

[23]The first four of Stendhal's quotations from*Don Juan,* all of which concern Juan and Julia, are applied to Julien and Mme de Rênal, the other three to Julien and Mathilde de la Mole. The order of the quotations is as follows: Canto I: 74, 73, 71, 170; Canto XIII: 1, 84; Canto I: 73 (once more). In a letter of 20 January 1838, Stendhal shows less than perfect regard for Byron's masterpiece: "Lord Byron's Don Juan is a mere Faublas, for whom the larks fall ready roasted . . . . Lord Byron's reputation and the scintillating beauty of his verse have disguised the weakness of his *Don Juan." To the Happy Few: Selected Letters of Stendhal,* trans. Norman Cameron (New York: Grove, 1955), 348.

[24]*Stendhal: Fiction and the Themes of Freedom,* 60. Robert M. Adams remarks that "whenever Julien shows any sensitivity, perceptiveness, or sincerity, he is stigmatized as foolish, ridiculous, weak, or naive."*Stendhal: Notes on a Novelist* (New York: Noonday, 1959), 65. (Of course Julien is also chastised at times for being imperceptive or theatrical.) Lloyd Bishop, emphasizing Stendhal's denigrations, claims that "the war between innocence and experience" in*Red and Black* "is waged not so much between Julien and himself as between the young and inexperienced Julien and his mature and experienced creator, Henri Beyle alias Stendhal." *Romantic Irony in French Literature,* 66. If this were true, the novel would be much less interesting than it is. Stendhal does not consistently rebuke Julien for being naive or ill-advised, though Bishop describes Stendhal's early attacks on his hero as "sarcastic" and "pitiless" (66-67). In any case, a worldly narrator berating his protagonist for all sorts of defects or misjudgments is not, as Bishop believes, evidence of romantic irony. (Bishop asserts that

"Stendhal also uses romantic irony as an exercise in sadomasochism. To compensate for his own disappointments, the author can revel in the discomfiture of his scapegoat hero" [79].)

²⁵F. W. J. Hemmings, *Stendhal: A Study of His Novels* (Oxford: Clarendon, 1964) 52.

²⁶Stendhal, *Red and Black*, ed. and trans. Robert M. Adams (New York: Norton, 1969) 204.

²⁷In connection with the theme of combined love and enmity, Victor Brombert cites Stendhal's fascination with the Clorinda-Tancredi relationship in Tasso's *Gerusalemme liberata. Stendhal: Fiction and the Themes of Freedom,* 83.

²⁸Dominick La Capra, *History, Politics, and the Novel* (Ithaca: Cornell UP, 1987) 18.

²⁹*Stendhal: Fiction and the Themes of Freedom,* 65-66.

³⁰Robert M. Adams, *Stendhal: Notes on a Novelist* (New York: Noonday, 1959) xviii.

³¹*Stendhal: Notes on a Novelist,* xviii.

³²Raymond Giraud, *The Unheroic Hero in the Novels of Stendhal, Balzac, and Flaubert* (New Brunswick: Rutgers UP, 1957) 69. Brombert, on the other hand, in his essay "Stendhal, Analyst or Amorist?" merely alludes to "the baffling romantic irony so typical of Stendhal." *Stendhal: A Collection of Critical Essays,* ed. Victor Brombert (Englewood Cliffs: Prentice, 1962) 166. In his introduction to this critical anthology, however, the idea of romantic irony (shorn of comedy) can be extracted from several of his comments. For example: "Prosaic precision and poetic vagueness, illusion and disenchantment, cynicism and idealism, negation and affirmation of values, parody and sentimental commitment – all coexist, clash, and somehow merge in a mercurial synthesis" (7). Other essayists in this collection make much the same point. In "A Theoretical Outline of 'Beylism' " Leon Blum speaks of the persistence in Stendhal of "the combination of a heart and a mind that contradict each other; of an intellect that believes in the necessity of order and the effectiveness of logic, that subjects everything to rational explanation and empirical verification; and of a sensibility that thirsts for, and values, only disinterested exaltation, free movement, and ineffable emotion" (109). In "Knowledge and Tenderness in Stendhal," Jean-Pierre Richard shows that Stendhal "presents a dual image: there is the lucid and logical mind, desirous of attaining truth even by the most arid paths of analysis; but there is also the chimerical dreamer, the passionate lover, swept away at the slightest pretext by romantic melancholy and by visions of bliss" (127).

Chapter 6

¹Roman S. Struc, "Pushkin, Lermontov, Gogol: Ironic Modes in Russian Romanticism," *Romantic Irony,* ed. Frederick Garber (Akadémiai Kiadó: Budapest, 1988) 249.

²Mihail Lermontov, *A Hero of Our Time,* trans. Vladimir Nabokov and Dmitri Nabokov (Garden City: Doubleday-Anchor, 1958) 41.

[3]John Garrard points out that "Grushnitsky's outlook represents an exaggeration of Pechorin's, and calls it into question. In crushing Grushnitsky, Pechorin is attacking himself by proxy." *Mikhail Lermontov* (Boston: Twayne, 1982), 141. He adds that "Pechorin is a 'Byronic' hero, but set in perspective by a *reductio ad absurdum* of the type 'Grushnitsky' " (141).

[4]Neither political nor religious fervor in this tale of the insurgency, in seventeenth-century Scotland, of hard-core Presbyterians against the authority of the royalist government would interest Pechorin as much as the love that Edith Bullenden inspires in two valorous young men, Henry Morton and Lord Evendale, who are on different sides of the novel's ideological conflict. There are also enough momentous military encounters in the novel to satisfy the warrior in Pechorin.

[5]Mihail Lermontov, *A Hero of Our Time,* trans. and introd. Paul Foote (Harmondsworth: Penguin, 1974) 13. Guy Daniels, who rightly describes Lermontov as a romantic ironist, applies to Pechorin's psychological state (as well as Lermontov's) certain statements by Camus in *L 'Homme révolté*: "The revolt of the 'dandy,' [Camus] tells us, begins with an excess of unemployable love, develops from this to the fury of 'outraged innocence,' and ends in satanism or 'demonism': a compulsion to do evil 'out of a nostalgia for an unattainable good' . . . . This entire description fits Lermontov's case exactly." *A Lermontov Reader,* ed., trans. and introd. Guy Daniels (New York: Macmillan, 1965), 16. In Maurice Bowra's simpler analysis, Lermontov "was cynical because he felt that the world had defeated him. In boyhood he had longed for some ideal, unattainable condition, and when he failed to find it, he compromised with the world and treated it, as he thought it deserves, by going further than most men in the reckless, hard-hearted spirit which prevailed in society. But behind this we can see that his cynicism was largely due to his bitter conviction that his most cherished hopes would never be fulfilled." Introduction, *The Demon and Other Poems,* by Mihail Lermontov, trans. Eugene M. Kayden (Yellow Springs: Antioch, 1965), xvii.

[6]John Mersereau, *Mihail Lermontov* (Carbondale: Southern Illinois UP, 1962) 150. Mersereau adds that Onegin "simply drifts through life yawning, disinterested even in himself. Pechorin plots, fights, and destroys, intensely interested in his own attitudes and emotions" (150). In Dostoevsky's somber view, Onegin and Pechorin represent an increasingly virulent crisis of the Russian spirit, "which, having steeped itself in European culture, realizes it has lost its native roots and accordingly turns back on itself with destructive scepticism." Onegin, Dostoevsky writes, "does not respect even his own thirst for life and truth . . . . He becomes an egotist and at the same time ridicules himself because he does not even know how to be that." In Pechorin, Dostoevsky comments, the Onegin type "reached a state of insatiable, bilious malice, and of a strange contrast, in the highest degree original and Russian, of a contradiction between two heterogeneous elements: an egotism extending to the limits of self-adoration and a malicious self-contempt . . . . Out of anger and as if in derision, Pechorin throws himself into outrageous, strange behavior that leads him to a stupid, ridiculous, and useless death." Quoted

in Joseph Frank, *Dostoevsky: The Miraculous Years 1865-1871* (Princeton: Princeton UP, 1995), 468. Frank points out that "the most extreme and uncompromising development of this type, who coldly experiments with the farthest reaches of perversity and self-degradation, is of course Stavrogin" (468).

⁷André Sinyavsky, *Strolls with Pushkin*, trans. C. T. Nepomnyashchy and S. I. Yastremski, introd. C. T. N. (New Haven: Yale UP, 1993) 50-51.

⁸Alexander Puskin, *Eugene Onegin*, trans. Charles Johnston (New York: Viking, 1978) 6.20. (Citations are to chapter and stanza.)

⁹John Bayley claims that "Lensky must remain a figure of the vaguest and most touchingly ideal potential. His pathos is only enhanced by the contrast between the pantheon of Chénier and the destiny of a Russian country gentleman." His possible surrender to ordinary, non-poetic life "must not be impugned by ironic authorial speculation." *Pushkin: A Comparative Commentary* (London: Cambridge UP, 1971), 244. It is hard to agree with this appraisal, especially when Bayley goes on to say that "the query of Pushkin's epitaph – would he have become a poet, or lapsed into the dressing gown of contented middle age? – is not so much antithetical as movingly elegiac. Immersed in life as he is, the two destinies for Lensky would have been the same" (258). Bayley, incidentally, uses the phrase "romantic double-take" (80) to denote a pendular swing between expressing feeling and then laughing at it.

¹⁰Richard Freeborn, *The Rise of the Russian Novel* (Cambridge: Cambridge UP, 1973) 27.

¹¹Monika Greenleaf, *Pushkin and Romantic Fashion: Fragment, Elegy, Orient, Irony* (Stanford: Stanford UP, 1994) 54. Mobility is also a vital theme in Aileen M. Kelly's commentary on Alexander Herzen in *Toward Another Shore: Russian Thinkers Between Necessity and Chance* (New Haven: Yale UP, 1998). Kelly cites René Wellek's summary of Schlegelian irony, which emphasizes the need for ambivalent attitudes in a paradoxical world. Yet she goes on to make "romantic irony" synonymous with "general irony" (308).

¹²Paul Foote, introduction to *A Hero of Our Time,* by Mihail Lermontov, trans. Paul Foote (Harmondsworth: Penguin, 1966) 16. Janko Lavrin has a similar comment: "As far as an insight into certain aspects of the psychology of nihilism is concerned, Lermontov anticipated Dostoevsky. After all, from Pechorin to Stavrogin . . . there is only one step; and not a big one at that." *Lermontov* (New York: Hillary, 1959), 91.

¹³Mihail Lermontov, *A Hero of Our Time,* trans. Vladimir Nabokov and Dmitri Nabokov, 127.

¹⁴Fyodor Dostoevsky, *Notes from Underground* and *The Grand Inquisitor,* ed. and trans. Ralph Matlaw (New York: Dutton, 1960) 42.

¹⁵Joseph Frank, *Dostoevsky: The Stir of Liberation 1860-1865* (Princeton: Princeton UP, 1986) 338. The function of Part II of *Notes from Underground,* Frank subsequently remarks, "is surely to drive home the contrast between imaginary, self-indulgent, self-glorifying, sentimental Social Romanticism and a genuine act of love – a love springing from that total forgetfulness of self which has now become Dostoevsky's highest value" (341).

Chapter 7

[1]Donald Fanger, *Dostoevsky and Romantic Realism: A Study of Dostoevsky in Relation to Balzac, Dickens, and Gogol* (Cambridge: Harvard UP, 1965) 257.

[2]Alex de Jonge, *Doestoevsky and the Age of Anxiety* (New York: St. Martin's 1975) 3.

[3]Joseph Frank's reservations about *Dostoevsky and the Age of Anxiety* basically concern the absence of discussion about Dostoevsky's shaping powers as an artist. But his final objection to the book is that de Jonge's attempt to "turn the greatest and most devastating opponent of moral nihilism in modern literature into its surreptitious advocate" is "meretricious and misleading."*Times Literary Supplement* 20 Feb. 1976: 200.

[4]D. J. Mossop, *Baudelaire's Tragic Hero: A Study of the Architecture of "Les Fleurs du Mal"* (London: Oxford UP, 1961) 105.

[5]Martin Turnell points out that ennui and spleen are "practically synonymous terms in 'Spleen and Ideal,' " but that "strictly speaking *spleen* seems to be a physical and *ennui* a moral malady." *Baudelaire: A Study of His Poetry* (New York: New Directions, 1953), 101. In Walter Benjamin's view, which is scarcely unique, spleen dominates the ideal: "the *ideal* supplies the power of remembrance; the *spleen* musters the multitude of the seconds against it. It is their commander, just as the devil is the lord of the flies." *Charles Baudelaire: A Lyric Poet in the Era of High Capitalism,* trans. Harry Zohn (London: NLB, 1973), 142.

[6]The letter is dated 30 Dec. 1857. Quoted in Lois Boe Hyslop, *Charles Baudelaire Revisited* (Boston: Twayne, 1992), 70.

[7]Jonathan Culler, introduction, *The Flowers of Evil,* by Charles Baudelaire, trans. James McGowan (New York: Oxford UP, 1993) xvii.

[8]*The Mirror of Art: Critical Studies by Charles Baudelaire,* ed. and trans. Jonathan Mayne (Garden City: Doubleday-Anchor, 1956) 441.

[9]*Baudelaire's Tragic Hero,* 235. Martin Turnell states that in his poetry Baudelaire is "constantly in search of something that he describes as the 'Ideal' or the 'Absolute,' but it is evident that he does not believe in its existence. His scepticism coupled with the ardour of his pursuit of the chimera gives his poetry its unending tension." *Baudelaire: A Study of His Poetry,* 33. A. E. Carter decisively deprecates the value of Baudelaire's idealism. In discussing the desanctification of ideal love in "Spleen and Ideal," he claims that "love is not an ideal, but a devouring lust over which man tries to throw an ideal veil. Inevitably the results are catastrophic." *Charles Baudelaire* (Boston: Twayne, 1977), 75. Enid Starkie suggests that Baudelaire's idealism "often took the form of torturing himself with contemplation of things which hurt and repelled him most." *Baudelaire* (London: Faber, 1957), 553.

[10]Nicole Ward Jouve remarks that "on solitude and communication, on spleen and ideal, on liberty and fatality, De Quincey makes a self-destructive choice between two opposites which to him are incompatible. Baudelaire reconciles the opposites into a synthesis which retains their antagonism, but makes each one appear as the necessary condition for the existence of the other." In this dialectical

pattern, "artifice and nature exclude each other, but also compensate for each other, complete each other, become each other." *Baudelaire: A Fire to Conquer Darkness* (New York: St. Martin's, 1980), 286-87.

[11]Charles Baudelaire, *The Painter of Modern Life, The Essence of Laughter and Other Essays, Journals, and Letters,* ed. and introd. Peter Quennell (New York: Meridian, 1956) 53, 55.

[12]M. H. Abrams notes this capability in "Coleridge, Baudelaire, and Modernist Poetics," *The Correspondent Breeze: Essays on English Romanticism*(New York: Norton, 1984), 122.

[13]Charles Baudelaire, *The Flowers of Evil,* trans. Richard Howard (Boston: Godine, 1983) 58. All quotations from Baudelaire's poetry are taken from this text. Where English titles of poems differ significantly from the French, the French titles have also been included.

[14]Erich Auerbach, "The Aesthetic Dignity of *The Flowers of Evil,"* *Baudelaire: A Collection of Critical Essays,* ed. Henri Peyre (Englewood Cliffs: Prentice, 1962) 168.

[15]In *Baudelaire and Schizophrenia: The Sociopoetics of Modernism* (Cambridge: Cambridge UP, 1993), Eugene W. Holland argues that "Hymne à la beauté" "goes beyond the reversal of value-hierarchies to subvert the metaphoric logic of binary opposition underlying hierarchy itself" (59).

[16]Mario Praz, *The Romantic Agony,* 2nd ed.., trans. Angus Davidson (London: Oxford UP, 1970) 40.

[17]This association is pinpointed on p. 27, where Praz comments on Jules Janin's *L'Âne mort et la femme guillotinée* (1829), and on p. 135, where he discusses Pétrus Borel's "Dina la belle juive," one of the stories in*Champavert, contes immoraux* (1833).

[18]In his essay "Immortal Rot: A Reading of 'Une Charogne' " William Olmstead writes that "whatever the 'sunny' woman may once have meant to the poet, inevitably her effect on him will be like the cadaver's, a stimulus for disgust," though "the prospect of her decay excites the speaker and adds a certain zest to his present passion." *Understanding "Les Fleurs du Mal": Critical Readings,* ed. William J. Thompson (Nashville: Vanderbilt UP, 1997), 63.

[19]Quoted in Praz, *The Romantic Agony,* 43.

[20]This is the assessment of Enid Starkie, who declares that the poem "could be used as a text for an orthodox sermon on the theme that everything here below is vanity and will inevitably turn to dust and ashes . . . . For him, however, as a poet, there remains the consolation" of eternalizing art. *Baudelaire* (London: Faber, 1951), 119.

[21]*The Intimate Journals of Charles Baudelaire,* trans. Christopher Isherwood, introd. W. H. Auden (Boston: Beacon, 1957) 4.

[22]Lois Boe Hyslop, *Baudelaire: Man of His Time* (New Haven: Yale UP, 1980) 84. In her later work, *Charles Baudelaire Revisited* (1992), Hyslop reaffirms the importance of duality in Baudelaire: "The unifying theme running throughout the six sections of *Les Fleurs du Mal* is that of the conflict between good and evil, spleen and ideal, dream and reality" (55-56).

[23]Leo Bersani, *Baudelaire and Freud* (Berkeley: U of California P, 1977) 2-3.

[24]*Baudelaire and Freud*, 15.

[25]James R. Lawlor, *Poetry and Moral Dialectic: Baudelaire's "Secret Architecture"* (Teaneck: Fairleigh Dickinson UP, 1997) 116.

[26]Jonathan Culler, introduction, *The Flowers of Evil,* by Charles Baudelaire, trans. James McGowan (Oxford: Oxford UP, 1993) xx. Walter Benjamin notes the "profound duplicity which animates Baudelaire's . . . poetry." Yet Benjamin also suggests that Baudelaire "assumed ever new forms" because "he did not have any convictions." *Baudelaire: A Lyric Poet in the Era of High Capitalism,* 26, 97. Anna Balakian remarks that Baudelaire's "most salient characteristic is his diversity, his very lack of a salient trait, his virtual reversibility of character."*The Symbolist Movement: A Critical Appraisal* (New York: Random, 1967), 31. But she also stresses the poet's duality: "Now he believes, now he does not; now he soars with the ideal, now he plunges with the spleen" (33).

[27]Martin Turnell suggests that "in the last resort it is not the horrors of contemporary civilization but an inner spiritual malady which drives" the voyagers on. *Baudelaire: A Study of His Poetry,* 84.

[28]F. W. Leakey poses the following question in *Baudelaire and Nature* (Manchester UP, 1969): "if, in the perspective of Death, the poet of "Le Voyage" turns so eagerly toward the New, is this not simply because he has lost all taste for life and conserves only the 'taste for nothingness?' " (309) Not quite, is Leakey's answer, inasmuch as the poet also exhibits "an infectious, almost 'optimistic' *conviction . . .* a paradoxical nobility and ardour" (317). On this issue, Jouve offers an inconsistent reading. At one point, he claims that "as happens with beauty, love, wine, embarking on death as a door to the infinite is a self-damning delusion" heading straight towards hell. *Beaudelaire: A Fire to Conquer Darkness,* 184. Later Jouve writes that the final plunge into death reveals "no... recklessness, nihilism or pride"; it is a "vibrant assertion of the spirit's need to go on perpetuating itself and tending towards a future" (288). Richard D. F. Burton thinks that the last lines of the poem, far from being a "cry of nihilistic defiance," are "an affirmation of life whatever it may bring, a triumph for the lyricist's passionate espousal of life over the moralist's horrified recoil from it"*Baudelaire in 1859: A Study of the Sources of Poetic Creativity* (Cambridge: Cambridge UP, 1988), 89.

[29]References are to Charles Baudelaire, *Paris Spleen,* trans. Louise Varèse (New York: New Directions, 1970).

[30]What J. A. Hiddleston, in *Baudelaire and "Le Spleen de Paris"* (Oxford: Clarendon, 1987) calls the "intoxication of the absurd" – "an ecstasy at the horrific and gratuitous presence of things" (97) – has more than a slight bearing on the black comedy of "The Bad Glazier." Hiddleston makes a rigid distinction, however, between *Les Fleurs du mal* and *Le Spleen de Paris.* He believes that "the highest flights of lyricism in *Les Fleurs du mal* point to a . . . vision of oneness where contradiction is overcome," whereas the lyricism of *Le Spleen de Paris* is an " 'ecstasy' before the irrational in which mere juxtaposition has stunned and paralyzed the mind into a sense of infernal stasis and timelessness" (97-98). Yet

in a number of poems in *Le Spleen de Paris,* that presumptive paralysis yields either to moral commitment or to the flexible wisdom of buffoonery. Edward K. Kaplan thinks that the narrator of "The Bad Glazier," having become a "satanic esthete," unconsciously confuses "true art with selfish pleasure" and "claims to create beauty through violence." *Baudelaire's Prose Poems: The Esthetic, the Ethical, and the Religious in "The Parisian Prowler"* (Athens: U of Georgia P, 1990), 43-45. Enid Starkie believes that *Paris Spleen* is on the whole more mature in conception than *The Flowers of Evil,* "or more consistently so – containing less turmoil and strife, more peace and serenity, and also more harmony in the contrast between spleen and ideal, between the flesh and the spirit." *Baudelaire,* 458. Eugene W. Holland claims that "rather than narrate a final passage from one state to the other, the prose poems oscillate 'undecidedly' between the extremes of idealization and cynicism, which form the axes of the collection." *Baudelaire and Schizophrenia,* 201.

[31]"Ostensibly," Roger Shattuck points out, "Fancioulle dies for political reasons. But the eyewitness narrator tells us insistently that Fancioulle has made the prince jealous by acting too well, by displaying a competing source of power." *The Innocent Eye: On Modern Literature and the Arts* (New York: Farrar, 1984), 110. Even if it does not prove to be impregnable, the clowning that is crucial in "A Heroic Death" retains a strong affirmative quality. The clowning of Baudelaire's successor, Jules Laforgue, tends to submerge affirmation – this is true especially of the *Moralités légendaires* – in iconoclastic, flippantly decadent ironies. That is why Jules Laforgue is a shaky romantic ironist at best. "In *Moralités légendaires* Laforgue amuses himself," Michael Collie writes, "by giving popular stories or myths an extravagantly anti-romantic treatment. In each case the story is turned upside down, its heroic or cosmic 'meaning' made fun of and its plot given ironic or sardonic twists that negate the idealizations of the original." *Jules Laforgue* (London: Athlone, 1977), 50-51.

[32]*Baudelaire's Prose Poems,* 52. Kaplan, who believes that "A Heroic Death" has affinities with both German romantic irony and the "absolutely comic," asserts that the final ironies of the poem correspond to Wayne Booth's "irony of infinite instabilities" and that the martyrdom of the artist derives ultimately from "cosmic injustice or meaninglessness" (55). In his discussion of Baudelaire in *Romantic Irony in French Literature,* Lloyd Bishop accepts the following contraries as manifestations of romantic irony: pity and revulsion, filth and grandeur, illness and health, guilt and self-indulgence, tenderness and contempt, heaven and hell, beauty and horror, pleasure and pain, love and abhorrence, torture and self-victimization (99-100). These contraries, Bishop (understandably) states, may convey a tone of pain and anguish. Bishop also notes that Baudelaire's sense of irony is usually sardonic, and that his laughter is grim and bitter (104). But Bishop's considerable addition to the romantic ironist's thematic and tonal ambivalence once again overloads and imperils the concept of romantic irony.

[33]This review may be found in the Essays in Criticism section (336-43) in *Madame Bovary,* ed. Paul de Man (New York: Norton, 1965). Quotations from the novel, and from Flaubert's correspondence, are taken from this edition.

[34]Though Harry Levin identifies Madame Bovary as "the female Quixote," he differentiates between Quixote's intellectual, altruistic vagaries of chivalry and Madame Bovary's emotional, egoistic addiction to the romance of love.*The Gates of Horn,* 47. Levin does not use the phrase "romantic irony," but he approves of Albert Thibaudet's term "binocular vision" to describe Flaubert's juxtaposition of lyrical affirmation and satiric negation (232). Earlier in his study, Levin suggests that Stendhal, Byron, Pushkin, and Heine may be viewed as "counter-romanticists": "All four, in contradistinction to the romanticist, preferred cosmopolitanism to nationalism, rationalism to mysticism, irony to sentiment. They professed the culture of the Enlightenment, the cult of Napoleon, and the pose of a dandy" (111). Had Levin emphasized what he was thoroughly aware of, that is, that the counter-romantics were also profoundly romantic, and had he highlighted their comic disposition, he would have provided the basic elements of European romantic irony.

Harold Bloom has more recently associated Madame Bovary with Don Quixote. Madame Bovary, he writes, "is to the ideal of erotic passion what Don Quixote was to the ideal of playfulness, and like the Don she is at last murdered by reality, whose name is Flaubert, or Cervantes .... Emma has fed herself on the erotic debasement of popular romances even as Don Quixote has sustained himself upon romances of knight-errantry. The Don is sublimely crazed, in terms of the order of reality, but he is sublime in the order of play. No order of play is available for Emma, and in the world of reality-testing she is absurdly suicidal."*Emma Bovary,* ed. and introd. Harold Bloom (New York: Chelsea, 1994), 2. Pushkin's Tatyana and Flaubert's Emma may also be compared. Both, for all their social and psychological dissimilarities, are avid consumers (and victims) of romantic literature. Tatyana ultimately has the will to extricate herself from the perils of romantic illusion. (Yet her love for Onegin is never dismissed as a juvenile folly.) Emma, however, remains ensnared by them to the end. The narrator of*Eugene Onegin* benignly accepts (although he also wittily deprecates) the frailties and contradictions of human nature. Flaubert's narrator, however, has a prickly (though at times empathetic) attitude toward those who covet the treasures dangled by romantic illusion. Yet he exhibits an even more mordant attitude toward the gross middle class imperatives – these do not contaminate the earlier*Onegin* – that drive sensitive, non-bourgeois beings toward romantic escape.

[35]*Madame Bovary,* 311.

[36]*Madame Bovary,* 309.

[37]Peter Gay, after noting that Flaubert's "severe antiromanticism was, as Bourget had already seen, a way of warding off a seductive romantic streak" declares that "Flaubert's disavowal of his own [bourgeois] class looks like a response to the fear that he had not really escaped it. He was, it seems, projecting onto his fellow bourgeois qualities he detected in himself, making enough noise to drown out his anxiety."*Pleasure Wars* (New York: Norton, 1998), 32. Stephen Heath, in *Gustave Flaubert: "Madame Bovary"* (Cambridge: Cambridge UP, 1992) observes that Flaubert operates "what the critic Georg Lukács calls a 'dual critique': ironic detachment from his own ineradicable Romanticism is coupled

with rejection of a bourgeois world condemned by the standards of this same Romanticism" (14).

[38]Margaret G. Tillett, *On Reading Flaubert* (London: Oxford UP, 1961) 14-15.

[39]In his discussion of the agricultural fair, Eric Gans suggests, somewhat wickedly, that the image of two hogs tied for first prize "offers a burlesque parallel with the couple who, despite the apparent difference of their roles, may be said to be equally wallowing in sensuality." *"Madame Bovary": The End of Romance* (Boston: Twayne, 1989), 101. Gans had earlier stated that "by refusing either to endorse or to condemn" Emma's romantic dreams, Flaubert "suggests that within the world no truer perspective is available. *Madame Bovary* is a study in the futility and the necessity of worldly desire" (7).

[40]Victor Brombert, *The Novels of Flaubert: A Study of Themes and Techniques* (Princeton: Princeton UP, 1966) 72.

[41]Dacia Maraini, who is convinced, in *Searching for Emma: Gustave Flaubert and "Madame Bovary,"* trans. Vincent J. Bertolini (Chicago: U of Chicago P, 1998), that Flaubert pursues Emma "with a ruthlessness and tenacity that verge on the grotesque" (1), and that he cruelly leaves her "without a single good quality, not one" (2), claims that both Emma and Bournisien "are both made fun of, but Flaubert has a greater appreciation for the priest, who has his feet firmly planted on the ground and his head on straight, than for the young woman, whose foolish and arrogant pretenses outweigh her sufferings, however real and painful they may appear to her" (46). Maraini is obliged to concede that "Flaubert writes of his Emma as of a creature who is indeed vile but also beloved or, at the very least, tolerated – too deeply sympathized with and abhorred not to have been in some way an influence on him. So much so, perhaps, that he confuses himself with her, believes himself her brother, her equal" (23). Rosemary Lloyd is convinced that even Flaubert's defense of Emma's hackneyed language of love (disparaged by Rodolphe) is highly suspect: "what appears to be a narrative, even an authorial judgment, is couched in what appears to be yet another pastiche of Chateaubriand." *Madame Bovary* (London: Unwin, 1990), 89. Roberto Speziale-Bagliacca, in *The King and the Adulteress: A Psychoanalytic and Literary Reinterpretation of "Madame Bovary" and "King Lear,"* English version ed. Colin Rice (Durham: Duke UP, 1998), is less interested in observing Flaubert's dualistic attitudes than in detecting (or inventing) Charles's ambivalence toward Emma. Speziale-Bagliacca claims that Charles idealizes Emma in his love for her, but at the same time he wishes sadistically "only to destroy" her (40).

[42]Levin, *The Gates of Horn*, 263.

[43]D. H. Lawrence, "Pornography and Obscenity," *The Portable D. H. Lawrence,* ed. and introd. Diana Trilling (New York: Viking, 1947) 661-62. Flaubert has his own penetrating comment on the question of lyrical idealism and extreme sensuality: "I am convinced that the most raging material appetites express themselves unwittingly in outbursts of idealism, just as the most obscene carnal excesses are engendered by pure desire for the impossible, ethereal aspiration toward supreme bliss." Letter to Mlle Leroyer de Chantepie, 18 Feb.

1859, *The Letters of Gustave Flaubert 1857-1880,* ed. and trans. Francis Steegmuller (Cambridge: Harvard UP, 1982), 15-16.

[44]*The Letters of Gustave Flaubert 1830-1857,* ed. and trans. Francis Steegmuller (Cambridge: Harvard UP, 1980) xix.

[45]Lilian R. Furst, *Fictions of Romantic Irony* (Cambridge: Harvard UP, 1984) 61.

[46]Jonathan Culler, *Flaubert: The Uses of Uncertainty* (Ithaca: Cornell UP, 1974) 202.

[47]Erich Auerbach, *Mimesis: The Representation of Reality in Western Literature,* trans. Willard Trask (Garden City, NY: Doubleday-Anchor, 1957) 482.

[48]*Fictions of Romantic Irony,* 91.

[49]*Romantic Irony in French Literature from Diderot to Beckett,* 122.

Appendix

[1]Ernest J. Lovell, "Irony and Image in Don Juan," *The Major English Romantic Poets: A Symposium,* ed. Clarence D. Thorpe, Carlos Baker, and Bennet Weaver (Carbondale: Southern Illinois UP, 1957) 141. According to Winters, the essence of romantic irony is "that the poet ridicules himself for a kind or degree of feeling which he can neither approve nor control; so that the irony is simply the act of confessing a state of moral insecurity which the poet sees no way to improve." *In Defence of Reason* (New York: Swallow, 1947), 70. Winters indicates that he is partially indebted to Irving Babbitt for his animadversions. He also cites Kenneth Burke's essay "Thomas Mann and André Gide" in *Counterstatement* as an excellent defence of the attitudes he is objecting to – attitudes adding up to a species of "adolescent disillusionment" (65). Burke writes that "the ironist is essentially impure, even in the chemical sense of purity, since he is divided. He must deprecate his own enthusiasm, and distrust his own resentments" (quoted, 72).

[2]Robson's essay, finally titled "Byron the Poet," was published in its entirety in his *Critical Essays* (London: Routledge, 1966). References, however, are to "Byron and Sincerity," *The English Romantic Poets: Modern Essays in Criticism,* 2nd ed., ed. M. H. Abrams (Oxford: Oxford UP, 1975).

[3]Truman Guy Steffan, *The Making of a Masterpiece,* 2nd ed. (Austin: U of Texas P, 1971) x.

[4]Paul West, *Byron and the Spoiler's Art* (London: Chatto, 1960) 12.

[5]In his introduction to *Byron: A Collection of Critical Essays,* ed. Paul West (Englewood Cliffs: Prentice, 1963), West again emphasizes Byron's antic unpredictability and noncommitment: "the humor of *Don Juan* . . . has persuaded people he is writing satire. On the contrary, he is almost entirely non-reformist. The inveterate man not of parts, but of fragments, he is a true schizophrenic. The romantic and the humorist are not his alternatives at all" (12-13).

[6]George Ridenour, *The Style of "Don Juan"* (New Haven: Yale UP, 1960) 122.

[7]David V. Erdman, "Byron's Flirtation with the Muses,"*Rereading Byron: Essays Selected from Hofstra University's Byron Centennial Conference*, ed. Alice Levine and Robert N. Keane (New York: Garland, 1993) 126.

[8]Thomas Greene, for example, evokes "the famous irony which every critic has enlarged upon, that divinely enigmatic smile which seems to permit everything and believe in nothing." *The Descent from Heaven: A Study in Epic Continuity* (New Haven: Yale UP, 1970), 130. "Skepticism, in one form or another," he goes on, "pervades most of the poem [*Orlando Furioso*] . . . skepticism of the very chivalric work which was the very fabric of his art" (130).

[9]Brian Wilkie, *Romantic Poets and the Epic Tradition* (Madison: U of Wisconsin P, 1965) 257n5.

[10]M. K. Joseph, *Byron the Poet* (London: Gollancz, 1964) 273.

[11]Knight remarks portentously that apparent Byronic anomalies – "switching from agonies of spiritual guilt to wild buffoonery" is a highly significant example – "await an integration in some future order of man at present hard to conceive." *Byron and Shakespeare* (London: Routledge, 1966), 135.

[12]Alvin B. Kernan, *The Plot of Satire* (New Haven: Yale UP, 1965) 185. Kernan's discussion of *Don Juan* was subsequently reprinted in *Romanticism and Consciousness*, ed. Harold Bloom (New York: Norton, 1970).

[13]Kernan's categories at times prove troublesome. *Volpone* is labeled a satire, *The Alchemist* a comedy. Kernan concedes, however, that Jonson's comedies have a "strong satiric quality" (221).

[14]Jerome J. McGann, *Fiery Dust: Byron's Poetic Development* (Chicago: U of Chicago P, 1968) ix.

[15]Robert F. Gleckner, *Byron and the Ruins of Paradise* (Baltimore: Johns Hopkins UP, 1967) 297.

[16]Cf. Donald H. Reiman on the significance of tone: "As the mainspring of great poetry is always feelings, not ideas, tone is more important to the meaning than the denotation of words." "Byron and the Uses of Refamiliarization," *Rereading Byron*, 3.

[17]Northrop Frye, *A Study of English Romanticism* (New York: Random, 1968) 43-44.

[18]Jerome J. McGann, *"Don Juan" in Context* (Chicago: U of Chicago P, 1976) 55.

[19]Jerome J. McGann, "Formalism, Savagery, and Care: or, The Function of Criticism Once Again," *Critical Inquiry* 2 (1976): 613.

[20]M. C. Cooke, *The Blind Man Traces the Circle: On the Patterns and Philosophy of Byron's Poetry* (Princeton: Princeton UP, 1969) 44.

[21]M. H. Abrams, *Natural Supernaturalism: Tradition and Revolt in Romantic Literature* (New York: Norton, 1971) 12.

[22]Abrams, *Natural Supernaturalism*, 13.

[23]M. H. Abrams, "Rationality and Imagination in Cultural History," in Wayne C. Booth, *Critical Understanding: The Powers and Limits of Pluralism* (Chicago: U of Chicago P, 1979) 189.

[24]M. H. Abrams, "Rationality and Imagination in Cultural History," 188-89.

[25]M. H. Abrams, "Construing and Deconstructing," *Romanticism and Contemporary Criticism,* ed. Morris Eaves and Michael Fischer (Ithaca: Cornell UP, 1986) 169.

[26]Charles Rosen, "The Intense Inane: Religious Revival in English, French, and German Romanticism," *Romantic Poets, Critics, and Other Madmen* (Cambridge: Harvard UP, 1998) 45-46.

[27]Stuart M. Sperry, *Keats the Poet* (Princeton: Princeton, UP 1973) 245.

[28]Stuart M. Sperry, "Toward a Definition of Romantic Irony in English Literature," *Romantic and Modern: Revaluations of Literary Tradition* (Pittsburgh: U of Pittsburgh P, 1977) 3. Susan J. Wolfson claims that in "Towards a Definition of Romantic Irony," Sperry reassesses his view of Keats's commitment to perpetual indeterminacy, arguing instead that Keats entertained indeterminacy as a necessary phase in a dialectic ultimately 'intent on achieving through poetry something more definite' [6-7], especially as he moved out of the contained forms of the odes into epic and allegory. Indeterminacy itself, especially when confronted in existential rather than aesthetic forms, becomes subject to ironic review." *Formal Charges: The Shaping of Poetry in British Romanticism* (Stanford: Stanford UP, 1997) 284n28. Yet note what Sperry says, in "Towards a Definition of Romantic Irony," about Keats's changes in the aborted*Hyperion* epics: "More than a poem he was unable to finish, what we have in*Hyperion* is a work whose conceptual grounds underwent a total alteration as it proceeded through a deepening of human awareness. It distills that kind of indeterminacy that I have been attempting to define as peculiarly Romantic" (11).

[29]By 1988 Sperry was convinced that the idea of indeterminacy had become all too negative in its skepticism. In his contribution to the MLA 1988 program, "The Background and Significance of Indeterminacy as a Critical Concept," Sperry notes that while the concept of irony in the New Criticism was enriching (before it ballooned into over-pervasiveness or collapsed into banality), and while Schlegelian romantic irony had a positive, even exhilarating side, as well as a disintegrative one, the concept of indeterminacy in our own day has become "sad, confused, deconstructive or self-destructive" (2).

[30]Peter Conrad, *Shandyism: The Character of Romantic Irony* (New York: Barnes, 1978) vii.

[31]David Simpson, *Irony and Authority in Romantic Poetry* (Totowa: Rowman, 1979) ix.

[32]Anne K. Mellor, *English Romantic Irony* (Cambridge: Harvard UP, 1980) vii.

[33]In *"Kubla Khan" and the Fall of Jerusalem: The Mythological School in Biblical Criticism and Secular Literature 1770-1880* (Cambridge: Cambridge UP, 1975), Elinor Shaffer twice refers to romantic irony. She remarks that "the style of the apologists for Christianity partook of the subtle obliquities of their ironic Enlightenment opponents"; this apologetical style, this mode of affirmation and self-critique, "is a form of romantic irony" (8). A comparable point is made later: "the solutions of the higher criticism were bound up with the dialectics of romantic irony" (213); that is, "the higher criticism transformed its own minute

destructive scrutiny of event and person into a new bulwark of faith" (215). (Shaffer does not, however, trace any influence exerted by the higher criticism on identifiable romantic ironists in England.)

[34]Lilian R. Furst, *The Contours of European Romanticism* (Lincoln: U of Nebraska P, 1979) 26.

[35]Lilian R. Furst, *Fictions of Romantic Irony* (Cambridge: Harvard UP, 1984) 9. Presumably Furst would not be delighted by her earlier comments on Schlegelian irony in *Romanticism in Perspective: A Comparative Study of Aspects of the Romantic Movements in England, France, and Germany* (New York: Humanities, 1970). In this earlier study, Furst underlines Schlegel's metaphysical woolliness (143) and notes that "throughout his theories the connotation of the term [Romanticism] fluctuates disconcertingly" (18); indeed, Schlegel's "unpredictability is that of a weather-vane, blown hither and thither by the wind of his whims" (19). Most interesting is Furst's remark that "unfortunately Friedrich Schlegel's aphorisms, hardly models of clarity at any time, seem particularly opaque on the subject of irony" (243).

[36]Furst nevertheless commends Mellor for "showing the presence of irony [that is, romantic irony] in Byron, Coleridge, Keats, Carlyle, and Lewis Carroll"; Mellor thus "redresses" the "misconception" (245n6) that irony is "alien to the Romantics' engagement in feeling" (43).

[37]Yet Furst, who does not for the most part overly insist on the transfiguring power of Schlegelian irony, declares on the preceding page that the artistic irony of the German romantics "was the essential dynamic force in a progressive process in which the work of art was to be deconstructed and re-constructed into a closer approximation of the ideal. Irony is thus one of the major instruments of Romantic idealism." *Fictions of Romantic Irony,* 238.

[38]Frederick Garber, *Autonomy of the Self from Richardson to Huysmans* (Princeton: Princeton UP, 1982) 115.

[39]Frederick Garber, *Self, Text, and Romantic Irony: The Example of Byron* (Princeton: Princeton UP, 1988) 186.

[40]Peter W. Graham, *"Don Juan" and Regency England* (Charlottesville: UP of Virginia, 1990) 7.

[41]In *Satire and Romanticism* (New York: St. Martin's, 2000), Steven E. Jones relies a good deal on Graham's approach. Jones sees romantic irony as rooted in the tradition of pantomime, which he describes as "the performative satiric" (173). This perspective is offered as an "antidote to overly philosophical notions of Romantic irony" (173). But Jones himself surrenders to excess when he states that Schlegelian romantic irony is inspired above all by the commedia dell'arte (helped along by Aristophanes, Gozzi, and Tieck), Schlegel's theory, he declares, "is grounded in the example of the pantomime theater – especially the practice of Ludwig Tieck" (186). (The Tieck linkage has been shown by a number of scholars to be erroneous.) According to Jones, Byron's *Don Juan* is also vitally sustained by pantomimic conventions: comic rhymes are trapdoors, masking and unmasking are constants, characters are preternaturally mobile, and transformations – for example, romance becomes satire, and satire turns into romance – abound. (In the

Juan-Haidée episode, Juan is Harlequin, Haidée is Columbine, and Lambro is Pantaloon.) Byron's allegedly pantomimic romantic irony, it must be noted, is defined by Jones as a mode of satire, corrosively caricatural and darkly sceptical.

[42]Frederick W. Shilstone, *Byron and the Myth of Tradition* (Lincoln: U of Nebraska P, 1988) xii.

[43]*The English Romantic Poets: A Review of Research and Criticism,* ed. Frank Jordan (New York: MLA, 1985) 12.

[44]Ann Barton, *Byron: Don Juan* (Cambridge: Cambridge UP, 1992) 42.

[45]Caroline Franklin, *Byron's Heroines* (Oxford: Clarendon, 1992) 144-45.

[46]Malcolm Kelsall, "Byron and the Romantic Heroine,"*Byron: Augustan and Romantic,* ed. Andrew Rutherford (New York: St. Martin's, 1990) 56.

[47]David Simpson, "Romanticism, Criticism, Theory," *The Cambridge Companion to British Romanticism,* ed. Stuart Curran (Cambridge: Cambridge UP, 1993) 11, 24.

[48]Those few lines occur in an essay ("The Romantic Fragment") by Ann Janowitz, who defines Schlegelian romantic irony (her source is Mellor) as "the simultaneous operation in literary production of creation and destruction and joy and scepticism. This co-existent de-creative and re-creative action attests to the vitality of the imagination, and its ability to see the world as passing both into and out of form." *A Companion to Romanticism,* ed. Duncan Wu (Oxford: Blackwell, 1998), 448. In the volume's only essay on *Don Juan,* Jane Stabler writes, merely parenthetically, that the undercutting function of the ottava rima's final couplet reveals "romantic irony in performance" (249). Much of the significance of romantic irony is lopped off in this remark. The sudden subversion of pathos, for example, does not constitute romantic irony.

[49]Josie Dixon, "Revolutionary Ideals and Romantic Irony: The Godwinian Inheritance in Literature," *Revolution and English Romanticism: Politics and Rhetoric,* ed. Keith Hanley and Raman Seldan (New York: St. Martin's, 1990) 163.

[50]Greg Kucick, "Ironic Apocalypse in Romanticism and the French Revolution," *Revolution and English Romanticism: Politics and Rhetoric,* 67.

[51]Jerome J. McGann, *The Beauty of Inflections: Literary Investigations in Historical Method and Theory* (Oxford: Clarendon, 1985) 335.

[52]Jerome J. McGann, *Towards A Literature of Knowledge* (Chicago: U of Chicago P, 1989) 55.

[53]Jerome J. McGann, "Byron and the Anonymous Lyric,"*Romanticism: A Critical Reader,* ed. Duncan Wu (Oxford: Blackwell, 1995) 245.

[54]In an impressive work, *Lord Byron's Strength: Romantic Writing and Commercial Society* (Baltimore: Johns Hopkins UP, 1993), Jerome Christensen indicates that he does not believe in McGann's account of Byronic romantic irony (in *"Don Juan" in Context*) as a clash between the Horatian-conversational and Juvenalian-sublime styles; the "heterogeneous ferment" of *Don Juan,* Christensen declares, cannot support such simplifying dualism (214). Later, Christensen describes this dualistic critical aberration rather differently: he now refers to "the antithetical formation that criticism, more naïve than the poem it engages, has

thought *Juan* to embody: the mating of the egotistical sublime to Romantic irony" (316). Christensen's own sense of romantic irony, at least at one point, finds its self-reflexivity to be akin to the self-referentiality of paranoia (98). Christensen of course recognizes Byron's intensifying ironic consciousness; but he does not identify *Don Juan*'s abundant circumstantiality as either largely or partially romantic-ironic. The only work of Byron's that is so labeled is *Sardanapalus,* a play which "turns back on itself," presumably because its "ironic critique of Asiatic despotism" is itself subjected to irony. Moreover, it is *Sardanapalus,* not *Don Juan,* that in Christensen's view exemplifies Schlegel's concept of romantic poetry, which " 'alone can become, like the epic, a mirror of the whole circumambient world, an image of the age. And it can also – more than any other form – hover at the midpoint between the portrayed and the portrayer, free of all real and ideal self-interest, on the wings of poetic reflection, and can raise that reflection again and again to a higher power, can multiply it in an endless succession of mirrors.' " (295).

⁵⁵Drummond Bone, "The Question of a European Romanticism,"*Questioning Romanticism,* ed. John Beer (Baltimore: Johnson Hopkins, 1995) 130. Malcolm Kelsall's chapter on Byron in *The Romantic Period,* ed. David B. Pirie (Harmondsworth: Penguin, 1994) does not raise the question of romantic irony. But Kelsall observes that "the poet is subversive of his own ideals even while (and because) most idealistic" (307).

⁵⁶Eric Gans, *Signs of Paradox: Irony, Resentment, and Other Mimetic Structures* (Stanford: Stanford UP, 1997) 64.

⁵⁷It is almost a relief to turn to Linda Hutcheon's more conservative view of romantic irony in *Irony's Edge: The Theory and Politics of Irony* (London: Routledge, 1994), though Hutcheon does not have a tender regard for the subject. She promises very early in *Irony's Edge* that the over-rated "power of romantic irony (in terms of freedom, pleasure, psychic health, intellectual stimulation, and so on) will be dealt with where relevant to the discussion of irony's politics" (3). (Hutcheon is presumably knocking Mellor's paean to the therapeutic glory of romantic irony.) This "power" is not in fact dealt with. Romantic irony itself is defined by Hutcheon as "the perception and transcendence of the epistemological, ethical, or experiential paradox of appearance vs. reality" (2). The Schlegelian resonance of this definition is undeniable, though it is oddly diluted by its association with circumstantial irony.

According to Richard D. McGhee, author of the article on irony in the *Encyclopedia of Romanticism: Culture in Britain, 1780s-1830s,* ed. Laura A. Dabundo (New York: Garland, 1992), all romantic writers, being determinedly anti-conventional, "bring chaos out of order to make clear the essential irony of sincerity in human existence" (291). More lucidly, McGhee claims that all great romantic poets are romantic ironists because they reject commitments to absolutes and cultivate uncertainty, relativity, and unbounded process. "Wordsworth and Keats are masters of the speculative interrogative" (290). "Blake and Shelley are artists of irony as a dialectic of contraries" (291). Coleridge and Byron disclose in their writings "unbounded developments of versatile styles" which express their "improvisational answers to provisional existences" (291). In sum, the greatness of romantic poetry is inviolably wedded to the essence (a fluctuating essence) of romantic irony. In another volume that has a stake in pedagogy, *Lessons of Romanticism: A Critical Companion*, ed. Thomas Pfau and Robert F. Gleckner (Durham: Duke UP, 1998), there is a tantalizing allusion to the "tensions and impasses" of romantic irony (129) and a statement (in the vein of Kierkegaard) that "the Romantic New Historicists, and some others, have found Romantic irony impotent and sorely unanswerable to the pressures of historical actuality" (82). In his introduction ("General Studies of the Romantic Period") to *Literature of the Romantic Period: A Bibliographical Guide* (Oxford: Clarendon, 1998), Michael O'Neill tersely declares that "a major idea from German Romanticism to affect studies of English authors is 'Romantic Irony,' the ability of a writer and text simultaneously to hold an idea or attitude and undercut it in the name of creative freedom" (13).

Index